THE UNCERTAIN GIANT: 1921–1941

American Foreign Policy Between the Wars

AMERICAN DIPLOMATIC HISTORY SERIES

GENERAL EDITOR: *Armin Rappaport*

THE
UNCERTAIN GIANT:
1921–1941

American Foreign Policy Between the Wars

Selig Adler

SAMUEL PAUL CAPEN PROFESSOR OF
AMERICAN HISTORY, STATE UNIVERSITY
OF NEW YORK AT BUFFALO

THE   MACMILLAN COMPANY, NEW YORK
COLLIER-MACMILLAN LIMITED, LONDON

First Printing

The Macmillan Company, New York
Collier-Macmillan Canada, Ltd., Toronto, Ontario

Library of Congress catalog card number: 66–10257

Printed in the United States of America

For my granddaughter,

RACHEL CATHERINE KRANTZ

Preface

The course of American diplomacy during the interlude between World Wars has stimulated the efforts of many gifted historians. This should occasion little surprise, for the period is rich in glaring contrasts and is marked by constant gyrations of public opinion around foreign affairs. The Versailles Peace Conference was followed by general recovery from the dislocations of war and a business bonanza throughout the industrialized world. During these years the League of Nations experiment in collective security proved a partial success. Then the Great Depression transfixed the glittering prosperity, revived the law of the jungle in world politics and turned the attention of men from liquidating the results of one war to preparing for another.

This swift-moving and variegated panorama of events invites historical investigation and elucidation. Another unusual factor magnetizes the attention of scholars to the decades separating the great wars of our century. Prior to 1914 the pace of international happenings was seemingly slow—slow enough to allow historians to periodize its epochs in terms of fractions of centuries. Following the Second World War, however, the rate of scientific and territorial upheaval staggers human comprehension. Hence, the years chronicled in this volume constitute the last definable period when international happenings can be weighed without reckoning the repercussions of the nuclear breakthrough and the wholesale uprising of the colonial peoples.

Viewed in this light the years of the Long Armistice form a transition between the relative tranquillity of the protracted Victorian Era and the ominous volatility of our own Atomic Age. Like every other segment of history, the period from 1921 to 1941 constitutes an integral part of the past from which it sprang and of the future with which it was to merge. Probably it was the last time when a substantial majority of Americans could believe that it was possible to plan the future of their country regardless of overseas turmoil and confusion. Yet, save for a few years in the mid-1930's, there was never a clear-cut consensus on this point. An articulate minority repeatedly insisted that a prime world power could abdicate international leadership only at its own peril. The net result was an uncertainty as to whether the United States should ignore global disorder or lead the movement to curb it. This basic irresolution of purpose limited American efforts to divert the ghastly tragedy of the Second World War.

Intended primarily for the nonspecialist, this book blazes few new paths. I do hope, however, that I have supplied an intelligible road map through a score of history-packed years. While the volume rests in part on my own researches in unprinted source material, my chief aim has been to provide a synopsis of the best findings in secondary works on the period. Therefore I am heavily obligated for the spade-work of many scholars who have diligently probed the primary sources for fresh insights and facts on specialized portions. My synthesis has been created out of their efforts.

To suit the purpose of the present series I have found it necessary to limit footnotes to arresting primary sources and to books and articles to which I was especially indebted. From the reading of such works I have absorbed many facts and ideas. These I have tried to acknowledge in the annotated bibliography.

A grant from the Committee on the Allocation of Research Funds of the State University of New York at Buffalo greatly eased the completion of my task. I also wish to express my gratitude to Dean Milton C. Albrecht and Associate Dean Myles Slatin of the

College of Arts and Sciences for their unfailing help and generosity.

My heaviest debt is to my research assistant, Mrs. Myra S. Goldstein, who painstakingly worked over the first draft of my chapters, making many improvements in organization and style. With similar skill and devotion, Mrs. Goldstein prepared the index to this volume.

I gratefully acknowledge the many suggestions of my teacher, friend, and long-time colleague, Professor Julius W. Pratt. Dr. Pratt read the entire manuscript and placed at my disposal his impressive knowledge of American diplomatic history, the fruit of a lifetime of creative teaching and thought-provoking research. The editor of this series, Professor Armin Rappaport, pruned all of my chapters and likewise spared me inadvertent slips and omissions. For remaining errors of judgment, interpretation and fact I, of course, am alone responsible.

Thanks are also due to Professor Joseph Laufer of the law faculty of the State University of New York at Buffalo. He presented me with a sheaf of transcripts from contemporary publications which he collected during the years of the Axis crisis. This material reinforced my own investigations and brought to my desk many items that easily could have been overlooked.

I also wish to thank my colleagues for generous help and advice on aspects of my research related to their own specialties. This list includes the chairman of my department, Professor John T. Horton; and Professors George A. Brubaker, Theodore W. Friend, Robert L. Canyard, Karel Hulicka, John D. Milligan, Milton Pleaur, and Melvin J. Tucker. Two graduate students in this department, Mr. Carmen A. Notaro and Mr. Barrett G. Potter, helped assemble and check my bibliographical references. A word of appreciation is also due to my typist, Mrs. N. Evelyn Tucker, who readied this manuscript for publication with a minimum of burden upon the author. Mr. Frederick K. Henrich and Miss Virginia B. Thweatt of the Lockwood Memorial Library aided me with countless acts of friendly assistance.

Two members of my immediate family speeded the completion of this project. My son, Joseph G. Adler, ran many errands to the library, checking my findings and unearthing new references. Finally my wife, Janet S. Adler, watched carefully over stylistic details with a critical eye and an ever-ready blue pencil.

SELIG ADLER

Contents

CHAPTER I

The Tottering of Idealism

November 2, 1920, should have been the day of days for Warren G. Harding. On this Tuesday, his fifty-fifth birthday, Warren Harding had been elected President of the United States by a breath-taking majority. Observers noted, however, that the Senator did not share the exultation of his domineering wife and self-seeking political cronies. Inherently modest, Harding was overawed by his triumph. He understood the political jungle too well to mistake the avalanche of Republican ballots for a personal endorsement. Just a year before, his name scarcely would have been recognized outside his native Ohio; now he was the first man in history sent by the people from the Senate to the White House. Aware of the political accident which made this possible, Harding asked his friends to beseech for him the divine guidance that he so surely needed.

Which combination of circumstances bestowed upon this semi-educated politico a signal honor denied to Senators Clay, Calhoun, and Webster? Harding owed his good fortune primarily to the GOP high command's decision to toss him the nomination in a strongly Republican year, a choice made because the handsome Senator was available and could be counted on to take orders from Capitol Hill. Harding's newly coined slogan, "Back to Normalcy," caught fire among millions of voters who yearned to turn the clock back to an era undisturbed by industry-wide collective bargaining, soaring costs of living, demands for self-determination on the part of oppressed nationalities, Red scares, and unwelcome foreign entanglements. "We aren't thinking in terms of a better tomorrow," reasoned the astute Kansas editor, William Allen White, "but merely trying to make a bridge back to yesterday."

Mr. White sensed the gigantic recoil against the war and the spirit of internationalism it had engendered. In the exuberant and confident days of 1918, Woodrow Wilson's call for world organization had captured the public mind. The President came home from Versailles with a League of Nations blueprint that was widely hailed. Only when his opponents dissected his plan did it become evident that he faced an uphill fight for senatorial approval.

At first Wilson's critics were only special interest groups: the GOP cadre longing to reclaim the White House, flag-waving patrioteers demanding that the United States go it alone in the postwar world, liberals disillusioned by the hard facts of war, and immigrant hyphenate groups indignant at the terms meted out to their native lands at Paris. The majority still agreed with their President that a workable collective security system would have to compensate the world for the agony of its four-year strife. As Wilson sought to translate his ideals into concrete terms, his critics gained momentum.

The conventional reasons recited for this sharp slump in idealism are often superficial. A junto of willful senators, so the story goes, forced upon the President the bad choice of either accepting reservations that would seriously weaken the Covenant of the League or else facing the outright defeat of the entire treaty. A headstrong Wilson refused to make concessions, staked his program on the outcome of the 1920 election, and lost to the Republicans, who rejected the League. Actually the public was not completely won over by Wilson's arguments that League membership would promote American security. Rather, popular opinion reverted to the older concept of peace through separation from European power politics. Probably a majority was ready in 1920 to accept the League with reservations limiting future American commitments, but such a compromise proved impossible and subsequently the drift toward the postwar spell of isolationism became irreversible.

The "over there" spirit waned rapidly as Wilson's war "to save democracy" began to recede into memory. "The Great War was," writes William E. Leuchtenburg, "a dirty, unheroic war which few men remembered with any emotion save distaste." The tedium of trench fighting had not been relieved by gallant charges, and the whole affair had about it the impersonality of the unknown soldier soon to be entombed at Arlington. To be sure, four ancient dynasties long regarded as hallmarks of European tyranny had been toppled, but the new order created at Versailles only confounded the political and economic confusion. In place of the glad certainty that the fall of Kaiserdom would usher in a millennial dawn, came renewed Old World turbulence, revolutionary uprisings, economic discontent, blighted hopes, and fresh bickerings between the nations. Bolshevism, so it seemed in 1919, was spreading rapidly beyond the borders of strife-torn Russia. The news picture lent substance to Senator Harding's banal remark that the United States needed "sustainment in triumphant nationality" rather than "submergence in internationality." "If all the Armenians were to be killed tomorrow and if half of Russia were to starve to death the day after," George Nathan remarked with majestic indifference, "it would not matter to me in the least. . . . For all I care the rest of the world may go to hell at today's sunset."

In answer to the self-complacent and the hypercritical, fair-minded men insisted that Wilson had achieved many of his goals at Paris, that the new boundaries were an improvement over the old European piebald map, and that there could be no lasting American security without a viable League. Even the generous, however, found much justifiable complaint with the treaty settlement. The reparations about to be levied against Germany were unjust and impossible to collect; and this indemnification was based upon the treaty's war-guilt article which distorted the facts of history. Now there were new *irredentas,* for most boundary questions had been settled in favor of the victors. "Is it," Lloyd George was reported to have asked cynically, "Upper or Lower Silesia that we are giving away?" In the light of history, the peace was too harsh to regenerate the Reich, and too soft to prevent a revival of Junker militarism.

President Wilson understood the imperfections of the treaty that he had signed. He failed, however, to persuade his questioners that the League would provide an "ultimate corrective" for certain temporary injustices. The American people, too long insulated from the hard ways of international politics, were unprepared for the give-and-take bargaining of the peace table. Unfortunately both the war and the peace had been badly oversold on this side of the water. George Creel, in charge of Wilson's propaganda machine, boasted that the war was "the world's greatest adventure in advertising." Hence the exaggerated dismay when his fellow citizens discovered that the rest of the world was not ready for open diplomacy or instant democracy. As the crusading spirit of 1917 spent itself, it left Americans with an overwhelming desire to save themselves from European wiles.

Such sentiments led to the demand for a return to "one hundred per cent Americanism." This red-blooded slogan was particularly attractive to older men, whose impressionable years had been spent during that marvelous spurt of American energy which followed the Civil War. This older generation was now loath to share its hard-earned good fortune or to surrender its privileged geographic position. Is Fiume, asked former Senator Albert J. Beveridge, "worth the life of a single American boy or a dollar of the American people's money?" "We do not begrudge the billions we loaned to the others who were fighting the same enemy," he added later, "but have we not at least earned the right to be left alone henceforth?" "No foreign alliances, no entangling leagues," demanded the American Club of Minneapolis. Similar "save the republic" groups labeled the League a superstate that could summon American boys to battle at the whim of a peevish Balkan king. We should not, said a chauvinist, swap the "Aladdin's lamp of nationalism" for "a newfangled . . . foreign-made lamp of internationalism." More penetrating thinkers wrote off Victorian world stability as a casualty of war and insisted that an enlightened self-interest demanded an American hand in the restoration of world peace. The uncritical masses, however, were beguiled by the more simple expedient of just closing the doors against overseas commotion.

To dispel this growing myopia, strong and plain language was needed. But Woodrow Wilson never made explicit the relationship of American security to the new balance of power. Instead he promised that the very existence of the League would make such a balance or any peacetime system of alliances unnecessary. Seldom was the essential point made that the United States, now a prime power in a science-shrunken globe, could not escape involvement in major foreign wars. Was it not, then, in our material interest to join a coalition of like-minded nations to curb aggression and war? Rarely was the question posed in such realistic form.

The President's critics had the advantage of a clear-cut program streamlined for popular comprehension. For a short spell after the Armistice, collective security sounded attractive. On second thought, however, Americans began to hesitate on the vital matter of advance commitments in the event of violations of the Covenant. This controversy soon centered around Article X, which obliged member states "to respect and preserve as against external aggression the territorial and existing political independence" of all signatories to the Covenant. Nor were the ingrained isolationists alone in opposing a blank check guarantee of the boundaries and independence of a score of remote nations. Sincere internationalists, headed by the Republican Nestor, Elihu Root, felt Article X too drastic a departure from American tradition. Although the Covenant of the League contemplated police action against an outlaw state rather than actual warfare, the distinction seemed academic. This was a serious problem for men of the Root school who had long argued that peace must be maintained, not by physical coercion, but by moral suasion, increased respect for international law and improved arbitrational machinery. Wilson replied to such critics that, minus the force provisions of Article X, world security would be illusion rather than reality. Senator William E. Borah, leader of the bitter-end isolationists, pointed up the President's dilemma when he asked publicly: "What will your league amount to if it does not contain powers that no one dreams of giving it?" History does not record a direct answer, but the President labored to explain that Article X involved a *moral* rather than a *legal* obligation to the League.

Because the President failed to make due allowance for the inbred prejudice against advance commitments, he lost the support of many sincere Republican friends of international cooperation. Had illness not impaired Wilson's political judgment, it is possible that he might have quieted some genuine fears against perpetual involvement in Europe's squabbles.

Apprehension for the future fate of the Monroe Doctrine also widened the breach between the President and the restrained internationalists, whose support was essential to his success. The impression was rampant that the League meant the end of Washington's traditional leadership in Western Hemisphere affairs. This control had long been associated with the older policy of nonentanglement; now it was argued that both traditions were headed for the same scrap heap. Henceforth, would the League rather than the United States guard the New World against foreign encroachment? Under the Covenant, could a Latin American country appeal against our own interpretation of the Monroe Doctrine? At Versailles, President Wilson had been persuaded by friendly critics to add to the charter a backhanded recognition of "such regional understandings" as the Monroe Doctrine. But this concession did not satisfy men who wished to insure complete American control over the Monroe Doctrine. The worst fears of the nationalists were confirmed when the most renowned American authority on international law, John Bassett Moore, predicted that if the Monroe Doctrine was cast into the caldron of world politics, it would lose its unique connotation.

While the undecided followed the wearisome polemics over the treaty, events overseas played into the hands of Wilson's foes. Time was working for the isolationists, for the longer the argument lasted, the less attractive League membership appeared. New European disorders and uprisings helped the doubters make up their minds.

The isolationist wave mounted amidst growing resentment against our erstwhile allies and the new succession states created

at Versailles. This growing anti-foreign feeling was intensified by
a spate of petty wars which plagued Europe for half a decade.
Newly liberated states, often aided and abetted by France, seized
disputed territory. These local wars, which raged while the treaty
was before the Senate, provided splendid ammunition for the anti-
leaguists. Pro-Polish sentiment, so marked during wartime, was
dissipated as the Warsaw government persecuted racial minorities
and pushed its boundaries eastward in blatant violation of the
principle of national self-determination. "The uprising in Hungary
and the mix up with the Czecho-Slovaks," Beveridge wrote Senator Borah, gives "a crushing argument against *any League whatever*. All you have to do is to ask the people whether they want
their boys to be sent into such a maelstrom of blood and death
as that."

Hunting for two-inch captions to replace the headlines of battle,
the press hawked extra editions telling of new European intrigues
and coups. There was talk of a new major conflict even before the
Senate voted on the treaty. Overseas correspondents warned that
no league could hold in check the stormy forces which comprised
the backwash of war. They insisted that a thousand years of inbred
hate and fear had poisoned the European bloodstream. The minority against the League was mushrooming into a majority.

Returning doughboys helped swell this sentiment. They came
back jingoistic, anti-foreign, and determined almost to a man to
make no more troopship crossings. Before the year 1919 was over,
the American Legion was organized with "hundred per cent
Americanism" as one of its watchwords. To make matters even
worse, soldiers and sailors were mustered out at a time when the
index of wholesale prices stood at double its prewar level. Where
was the peace or any other tangible profit to compensate for the
lost months spent in drafty barracks or mud-filled trenches? The
isolationists alone seemed to have an answer for the European
problem: if we got nothing else out of the war, at least let it serve
as an experience to be remembered.

Despite evidence of widespread irritation with the administration, the League still had many devotees. There was an excellent
chance that popular opinion might force positive Senate action on

the treaty if the gap between the President and the middle-road-
ing Republicans could be bridged by compromise. To prevent
such a possibility, some fourteen Irreconcilables, as the cadre of
bitter-end isolationist senators was called, played masterful politics to cement together all segments of opinion opposed to the
original treaty. Judging by end results, these men did more than
defeat the treaty; they created an isolationist phalanx which was
to determine the foreign policy mood of the country for two
decades.

The logic of history, it has oft been noted, is coincidence. A
combination of circumstances during the postwar period gave an
unexpected fillip to the recoil against international organization.
First of all, we must reckon with the intensified isolationism of the
upper Mississippi Valley, a regional sentiment scarcely noticeable
before Wilson's day. Many scholars have weighed the fundamental
causes of this midwestern attitude. Geography was undoubtedly
important, for this region was far removed from salt water and its
inhabitants had been less disturbed by the fighting than were men
of the Atlantic states. Furthermore, deeply rooted economic prejudices, a vestige of the Populist commotion of the 1890's, led to the
belief that our neutrality had been undermined by greedy eastern
bankers and cold-blooded munitions makers. This interpretation of
American intervention in the war was congenial to a rural folk
composed in large measure of German and Scandinavian ethnic
groups, many of whom had brought with them from Europe
pacifist and socialist orientations. However, in assessing the importance of midwestern isolationism, one should not overlook the
fact that many of Wilson's most influential opponents came from
other parts of the country. Only in the South was there no measurable isolationist upsurge, for Dixie had few immigrants with a
divided emotional allegiance and no Republican state organizations in a position to exploit opposition to the President's foreign
policy.

Elsewhere, especially in the crowded eastern cities, Wilson had
alienated a number of key voting blocs. German and Austrian
stocks blamed him for making war against their fatherlands and
then forcing upon these countries a humiliating peace. During the

Versailles Conference, the President lost his hold on Italo-Americans by opposing some of Rome's exaggerated war aims. These factors alone made serious inroads on Democratic strength, but even more dangerous to the President's success was the revolt of the Irish Democrats. While fighting the Kaiser, England had drifted into civil war with the Sinn Fein, the Irish revolutionary junto, which had a host of sympathizers in the United States. The Irish-Americans were baffled. How could the President demand self-determination for every oppressed nationality save their own?

Putting the cards together, all foreign-oriented elements had suffered rebuffs at the hands of old-stock Americans and Wilson served as a convenient symbol of the latter. This hated "Establishment" was blamed for leading the country into war on the side of the unpopular English, and then capping the alliance with a treaty of peace that subjugated other nations for the sake of the British and the French. Albeit Henry Cabot Lodge, leader of the Senate opposition to Wilson, was a frosty Yankee with ingrained prejudices against newer Americans; nevertheless he now lent a willing ear to their grievances.

To insure success, Senator Lodge extended the hand of fellowship to still another uncongenial group—liberals who had deserted the President. In sharp contrast to the reactionary Massachusetts senator, these men were political independents, staunch anti-imperialists and lifelong friends of reform. Their disillusion with Wilson stemmed originally from the way the administration had curbed wartime domestic dissent. Nor did the witch hunt abate after the Armistice, for the most severe suppressions of civil liberties came during the Red scare of 1919–1920. While the President was only indirectly responsible for some inexcusable injustices on the part of his subordinates, he never publicly rebuked them and his pro-League speeches occasionally contained undercuts aimed at unpopular dissident minorities. Meanwhile many additional liberals had broken with Wilson over peace terms which they called "purple with revenge." Although some independents were isolationists by choice, the majority were internationalists who demanded a League based upon the rule of reason rather than on sanctions envisioning physical coercion. "They are not," said one liberal quoting Nikolai Lenin, "forming a league of nations, but a league of imperialists to strangle the nations." With the Democrats weakened by the defection of the independent and hyphenate vote, the 1920 Republican presidential candidate seemed certain of an easy victory.

While the GOP top command was happily contemplating the outcome of the next election, Republican senatorial chieftains were occupied in attaching strong reservations to the treaty. As the debate progressed, the public tired of endless haggling on foreign matters that were, in those pre-atomic days, of no pressing concern to ordinary citizens. With domestic tensions, strikes, Red hunts, and the White Sox baseball scandal crowding Europe out of the headlines, people became increasingly indifferent to plans for international association. The simplest remedy for overseas confusion seemed the most attractive. Perplexed by continental disorders? queried the isolationists. Solve the problem by "dealing us out" and insisting that other nations let Uncle Sam mind his own business. To the unreflective millions far more interested in the new sport idols Babe Ruth and Jack Dempsey than in Shantung or Danzig, this advice made good sense.

Because Lodge was busy in Washington tailoring the treaty to suit Republican inclinations, the task of mustering the support of the country fell into the willing hands of the outright isolationists. William Edgar Borah was the original Irreconcilable, leader of the small band of senators who equated any compromise whatsoever on the League question with treason. Faithful to the progressive tradition in his own quixotic fashion, Borah had not joined the Bull Moose revolt of 1912 and so was on congenial terms with all Republican factions. Although he had valuable German and Irish grass roots associations, Borah had been a 1917 War Hawk with an unassailable war record. An incomparable orator, the Senator was an old hand at parliamentary obstructionism, experience which he now found invaluable. Putting his inexhaustible energy, contagious enthusiasm, and country-wide connections to full use, Borah fanned opposition to the treaty. Characteristically the Senator did not consider himself an isolationist, for he had hazy notions of keeping peace through educating world opinion to the point where it would accept the tenets of international law. Such an advance, he maintained, would be more effective than any formal association of nations. Returned to the Senate term after term by rustic constituents who gloried in his fame, the "Lion of Idaho" held a leverage on foreign policy making for a score of years.

When Borah began to battle the League in forty-eight states, he challenged a powerful President standing at the pinnacle of his fame. The Senator's chances of success seemed slim in the spring of 1919, for his only allies were a handful of like-minded senators plus some friendly newspaper editors. The recalcitrant senators needed money to finance their propaganda. Ample funds were soon forthcoming from a brace of Pittsburgh multimillionaires—Henry Clay Frick of coke and steel fame, and Andrew W. Mellon, aluminum and banking magnate. Now the "Battalion of Death," as Borah's associates were called, could wage a nationwide campaign using traveling orators and the far-flung distribution of every variety of printed matter.

As a result of this campaign, Senator Hiram W. Johnson emerged as a leading contender for first place on the 1920 Republican ticket. Unlike that of his ally and campaign manager, Borah, the California senator's flag-waving nationalism was unmarred by even a token gesture toward world cooperation. "Let's have peace and get out of Europe," was Johnson's message to the American people. "This league means that American boys shall police the world; that all tottering nations of the earth shall be upheld by our blood and our bone." Johnson was to remain in the Senate to harass all efforts toward international cooperation until the very eve of the Atomic Age.

There was a marked difference in attitude toward the League experiment on the part of European and American skeptics. Overseas the fires of war had burned so deeply that even stern-jawed realists were willing to weigh the merits of any plan that might possibly prevent another holocaust. The Earl of Avon (Anthony Eden) relates in his *Memoirs* that he returned to civilian life in 1919 to find "every single male member of [my] family, with whom I had spent my life before . . . dead, wounded, or captured." Even the dour Clemenceau was willing to try collective security, provided that France's safety was also buttressed by a large standing army and a string of conventional alliances. Americans, however, naïvely regarded the League as a complete revolution in the conduct of international relations. Wilsonians viewed the Covenant as an epoch-making *démarche* that outmoded war-breeding balances of power and rival alliance blocs. Their opponents likewise made the mistake of taking the new departure at face value; they feared that League membership would undermine their country's sovereignty.

Blessed with the vantage of hindsight, the historian is tempted to speculate on one of the important "ifs" of twentieth-century history. Would the decision have been for League membership had Americans of Wilson's day realized that Great Britain could no longer balance European power without our help? Would such a step merely have resulted in the same chaos that followed our wholehearted participation in the United Nations? There can be no positive answers to these tantalizing questions, but it is safe to say that the chances for a successful system of collective security were markedly better in the earlier period. In 1919 the British Empire still stood intact; Washington and London could have compromised certain minor diplomatic differences in order to make the League genuinely workable. With Germany momentarily powerless and the Soviets not yet ready to spread Communism by force or threat of force, an Anglo-American partnership designed to uphold the peace would have had an excellent chance of success. It is one of the major tragedies of our troubled century that this golden opportunity, never destined to recur, was rejected by the United States.

The denouement of this tragedy is familiar history; the Irreconcilables triumphed when, on two separate occasions, the Senate voted down the treaty. With the assistance of Borah's "Battalion of Death," the Republican majority eventually freighted the treaty with fourteen reservations, the number serving as a convenient reminder of Wilson's Fourteen Points. When the amended treaty came to a Senate vote on November 19, 1919, the Irreconcilables joined the Wilsonian Democrats in the "nays"; minutes later these strong-willed men united with the Republican majority to vote down the settlement in its original form. In the ensuing months, all attempts to reconcile the differences between the White House and Capitol Hill failed, for neither the ailing President nor the GOP leadership would yield sufficient ground. So the treaty, under virtually similar circumstances, failed again in the Senate on March 19, 1920. The final tally revealed that more than a majority of senators, but not quite the required two-thirds, were willing to accept the treaty with the Lodge reservations.

Two months before this final Senate action on the treaty, President Wilson made a colossal political mistake. He asked, in the event of a second Senate refusal, that the upcoming presidential election constitute "a great and solemn referendum" on the League issue.[1] "I suggest," Wilson added on the eve of the 1920 election, "that the candidacy of every candidate for whatever office be tested by this question—'Shall we, or shall we not, redeem the great moral obligation of the United States?' "

No completely satisfactory explanation can be given for Wilson's desperate gamble, a mad venture for one so steeped in the ways of politics. The President must have known that in all American elections foreign policy issues are always hopelessly entangled with pressing domestic questions. The congressional elections of 1918, held during the height of the war hysteria, had been won by the Republicans amidst telling portents of a rising GOP tide. Moreover, eight years of Democratic rule had built up a host of resentments against the incumbents. Usual irritations with the

---

[1] Following the initial defeat of the Treaty of Versailles in the Senate, Wilson thought seriously of challenging the fifty-seven opposition senators to resign their seats immediately and to ask the voters of their states for re-election. The President's scheme was to assure the opposition that if a majority of the resigning senators were re-elected, he and the Vice-President would resign after he had appointed a leader in the opposition as Secretary of State so that he could succeed to the presidency. The plan was abandoned in January, 1920, because it involved too many difficulties. It is important to note, however, that Wilson first used the term "solemn referendum" in relation to this direct appeal to the people and only later did he use it in relation to the upcoming presidential election of 1920. Wilson, apparently, was aware of the difficulties inherent in boiling down the 1920 election to a single major issue, but with the failure of his first plan, he thought that he had no alternative. Kurt Wimer, "Woodrow Wilson's Plan for a Vote of Confidence," *Pennsylvania History*, XXVIII (January, 1961), 2–16.

party in power had been multiplied by the inconveniences of war and the dislocations of reconstruction. Wilson had demanded the impossible, for the League issue could not be separated from the general reaction against the administration.

As the President might have foreseen, had not illness blurred his political vision, the GOP would not risk the loss of its internationalist wing by permitting the election to become a "yes" or "no" plebiscite on collective security. When the Republican delegates swarmed into Chicago to choose the ticket, Elihu Root and Ogden Mills drafted a foreign policy plank sufficiently vague to hold together both GOP treaty reservationists and classic isolationists. One stout prejudice united all the hot, collar-wilted politicos. They cheered to the rafters the incomparable octogenarian spellbinder, Chauncey M. Depew, when he characterized Woodrow Wilson as "a babe confident of himself," an innocent abroad fleeced by a crew of wily European "gamblers in international politics."

Inasmuch as the Republican nomination seemed tantamount to election, the battle on the convention floor was a lively one. When the front-runners deadlocked in the opening ballots, Chairman Lodge pounded his gavel and declared a recess. That night, in the most famous of all smoke-filled rooms, the party leadership, dominated by a handful of veteran senators, decided upon Warren Harding. Six years of experience with the affable Ohioan in the clubby atmosphere of the Senate must have given them some clue as to the limited abilities of their man. However, in searching for a second-rater who could be managed, the senators settled for something much less. On the other hand, the Ohio senator seemed to fit all the necessary requirements: he looked like a President, could deliver a ghost-written speech in acceptable if flamboyant manner, and his stand on the treaty was wobbling enough to maintain party unity.

The Democrats, meeting at San Francisco, did little better. True to long party habit, they fought it out for forty-six tedious ballots and then handed the nomination to another Ohio newspaper editor, the lackluster James M. Cox. Happily for the country, so a quipster remarked, "they both can't win." Governor Cox was not

enthusiastic about burdening himself with Wilson's political lia-
bilities, but a visit to the White House turned him into a forth-
right, if reluctant, warrior for the League. Like its Republican
counterpart, the Democratic foreign policy plank invited contradictory interpretations. At first glance a reader might gather
that the Democrats stood firmly behind the President, but closer
examination would reveal clear hints that the party would not
oppose reservations spelling out the exact obligations of the United
States to the League. Facing almost certain defeat late in the
campaign, Cox clutched at straws. He abandoned Wilson's uncompromising position and declared himself willing to accept
"good" reservations which would include a stipulation that the
United States bore no obligation to lend military assistance to the
League without the consent of Congress.

Because Harding's victory was regarded as certain, his sonorous
platitudes were more closely scrutinized than Cox's colorless effusions. Whatever his shortcomings for high office, the Senator
showed special talent in holding together the opposing wings of
his party for the duration of the campaign. The Republican candidate's foreign policy statements reflected the pressure put on him
by the Borah-Johnson coalition. Harding publicly confessed that
he had reluctantly voted for the treaty with reservations and stated
that he now was not in favor of joining the League on any basis
proposed by Wilson.

There was, however, another side to the Republican coin. Prominent Republican leaders, including William H. Taft, Charles Evans
Hughes, and President Nicholas Murray Butler of Columbia, had
pioneered the concept of collective security long before Woodrow
Wilson had become a convert to the cause. It would have been
difficult for these GOP elder statesmen to swallow their words
even had they now been so minded. But they were not by habit
"gut" political fighters, and in 1920 they so detested Wilson that
they were willing to yield too much in the interest of a resounding
Republican victory. Nevertheless, Harding's isolationist speeches
alarmed the moderates and they wished to force the Senator to
take a pro-internationalist stand prior to his anticipated victory.
Elihu Root penned the demands of the GOP internationalists in

the famous manifesto of the Committee of Thirty-One. Essentially this statement mirrored the views of eastern conservative intellectuals who wanted to join the existing League providing that the entangling obligations of Article X were removed. In their statement to the country, the committee explained that Harding's election would break the deadlock between the President and Congress and thus make possible a revision of the Covenant that would satisfy the American people. A vote for Harding, according to this logic, would therefore be a vote for the League. Senator Harding lost none of his aplomb and explained away his party's predicament in a confusing flow of words. Some Republican independents were satisfied. Others held their noses and stood by the Grand Old Party, while some dissidents joined the pro-League independents who supported the colorless Cox. In the end, Governor Cox agreed to accept any reservation necessary to secure Senate consent to the treaty. Thus, by Election Day, the distinction between the League stand of the two parties was blurred to the point where a referendum on the issue was well-nigh impossible.

Probably all this campaign oratory and interparty maneuvering had little effect on the final result, which proved to be an epoch-making majority for Harding and Coolidge. Wearied by two years of haggling over a foreign question that bore little relation to immediate personal interests, voters were out to punish the incumbents for an uncomfortably high cost of consumer goods and other annoyances stemming from a "Democratic" war. The critical independent vote, which had re-elected Wilson four years earlier, wished to rebuke the President and his subordinates for a callous disregard of civil liberties during the war and the Red Scare. Foreign-oriented groups voiced their protest against the war and the treaty. In addition the new prosperity had dispelled the old fear of Big Business among many erstwhile progressives, and this group, grown property-conscious, now favored the more conservative candidate. Hence it is not surprising that the election of 1920 marked the greatest shift of votes from one party to another in any presidential contest held since Lincoln's day.

The majority of contemporary and subsequent observers have concluded that Harding's landslide was not equivalent to a popular repudiation of collective security. Instead it is more reasonable to argue that a naïve electorate was beguiled into believing that Harding could cooperate with other nations to preserve the peace, and at the same time make life more agreeable by ending the sense of perpetual crisis. By returning to "normalcy," it was believed, America could slide back into its old comfortable way of life and at the same time pay sufficient attention to foreign affairs to avert another collapse of the peace. These goals were to prove contradictory.

President-elect Harding encouraged unrealistic thinking by a vastly oversimplified interpretation of his mandate. Only two days after the polls closed, he declared the question of joining the League deceased and, in practice, he was to regard the issue as "dead as slavery." In a flowery inaugural address, he insisted that "in a public mandate" Americans had voted the League down and he promised that his administration would accept no overseas responsibility "except as our own conscience and judgment, in each instance may determine." Five weeks later he told Congress that the League was a "super-power" that "can have no sanction by us." In all fairness it should be conceded that isolationist sentiment had mounted so rapidly by the spring of 1921 that the new President, even had he so desired, could not have secured Senate consent for the treaty. So whatever the verdict of 1920 was intended to mean in regard to collective security, in practice the election was regarded as a popular repudiation of Wilson's plan for enduring peace.

Privately Democratic leaders shared Harding's belief that the electorate had repudiated the League. Stunned by its overwhelming defeat at the polls, Wilson's party would not give another outright endorsement to a plan for world organization until the virtual end of the Second World War. As Democratic politicians retired to their provincial lairs to lick their wounds, the League of Nations loomed as an obstacle to party reunification. The real import of the election of 1920 for the student of American foreign policy is not the actual verdict of the voters on Election Day, but rather the fact that both parties convinced themselves that an advocacy of collective security was an invitation to political disaster. Following 1920, an isolationist mood, strongly bipartisan in nature, swept the country.

Reading of the European complex of petty wars, tyrant-cursed governments, ruinous currency inflations and congenital hatreds, "Main Streeters" felt safe, superior, and smug. Harding, whose small-town associations had brought him initiation into the orders of the Elks, Hoo Hoose, Moose, and Red Men, spoke a language congenial to millions of fellow joiners. "You just didn't want a surrender of the United States of America," he declared. "You wanted America to go under American ideals." On this essential point the President was adamant; in other details of foreign policy he was willing to grant Secretary of State Charles E. Hughes unprecedented freedom of action.

Although Hughes was inclined toward international cooperation, his deft hand was to be stayed by the popular wave of self-complacency and xenophobia that accompanied the Republican Restoration. "America for the Americans," said a spokesman for the hypernationalists, and he added that the rest of mankind was free "to seek its safety and happiness by the methods its reason may dictate." In all probability the vast majority of the sixteen million voters who elected Harding were willing to let the matter rest there. A group of uncritical nationalists, however, carried their chauvinism far enough to make it appear a harbinger of a home-grown Fascism. This reaction stemmed in part from an exaggerated notion of American superiority; in other measure, it was an answer to a spate of crippling postwar strikes precipitated by an ambitious labor movement said to be under radical domination. Many varieties of superpatriotic organizations sprang up to hurl back these forces of "un-Americanism." The League of Loyal Americans vowed to fight for "One Tongue, One Ideal and One Flag." In Boston the biographer Louis A. Coolidge headed the Sentinels of the Republic. Elsewhere members of the American Flag Movement made it their mission to place the national colors in every home. Whatever their immediate purpose or pet phobia, all nativist organizations of the day preached a "red-blooded" nationalism designed to restore the values of an earlier rural society allegedly corroded by Wilsonian internationalism.

When prosperity returned after the sharp recession of 1921–
1922, most of these postwar organizations dissolved or else ran
out of gas. A notable exception was the Ku Klux Klan, which
proved to be of more than ephemeral importance. The Klan had
been revived in 1915 by William J. Simmons, oddball Methodist
circuit rider and backwoods history professor, whose breath
exuded a refreshing mixture of mint, cloves, and bourbon. The
Klan attracted but little attention until the post-armistice Red
hysteria when its members laid violent hands on Negroes, aliens,
and social nonconformists. Reorganized by Edward Y. Clarke and
the blowzy Mrs. Elizabeth Tyler, the organization found its place
in the rustic, lodge-minded town life of the 1920's. The Klan's new
commercially minded leaders saw the possibilities of the ten-dollar
membership fee paid by members who formed Realms, Provinces,
and Klans. These in turn were headed by officers bearing the weird
titles of Wizards, Goblins, Great Titans, and Exalted Cyclopes.

In 1922 a Texan dentist, Dr. Hiram W. Evans, replaced Simmons as Grand Wizard. Under more sober but more sinister leadership, the Klan expanded its political front northward into Indiana
and other midwestern states where racial tensions had been made
acute by the arrival of southern Negroes seeking jobs in war
plants. Estimated at a total of five million members at the height
of its power, the Klan's strength derived from an exploitation of
regional prejudices. For the Klansman, "alien" meant Negro in
the South, Jew in New York, Oriental on the West Coast and
Catholic in the Bible Belt. In general the organization drew its
members from lower-middle-class, old-stock Americans, who
dominated village and town life. This element, North and South,
was hyper-resistant to the new forces of urbanism, industrialism,
and cosmopolitanism which were then playing havoc with Victorian habits and mores. While Klansmen were primarily absorbed
in domestic affairs, their organization formed the extreme right
wing of the isolationist phalanx, for their brand of twentieth-
century know-nothingism put a curse on all traffic with foreigners.

Weakened by press exposures of its violent tactics and internal
venality, the Klan declined rapidly after 1925 as middle-class
America regained its balance. Meanwhile an offshoot of the Klan's

spirit had been incorporated into the permanent immigration policy of the United States. Shortly after Harding's inauguration, Congress passed an emergency act which sharply limited immigration and which discriminated against would-be migrants from southern and eastern Europe. In 1924 the racists won a clear-cut victory with the passage of the Johnson Act. The new law, a concomitant to the neo-isolationism of the day, sealed immigration at 150,000 entrants per year and provided for a future "National Origins" scheme heavily weighted in favor of the Nordic European countries. Ignoring the protests of the President and his Secretary of State, Congress excluded from entry all Orientals ineligible for citizenship under American law. Japan was deeply injured by this widely advertised loss of face. The insult was all the more biting because Tokyo had scrupulously observed the Gentlemen's Agreement of 1907, whereby the Japanese themselves had limited Nipponese emigration to the United States.

The relationship between the Johnson Act and an intensified isolationism is readily apparent. In Coolidge's day, the United States was filled with racial theoreticians who emphasized heredity at the expense of environment, who overglorified Anglo-Saxon virtues, and who felt that immigrants from other countries were but "half-civilized." The prolific writer Lothrop Stoddard recklessly used wartime IQ army statistics to depreciate the intellectual potential of recent immigrant strains and to pin the blame on these nationalities for recent revolutionary upheavals. Representative Jasper Napoleon Tincher of Kansas summed up this widespread prejudice when he told Congress: "On the one side is beer, bolshevism, unassimilating elements and perhaps many flags—on the other side is constitutional government; one flag, [the] stars and stripes."

It is a cruel paradox that a war waged in the name of world democracy set in motion a nationalist wave that proved inimical to this cause. By 1921 the great isolationist front stood as a roadblock to the formation of an enlightened American foreign policy which conceivably might have prevented the Fascist nightmare. This isolationist combine, destined to plague all Presidents of the interwar decades, was made up of many diverse elements. Its liberal segment wished no traffic with a League allegedly formed to perpetuate the iniquities of an unjust peace. Communist isolationists, small in number but prolific in argument, insisted that the League lay as a dangerous derelict athwart the path to a globe-wide economic unity of Marxist orientation. Perversely enough, some American immigrant blocs were isolationists because of strong European attachments. Added to these elements were the flag-waving patrioteers who looked askance at all things foreign and who regarded our ocean moats as an American counterpart for the Great Wall of China.

Despite the widespread prevalence of parochial thought in the postwar decade, isolationism was to prove stronger in theory than in practice, for its pristine form failed to make room for the new power position thrust upon the United States by the whirlwind of history. Outside of the isolationist ranks stood a substantial minority of vigorous and articulate champions of policies better attuned to the needs of the day. These divergent views must be explored prior to an appraisal of the official Republican alternative to the membership in the League of Nations proposed by Woodrow Wilson.

CHAPTER II

Blueprints for Peace

As the smoke settled over the wearisome League of Nations battle, thoughtful persons pondered the next step in foreign policy. Men of perception realized that there could be no return to "the safe and sane nineteenth century"; this sanctuary had been consumed by the fires of war. Nor was it possible to ignore the turmoil of a Europe in disarray. In or out of the League, there was no escape from the reality of the situation.

In addition, the professional diplomats now had to reckon with still another new development, the active intrusion of public opinion into the realm of foreign affairs. The Republican elder statesman Elihu Root waxed philosophical on this challenge. Although Root had done more than his share to defeat the Treaty of Versailles, he was experienced enough to grasp that his own party had inherited the same foreign problems which had vexed the discredited Democrats. Repeatedly he told the victory-flushed Republicans that the war had interested the masses in diplomatic affairs and that GOP politicians could not continue their traditional overemphasis on domestic questions. This was impossible, said Root, for Americans had learned more about international relations in "the past eight years than they had learned in the preceding eighty." Therefore a conscious effort must be made to develop the international mind lest ignorance and error "make wild

with foreign relations." "The masses of the people," commented
The New Republic, "think a thousand times more about peace and
war than they did in 1913." A broadened realization of the complexities of the international situation manifested itself in a new
popular concern for world peace.

Hence, the postwar decline in international zeal was relative rather than absolute. Educators, liberal clergymen, club
women, idealistic journalists, public officials, and enlightened businessmen continuously questioned the basic concepts of the new
isolationism. Now critical decisions in American foreign policy
could be made only after divergent shades of opinion had been
taken into consideration. While the war had taught many people
to rationalize their isolationist convictions, the years of strife had
also reinforced internationalist thought. The net result was an ambivalence of opinion, with both sides forced to pay heed to the
regnant convictions of the majority hatred of war and a desire
to avoid further foreign embroilments.

In evaluating the various schools that held contrasting views
on postwar diplomacy, it is best to begin with the confirmed isolationists. This group enjoyed a great advantage, for its gospel was
simple, direct, easy to comprehend, and therefore palatable to
the public. Above all, the isolationists were able to resolve differences among themselves. It is always easier to unite against some
particular course of action than to arouse enthusiasm for so specific a cause as League affiliation.

Pristine isolationists were unilateralists who maintained that foreign wars would not be prevented by cooperative action. Such
association, either with the League or with some substitute organization, would ensnare the country in overseas traps fraught
with danger. Much more could be done for world peace, they
argued, if we retained our freedom of action for profit in future
emergencies. In addition, by "going it alone" the United States
could promote prosperity and thus serve as an example for Europe, a troubled continent seeking its way out of a morass of ingrained hatreds and rivalries. To dismiss holders of such views
as dogged "isolationists," Wayne S. Cole reminds us, is misleading, for no responsible person wished to isolate the country cul-

turally or commercially. Moreover, the so-called isolationists ordinarily did not extend their aloofness to Asia or Latin America, for they were primarily concerned with separation from European power politics.[1]

In an age of rapid centralization, mechanization, urbanization, and secularization, many isolationists (to use the most convenient term) still clung to the old American values formulated in a day of agrarian decentralization and small-town experiences. Hyperresistance to twentieth-century changes was especially strong in the Midwest, where petty capitalists, farmers, and workers continued to cherish the time-honored worths of individualism and free competition. Fear of modern businesss trends was intensified by the failure of the North Central states to share fully the new urban-based prosperity. As European soldiers returned to the plow and competed once more against American agricultural products, the interior states failed to recover from the postwar recession. The congressional farm bloc, devoted almost as much to isolationism as to the interests of agriculture, was formed by 1921 and met regularly in the Washington offices of the American Farm Bureau. A fleeting wartime prosperity for the American farmer was followed by long years of "deflation, tight credit, falling prices, high taxes and mortgage foreclosures." This ordeal of American agriculture came during a decade in which the industrial and financial giants of the eastern cities were consolidating their control over the country's businesses. Little wonder, then, that the old Populist prejudices were voiced once more against the international money-changers, men now identified as Wilsonian internationalists.

The country did not lack for city-bred isolationists, but this variety usually showed more comprehension of the integrating forces of the twentieth century. They understood, if at times only vaguely, that the powerful creditor nation that emerged unscathed from the war could not crawl back into the garden of international innocence. No longer could the sending of a missionary

[1] For an exploration of the technical terms "isolationists" and "internationalists" in the interwar years, see Wayne S. Cole, *Senator Gerald P. Nye and American Foreign Relations* (Minneapolis, 1962), pp. 4–5.

box to China once a year satisfy popular curiosity on foreign matters. Provincialism shrank with the ever-increasing flow of summer tourists to Europe, the viewing of movies filmed in Shanghai
or in Calcutta, and with foreign radio broadcasts tuned in by
sleepy Americans during the wee hours of the morning.

The term "internationalist," generally used to designate individuals who believed that our national security could best be preserved by cooperating with other nations to ensure a stable world
order, came to be applied to men espousing a wide variety of programs.[2] The array of internationally minded organizations in the
twenties grew large and impressive. At the core of the movement
stood the persistent Wilsonians—iron-willed individuals who insisted that a durable peace without effective world organization
was a deceptive illusion. The strenuous efforts of the hard-core
leaguists bore few immediate results. They would, of course, have
accomplished much more had all American internationalists
agreed that no feasible substitute for the League existed within
the realm of political possibility. Because a renewed campaign to
join the League would certainly be opposed by a coalition of un-
bending isolationists and contrary-minded internationalists, the
Wilsonians were repeatedly forced to pare down their program.
A goodly number of business and professional men, clergymen,
and professors, who had previously affiliated Republican, turned
to the Democrats in protest against the unimaginative diplomacy
of the Harding-Coolidge Era. In 1923 this group coalesced with
the Wilsonian Democrats to form the League of Nations Non-
Partisan Association, but its initial campaign thrust, backed by a
cadre of outstanding civic leaders, yielded less than 50,000 en-
rolled members. In practice the new association argued for "cooperation with the League" rather than outright membership. Its
prolific propaganda, Richard W. Leopold points out, was emotional rather than realistic. Regarding the League as "an article of
faith, not a reasoned conviction," its officers seldom asked the
question that would have appealed most to our own crisis-hard-

---

[2] The term "internationalist" is just as unsatisfactory as its antithesis, "isolationist." Nevertheless, for want of better classification, the use of these
terms has been retained throughout.

ened generation: would American membership in the League *help* or *injure* our long-run enlightened self-interest?

The long patient work of the Wilsonians did not go entirely unrewarded. Their conversion of the teaching profession resulted in a spate of social science textbooks with strong internationalist overtones. In an era when the outlook for their cause appeared hopeless, the internationalists reached many young Americans of an impressionable age through their sway among the schools, colleges, and churches. This influence was exerted at a time when an ever-increasing number of youngsters completed high school to go on to college and even to graduate school, where their mentors usually exposed them to the nonisolationist point of view. In this way Wilson's heirs helped rear a generation that, faced by the Axis threat, accepted and promoted American leadership in world politics.

College-bred women, whose interest in public affairs had been stimulated by their recent victory in the Women's Suffrage Amendment, did much of the tedious leg-work for the cosmopolitan-oriented groups. Limitation of families, midget-sized apartments, pre-cooked foods, and labor-saving household gadgets left many educated women with too much leisure time on their hands. By 1928 the Federation of Women's Clubs had a combined membership of over five million. While the League idea enjoyed great popularity in silk-stocking suburban areas, such an outlook was by no means acceptable to all women who spent time in reflective thinking. The newly formed League of Women Voters, for instance, soon discovered that the disarmament crusade held far more attraction for its members; other groups actively opposed collective security. Nevertheless, the Chicago *Tribune* noted with alarm the number of female internationalists and observed that women, so long shielded from the hard facts of life, fell easy victims to the delusion that a League of Nations could bring order to a world plagued by seething national rivalries.

Although a goodly proportion of the leaguists were domestic reformers of the liberal tradition, their ranks included some economic stand-patters. Some industrial bigwigs and metropolitan bankers were cosmopolites whose horizons had been widened by travel abroad; others hoped to make their overseas investments secure by promoting world stability. Some capitalists, their feelings injured by charges hurled against them during the Populist-Progressive Era, wished to transform their reactionary image by embracing the cause of liberal internationalism.

The effort to sustain interest in collective security had a wider front than the League of Nations Non-Partisan Association, which soon settled down to become a New York City outfit with branches located in the larger university centers. Franklin Roosevelt, in semi-retirement to overcome his paralysis, had plenty of time to meditate the next step. Repeated queries to friends and acquaintances on an appropriate tribute to former President Wilson led to the creation of the Woodrow Wilson Foundation. The founding trustees originally thought of an American version of the Nobel Peace Prize, but the experiment proved abortive. Eventually the Foundation turned to the promotion of essay contests and the establishment of the Woodrow Wilson Library in New York City.

Some internationalists, sharing the materialistic outlook of the affluent 1920's, sought to advance their cause by promoting competition in cash prize contests. Perhaps the most widely advertised of these endeavors was the 1924 Bok Peace Award, which was sponsored by Edward W. Bok, the Dutch-born millionaire publisher, whose autobiography had gained him Pulitzer recognition. Bok wished to revive American international idealism "by the golden spur of self-interest." This decision led to a national contest designed to procure, through the workings of many minds, a peace plan acceptable to all segments of enlightened opinion. The jury of award sifted 22,165 individual peace formulas before handing the $50,000 prize to the elderly Charles E. Levermore, former college president and veteran peace crusader. Levermore's blueprint called for immediate American entry into the World Court, subject to the reservations advocated by Secretary of State Hughes. Although remaining out of the League for the time being, the United States should cooperate fully with Geneva in its nonforce activities. The League, in turn, was to be asked to reconsider the question of sanctions based on force and urged to devote additional effort to the development of international law.

The only noticeable effect of Bok's contest was a stiffening of senatorial opposition to any possible "back-door entry" into the League.

In retrospect, the Herculean efforts of the internationalists were hindered by three factors. First of all, they could never agree upon support for the League, the most hopeful peace organization of the day. Secondly, the confirmed internationalists lacked the support of either major party. The Republican incumbents were searching for a spineless substitute for the Geneva experiment, while most Democratic politicians regarded the League issue as a political albatross. The simon-pure Wilsonian Democrats, a minority in their own party, had to labor without any real expectation that even a political upheaval would fulfill their fondest hopes.

Finally, all efforts toward international accord had to reckon with the nature of our government, for no program had any chance of success without congressional and popular support. Because each of the states had an equal number of senators, hinterland constituencies with ingrained isolationist prejudices were over-represented in the Senate, while failure to reapportion congressional districts to mirror urban population changes led to like consequences in the House of Representatives. Moreover, both Republicans and Democrats realized that political bromides yielded more votes than the presentation of the grim facts of international existence to the fun-loving electorate of the Jazz Age. Only a small fraction of the voting public understood that if a volatile Europe was allowed to erupt once more, the United States would find it virtually impossible to escape involvement.

There were, of course, men and organizations who understood the true nature of the situation, but often their views contrasted sharply with those of the theoretical internationalists. Therefore the advocates of military preparedness were more often allied with the isolationists than with their opponents. Ultranationalists conjured up all sorts of hypothetical cases to illustrate how League machinations might undermine the Monroe Doctrine. What would happen if Mexico invaded Guatemala and the League applied sanctions? Would the Latin American states, with their nervous suspicion of the Colossus of the North, turn to Geneva or the World Court to settle their disputes and thus jeopardize the dominant position of the United States in the New World?

Yet in contrast to the hard-core isolationists, the pro-preparedness groups thought in terms of an expanded rather than a contracted American role in world politics. They therefore refused to concede that a supposedly insularized country required only a minimum of armed protection, for their philosophy was based on the premise that war rather than peace was the ordinary habit of mankind. Generally speaking, they paid more attention to naval than to military preparedness, for they believed that a wall of battleships guarding our shore lines would add substantially to the protective powers of our ocean breakers.

This argument was embellished by the Navy League of the United States, a civilian pressure group dating from 1902 that had made many converts during the war. Its plans to equal or surpass British tonnage found many sympathizers in German-American and Irish-American circles. Professor Armin Rappaport has destroyed the hoary myth that, prior to World War II, the Navy League was a mouthpiece for ambitious admirals or the tool of special economic interests who stood to gain by a naval build-up. In the light of his research, the Navy League appears, not as a sinister group, but rather as a ludicrous and ineffective organization of noisy civilian patrioteers whose propaganda efforts did little for the cause of naval strength. In time its leaders became ever more suspicious of the subversive activities of pacifists, defeatists, internationalists, and radicals, who, it was charged, "are guiding our adolescent youth into patricide."

With a handful of notable exceptions, army career men opposed collective security because its concepts contradicted their own program: peace as the offspring of national power. Their civilian counterpart, the National Security League, had shriveled with the restoration of peace after the Armistice. Nevertheless, its cardinal ideas survived. In the 1920's the demand for stronger land forces was left to the professional militarists, who scoffed at the very idea that conflicting national rivalries could be settled without resort to a strong infantry. Dominance through fear, an idea seldom hitherto advocated in peacetime, was set forth by one articulate minority as an alternative to world cooperation.

The religious groups, even in an era whose culture reflected an acquisitive materialism, were more influential, better organized, and more liberally financed than organizations founded to uphold the peace by means of military deterrence. In a population of some 106,000,000 souls, with religious affiliation splintered into countless Protestant denominations plus the Catholic and Jewish minorities, no unity could be expected on so vital a subject as foreign policy.

Generally speaking, American Catholics were isolationist-oriented because of the Irish and German affinities of so many communicants. In contrast, the more worldly Protestant ministers serving metropolitan parishes usually favored international cooperation or else were uncompromising pacifists. The motives of these preachers were varied. In some cases the old missionary spirit was now channeled into work for the League of Nations in order to ameliorate the plight of suppressed nationalities, a concern that had long held the interest of American Protestantism. Religion's permanent duty, said the nonfundamentalist Protestants, was to conquer war by making the world masses conscious of the stark necessity for international harmony and order. Unfortunately even the modernists were unable to rally around any one program; time and again disjointed action foiled the efforts of these dispensers of good will.

Bible Belt Christianity was still a powerful national force in the 1920's. The celebrated Scopes trial over the teaching of evolution bears full witness to this fact. For rural churchmen the recent war had accentuated resented changes in the older American way of life. Insulated by geography, unsympathetic to foreign nations, prejudiced against liberals who were promoting internationalism, neither fundamentalist ministers nor their flocks found room in their tunnel-vision for the "foreign-dominated" League. On the other hand, the movement to outlaw war did penetrate the ranks of the ultra-conservative religionists. Fundamentalists proclaimed that this was God's world and the war system would have to follow slavery and the saloon into limbo.

Along with nationalists and religious leaders, ordinary citizens sought as never before to influence the formulation of foreign policy. Often, however, the activities of schools, colleges, churches, and service clubs confused rather than clarified the essential issues at stake. Peace, rather than abiding national security, was set forth as the ultimate goal of diplomacy. Headlines and digests frequently oversimplified complex situations. Nevertheless, press releases reflected the quickened interest in foreign affairs that had been stimulated by America's first overseas war. On the other hand, mergers and consolidations in the newspaper world of the 1920's led, through the use of syndicated pieces, to a monotonous standardization of press opinion. This united press wielded a terrific influence on the dispensation of news, an influence largely undiminished by the advent of the radio because so many broadcasting systems were dependent upon the news-gathering agencies of the metropolitan dailies.

Some important exceptions aside, most of the giant newspaper chains had strong isolationist leanings. With the current upheaval in ownership, many old-time Democratic papers were bought up by these chains or else were acquired by independent Republican owners. These publishers, or their editors, accepted the new isolationism as a tenet of GOP orthodoxy.

Among the press moguls who rapidly expanded their dominions were many veteran enemies of the League. Frank A. Munsey, who controlled the *Sun, Telegram,* and *Herald* in New York City alone, had done yeoman work for the Irreconcilable cause. The king titan, William Randolph Hearst, was even more influential in the press crusade against world organization. Possessed of an exaggerated nationalism which blended well with isolationism, Hearst's sole consistency was a vicious America-first parochialism.[3] Possibly such press tycoons as Hearst and Munsey reflected, rather than shaped, the opinions of the bulk of their readers. Nonetheless, their editorials gave a fillip to the prevailing tendency in Ameri-

[3] By 1923 Hearst had accumulated twenty-two newspapers, seven American and two British magazines, his own news services and the King Features Syndicate, to which many independent publications subscribed. The biggest consumer of paper in the world, Hearst claimed to reach seven million readers, and his octopus clutch was steadily reaching out for new publications.

can foreign policy by constantly contrasting our own moral superiority with the congenital wickedness of other folk.

Two strong papers that maintained their independence in this decade of mergers merit special attention. The Chicago *Tribune* and the Kansas City *Star*, the leading isolationist journals of the nation's heartland, penetrated the countryside far from their home offices. Colonel Robert R. McCormick, long-time czar of the *Tribune*, was noted for his cynicism, arrogance, jingoism, and pretentious patriotism. William Rockhill Nelson's Kansas City *Star*, on the other hand, was conceded to be "clean, brave and fair," even by men who resented its isolationist obsession.

There was, of course, a strong minority to countervail isolationist press leanings. Adolph Ochs's New York *Times*, reflecting the views of the eastern business groups and the well-informed intelligentsia, carried a torch for the cause of collective security. When Munsey sold the *Herald* to Ogden Mills, the newly combined *Herald Tribune* backed the *Times* in pleading for a broader world outlook; their joint effort helped neutralize the Hearst-Munsey influence along the Atlantic seaboard.

In the Midwest, Victor Fremont Lawson, owner of the Chicago *Daily News*, stinted no effort to combat the Chicago *Tribune*'s exasperating editorials. Lawson had a European staff headed by Edward Price Bell which included such able men as Raymond Gram Swing, and the two Mowrer brothers, Paul Scott, and Edgar Ansel. Lawson was genuinely interested in promoting the cause of world organization, and at times he and his colleagues ran their foreign service at a loss merely for the sake of curbing Colonel McCormick's growing national influence.

Except for the Lawson outfit and the European staff of the New York *Times*, the foreign news guild usually cabled home chits which bristled with prejudice. Reports on foreign convulsions were frequently unsympathetic in tone, and often larded with prayers of thanks for the wise Republican statesmanship that had prevented continuous entanglements. Some objective observers noted that many of these correspondents deteriorated in foreign climes and took just enough time off from the pursuit of masculine happiness to make carbon copies of each other's communications.

Perhaps the rise in importance of the professional newspaper columnist, whose writing reflected the new interest in overseas affairs, was of greater consequence than the views of the press magnate who employed him. By 1920, nineteenth-century personal journalism, with its lively polemics, had given way to a deceivingly objective listing of facts. The answer to this type of dead-pan journalism was the syndicated column, which has done so much to shape public opinion in contemporary America. The pioneers of this genre were Arthur Brisbane, Heywood Broun, and Walter Lippmann. Brisbane's "Today," dating from 1917, was later pushed by Hearst to the point where its isolationist-minded author wrote 500,000 words a year and reached millions of readers. Lippmann and Broun were much more mindful of foreign complexities but they were prone to scold European statesmen and their barbs were more effective than their occasional reminders that America did not enjoy a monopoly on the desire for peace.

It is obvious, therefore, that the isolationist cause enjoyed a very good press. Though there were attempts to offset this advantage by partially effective internationalist counterpropaganda, the voice of the opposition was apologetic and hesitant. Certainly no peace plan to rival the League resulted from journalistic efforts.

If the guiding lights of the Republican Restoration had searched diligently for new dynamic plans, they would have found many in the platforms of the peace societies of the day. Since the great reformatory period which we loosely term "Jacksonian Democracy," the United States had spawned most of the modern peace movements. Prior to the 1914 holocaust, these societies were fostered by large endowments from philanthropic-minded capitalists and worked leisurely toward their common goal of world peace. American intervention in the Kaiser War revived the activities of the older organizations and gave birth to some forty new outfits which carried on their programs after the Armistice. In a decade when messianic reforms sparked little enthusiasm, the peace movement flourished.

Professor Robert H. Ferrell, to whom we are indebted for so much light on the inner workings of the peace movements of the 1920's, has conveniently classified the societies as conservative or radical (nonconformist) organizations. The older groups, which belonged to the first division, were usually eastern in origin and appeal, well-financed by large gifts, restrained in propaganda efforts, and they seldom actively promoted membership campaigns.

The World Peace Foundation belonged to this conservative category. Established in 1910 by the textbook king Edwin Ginn, it found a certain amount of neutrality on vital issues prudent. Nevertheless, the Foundation did become the official distributor for all League publications. Also belonging to the conservative group was the Carnegie Endowment for International Peace. Following the Armistice it had more assets than ever with which to pursue its elusive goal, for the war had greatly increased the value of Carnegie's initial gift of ten million dollars in U.S. Steel bonds. Thus, *International Conciliation* was distributed at nominal rates, one thousand International Relations Clubs were sponsored, and "International Mind" alcoves in countless small libraries were well stocked. The Endowment's officers and paid personnel were all friends of world organization. However, such institutions designed to promote international accord had to handle the League issue with kid gloves, and this very fact is a pointed reflection on the spirit of the day. Furthermore, as time went on, even the pro-League conservative organizations tempered their demands for unqualified American participation for they were run by men not given to trust in political miracles.[4]

Also belonging to the conservative category were certain postwar organizations whose purpose it was to provide objective nonpartisan information to their constituents. Most noteworthy of these news-dispensing agencies were the Foreign Policy Association and the Council on Foreign Relations, both of which evolved from wartime groups. In 1921 the Foreign Policy Association began to publish its celebrated *Bulletin,* a four-page weekly which provided information that the public could not conveniently find

[4] In queer fashion, the venerable American Peace Society, dating from 1828, opposed collective security of the League variety because its officers were unwilling to approve of any plan whose sanctions rested upon physical coercion.

elsewhere. For a short spell the revamped FPA continued its original pro-League propaganda efforts, but it soon specialized in purely educational work, establishing branches in leading cities and providing a Speakers' Bureau to foster local discussions of world affairs.

The Council on Foreign Relations was a more exclusive organization with high dues and membership only by invitation. One of its leading contributions was the sponsorship of *Foreign Affairs*, an elitist quarterly which dealt with international relations on a sophisticated level. *Foreign Affairs* was launched with the "conviction that isolationism had died with the last doughboy." Significantly, its first editor was the hard-nosed Yankee professor Archibald Cary Coolidge, whose 1910 volume, *America as a World Power*, had been heralded as an academic recognition of the end of isolationism. It is, therefore, noteworthy that Professor Coolidge's editorial neutrality on the League issue (continued by his successor, Hamilton Fish Armstrong) was not conducive to complete unity in the Council. Apparently it was difficult for the internationalists to agree, even when their avowed purpose was simply educational enlightenment.

By 1926 there were some twelve hundred organized groups in the land dealing with the promotion of peace and a better understanding of international relations. The energy expended in prewar years on domestic reforms had now been sublimated into world affairs. This fact alone is enough to warrant reconsideration of the hasty judgment that all Americans of the Jazz Decade were "money-hungry Babbitts" or disillusioned idealists seeking refuge in Europe from prohibition and the tedium of existence under Coolidge. Dexter Perkins has observed that the passion for peace stimulated by Wilson now took many forms—some realistic and others visionary. Viewed in this light, the peace movements of the day mark a period of adjustment to America's new world role; and in the manner of such periods, they provided more confusion than enlightenment. This was especially true of the newly founded peace organizations of the nonconformist variety. These organizations worked on shoestring budgets and were prone to emphasize a single panacea for complex questions. To attain their goals, they employed every possible propaganda device, including mass petitions and letters addressed to public officials. They specialized in appeals to the newly enfranchised women voters.[5] On the whole, the failures of these peace enthusiasts are more apparent than their achievements. Nevertheless, their very existence kept the country from sinking even further into a twentieth-century variant of know-nothingism.

Thus, organizations multiplied with obtrusive names, gaudy stationery, annoying fund-raising campaigns, inane conventions, and irritating pressure techniques. All in all, the radical groups had about one hundred full-time bureaucrats, stationed at Washington or New York, running the organizations while most of their constituents satisfied their consciences merely by providing financial support. Frequently, hired personnel and fanatical volunteer workers resisted cooperative action with rival groups that might impinge upon the autonomy of their own organizations. Invariably more thought was given to immediate programs than to ultimate ends. Despite widespread futile and overlapping action, they did manage to reach, in one form or another, about a third of the country's population.

Significantly, in Europe utopian peace organizations were fewer in number and less influential. Overseas, firsthand experience with the desolation of war had convinced realistic men of the necessity for backing the League, imperfect though it was. But American peace groups were torn by divided counsels and their efforts vitiated by visionary proposals. In reality, writes John E. Stoner, some American peace advocates wanted to attain their goal "but were not particular what road they took to reach it; others . . . wanted peace but would consent to approach it only by a road of their own choosing." Some utopians even argued that a universal grass-roots reform movement would render peace

[5] Their most important units were the Women's International League for Peace and Freedom, the American Committee for the Cause and Cure of War, the National Committee for the Prevention of War, the Parliament of Peace, the War Resister's League, and the American Committee for the Outlawry of War, whose startling success warrants further consideration later in this volume.

machinery superfluous, for newly inspired peoples would prevent rapacious governments from waging war.

In the United States, the world reform movement that captured the imagination of a major sector of influential internationalists was the call for the enthronement of international law. During the century of peace that followed the fall of Napoleon, modern international law had evolved through treaties, conventions, common practice, and sporadic attempts at the codification of its principles. While its sanctions were frequently challenged, the system functioned with considerable efficiency until the Great War of 1914 blurred the distinctions between armed and unarmed individuals, between contraband and noncontraband goods. Nevertheless, some of the best legal minds in America still held high hopes for the future of international law, for even amidst the havoc of war, it had provided a modicum of help for occupied nations and individuals deprived of property rights.

In view of its recent deterioration it is difficult to explain the former hold of the law of nations upon many American experts. Such men were impressed by the legal background of United States history and they maintained that if the world would accept the sanction of international law, help perfect its codification, and provide a universal court for the judicial settlement of global disputes, twentieth-century civilization could exorcise the demon of war.

This argument was the favorite of legal-minded experts who, in retrospect, underestimated some formidable obstacles. To begin with, the League Covenant had executive, legislative, and judicial branches, while the blueprints of international lawyers usually failed to provide for a world legislature to formulate new law or an executive to administer commonly accepted principles. Secondly, while judicial methods of settling disputes proved satisfactory in minor altercations over diplomatic immunity or treaty ratifications, the World Court established by the League was all but helpless when it attempted to settle major arguments that impinged upon national sovereignty or where its decisions might jeopardize the supposed security interests of the litigant states. Finally, the concept of international law was undermined by the very nature of modern total war. Under such circumstances, it was virtually impossible to add to the existing body of international law, to codify it or to endow it with proper sanctions.

Undaunted by these obstacles, prominent American jurists pressured their government to promote the cause of international law. Often these lawyers were Republican opponents of the League who displayed only a lukewarm interest in Geneva's non-judicial activities. Hence the insistent requests for a new meeting at The Hague to continue the work started at the two prewar international conferences in the Dutch capital. It was freely predicted that a postwar Hague conference would systematize the law of nations and replace League power politics with international morality. A persisting nineteenth-century optimism overestimated the better side of human nature, a wishful thought to be dispelled by the rise of the Fascist dictators.

In addition to the promotion of international law as a substitute for League membership, legalists also advocated the expansion of other conventional methods of settling disputes—direct diplomatic negotiations, the use of mixed commissions, mediation, and good offices, and the overhaul of our outdated string of treaties providing for arbitration and conciliation. These abortive efforts reflected still another carry-over of the thinking of the nineteenth century. Sponsors of these attempts often must have worked in halfhearted fashion, for they knew full well that war had come in 1914 without any serious effort to utilize the some hundred agreements negotiated to avoid it. Yet American statesmen continued to explore discredited paths to peace because of public demand and because these efforts helped ease bad conscience over the League rejection. New treaties were a free advertisement of the American will for world peace and were based on long-standing precedent that did not run counter to the traditions of neutrality and nonentanglement. Hence, beginning with the secretaryship of Frank B. Kellogg (1925–1929), many new bilateral treaties of arbitration (supplanting the Root series of Theodore Roosevelt's day) were negotiated. Also signed were a series of cooling-off conciliation agreements which supposedly improved upon the prewar labors of Secretary of State William J. Bryan.

Marshaled together, these new pacts accomplished nothing. Though Secretary Kellogg's arbitration and conciliation treaties sounded more impressive than the best wording that Root and Bryan could get through the Senate, in actuality these series left open just as many loopholes and similarly ignored the all-important question of enforcement. Kellogg's efforts were widely hailed, but not a single sentence of these wordy pacts was ever invoked in the crisis-ridden years that preceded Hitler's blitz against Poland.

Meanwhile a curious mixture of idealism and irresponsibility prevailed in the American mind. A major cleavage existed between those groups who wanted to enforce peace and those who eschewed coercion whether used by a nation, alliance, or international body. While in most instances devotees of international law and arbitrational machinery were sober-minded thinkers honestly groping for a plan to end war, Pollyanna schemes multiplied among the parvenu peace groups. With the exception of the outlawry of war, most important among these amateur efforts were pacifism and plans for universal disarmament.

The unswerving pacifists formed a small but obstreperous minority. Their solution to the problem of war was as simple as it was whimsical: let the United States resolve never again under any circumstances to resort to armed strife. Frequently, dedicated pacifists made common cause with militaristic superpatriots to denounce the Republican tendency to establish unofficial rapport with League agencies. For twenty years following the Armistice, American peace crusaders celebrated "No More War Days," distributed "Disarm or Die" handbills, and held endless parades, discussions, and prayer meetings. Not all pacifists were ultraists, for since the days of Andrew Jackson, their ranks had broken after each actual outbreak of hostilities. Then a majority of their members would rationalize the present war as unique in nature and, therefore, deserving of support. This phenomenon was destined to be repeated in the era of the Second World War.

Meanwhile there was more general agreement on disarmament than on any other corrective of the postwar era. The popularity of this panacea stemmed from a complex of factors. A superficial analysis of the causes of Europe's 1914 tragedy created the impression that war came because of the inevitable collision of two rival alliances armed to the teeth.[6] Some American statesmen encouraged the disarmament crusade in the belief that the United States might set an example for Europe in the reduction of military budgets, thereby making it possible for our debtors to pay their war debts. Discouraged leaguists boosted American leadership in disarmament in the hope that it would stimulate further action leading to international cooperation. The disarmament coalition also contained some undeviating isolationists who hoped that the resulting *détente* might make peace so secure that the League would wither on the vine, thus removing any temptation for future American affiliation. Here, at last, was something upon which the vast majority could agree. This fact made disarmament the starting point in the postwar drive for peace.

Accordingly, when the triumphant Republicans returned to power, they found a broad popular front combating "The Crime of Competitive Armament." The New York *World* made press history by launching a gigantic newspaper campaign which included the appointment of a special "disarmament editor." The campaign was given terrific impetus when President Harding overcame some initial doubts and convened the Washington Naval Arms Conference, details of which belong to the ensuing chapter. An analysis of the disarmament combine is pertinent here, however, for it serves as a convenient illustration of the workings of the peace societies who momentarily buried ideological quarrels to concentrate on "a world-wide war against war."

The most effective body behind this purpose was the National Council for the Limitation of Armament, a federation of religious, labor, educational, and women's groups. Started as a makeshift body to marshal public opinion behind the 1921 Washington conclave, it later became a permanent organization known as the National Council for Prevention of War. Its headquarters were located across the street from the State, War, and Navy depart-

[6] For instance, the American League to Limit Armaments was organized late in 1914. The Disarmament Education Association was formed seven years later.

ments. It had a formidable budget and Frederick J. Libby, a Republican Congregationalist minister turned Quaker, was its presiding genius. It sponsored about four thousand local conferences and eventually distributed its fortnightly publication, *Disarmament Clipsheet,* to some twenty-five hundred newspapers. Libby's religious convictions made him an avowed enemy of a League whose Covenant approved of war to deter aggression, but he did throw his enormous influence behind the movement for qualified American affiliation with the World Court.

Paralleling the work of the NCPW were two women's organizations. Jane Addams, who had pioneered settlement work in Chicago's ghettos, dominated the American branch of the Women's International League for Peace and Freedom (WILPF). Like her Quaker coreligionist, Libby, Miss Addams condemned the League of Nations. Devotion to the cause of peace did not preserve tranquility in the inner councils of WILPF. Miss Addams's leadership was contested by Mrs. Carrie Chapman Catt, whose ambition had been whetted by success in the prohibition and suffrage movements and on the lecture platform. Eventually Mrs Catt left the movement to federate nine women's groups into the National Council on the Cause and Cure of War. Far less inclined toward pacifism than WILPF, Mrs. Catt's pro-League faction captured control of the secessionist organization and devoted its efforts toward lifting the country's insular mood.

Both the ultrapacifists and the moderate disarmament groups originally contained many theoretical internationalists. Most of their organizations, however, incessantly castigated Europe for its standing armies, unrealistically viewed the problem of national security, and glibly oversimplified complex causes for world disorder.

The numerous crackpot schemes for peace that flourished in the interwar years defy precise enumeration. Men of good will sought immortality by trying to solve a problem that had frustrated the best minds of countless generations. The Michigan Council for Peace drafted a plan for world government. A committee of one hundred paraded in Washington "For Law Not War." The socially prominent Mrs. Frank A. Vanderlip promoted a peace pageant called the March of Mankind. Only three years prior to his burial in the full regalia of a colonel of Nebraska volunteers, William J. Bryan came out in support of a constitutional amendment that would make the declaration of war, except in case of invasion, subject to a popular referendum. Here was the gist of the later famous Ludlow Amendment.

These far-fetched plans reflected American schizoid thinking, predominantly isolationist, overwhelmingly devoted to the cause of peace and yet unwilling to take the immediate risks that might have prevented a second global catastrophe. All groups, including the unchanging isolationists, wished to follow the arrow marked "To Peace." Even the world-minded cliques, unable to bridge differences in the interest of a workable peace plan, shared the dangerous illusion of American invulnerability. Little wonder, then, that their cosmopolitan talk lacked a sense of urgency as long as an exhausted Europe was too busy licking war wounds to launch new aggressions. The Harding administration came to power in the infancy of the long armistice. As the President's surrogate in foreign affairs, Secretary Hughes had to grope his way amidst a deceiving calm whose superficial nature was seldom disturbed by penetrating thought. Hence, there was little chance for creative diplomacy; Hughes would have to be content with the compromise between the old order and the new that we call neo-isolationism.

CHAPTER III

Midstream Diplomacy

Wilson's successors faced a knotty problem which they themselves had created. An intelligentsia devoted to the advancement of peace kept a careful watch on the diplomatic maneuvers of the incoming Republicans. Yet the country at large had rejected mem bership in the single world organization which bore any promise of success. As a candidate, Senator Harding had suggested an "Association of Nations" as a substitute system of collective security, but this campaign trick had to be discarded when Wilson's League blueprint was put into operation by the Allied coalition.

The new League faced great difficulty at first, for America's abandonment of the project nearly proved fatal. Europeans, however, clung to the experiment in the desperate belief that its survival betokened the single tangible hope of preventing another ghastly war. Hence, the Allies vitalized the Covenant under the skillful direction of Secretary-General Sir James Eric Drummond, a veteran diplomat who had learned his art in the service of the British Foreign Office. Shortly after Harding's election, the League Assembly held its constituent meeting, attended by delegates from forty-eight countries. On Inauguration Day, 1921, Harding and Hughes faced a going concern that was struggling to find its way in a war-scarred, unstable, and rancorous world.

The new administration would also have to bring its chosen

43

policy of nonentanglement into harmony with the fact that its government had emerged from the war as potentially the strongest power on earth. The new interests and unwanted responsibilities thrust upon the United States by the relentless course of history could not be ignored. The Republican Restoration, therefore, was compelled to meld into one concordant policy the concepts of nonentanglement and acceptance of the League's existence, as well as the irreversible necessity of playing the part of a superpower.

This formidable task, demanding superb manipulation, resulted in some basic inconsistencies. The United States continued to profess its aloofness from global politics, for no statesman on a decision-making level advocated any prior commitment to the use of force to maintain world peace. On the other hand, Washington was often forced, albeit grudgingly, to cooperate in order that the Versailles settlement remain intact and, simultaneously, to create new machinery to preserve world order. By common consent, this curious mixture of the new and the old is called neo-isolationism.

Professor Richard W. Leopold reminds us that the foundation for the basic interwar diplomacy was laid during President Harding's brief twenty-nine-month tenure. Supported by the vast bulk of public opinion, the Republicans refused to depart in theory from fundamental isolationist maxims, but, at the same time, they had to make certain concessions to the reality of the situation. These compromises bore the approval of the great majority which earnestly sought peace but was unprepared to make the necessary sacrifices to insure its blessings.

This uphill task of trying to reconcile the irreconcilable led to many incongruities, which were glossed over by pious platitudes designed to stimulate national egotism. Neo-isolationists argued that our motives were so pure and unselfish that we should not be freighted down with binding commitments which might impede our future efforts on behalf of humanity. "America first," said Calvin Coolidge, "is not selfishness; it is the righteous demand for strength to serve."

Personalities as well as the pace of events determined the nature of the country's postwar foreign policy. Secretary of State Charles E. Hughes belonged to the Atlantic seaboard intelligentsia which,

John Braeman has noted, "realized isolation was no longer possible, that the free security afforded by the ocean and the British
navy was drawing to a close, [and] that the outcome of a far-off
war might have grave consequences for this country." These Republicans were activists, but their internationalist orientation was
founded upon a belief in law and moral suasion rather than upon
the sanction of force. Hughes's legal, judicial, and political career
had brought him into intimate contact with Wall Street business
tycoons whose overseas economic interests long predated the Great
War. Such men naturally longed for a speedy European recovery
that would quicken the old import-export trade. Metropolitan
bankers, accustomed to financing these transactions, also had a
vested stake in global stabilization. The war had convinced many
eastern businessmen and corporation lawyers, including Hughes,
of the necessity of world association. Yet when Wilson's plans were
put on paper, the future Secretary dissented, for his legalized mind
inclined toward a judicial rather than a political settlement of disputes between nations. "Independence—" he once said, "that does
not mean and never has meant Isolation. Co-operation—that does
not mean and never has meant alliances or political entanglements." Although originally a treaty reservationist and a signer of
the Manifesto of the Committee of Thirty-One, Hughes's chief ar
gument with the chauvinists of his party was that he thought Wilson's plans had some redeemable features. But J. Chal Vinson has
noted that "his search for legal and judicial substitutes for the
League's power made him far more the critic than the exponent of
the principles of Woodrow Wilson." Blessed with an acute sense
of the possible, Hughes preferred limited triumphs to championing
lost causes aimed at remaking the world. Hamstrung by presidential apathy, congressional hostility, and mounting anti-foreignism
on the part of the public, Hughes chose the role of statesman-
politician rather than that of perfectionist.

At first Hughes seriously considered adhering to his stand during
the recent campaign, i.e., joining the League with reservations
eliminating the entangling Article X of the Covenant. He quickly
abandoned such thoughts, for on April 12, 1921, President Harding
told an applauding Congress that we wanted no part in the "world-

governing" Geneva organization which was endowed with "super-powers." The Secretary then faithfully explored the possibilities of redeeming his party's 1920 promise for a substitute Association of Nations, but he quickly saw the futility of a scheme that would invite scorn abroad and would draw the fire of Republican stalwarts and Wilsonian Democrats at home. "There is," he reasoned, "a middle ground between aloofness and injurious commitments." And so Hughes headed the ship of state for midstream. To be sure, there would be scorn and jeers from the extremists on both sides but the Secretary set his stern jaw and prepared himself for the stormy voyage.

Although delegating unusual powers to his brilliant Secretary of State, the new President also helped shape the diplomacy of his brief incumbency. Essentially a humble man, handsome, polite, easygoing, and pliable, Harding displayed no real interest in international affairs. When questioned about world conditions, he usually told curious reporters "to see Mr. Hughes about that." Yet the President did not completely surrender his prerogatives as chief executive. Furthermore, his Senate experience had conditioned him to be overly cautious in handling its bumptious nationalists. Harding absolutely vetoed any fresh proposition to come to terms with the Treaty of Versailles, for he was well aware that he could not carry the new Senate with him. Moreover, every faltering step taken in the direction of creating unofficial rapport with Geneva was followed by a quick visit to the White House on the part of Harding's isolationist confidants. The most influential members of this group were Senator Medill McCormick, soured by three visits to restless Europe, the waspish Senator George H. Moses, and Richard Washburn Child, diplomat, journalist, and propagandist.

Nevertheless, President Harding soon discovered that the past was irretrievable. If the United States could make its way in the postwar world without Geneva, our erstwhile allies could not. Lack of any world organization whatsoever might upset Europe's delicate equilibrium. The riddle now posed was how much recognition of the existing League and cooperation with its peace machinery were absolutely necessary. Consequently Harding's pompous and

platitudinous utterances lacked congruity. From one side of his
mouth he repeated the hackneyed clichés of the ingrained isolationists; from the other came hazy assurances that the United
States would accept the world responsibilities thrust upon her by
the global upheaval. Despite this proclivity for double talk, the
presidency widened the chief executive's world view. By 1923 he
admitted that it was impossible for the country to maintain a cold
aloofness from problems of an international nature, although, he
added, we would never abandon the "cherished policy to which
we are long and strongly committed." In the course of the trans-
continental trip that terminated with his death in San Francisco,
President Harding urged qualified American entry into the World
Court established by the League.

That two individuals so entirely different in mental endowment
as Harding and Hughes could reach essential agreement on foreign
affairs is proof of how particular circumstances, working in a given
period of history, mold the course of events. During the four years
in which he presided over the State Department, Hughes enjoyed
a freedom of action seldom granted a Secretary. He found Harding
"a most agreeable chief" who never disapproved his plans except
in cases where they would surely send the Senate's rear guard
battalion on the warpath. Nor was the situation much different
after the accession of Coolidge in August, 1923, for this Yankee
President expended his shortsighted vision and limited energy on
the management of domestic policies. Hence, the diplomacy of the
early 1920's was largely the work of Hughes. While the Secretary
shaped American foreign policy, he could not count on the usual
White House influence upon Congress. This was especially true
in his endless duel with the Senate's band of Irreconcilables who
sought always to reduce the ambit of his diplomacy.

The GOP moderates were also handicapped by a renewed upsurge of anti-foreign sentiment. Distrust of trouble-breeding
Europe had grown so rapidly since Harding's electoral triumph
that it is doubtful if even a more gifted President could have
achieved a truly creative diplomacy. John Foster Bass, seasoned
war correspondent, argued that if foreigners were wedded to a
program of conquest and revenge, the best that we could do was

remain on the side lines during the new turbulence. An ultra-dry Anglophobe, charging a world conspiracy against prohibition, introduced a ditty of King George V into the *Congressional Record:*

> Four and twenty Yankees
>   Feeling mighty dry
> Took a trip to Canada
>   And bought a case of rye
> When the case was opened
>   The Yanks began to sing—
> "To hell with the President
>   God Save the King!"

Secretary of Commerce Herbert Hoover, whose wartime reputation gave him extraordinary influence in the Cabinet, waxed hypercritical over "the eternal malign forces of Europe." The war, said a leading educator, had killed the best of Europe's breed; now we had to deal with a band of surviving unscrupulous upstarts who ruled the continent. Will Rogers's comment reflected the general prejudice: "Why, if they had Niagara Falls, they would have had 85 wars over it at various times to see who would be allowed to charge admission to see it."

Europe returned sneer for sneer. A gifted cartoonist depicted "Uncle Shylock" rifling the pockets of European nations sandbagged by Mars. Foreign writers were prone to embellish tales of American materialism and monetary greed. The United States, they insisted, was the most difficult nation in the world to influence by reason because Yankees were at all times persuaded that they had a monopoly on the instinct for righteous conduct.

Across the water Americans felt that to chaffer with Europe meant to be hornswoggled. Even Woodrow Wilson came to share this popular intolerance. Five months before he left office he praised his Secretary of State's efforts to cement the Pan-American Union as "the only available offset to the follies of Europe."

Every President and Secretary of State during the interwar years had to abide by this dominant mood of withdrawal. Charles E. Hughes was forced to weigh carefully even the slightest overture in the direction of international cooperation. He had taken office at a time when Congress was trying to regain the power and influence which it had lost to Wilson amidst the crisis of war. Hence, every international agreement that came from the White House in the 1920's was put under the microscope. The Senate, said the New York *Times*, was studded with "chartered libertines" who obstructed every move toward decent international cooperation. Such men were in the habit of opposing all agreements that were not one-sidedly to our advantage. It required all of Hughes's finesse to outflank the Senate obstructionists on measures which now seem as innocuous as they were futile. If Americans took it for granted that we were the supreme power on earth, all too few of them were willing to assume the responsibilities that went with this position. Generally speaking, those who knew the least feared the most.

Thore was, however, another side to the coin. If certain influences stayed Secretary Hughes's hand, there were also countervailing forces exerting pressure in the opposite direction. Influential Republicans who wanted to salvage at least part of Wilson's program were often as articulate as the GOP isolationists. Eastern money interests urged a foreign policy that would take into account America's postwar industrial and financial might, and an administration that courted big business had to pay some attention to such arguments. Republican internationalists of this school, albeit anxious to protect our global economic welfare, also wished to make no commitments that would impinge on national sovereignty, future freedom of action, or unilateral control over the Monroe Doctrine. This attitude was entirely in harmony with the moderate course plotted by Hughes which ran midway between Wilson and Borah.

The first task faced by the new administration was to end the war officially. The defiant Wilson had vetoed a joint congressional resolution which repealed the 1917 declaration of war against Germany. Congress then repassed this Knox Resolution and President Harding affixed his signature to it. Seven weeks later the administration negotiated the Treaty of Berlin with the Reich and made similar agreements with Austria and Hungary. We insisted upon every benefit that the Allies had gained at Versailles, but disclaimed all obligations which the earlier negotiations had entailed. The liberals were dissatisfied with the administration's policy, and Hughes himself would have preferred to do otherwise. He had wanted a simple ratification of the Treaty of Versailles without the appending Covenant. But in 1921 Versailles was a tainted word, and the Secretary had been forced to retreat under senatorial fire. "While . . . our action may be swallowed with a wry face," Hughes wrote apologetically, "it is the best that could be done."

This very practical point of view also characterized Secretary Hughes's approach to American-Soviet relations. Although in this area Hughes set some precedents that were not reversed until the 1932 Democratic triumph, in the main he followed and refurbished President Wilson's vacillating policies. It is, therefore, necessary to review the complicated dealings with Russia which followed the Communist revolution in that country.

Owing to complex and unusual circumstances, President Wilson had decided, in July of 1918, to land American troops in northern Russia and southeastern Siberia as part of a joint Allied intervention. It is certain that Wilson most reluctantly overruled the objections of his military advisers when, after repeated entreaties from the Allied Supreme War Council, he decided upon this step. The reasons attributed for Wilson's action are various and tangled. George F. Kennan warns that the confusion of the story forces the historian "to simplify, to generalize, and to ask the reader to lean on his judgment." Hence, nonspecialists must telescope the thorny details of the views of both Kennan and those authorities who question his conclusions.

For three years following the Leninist coup of November, 1917, Russia was locked in bloody civil wars between the Red Soviets and a succession of White counterrevolutionary despots. Possibly deep in Wilson's mind was the desire, openly expressed by the French, for a joint intervention that might speed the fall of a Communist regime devoted to the spread of class warfare and a general upheaval of capitalist governments. Also, the President acted when the 1918 German drive, begun after the separate Bolshevist peace with Germany, had jeopardized the safety of Paris. Under such circumstances it seemed logical to keep Allied supply depots in northern Russia and Vladivostok from falling into enemy hands and to reopen a diversionary eastern front against the Boche. In regard to the Siberian landings, Betty M. Unterberger insists that Wilson's overriding motive was to prevent unilateral Japanese intervention which might well have led to permanent control of southeastern Siberia and northern Manchuria. As a matter of fact, Wilson's ultimate decision in favor of a combined intervention was made subject to a Japanese promise to respect Russian territorial sovereignty. On the other hand, Kennan takes at full value the reasons stated at the time by the Wilson administration. According to this rationale, the President feared for the fate of the anti-Hapsburg prisoners of war loose in Russia. They had formed a Czech Legion and were making their way by the Trans-Siberian Railroad to Vladivostok to take ship for future fighting on behalf of the Allies. There was some reason to believe that this unarmed Czech Legion might be overcome by loyal German-Austrian PW's, and Siberia might fall into German hands. Probably all of these factors played some part in Wilson's ultimate decision for joint intervention.

Wilson was soon to deplore his stand. It proved impossible to maintain our troops in Siberia without indirectly helping the reactionary White Russian leader in those parts, Admiral Alexander V. Kolchak. The other alternative was withdrawal, and this step would surrender a strategic area to Japanese control. At the Versailles Conference, there was much talk of solving the Soviet question, but all plans were aborted. Before Wilson returned to the United States he ordered the withdrawal of troops from northern Russia, but fear of Japan made him hesitate in regard to Siberia. Finally, however, admitting that it was harder to get out of Russia than to get in, Wilson ordered the Siberian contingent home.

The American intervention had kept Murmansk in northern Russia from falling into German hands, but otherwise it had done much harm. The rescue of the Czech Legion proved unnecessary, the Japanese were not restrained to any measurable degree, and the Whites did not save the world from the Bolshevist experiment. Wilson's intervention was destined to have a lasting psychological effect upon our relations with the victorious Reds, and it impeded a cool-headed evaluation of the diplomatic turmoil which formed the backwash of the Russian Revolution.

By the end of 1920 the Reds had consolidated their control, subduing all counterrevolutionary armies and hurling the Polish invaders back to Warsaw. However, neither Wilson nor his confidants were willing to grant even *de facto* recognition to a government that rested on "the negation of every principle of honor and good faith." No Washington official grasped the essence of the problem, i.e., that the question of recognition should have hinged, not upon the kind of government that the Soviets had, but rather upon the nature of Communist behavior toward other nations. Owing to special circumstances, Wilson's policy stiffened during his last year in the White House. First of all, the Reds callously repudiated their American debts, an act that shocked a generation accustomed to even revolutionary leaders' honoring international obligations. In any event, American public opinion would not have approved an alternative policy, for the Soviets had made a separate peace with Germany which imperiled the Allied armies in the West. Complicating this was the popular but erroneous opinion that Lenin and Trotsky were German tools, for it had been the Reich which made possible their return from exile to Russian soil. Further, Wilson shared the popular belief that the overthrow of the proletarian dictatorship was only a matter of time, a prediction announced ninety-one times within two years by so cautious a newspaper as the New York *Times*. Finally, Lenin's statements and deeds justified, in part, Wilson's refusal to traffic with him.

The Republicans inherited from Wilson a fourfold Soviet platform: (1) friendship for the Russian people but hostility to the Moscow dictatorship; (2) opposition to any new outside force mustered to overthrow a regime that was believed to be on the verge of collapse; (3) an insistence that Russia was entitled to her 1914 boundaries; (4) no official recognition as long as the Reds were "determined and bound to conspire against our institutions." Secretary Hughes not only accepted this program, but in the face of solid, if unpleasant, evidence that the Kremlin was here to stay, held inflexibly to nonrecognition and incorporated it into the Republican creed. Nevertheless, Hughes followed Wilson's policy of differentiating hostility to the Soviet regime from animosity to the Russian people and the Secretary often upheld legitimate Russian territorial claims in his diplomatic correspondence.

The Harding administration also implemented Wilson's plan to ship food and supplies into starving Russia. In 1921 the situation became acute when a great famine threatened thirty million people with hunger and death. To their credit, the anti-Bolshevist GOP leaders did not follow the pattern of our erstwhile Allies, who made aid contingent upon debt settlements. Headed by Secretary of Commerce Hoover, the American Relief Administration spent some fifty million dollars in private and government funds on food, supplies, and seed plantings for stricken Russia. Three decades later Hoover asserted that his humanitarian efforts, which he claimed were devoid of political implications, received only a minimum of Soviet cooperation. The Kremlin's anxiety about Hoover's ultimate purpose, however, was not relieved by Hughes's public admission that the ARA was a "peephole" into dark Russia which substituted for the consular reports denied us by nonrecognition. While the ARA's twenty-two months of aid did little to ease American-Soviet tensions, the organization did remove a State Department roadblock to economic penetration— an ingress that in time was to pave the way for diplomatic recognition.

In the 1920's no direct power confrontations were likely between the United States and the Soviets, for we were concentrating our interests in the New World, and after the speedy collapse of some radical-inspired revolts in Central Europe, it was evident that for the time being Communism was contained within Russia. To be sure, the Kremlin's conduct was rude and the duality of Soviet foreign policy most bewildering to practitioners of traditional diplomacy. Nevertheless, Lenin made repeated attempts to regularize relations with Hughes's State Department. Later an Iron Curtain reserve was to bar frank communications with the outside world, but most of the pioneer Bolsheviks, broadened by years in exile and proficient in foreign tongues, understood the thought patterns of the outside world. Hence, Moscow was willing to make genuine concessions in the hope of reaching accord with Hughes. This flexibility, of course, was based upon self-interest, for the Kremlin sorely needed American goods and hoped that American power would balance Japanese might in the Far East. In December, 1923, Russia hinted that she was willing to talk about her Washington debts in order to reach an agreement, but this overture, like all the rest, was coldly spurned. A handful of American historians have argued that Wilson and Hughes should not have rejected these early Soviet olive branches.[1] The great majority, however, including Kennan, conclude that existing circumstances allowed befuddled American diplomats no other choice.

Nevertheless, Hughes's dogmatic stand was roundly criticized by two American groups. Some senators with liberal inclinations agreed with Borah that the Russians had as much right to establish a socialist state in a capitalist world as America had to choose republicanism over the prevailing monarchial tradition of 1776. Borah and other pro-recognition senators were aided by some private individuals, particularly Raymond Robins, Progressive political worker and social reformer. Robins, a Red Cross representative in Russia shortly after the Revolution, pressured for recognition on the threefold grounds that the Soviet regime would endure, that it would eventually secure a higher standard of living for the Russian masses, and that unless Washington acted, German influence would predominate in the reconstruction of titanic Russia.

Also in favor of recognition were businessmen who had been promised a "gigantic role" in the process of Soviet economic recovery. The opportunity was attractive, for after Washington lifted wartime trade restrictions with Russia (except armaments) in the summer of 1921, the Soviets became good customers. While

[1] In his *American-Russian Relations, 1781–1947* (New York, 1952), William A. Williams strongly indicts American handling of the problems arising from the Russian Revolution. He suggests that a friendlier attitude might have forestalled Japanese aggressions and might have curbed the Kremlin's dangerous emphasis upon the production of military equipment and nonconsumer goods.

the government lent no help to the promotion of trade by a commercial treaty that would have followed the exchange of ambassadors, it permitted trade, and even loans, on a private basis. Many American firms participated in an international corporation formed to foster the sale of goods to the Soviets. From 1923 to 1925 our exports to Russia multiplied ninefold; thereafter we sent more goods than did Great Britain, which had recognized the "outlaw" Red government. Many business tycoons visited the USSR and came home enthusiastic. Some even argued that the expected increase of trade that would follow recognition might strengthen the current Russian New Economic Policy retreat, a recession from Marxist dogma which planed down the rougher edges of Communism. However, these pro-recognition and pro-trade groups failed to join forces until the advent of the Great Depression and were thus unable to counterbalance official hostility toward "unregenerate Russia."

In his first annual message to Congress, President Coolidge, reiterating Hughes's position, said: "I do not propose to barter away for the privilege of trade any of the cherished rights of humanity." Three Republican administrations in succession rigidly opposed recognition of Moscow on the following grounds: (1) Soviet actions in repudiating pre-1917 Russian debts and uncompensated confiscation of property had involved a loss of over one-third of a billion dollars to the United States and its citizens. (2) In its attempt to Bolshevize the world, the Soviet-sponsored Third International and its agent, the American Communist Party, were undermining the American form of government. (3) The Kremlin promoted atheism by a studied hostility against organized religious groups within and without the borders of Russia. (4) A profitable trade with the Soviets could not flourish so long as the Reds refused to recognize the rights of private property. In other words, no accommodation with the Kremlin was possible until the Red commissars made basic economic changes that would repudiate Marxist axioms. Such a demand for the reversal of the Revolution precluded any possibility of Soviet acceptance. This was the strait jacket which bound American-Russian relations. Only an unprecedented business slump and a major political upheaval were able to break its hold.

American international relations in other areas during the Harding administration were generally guided by a spirit of compromise. Taken with the embellishments made during Coolidge's incumbency, which will be detailed in the ensuing chapter, the *démarche* included: (1) peace by unofficial cooperation with the nonforce activities of the League; (2) peace by disarmament agreements; (3) peace by legal means through qualified acceptance of the World Court Protocol; (4) peace by promoting the international outlawry of war.[2]

Secretary Hughes did not immediately attempt to insure peace by the first method, unofficial cooperation with the nonforce activities of the League. As a matter of fact early American relations with Geneva were marred by some unfortunate incidents that made Hughes the chief target of the frustrated internationalists. Late in the Wilson administration, fifteen communications from Geneva (some of them important because they dealt with mandate problems) had not been acknowledged. A minor State Department official had thoughtlessly put these missives in the dead letter file. Further, during the Harding administration's shakedown period, Secretary Hughes had treated "the League at Geneva" with bad grace. He advised American jurists against accepting judgeships on the League's World Court, dictated several rude refusals to join in a proposed arms-traffic conference, and dealt separately with each of the powers concerned in League correspondence involving American interests. Although his official biographer, Merlo J. Pusey, passes lightly over these episodes, Hughes did not improve his manners until he was roundly denounced by the New York *Times*. On July 18, 1921, Edwin L. James of the *Times* European staff began a series of sensational dispatches charging the State Department with studied hostility to the fledgling League organization, including the refusal to reply to letters received. The cry was taken up by a half-dozen internationalist associations. Hughes finally attempted to explain the

2 See Richard W. Leopold, *The Growth of American Foreign Policy: A History* (New York, 1962), pp. 426–427.

mistake of his bungling subordinate, whom, by the way, he banished to a post in Egypt. Also, Hughes began to answer Geneva's inquiries, although in a perfunctory manner. It is fair to say that for several years Hughes's department treated the League as an unwanted stepchild.

Hughes overcame his initial inclination to disassociate American policy from the League because he realized that Geneva was shouldering many tasks indispensable to the restoration of an orderly world. As a matter of fact, the very existence of the League facilitated the American withdrawal from Old World affairs, for Geneva liquidated many residual wartime problems that might otherwise have absolutely necessitated our interference. This fact was not lost upon the astute Secretary, nor even upon his impassive chief. The League, Harding admitted shortly before his death, was good for Europe, but he hastened to add that "it is not for us."

By the time Harding reached this conclusion, it was apparent to realists that the League was neither the millennium envisaged by the messianic Wilsonians, nor the dangerous Goliath so dreaded by the ultranationalists. Instead the new organization was struggling to cut its milk teeth on some essential but nonmomentous problems. To Hughes's disciplined mind, the facts dictated but one policy—countenance without plaguesome political involvements. This compromise satisfied all but the extremist wing of his party. "Simply because the United States did not enter the League of Nations," said the GOP's national chairman, "it does not mean that the United States is going to withhold its support of the good that the League will accomplish."

We know today that this straddle failed. Because the selfish, myopic diplomacy of all the Atlantic powers failed to prevent or halt Axis aggressions which culminated in our second overseas crusade, it is commonplace to condemn the statesmen of the interwar period who failed to insure peace in their time. As far as the United States is concerned, Hughes's ambivalent policy must be judged within the setting in which it was formulated. The dismal outlines of the future still remained veiled. Some of the best minds of the day, including the penetrating thinker John Dewey, insisted that America must refrain from the European experiment with collective security until the Old World nations mended their ways. More to the point, Hughes, like Wilson before him, could not have done much more without outrunning the possibilities of domestic politics.

Slowly Hughes worked out his golden mean policy toward Geneva, running the straits between nonrecognition of its existence and membership involving concrete commitments. This approach was expanded by his successors and endured until the end of the League's existence. The first step was taken when silent "unofficial observers" were sent to nonpolitical conferences sponsored by the League. This "peephole" diplomacy was gradually abandoned, and by the mid-twenties American delegates participated fully in certain areas of the League's work and served on its key committees.

Examining the functions of the League from a ringside seat at the University of Geneva, Professor William E. Rappard pointed out that they could be divided into three categories: A League to Enforce Peace, A League to Execute the Peace Treaties, and A League to Promote International Cooperation. American statesmen readily comprehended this threefold division, and they confined our participation to the League's humanitarian endeavors. Thus, by 1930 we had taken part in forty conferences devoted to matters of economic, social, and technical concern, carefully refraining (until 1931) from any colloquy involving collective security measures. Such cooperation, of course, ignored the fact that the League's *raison d'être* was the enforcement of peace.

Hence, all League overtures to the United States relating to the paramount question of limiting war were rebuffed until the 1931 Manchurian invasion. The Senate stubbornly refused to approve an agreement to strengthen international control over the private munitions trade, an item which was to command so much American interest in Franklin D. Roosevelt's day. Nor would Washington lend a hand in the League's attempt to strengthen its peace machinery. In 1923 Geneva tried to repair defects in the Covenant by a Draft Treaty of Mutual Assistance that vested the Council with additional power and improved methods for identifying and punishing an aggressor state. League officials courted American support by stipulating that no signatory was obliged to help execute sanctions against aggressors operating outside of its own continent. Hughes waited five months before he reacted to this proposal, and then dismissed it curtly on constitutional grounds.

The next year the League made another attempt at self-improvement by drawing up the Geneva Protocol for the Pacific Settlement of International Disputes, which was open to non-League states. Under its terms, adhering nations would be forced to submit all disputes to pacific settlement before resorting to war; recalcitrant nations would be branded aggressors and would be dealt with by ironclad economic sanctions. Hughes's enthusiasm for the plan waned rapidly when the outstanding international lawyer in the State Department, Charles C. Hyde, advised him that adherence would jeopardize our freedom of action in the troublesome Caribbean area and would limit our neutrality in future conflicts. Hughes finally dismissed the proposed European concert in a cold interchange with the British ambassador. It is quite possible that the Protocol would have failed in any event, for a British party revolution brought in the Conservatives, who shared a lack of enthusiasm for the plan with the dominions. National selfishness was not an exclusively American state of mind; British Tories were likewise anxious not to multiply their international responsibilities. Geneva's status dropped sharply with the rejection of the Protocol.

Then help came from a most unexpected quarter when Foreign Minister Gustav Stresemann of the German Republic began the diplomatic maneuvers that led to the 1925 Peace of Locarno. In some respects this pact, drawn up at a Swiss lakeside resort, took the place of the ill-fated Protocol, for it preserved the territorial status quo in the West and effected a *détente* in central Europe by providing for arbitration treaties between the Reich and her eastern neighbors. In addition the agreement paved the way for a German entry into the League with a permanent seat on its Council. "These recent Locarno agreements," President Coolidge told Congress with obvious self-satisfaction, "represent the success of this policy which we have been insisting ought to be adopted, of having European countries settle their own political problems without involving this country." If neo-isolationism had a rationale, observes the British historian Max Beloff, it was based upon the belief that somehow Europe could maintain its own equilibrium. The prestige of the League soared on the morrow of the Pact of Locarno. Until 1925 France. was the paramount power in Europe, a position made possible by her Little Entente with the small powers that lay between Weimar Germany and Soviet Russia. When the major powers recuperated from the devastation of war, Paris began to take the League more seriously in order to see "what could be made of its novel machinery for . . . enforcing the peace."[3] Actually the League's heyday came in the later 1920's. Geneva began to assume the trappings of a world capital and Assembly meetings at the Palace of Nations sparkled with the presence of illustrious statesmen. American skeptics suspended judgment, for as yet the League had merely demonstrated that it could handle small disputes between large nations and crucial ones between small countries. Philanthropists, however, gave the experiment the benefit of the doubt. The Rockefeller Foundation contributed over half a million dollars to the. League's Health Service, while other American funds helped support the publication of treaties, Albanian and Near Eastern Relief, and the work of the White Slave inquiry. Legal experts worked on the codification of international law under League auspices, and eminent American jurists (Hughes was later to be included among them) sat on the World Court.

After Locarno, Americans accepted the League as indigenous to the new placid Europe of a prosperous era. The bitter-enders were not won over, but an impressive group of Wilson's 1919 critics were loud in their praises of Geneva's accomplishments. While it was generally conceded that the day for full American participation had passed, the overwhelming majority of civic leaders was willing to support the League's program, strengthen its hands, and applaud its mounting successes. The United States, declared Charles A. Beard with approval in 1929, was a member of the League without the benefit of "parchment and seals." This was the same Beard who soon was to become an outstanding

3 H. Stuart Hughes, Contemporary Europe: A History (Englewood Cliffs, N.J., 1961), p. 145.

spokesman for the cross-grained isolationists of the New Deal Era. By the eve of the Great Depression, most Americans believed that collective security was an excellent device for foreigners who must needs curb their own turbulence. With every major European nation a League member save the pariah Soviets, it seemed reasonable to hope that Geneva could quash Old World quarrels. The United States, it was assumed, would keep order in its own hemisphere, while the Washington treaties of 1921–1922 would prevent eruptions in the Far East.

The crowning achievement of Hughes's diplomatic career was the Washington Naval Arms Conference (1921–1922). It represents the major American effort to attain peace by the second method, through disarmament agreements, and it was actually convened before the administration had decided upon informal coordination with the nonforce activities of the League. During Hughes's apprenticeship as Secretary of State, both the international situation and the domestic passion for a bold disarmament venture provided the Republicans an opportunity to champion peace while, for the nonce, ignoring the League's existence. Disarmament was the perfect scheme to draw support from virtually all segments of public opinion—Republican moderates, disappointed Wilsonians, and political independents who were clamoring for an international *détente* divorced from the League's coercive sanctions. At the same time the plan conformed to the neo-isolationist bent, for it concurred with the theory that an insulated country needed a navy sufficient only for self-defense. Moreover, any move that would save public money was welcome to Harding's tax-conscious mentors. An across-the-board reduction in armament was bound to be hailed with delight by millions, although choleric senators were certain to resent the international understandings that must be joined to the paring down of naval budgets.

A complex of circumstances led the Harding administration to call the conference. The unpredictable Borah pushed a resolution favoring a disarmament meeting through the newly elected Republican Congress at a time when President Harding was still annoyed by the suggestion. Soon, however, White House circles sensed a grass-roots opposition to the completion of the pending Gargantuan naval blueprint. As church and peace group pressures culminated in one of the most successful public opinion rallies in American history, the administration's interest grew in a proposal that would fulfill hopes for a "Republican Versailles."

Ultimately, however, the administration was goaded into action more by unresolved wartime international rivalries than by domestic demands. Burdened by debt, London had no stomach for a new naval race, despite the ancient British policy of maintaining the world's most powerful line of battleships. In an unofficial talk with the publisher of the New York *Times*, who was visiting London, the First Lord of the Admiralty suggested that, in the future, the British fleet might concentrate on the Atlantic, with American battlewagons guarding the Pacific. The proposal, transmitted by Mr. Adolph Ochs, was favorably received in Washington. On March 16, 1921, the Admiralty notified Washington that it was ready to concede naval parity to the United States. Nevertheless, there was still another obstacle to overcome—England's alliance with Japan was about to terminate and a refusal to continue the agreement might injure Anglo-Japanese relations. Hesitation on this score was removed at an Imperial Conference. The dominions, led by Canada, informed Prime Minister Lloyd George that they would not sanction the renewal of an alliance which appeared, at least on paper, as a threat to the United States. By the summer of 1921, London officials were enthusiastic for a meeting that might make unnecessary the implementation of new naval blueprints and rid them, with good grace, of an outworn Oriental alliance.

An American-Japanese rapprochement involved far more difficulties. Tokyo was anxious for a cutback in its post-armistice naval program, which consumed, by 1921, one third of the imperial budget. At the moment the United States fleet was stationed at Pearl Harbor. However, if Washington came to an agreement with London and built up bases at Guam and Manila to match those of Singapore, the Japanese would have to embark on military expenditures that their hard-pressed economy could ill afford. Nevertheless, Tokyo hesitated lest some acute arguments with the United States be lost amidst the give-and-take of the council table.

The Japanese held, under a League mandate, the island of Yap, upon whose shores two main trans-Pacific cables were joined. President Wilson had protested the Yap mandate, and his demand for international control of the island was renewed by his successor. In addition the Nipponese troops were still stationed in Russian Siberia, fomenting incidents so as to justify their presence long after Wilson had ordered the last American doughboys home from Vladivostok. Finally, Washington had become concerned about Japanese control of the former German possession of Shantung, for Tokyo had done nothing to implement her oral promise at Versailles to withdraw military occupation from that area, nor was she willing to do so without exacting a price from helpless China. An economic postwar slump had increased the attraction to some Japanese leaders of outlying Chinese provinces. Suspecting, with good reason, that the United States would demand further assurances of respect for Chinese territorial integrity as part of a general settlement, the Japanese procrastinated until Hughes promised Ambassador Kijuro Shidehara that he would not force a direct confrontation on certain delicate issues.

Meanwhile, on July 8, 1921, Secretary Hughes seized the initiative from Great Britain and convoked the conference. The astute London diplomats were willing enough that Washington issue the summons, for they understood that this action would lessen the hostility of chronic American Anglophobes. England, however, had suggested a meeting on Pacific and Far Eastern problems; the United States was intent upon broadening the agenda to include certain phases of disarmament. The net result was a package deal. The Japanese agreed to attend, with the proviso that problems of sole concern to individual powers be excluded from the discussions. Hughes, taking a cue from John Hay's 1899 legerdemain, slyly ignored these qualifications and sent out the invitations. To help Britain save face in shelving the Japanese alliance, all powers with Far Eastern concessions or interests, with the exception of the USSR, were invited. The Washington Conference opened on the morrow of Armistice Day, 1921. A stellar group of diplomats from nine nations added interest to the occasion.

The delegates settled down to business promptly. Taking a leaf from Woodrow Wilson on open diplomacy, Hughes stated bluntly that "the way to disarm is to disarm" and he made short work of the naval race by proposing to end it at once. Hughes had done his homework well, even to the point of getting American admirals to prepare the 5:5:3 proposed scale-down on capital ships for the three leading powers. Joined to this was a ten-year holiday on the construction of future battleships. The British and Japanese delegates were astounded as their stern-visaged host explained the details of his bold proposal. A contemporary source notes that Britain's First Sea Lord leaned forward in his chair "slightly staggered and deeply disturbed." His colleague, seated nearby, "turned red and then white, and sat immovable" as Hughes prepared to scrap more British bottoms than, it was said, had been sent to Davy Jones's locker by His Majesty's enemies in a "cycle of centuries." Meanwhile the Japanese delegation had "stirred in their seats and dropped close to the table."

Recovering their aplomb, the foreign diplomats bargained with skill. Hughes had to make concessions to the British in order to secure their control of European waters. As for Japan, the Secretary played with loaded dice. American cryptanalysts decoded Tokyo's communications with her conference delegates, and Hughes knew that Japan would hold firm on the completion of the super-dreadnought *Mutsu*. He yielded here in return for permission to retain two American ships almost ready for launching. The United States and Great Britain were also forced to promise Tokyo that neither country would build new fortifications or strengthen existing bases in the region of the western Pacific. Japan made a similar pledge to maintain the status quo in the Kuriles, the Bonins and Formosa. "The most important effect of this agreement," writes Dexter Perkins, "was that it virtually insured Japan against attack in the Orient."

The French and Italian emissaries, with competition for Mediterranean control in mind, reluctantly agreed to a 1.75-each ratio on battleships in relation to the 5:5:3 schedule for the United States, Great Britain, and Japan. The French delegates were so obdurate that Hughes had to appeal over their heads to the

Premier in Paris. In part a result of French opposition, no limitations were made on lighter ships—a decision that would ultimately lead to a new race in cruisers, destroyers, submarines, and other "defensive" craft.

The United States, which had made the greatest sacrifices in scrapping actual tonnage, predicated naval limitations upon agreements designed to preserve the status quo in the Far East. A Four-Power Pact (signed by the United States, Great Britain, France, and Japan) abrogated the Anglo-Japanese alliance and promised that the powers involved would respect each other's possessions "in the region of the Pacific Ocean." This far-reaching compact, supposedly guaranteeing our outlying Far Eastern possessions, was signed in the belief that moral suasion without commitments of any kind could prevent aggression. It was, writes J. Chal Vinson, "a peace conceived in the hope that pledges and public opinion unaided by international organizations and military force could meet the problems of a world power."

To justify our naval sacrifices, to satisfy American public opinion, and to yield something to the anxious Chinese delegation, some further assurances on the Open Door were necessary. The result was a Nine-Power Pact which pledged the signatories to respect China's integrity by a multilateral acceptance of the American Open Door formula. The public was delighted at the Nine-Power Pact, for, like the Four-Power Treaty, it was based upon moral restraint rather than upon collective safeguards. If either agreement was violated, we would talk rather than take actions that might lead to shooting. This assumption, says Foster Rhea Dulles, is a prime illustration of "that unhappy alliance of idealism and irresponsibility that so generally marked the . . . [current] American approach to international affairs." Only time would reveal the futility of moral assurance unbacked by force.[4]

This bundle of compromises now had to run the Senate gantlet. Partisan Democrats joined the Irreconcilable bloc in a broadside attack on the Four-Power Pact. "What I believed menacing and

---

[4] Other major accomplishments of the Washington Conference included satisfactory settlements of the Yap Island and Shantung problems and a public pledge on the part of Japan to withdraw from Siberia.

dangerous to the Republic under Democratic rule," said Senator Hiram Johnson, "I decline to accept under Republican rule." Was there not more to this agreement to preserve the status quo in the Pacific than appeared on paper? Why should the United States guarantee Tokyo's control over Pacific islands already secured by a League mandate? Was it reasonable to believe that the Japanese would relinquish their British alliance for a mere promise that no holdings in that area would be disturbed without prior consultation? In a decade where every molehill of a treaty loomed as a mountain of entanglements, the Republican senatorial leaders were hard pressed to explain. This was especially true inasmuch as Senator Lodge had been a delegate to the recent Washington Conference. The Versailles shoe was now on the other foot, and the resourceful Lodge was compelled to defend a pact that Senator James A. Reed labeled treacherous, damnable, and treasonable. "Who would have thought it," mused one senator. "Lodge is the father of a baby League of Nations."

Some of this protest was quashed when President Harding presented the treaty in person to his former Senate colleagues with an unqualified pledge that it constituted "no commitment to armed force, no alliance, no written or moral obligation to join in defense." Secretary Hughes found it necessary to state that we had told the powers before the conference convened that we could contemplate no alliance. Nevertheless, the apprehensive Foreign Relations Comittee recommended consent to the Four-Power Pact with a reservation attached that incorporated Harding's assurances. As one wit put it, in the 1920's the Senate would not have endorsed the Ten Commandments without stipulating qualifications!

The Senate voted first on the Four-Power Pact. The party whip cracked, and to the taunts of the Democrats, enough Irreconcilables yielded to allow the agreement to pass by the scant margin of five votes. The other treaties were then assured of easy passage.

There are many divergent evaluations of Hughes's accomplishments at the Washington Conference. Until the Japanese rode roughshod over the Pacific treaties, writers tended to hail Republican statesmanship as "an epochal contribution to peace." Then the fashion changed, and Hughes was charged with weakening the navy, abandoning the build-up of our Pacific outposts, and all the while allowing Tokyo to prepare its timetable of conquest. With the ebbing of the war hysteria evoked by the Pearl Harbor disaster, historical perspective returned. Viewed more objectively, the Washington settlement achieved significant though ephemeral successes. International tensions were relaxed for a decade—a respite not equaled by any of the Cold War's sporadic "thaws." Hughes began a naval disarmament regulation program, limited though it was, that lifted some burdens and lessened others. He delayed Japanese expansionism by giving the Tokyo liberals some additional years of power, and finally the Secretary managed to translate a fraction of American idealism into concrete action. Subsequently Hughes's work was to be vitiated by unforeseeable events, but in its own day it was grounded in realism. Had there been no limitations on battleships, it is most unlikely that a tight-fisted Congress would have made sufficient appropriations for the construction of capital ships, white elephants that General William ["Billy"] Mitchell demonstrated were outmoded by the advent of aerial warfare. Nor did our self-denying pledges at Washington impede adequate fortification of the Philippines and Guam, for such improvements were voted down in Congress long after the Nipponese had reduced their Washington pledges to mere scraps of paper.

The roaring twenties had opened with a wide gap between the ardent leaguists and the overzealous isolationists. Although other factors helped span this chasm, Hughes's efforts did much to build the vital bridge. But the Secretary's compromises were full of paradoxes. The United States would never join the League, but we would collaborate with it; we would never jeopardize our future neutrality by any prior commitment, but we condemned aggression on every possible occasion; we hallowed the creed of national isolation, but we were willing to depart from its tenets to achieve specific goals of an internationalist tendency. In other words, whereas we might have controlled events by taking a more active and straightforward stand, we now stood at their mercy.

Is it conceivable that Hughes, given the obstacles with which he had to contend, could have done more? His chief biographers think no, for they applaud his keen "sense of the possible" and his willingness to stay within its limits. Other writers argue that the Secretary's adaptability was also his greatest vice, for it was an anchor that chained him to the "stultifying tradition of Old Guard Republicanism." He was, moreover, usually deaf to the call of duty when political victory appeared improbable. On the other hand, if the Secretary fell short of farsighted statesmanship, one must remember that Hughes's brilliant analytical mind lacked "an auspicious era in which to perform."

CHAPTER IV

Makeshift Peace and Prosperity

President Harding, a veteran newspaperman, handled the press with an easy familiarity. One day a reporter asked his opinion of a pending bill that bore all the earmarks of McKinley's economic philosophy. "We should," he told his dumbfounded inquirer, "adopt a protective tariff of such a character as will help the struggling industries of Europe to get on their feet."[1] Perhaps no more could be expected of a man so obtuse to economic theory. Unfortunately, however, even his brilliant Cabinet triumvirate—Hughes, Mellon, and Hoover—failed to grasp the kaleidoscopic changes that mandated a reversal of our practice of sacrificing long-run diplomatic considerations for immediate economic gains.

This shift in world economic power came so swiftly that its full impact could not be comprehended immediately. For three centuries Americans had depended upon Europe's surplus capital to develop their new continent. At the same time the New World maintained a favorable trade balance by exporting to established nations more than was imported. However, a revolutionary reversion began with the outbreak of hostilities abroad. Pressed for funds, the Anglo-French holders of securities liquidated about 70 per cent of their American interests. Wall Street bankers loaned

---

[1] Eric F. Goldman, *Rendezvous With Destiny,* paperback ed. (New York, 1959), p. 221.

stupendous sums to the Allied governments before 1917, and in the following four years Uncle Sam advanced to friendly powers more than $10.5 billion. When the dogs of war were unloosed at Sarajevo in 1914, the United States was a debtor nation; six years later (without reckoning the war debts) this situation had been replaced by a favorable balance of some $3 billion. Nor did our creditor status remain stable. By the end of the Coolidge era, the world owed us about $21 billion.[2] "These figures," remarks William E. Leuchtenburg, "represent one of those great shifts of power that occur but rarely in the history of nations." Their impact, he adds, demanded a painstaking and concerted effort "to redredge the channels of world trade."

Had this effort been made, and had it been accompanied by an enlightened American policy at the council table of nations, the world might have settled down to a long era of tranquility. The failure to readjust our foreign economic relations proved to be the most perilous aspect of neo-isolationism, for this neglect was a prime factor in the coming of the Great Depression. This calamity, in turn, paved the way for the rise of reckless Fascist leaders whose wholesale aggressions culminated in another and more frightful world war. Thus, the entire League structure and the American policy of independent cooperation were to tumble down together.

It is easy today to speculate on the steps that might have prevented or mitigated global economic disaster. The unprecedented problem of reconstruction overtaxed the resources of devastated Europe. Instead of abdicating our wartime leadership by allowing private bankers to finance overseas recovery, we might have devised a Marshall Plan as we did after 1945. A partial precedent already existed. Great Britain, the world's previous creditor nation, had set a good example in the nineteenth century. Parliament adopted a free-trade policy; Britain took the goods of its debtors in repayment for loans, and reloaned the interest received in order to balance foreign economies. This farsighted program, however, required the sacrifice of the British farmer, who was permanently injured by competition from agricultural imports. Understandably

[2] This latter figure includes the funded war debts and foreign investments.

enough, no American party was willing to court political oblivion by the certain alienation of rural support. Nor was it politically possible to deny American industrialists the benefits of the home market by opening the tariff floodgates to foreign-made goods. Neither sector of our well-balanced economy would ever entertain the notion of becoming the scapegoat for European recovery. On the contrary, politicians gleefully let the genie out of the bottle to prepare a magic recipe to bring about the impossible. This formula provided that the United States could, at one and the same time, avoid foreign entanglements, monopolize the domestic market, collect our war debts, promote European markets for American goods, and build up our creditor holdings by further overseas loans. In truth, this economic delusion actually worked as long as American export capital covered up the cracks in the system. At the onset of the Great Depression, the United States was producing almost half of the world's manufactured goods. In 1929 our national income equaled the combined incomes of twenty-three countries, a list which included such nations as Great Britain, France, Germany, Canada, and Japan. To a nation of pragmatists, these figures answered skeptics who questioned the durability of this rickety economic structure.

The GOP economic take-off began with a tariff revision. One of Wilson's initial successes as President had been a lowering of the tariff boom which had long overprotected certain American industries. He ended his administration by sternly warning the country that a return to Republican tariff orthodoxy would impede the repayment of war debts, for, as he correctly insisted, our debtors needed an American market to fulfill their obligations. Wilson's admonition fell on deaf ears as a Republican Congress joyfully accepted Harding's charge "to Prosper America first." The Fordney-McCumber Act, which set new heights for tariff rates, was designed to please the farm bloc and certain wartime industries which feared that renewed European competition would endanger their recent gains. This was particularly true of the manufacturers of chemicals and dyes, who had expanded rapidly, thanks to heavy government subsidies and a free gift of confiscated German dye patents. Opposition to the Fordney-McCumber bill was minimal, for its passage through Congress was facilitated by Progressives in the vain hope that freedom from foreign competition would aid the surplus-laden farmers.

There is no question today that the rebuilding of this tariff wall was a blunder of the first magnitude. The American farmer gained little or nothing. The policy, swiftly followed by foreign reprisals, put a brake on our exports and curtailed European trade with the United States to the point where our debtors could not build up the dollar balances necessary to meet their war debt obligations. Moreover, the absence of a balanced two-way Atlantic trade forced Europe to spend too much on consumer goods, a step that impeded recovery in heavy industry. Thomas W. Lamont, a J. P. Morgan partner, wrote that the new tariff war begun by the United States was "fruitful of misunderstanding" and poisoning to genuine international accord.

In addition to the tariff, other American policies impeded European reconstruction. About a billion dollars a year in new private loans and investments steadily increased the interest obligations of the Old World. Forced to husband their gold lest they endanger local currency reserves, debtor nations depended in part upon selling services to the United States. While the American tourist trade was brisk in the 1920's, it was not heavy enough in those pre-jet days to build up sufficient dollar reserves. Prior to 1914 European maritime nations had enjoyed a near monopoly on transporting American goods. After the war, however, we decided to end this dependence on foreign bottoms, and Congress subsidized the domestic merchant marine. This American cargo competition, artificially stimulated by Congress, formed another hindrance to our major debtors.

In addition to these difficulties, Europeans were now faced with active American competition in their home markets. The United States was the only member of the victorious Allied coalition to emerge unscathed at the end of the war. At a time when Europe's production of finished goods dropped sharply, American firms, which had stepped up their output during the war, outran the demands of the domestic market. Big Business, cheerfully assuming that American withdrawal from the Old World was confined to political involvement, branched out to all portions of the globe. American industrialists came to hold interests in the textile center of Lodz, Poland. The Victor Talking Machine Company interlocked with a similar German concern, which was, in turn, affiliated with a corresponding Japanese interest. General Motors, Ford, IBM, International Harvester, and others spread out in all directions beyond our prized "ocean moats." At the same time, American capital financed railroad construction in Poland, harbor improvements in Yugoslavia, rubber production in Malaya, and the expansion of public utility services in Oriental countries. "Our financial mechanism," Herbert Feis later observed, "was busily creating future targets for our bombers."

Production overseas held a number of attractions for American firms—escape from local tariff barriers, a reservoir of cheap manpower, and a welcome reduction of income taxes. The federal government stimulated this economic invasion of foreign countries. Congress waived the anti-trust laws for exporting firms operating outside our borders and granted them liberal tax remissions and thinly disguised subsidies. Secretary Hoover's Bureau of Foreign and Domestic Commerce advertised business opportunities overseas. Hence, in the post-armistice decade, our foreign investments increased sixfold. Isolationist-minded government officials forgot that a nation can denounce an alliance or withdraw from a collective security concert with greater ease than a corporation can dismantle a three-million-dollar foreign plant.[3] The resulting situation was therefore paradoxical: as the Senate weighed simple international agreements on an apothecary's scale, business interests spun a wide web of economic entanglements.

The search for foreign markets and investments was paralleled by an American entry into the exploitation of distant sources of raw materials. A complex of factors set oil magnates at the vanguard of this race for concessions. During the Wilsonian Era, the navies of the world replaced coal with oil as fuel. In addition our 1917–1918 experience pointed up the importance of oil-fired planes, trucks, tanks, and submarines. Concurrently American geologists

[3] Thomas A. Bailey cites this comparison in *The Man in the Street* (New York, 1948), p. 252.

issued overly pessimistic predictions about domestic petroleum reserves. As a result, oilmen insisted that we must keep up with the British, who had secured their future supply of "liquid gold" by acquiring oil-rich reserves scattered over the globe. And so, with the government's blessing and diplomatic aid, several leading American producers worked their way into international combines operating in the Middle East, a penetration destined to create many acute headaches for future State Department personnel.

The outward thrust of American enterprise after 1920 ultimately rested upon the willingness of a handful of powerful banking houses to back the effort. This support was cheerfully given, for Morgan and his peers had garnered huge profits from foreign business following the outbreak of the European war and they now were eager to finance overseas recovery. These banking houses had surplus capital to lend, and the war had impoverished their Old World competitors. Nor were their motives entirely mercenary, for when Washington retired from the lending business in 1921, private bankers believed that their own risks would speed global recovery and stabilization. They failed to see, however, that the foreign trade which they sustained lacked a healthy balance because European buying power rested upon successive loans that would, in time, overburden the borrowers. Actually, part of the blame for these reckless foreign loans must rest with the Washington authorities. Since 1945 the government has tried to make private foreign loans serve the enlightened self-interest of the United States. In the twenties, however, the State Department reported only on the "political desirability" of foreign credits and on their "security and reproductive nature." Wall Street paid little attention to halfhearted warnings against excessive foreign borrowings, admonitions seldom heeded by rash bankers more interested in the immediate flotation of loans than in the long-range problem of repayment. In the bullish atmosphere of the day, bankers occasionally even bribed foreign agents to deal with their own houses and made it a habit to grant fresh credits when needed to pay the interest on older obligations. When this banking merry-go-round stopped, foreign debtors owed the United States and its citizens about twenty-one billion dollars.

Long before the Great Depression toppled this economic house of cards, the State Department had been forced to assist in settling European squabbles stemming from the punitive terms of the Treaty of Versailles. In 1921 the Reparations Commission levied the staggering sum of roughly thirty-three billion dollars in gold plus interest against the Weimar Republic. The first installment was paid; then a temporary moratorium was followed by a German default in December, 1922. Acting without British consent, the French and Belgian governments made it clear that they would enforce their claims by a military occupation of the highly industrialized Ruhr Valley. At this point Secretary of State Hughes decided upon action, for our Allied debtors had determined to pay Washington in war debts only what they received in reparations from Berlin. Hughes was, therefore, receptive to a British suggestion that American experts participate in an investigation into Germany's capacity to fulfill her financial obligations.

The adroit Secretary used the forum of an American Historical Association convention to air his plans. Warning that French occupation of the Ruhr would bring disaster without securing German reparations, he suggested that a mixed commission of experts on monetary matters, including some Americans, judge the reparations dispute. In time, this became the nucleus of the Dawes Plan. Adding that the United States wished neither German default nor the economic prostration of the Reich, Hughes predicated the adoption of his suggestion on the free consent of the European governments.

The immediate effects of Hughes's proposal were not encouraging. At home the isolationists beat their war drums loudly as French Premier Raymond Poincaré defiantly ordered his poilus to march into the Ruhr. This action split the American Anglophiles from the Francophiles. Since both groups had been internationally minded, the rupture threatened the unity of the pro-League bloc. The Ruhr episode also fractured the isolationist coalition, for France was defended by the heirs of Theodore Roosevelt, nationalists who understood Poincaré's show of force. On the other hand, the liberal isolationists joined with the German-American group in stoutly defending Germany's resistance.

For a season the Ruhr tangle promised to distract the country from the mah-jongg fad and the search for drinkable liquor. Current events, however, could only briefly distract the amusement-crazed America of the 1920's. As the dispute lagged, the public became bored with stories of German passive resistance and wild-cat inflation, French coercion and alleged brutality. With the waning of the summer of 1923, penny-pinching Frenchmen tired of the injurious and costly dispute. Following a political shakeup in Germany, Gustav Stresemann became chancellor and he gave the word to stop passive resistance to the French intruders.

Hughes had been careful not to irritate French feelings and his restraint was rewarded when the Reparations Committee agreed to the substance of his plan for a commission of experts. It took almost a year before the resulting work was accepted by the powers concerned. "If you turn this down," Hughes told Paris bluntly, "[then] America is through." So the French gave reluctant consent to the Dawes Plan. Under the terms of this agreement the Ruhr was evacuated and German reparations were put on "a plan payment." To enable Berlin to meet its obligations, the Reich's currency was to be stabilized and its economy revitalized by means of a $200 million loan, more than half of which was destined to come from the United States. Inasmuch as provisions for the total sum of reparations and the duration of installments were temporarily by-passed, further action was necessary. The Young Plan of 1929 scaled down reparations from $33 to $8 billion and provided that this smaller sum be payable over a period of 59 years at an interest rate of 5½ per cent.

The Dawes Plan, the Pact of Locarno, and the moderating influence of Foreign Minister Stresemann[4] ushered in a new period of German-American cordiality. As the Reich regained world respect, men began to suffer bad conscience concerning their erstwhile enemy. American tourists visited Germany in far greater numbers than in Hohenzollern days and came home impressed by the new dynamic culture that had arisen from the ashes of war.

[4] Stresemann was chancellor for only three months. From the latter part of 1923 to his death in 1929, he survived all the frequent changes in ministries to remain head of the Foreign Office.

Before leaving his Berlin post in 1925, Ambassador Alanson B. Houghton pronounced Junker militarism dead and declared Wilhelmstrasse's ambitions limited to economic rehabilitation. The press reflected this view, and pro-German editorials demanded either the modification or the end of the punishment meted out at Versailles.

German quiescence and American self-reproach only partially explained the prevalent good will. The United States was rapidly acquiring a heavy stake in the Reich's continued stability. The international loan which formed part of the Dawes Plan whetted an appetite for further German investments. American capitalists bought heavily into federal, state, and municipal Reich issues as well as German corporate stocks and bonds. Eventually over two billion dollars flowed from the United States into Germany. The wellsprings of German prosperity had been refreshed, but a significant question remained. How long would they gush without additional pump-priming?

Jacob Gould Schurman, Houghton's successor as Ambassador to Berlin, fostered this overconfidence in German investments. The Canadian-born Schurman, long-time President of Cornell University, was transferred in 1925 from war-torn China to the sophisticated society of the German capital. Seldom troubled by doubts, he always completely identified himself with the immediate project at hand. He was captivated by Stresemann's Germany and paid no attention to the ugly Nazi sore festering under the skin-deep prosperity. A man of forceful speech, abundant energy and great fervor—the Weimar Republic could not have asked for a better advertising agent. A distinguished academic figure, Schurman enjoyed excellent rapport with affluent American investors. On visits home he made charming after-dinner speeches which pointed up German business opportunities. In Berlin the Ambassador took pains to entertain visiting American industrialists. The State Department let Schurman know of its concern over the heavy American stake in the Reich's economy, but these admonitions, writes Herbert Feis, were based upon the wrong grounds. Washington showed little anxiety about the soundness of private credits. Instead the State Department feared that interest payments to private investors might jeopardize the fulfillment of German reparations and thus endanger our war debt installments from England and France.

To explore the economic network of those flush days it is necessary to fit the war debt question into the whole complicated picture. President Wilson had established the American case for full payment of the $10.5 billion advanced to erstwhile Allies and to the new states created by the partition of the polyglot Russian and Austro-Hungarian empires. Wilson insisted that inasmuch as the United States had received no reparations or territorial additions from the war, she was entitled to full repayment of these subsidies. He brusquely dismissed British proposals to forgive the debts in the interest of general recovery. Wilson's Republican successors remained firmly on the same ground. Indeed, they had no choice. The voting public knew that the dollars for these foreign loans had come from Liberty and Victory bonds purchased by Americans. Therefore, cancellation of the obligations was equivalent to placing a substantial part of the war cost upon the overburdened shoulders of the American taxpayer. Statesmen on both sides of the Atlantic failed to grasp the essence of the problem: Could these debts be repaid in view of the unfavorable export balance of European trade? Even the most ardent American internationalists were seldom cancellationists, for they failed to see that a clean sweep of the slate would be to the common interest of all concerned with speedy European recovery and political tranquilization.

On the other hand, in the four years following 1922, the World War Foreign Debt Commission did make funding agreements with thirteen debtor countries at interest rates lenient enough to equal the forgiveness of a substantial percentage of their entire obligations. This caused considerable grumbling when Congress was asked to approve these separate agreements, but consent came because, as Secretary of the Treasury Andrew W. Mellon observed, the administration had made "the most favorable settlements that could be obtained short of force."

Europeans hurled verbal brickbats across the Atlantic over this embittered question. They insisted that the monies advanced had gone for a common war effort toward which the United States had contributed little blood. They maintained that most of the dollars were spent in the United States for supplies purchased at war-inflated prices, and that cancellation was essential to the recovery of wrecked Allied economies. The French were particularly vindictive. Cartoonists portrayed Uncle Sam as "L'Oncle Shylock" with dollar signs replacing the stars on his traditional top hat.

Counterarguments were equally acrimonious. Americans charged that their money had been used for foreign propaganda rather than for relief, for liquor and armaments rather than for economic reconstruction. Next time, said a letter to the *Saturday Review*, "when they come whining and begging for men and ships and . . . foods . . . and '*give till it hurts*,' we will say, Like Hell, *Shylock holds on to his own!*" In the light of subsequent developments, the analogy may be carried a step further; like Shylock, Uncle Sam also did not get back his money.

By 1931 about two billion dollars had been paid to the United States on the war obligations, a sum almost equal to American governmental and private postwar loans to Germany. Unable to pay her creditors in gold, Berlin met reparations in foreign credits, most of which came from American sources. The dollar made the grand tour—it traveled to Germany as a loan, to Allied capitals as reparation, and back to Washington as a war debt installment. But perpetual motion is no more possible in the economic world than in the physical. These German securities dwindled in the days of Hitler, and so the American taxpayer, as the final creditor, footed the bill for a healthy share of the two billion dollar war debt installments in addition to the default of the balance of the Allied obligations. This round trip of the dollar contributed heavily to the rancorous isolationism of the New Deal Era.

Some prescient thinkers penetrated the neo-isolationist façade where the nonentanglement front covered up widespread economic involvement. For the most part it was the La Follette Progressives who denounced the crass moneylenders whose foreign concessions and investments "bind us . . . to hazardous agreements entirely alien to our traditions." The 1924 convention that nominated La Follette for President on a third-party ticket denounced in its platform "the mercenary system of foreign policies . . . in the interest of financial imperialists, oil monopolists and international bankers." "We get out of Europe," commented the Chicago *Evening Post*, "but we enter the race for that thing for which Europe cares most—trade supremacy." The return to national isolation, it was later discovered, did not halt economic explorers, their engineers, and financial backers, who extended American activities into the unexploited regions of the earth.[5]

The futile efforts of the business-minded Coolidge administration to promote peace free of meaningful obligations form an excellent example of the puzzling diplomacy of the 1920's. American tradition has depicted President Calvin Coolidge as the symbolic "Mr. Isolationist." This image is only partially correct. Actually the dour Yankee's original outlook on foreign affairs was broader than that of his amiable predecessor. Coolidge's concealed departures from isolationist tenets, made in response to Big Business's overseas needs, are often forgotten. At the same time, his laconic parochial platitudes on foreign affairs have left an indelible impression.

The new President was not an undeviating isolationist and he was usually at loggerheads with the Senate Irreconcilables. His pre-White House record reveals a cautious admiration for the League's noble aspirations. Yet, despite this passing flirtation with internationalism, Coolidge was too canny a politician to brave the

[5] Some recent writers, especially William A. Williams, have dismissed the isolationism of the 1920's as a figment of the historical imagination. It was a decade, writes Williams, "marked by express and extended involvement . . . in the affairs of other nations." Williams's theory has been rejected by the vast majority of diplomatic historians, who rightfully insist that we must give to isolationism the meaning that the isolationists themselves gave it, i.e., freedom from binding commitments that were intended to preserve world order. Moreover, Williams is too literal in his interpretation of that inexact word, isolation. It never meant, as Borah once explained, an autarkical insulation that would remove the United States from world channels of trade, finance, and culture. To be sure, at times the unplanned and uncontrolled economic expansion engendered by the war forced relaxations from isolationist theory. But whatever the temptations, Washington always stopped short of economic or military sanctions against would-be aggressors. For Williams's point of view see his "The Legend of Isolationism," *Science and Society*, XVIII (Winter, 1954), 1–20, and *The Tragedy of American Diplomacy* (Cleveland, 1959), pp. 77–118.

dominant bias of the day, a complete intolerance of advance contracts for collective action. Furthermore, his oft-quoted clichés on nonentanglement blended well with his public image of a Puritan relic in an age of jazz, flappers, and speakeasies.

Upon his accession, Coolidge promptly endorsed Secretary Hughes's modified isolationism. His first annual message to Congress promised that the United States would attend to its own affairs while recognizing its historic mission "to help others." He wished the "foreign agency" domiciled in Geneva well, but added that there was no reason to limit our own freedom and independence by joining in the venture. In the three-cornered presidential race of 1924, when Coolidge won handily over John W. Davis (Democrat) and Robert M. La Follette (Progressive), the President took full credit for the Republican *démarche* in foreign policy. He promised to continue a common sense foreign policy which, he boasted, had maintained our ancient traditions, lifted the burden of naval armaments, and helped Europe settle its own affairs.

The diplomacy of the Coolidge Era was unimaginative and dull. It has been aptly noted that "The shop was kept running, but few new goods were put on the shelves." No more could be expected in those smug but unexciting years when the President was a poorly read, lethargic man who limited his interest in foreign affairs to the needs of Big Business. An alert Secretary of State might have compensated for Coolidge's shortcomings, but when Hughes decided to retire in 1925, his chief showed no signs of dismay. Instead of filling this key post with another superior personality, the President chose a man who would be no threat to his own run-of-the-mill mentality. The naming of Frank B. Kellogg to the premier Cabinet post was Coolidge's cardinal error in the diplomatic field. The Kellogg years marked the nadir of Republican postwar statesmanship.

The new Secretary's education had been limited to reading law in a Rochester, Minnesota, law office. After making his mark as a local trust-buster, Kellogg found it more advantageous to work for the corporations than against them. As a United States senator, he had wished the Treaty of Versailles in hell rather than go on record for *or* against it, but he wound up supporting the Lodge reservations. Yet, for all his caution, Kellogg lost his Senate seat in 1922 to an ultra-isolationist Farmer-Labor Party candidate. During this time, however, Kellogg had treated the shy and retiring Vice-President kindly; his reward came when President Coolidge asked him to leave his London ambassadorship for the ranking Cabinet post.

The short, snow-haired Minnesotan with the ever-harried look stood out in glaring contrast to the forceful and austere Hughes. Nearing seventy, Kellogg replaced his former youthful daring with a caution that frequently hamstrung his efforts to adjust the neo-isolationist philosophy to ever-changing conditions abroad. His biographer, Professor L. Ethan Ellis, praises his subject's loyalty, personal integrity, experience, and industry. Nevertheless, Ellis's final verdict is that Kellogg was "a busy mediocrity" who spent "a maximum . . . of energy to produce a modest accomplishment."

In fairness to Coolidge and Kellogg, one must concede that they operated under a *Zeitgeist* that made constructive world leadership difficult, if not impossible. The American people, to whom they were ultimately accountable, were preoccupied with the comforts of a material existence. A stronger President than Harding might possibly have fanned the smoldering embers of wartime idealism. By the mid-twenties, however, internationalist zeal had waned, while the let-well-enough-alone spirit of boom times prevailed. The isolationist coalition now represented more than a pooling of groups who were disenchanted with Wilson. In Coolidge's day there were many varieties of isolationists: militarists and pacifists, reactionary Bourbons and dedicated Marxists, hyphenates and jingoists, polished New England congressmen and rough-hewn Solons from the hinterland. This motley group was united by a common fear of the "untouchable" League. An analysis of this fear yields a bundle of contradictions: Geneva was warlike, but joining it would destroy manly Americanism; it formed the path to socialism, but it had been designed to shackle the world in capitalist chains; it would fetter American business expansion, but it had put the world at the mercy of Wall Street. The contradictions are possibly more imposing in retrospect than they were at the time of utterance. In truth, ordinary Americans of Coolidge's years had tired of the reform spirit that preceded 1914 and the wartime perturbation that came after it. This prevailing mood explains the apathy of the masses far better than do any logical arguments for or against the League. It also explains the Coolidge conundrum. The President's feeble efforts in supporting some innocuous proposals to further international accord led Elihu Root to remark that Coolidge did not have an international hair on his head, while the Senate die-hards shivered lest the President be a Woodrow Wilson in Republican guise.

The Irreconcilables were equally suspicious of Secretary Kellogg, who, in turn, was so apprehensive of Capitol Hill that Washington reporters dubbed him "Nervous Nellie." In evaluating the reasons for his spiritless diplomacy, it is necessary to recall the power of the indomitable Borah, who succeeded Lodge as chairman of the Senate Foreign Relations Committee in 1924. This succession proved unfortunate, for the Idaho senator lacked finesse, leadership ability, and a capacity for teamwork. Borah, writes his most recent biographer, demonstrates "the dangers of good will undirected by an informed intelligence." An obstructionist who thought his main duty as chairman was to act as watchdog over the State Department, Borah was an obstacle that Kellogg feared to budge. An expert at detecting the slightest flaw in an opponent's argument, Borah was singularly incapable of proposing plans of his own. About all that party loyalty meant to him was a grudging support for the ticket in presidential years. Hence, Coolidge and Kellogg could not count upon their official Senate spokesman to push measures designed to perfect Hughes's plans. Borah was utterly impervious to the fact that the wealth, power, and far-flung business interests of the country entailed additional international responsibilities. To say the least, Kellogg found such an obdurate man difficult to work with and almost impossible to convince.

Each year the gap widened between the White House and the extreme isolationists. After the congressional elections of 1926, the two major parties were so closely balanced in the Senate that the liberal-progressives were in a position to block administration foreign policy aimed at loosening the manacles of isolationism. These Senate independents, writes John Braeman, held an archaic world view "based upon the vision of an innocent republic of happy artisans, prosperous yeomen, and thriving small business safe behind the impassable ocean from the crimes and follies of the Old World." The unflinching isolationists did their utmost to halt a closer understanding with Geneva's peace-preserving machinery. Their first direct confrontation with the Coolidge administration came over the issue of adherence to the World Court.

This protracted battle, destined to beset American politics for a dozen years, involved a proposal with deep-seated Republican roots. Two previous Republican Secretaries of State had urged the creation of a court of law designed to handle the judicial settlement of international disputes, a proposal heartily endorsed by outstanding members of the majority party, including Charles E. Hughes. American jurists had shown far more interest in such a court than in any alternative peace scheme, for they shared a widespread conviction that international law must be substituted for force as the ultimate arbiter in human affairs. The World Court front was broad and bipartisan. It included pacifists, GOP internationalists, and Wilsonian Democrats who regarded the Court campaign as a counterattack against the isolationist enemy.

Acting under League auspices, an Advisory Committee of Jurists (Elihu Root was a leading member) created the Permanent Court of International Justice to sit at The Hague. Although the new body was the League's godchild, Geneva opened membership to nations who remained outside of the League Covenant.

Secretary Hughes, friend and admirer of Root, did his best to overcome Senate objections to the World Court. When the political decks were clear of the Washington treaties, he formulated reservations to the protocol designed to cut the ground from under the opposition. In February, 1923, President Harding approved Hughes's qualifications and requested Senate consent to the protocol, subject to four explicit conditions designed to preserve American national sovereignty from League encroachments.[6]

Such precautions did not prevent a storm of protest on the op-

---

[6] Hughes proposed: (1) There were to be no legal relations with the League or assumptions of any obligations under the Covenant. (2) The United States was to participate on an equal basis with League members to elect the Court's judges. (3) Congress was to determine and pay a fair share of the Court's expenses. (4) No amendments were to be made to the protocol without our consent.

posite end of Pennsylvania Avenue. Faced with growing party discord, Harding retreated and gave additional assurances to the chary Irreconcilables. Hughes, however, stood his ground. He warned the Wilsonians that their hope of using the protocol as a wedge to reopen the League question was as preposterous as isolationist fears that The Hague was a stopover on the journey to Geneva.

Soon after entering the White House, President Coolidge announced his full support of Hughes's original conditions. Despite mounting evidence of popular support for the President's position, the Irreconcilables blocked Senate action on the question for two years. They employed the now familiar techniques of holding tedious public hearings and contriving alternate schemes to confuse the issue. Borah acted entirely in character; he originally supported the White House, then smelled collusion with Geneva, and ended up by demanding the rejection of THIS COURT in favor of A COURT endowed with "affirmative jurisdiction." The Republican landslide of 1924 followed a campaign in which both major parties endorsed the Court. This seemed to insure prompt action, but the opposition had enough obstructionist ammunition left for still another year. Finally the Court matter was placed high on the Senate agenda for the session which opened in December, 1925.

The legislative battle that ensued is deserving of attention only because it serves as a reminder of the fruitless peace gropings of the period. For the third time in seven years the church groups, the club women, and the peace and uplift societies launched an all-out pressure campaign for a single panacea. First there had been the 1919 League drive, then the 1921 disarmament campaign, and now the same people marshaled their forces under the World Court banner. In consequence, the benefits of joining were as fully magnified as the gloomy predictions of the isolationists. To be sure, some internationalist disputes could be settled by judicial means and the Permanent Court of International Justice provided a convenient means of facilitating such settlements. At best, however, the Court could not have realized the American objective of preserving the peace. Actually its activities were confined to minor affairs because it could assume jurisdiction only at the request of all participants—and requests were not likely to be made when vital national interests were at stake. Professor Robert H. Ferrell has aptly queried: How much do you hear today about the International Court of Justice of the United Nations to which virtually all nations belong?

The Senate extremists were so exasperated by the propaganda build-up that they threw caution and good taste to the winds. James A. Reed, crusty reactionary Democrat from Missouri, derided the World Court bench. "Rafael Altamira, of Spain," he asked, "now, just what does Rafael stand for? . . . Yorozu Oda, of Japan . . . Who are these who would place above the American flag the bastard banner of internationalism?"

When the administration made it crystal clear that there could hardly be an infringement on national sovereignty by a Court with so limited jurisdiction, the Irreconcilables blew up out of all proportion the question of advisory opinions. Curiously, they found an influential ally in Judge John Bassett Moore, who sat on the bench of the Permanent Court of International Justice. Moore told interested senators that there was some hazard to the United States in the power of the Court to render advisory opinions (which, contrary to the practice of American jurisprudence, might be given as to the right or wrong of a dispute before litigation). His suggestion aroused a number of latent fears concerning the Monroe Doctrine and our tight immigration laws. Furthermore Judge Moore argued that the United States would labor under a distinct disadvantage, for League members, unlike ourselves, could oppose requests for advisory opinions in the Council or Assembly.

With Moore's help, the Senate Foreign Relations Committee framed a fifth reservation to be tacked on to the resolution of adherence. This new condition, destined to form the actual roadblock to American adherence, demanded that advisory opinions involving American interests be guaranteed special treatment. Moreover, the committee specified that, contrary to usual treaty procedure, each of the forty-eight nations adhering to the protocol must acquiesce separately in the American reservations. For good measure, a few more stipulations were added providing for gratuitous treatment for Washington that other nations would be bound to resent. The more responsible isolationists now were satisfied, but the thoroughgoing Irreconcilables planned a last-ditch fight. Finally, goaded by the White House, the Senate took the rare step of preventing a filibuster by resorting to a closure motion which limited debate. The Senate then passed (76 to 17) the resolution of adherence, subject to the reservations recommended by its Foreign Relations Committee.

Even so, the ultimate victory went to the isolationists. The administration cooled its heels in getting the other nations to agree to the Senate's stipulations. Coolidge, says Professor Richard W. Leopold, displayed extraordinary bad manners by refusing to parley with Europe on possible compromise measures. During the ensuing impasse, the administration dropped the Court plan to opt for a far more chimerical scheme—the international outlawry of war.

For half a dozen years the State Department had kept the outlawry plan in the pigeonhole reserved for the multifarious peace nostrums of the day. Then, in 1927, a combination of circumstances forced Coolidge and Kellogg into an abrupt *volte-face*. First of all, they wished to reverse some striking setbacks on the diplomatic front. When the World Court issue became stalemated, the administration decided to renew the earlier drive for naval disarmament. During the years of the moratorium on battleship construction, a new race in cruisers had developed to the point where Coolidge was faced with the bad choice of either sacrificing his cherished economy program or else seriously handicapping our navy's striking power. To solve this dilemma, the President set the wheels in motion for a new naval conference, which met in Geneva in the summer of 1927. The second-raters that Secretary Kellogg sent abroad to represent his department were unable to break the deadlock that soon developed between the naval experts. France and Italy, rivals for control of the Mediterranean, blandly explained that they could send only "observers" to a non-League conference. Meanwhile the Japanese sat quietly on the side lines while the two Anglo-Saxon nations spent six weeks in futile argument. Leading American shipbuilders sent William B. Shearer to lobby against agreement. However, the real difficulty was the failure of the American and British conferees to compose their differences on cruiser limitations. Following this stillborn conference, Coolidge and Kellogg were searching for another peace plan to cover up previous diplomatic failures. By chance, just at this time, the bandwagon for the outlawry of war moved into high gear. Its proponents boasted of a simple, inexpensive way of permitting Americans to reconcile two incompatible longings—the preservation of nonentanglement and the desire to promote the cause of world peace.

A decade earlier a Chicago attorney, Salmon O. Levinson, had been amazed to discover that international law did not forbid the waging of war. He coined the captivating slogan, "outlawry of war," and propagated his scheme. As the years passed his converts splintered into three groups. One faction of the movement, dominated by Mr. Levinson, sacrificed enforcement machinery for the sake of winning over Senator Borah, who pressed the plan in Congress after assurance that the enforcement of outlawry would depend solely upon an aroused world opinion. The second sect was composed of collective security enthusiasts who reasoned that if the nations renounced recourse to war, a monopoly on the use of coercion would devolve upon the League. This segment was masterminded by Colonel Raymond Robins, a veteran of the Yukon diggings who later devoted his zeal to uplift movements; and both Nicholas Murray Butler and James T. Shotwell, who spoke for the Carnegie Endowment for International Peace. Finally, Levinson's plan spread to liberal circles then so strongly under the spell of John Dewey. Using the pages of *The New Republic* to air his views, Dewey argued that the chances for peace would be enhanced if it were made illegal to think in terms of military coercion. If Levinson's scheme would not work, said the illustrious philosopher, "the world will not get rid of war under any system." In an era when it was customary for the intelligentsia to suspend judgment on moot questions until Professor Dewey had spoken, the philosopher's endorsement of outlawry carried great weight. By the mid-twenties the advocates of Levinson's doctrine formed one of the most ebullient and persevering pressure groups in the land. This was true despite the fact that the coalition could never agree as to whether the outlawry scheme was to buttress the League's peace machinery or to replace it.

Weakened by divided counsels and repeated frustrations, the movement was languishing when the Shotwell-Butler faction saved it by a master stroke. On March 22, 1927, Shotwell was received by the French Foreign Minister, Aristide Briand. Briand was a self-made man who, in abandoning the Socialist orientation of his salad years, retained his youthful passion for universal peace. Shotwell promptly stated the purpose of his visit by proposing an American-French "Pact of Perpetual Friendship" that would set a precedent for the universal outlawry of war. Briand agreed, and on April 6, 1927 (the tenth anniversary of American intervention), the Foreign Minister transmitted this proposal for a bilateral pact through an announcement to the Associated Press. The Frenchman acted from mixed motives. He was devoted to peace, but he also saw a way of serving Paris's interests by improving strained relations with Washington and hedging against a diplomatic revolution that might put America on the German side in any future conflict.

Official Washington read Briand's offer with many misgivings. They disliked the way he had by-passed official diplomatic channels, and they were still smarting under France's refusal to participate in the Geneva Conference. Most important, they wanted no part of a treaty that would inform the world that in the next Franco-German round, America was bound by treaty not to intervene against a France that had branded Uncle Sam a Shylock.

Kellogg at first did not even reply to Briand's roundabout message. Under pressure from all sides, including a bill of indictment by Dr. Butler blazoned on the pages of the New York *Times*, Kellogg finally agreed to discuss the matter. Then fate intervened once more, for Lindbergh's solo flight to Paris (May 20–21, 1927) aroused a new cordiality for France. Within a month, Briand handed the United States ambassador the draft of a treaty whose wording was to become the distinctive feature of the celebrated Pact of Paris.

Still, Washington vacillated for six months. Then came the need for a diplomatic coup to offset criticism for the Geneva fiasco. Kellogg, however, refused to move until he found a way out of the perplexities stemming from a bilateral no-war treaty. We are not sure who first suggested the solution of offering the benefits of outlawry to the whole family of nations.[7] Certain it is, however, that Secretary Kellogg now pursued the matter with the newly found vigor of a frail cardinal just elected Pope. Curiously, the foreign ministries of three major powers assented to Kellogg's counterproposal before Briand agreed. Ultimately the 1928 Pact of Paris, which renounced war as an instrument of national policy, was ratified by sixty-four nations. Included in this tally were the very nations that would soon refine the art of aggression to a perfection never before achieved.

In the meantime, as Kellogg digested foreign and domestic qualifications of his proposal, it became apparent that only the naïve were willing to take the principle at face value. Faced with loading down the pact with reservations demanded by other nations, and inviting failure at home by providing enforcement machinery, the Secretary chose to keep the text simple and to ignore means for preventing violations. Hence, he consented to France's interpretation that the Pact permitted military action taken in self-defense or to honor her network of security agreements. Nor did he demur when London added to these stipulations that His Majesty's Government reserved full freedom of action in "certain British regions of the world." In Coolidge's day, these red-marked regions girded the global map.

Kellogg handled the inquisitorial Senate Foreign Relations Committee in similar fashion, accepting an American interpretation of the Pact in return for no formal reservations. The Committee then recommended Senate consent, subject to the understanding that it did not impinge upon the Monroe Doctrine. Adding this leeway to those granted other signatories, justification can be provided for the quip that the outlawry treaty was the most comprehensive agreement ever enacted to legalize certain categories of war!

[7] John Chalmers Vinson, *William E. Borah and the Outlawry of War* (Athens, Ga., 1957), p. 131 ff., assigns much of this credit to Borah. However, Kellogg also claimed credit for the idea while some writers suggest that it may have stemmed from underlings in the State Department.

Realism is not an exclusive gift of our own hard-boiled generation, for many contemporaries grumbled loudly as the Pact was
emasculated by understandings, qualifications, and interpretations.
Still more were rightfully skeptical of the notion that international
good will alone could sanction a fiat against war. Senator Reed
dismissed the entire proceedings as "an international kiss." Tart
old Carter Glass was unwilling that any of his Virginia constituents
should suppose that he thought it worth a postage stamp.

On the other hand, the Chicago *Tribune* was certain that Uncle
Sam, like the mighty Samson of old, was "walking into the barber
shop." On the Senate floor, the Big Navy proponents, isolationists
more rabid than Borah, and a sprinkling of outspoken realists
fought Kellogg to the last. This opposition was finally quelled by
last-minute concessions and White House influence. Kellogg gave
further assurances that the treaty involved no obligations of enforcement while Coolidge got the Vice-President to crack the party
whip. Ironically enough, Chairman Borah had to argue for a place
for the Pact on the Senate agenda with sponsors of a bill providing
for the largest naval build-up since the armistice. With a straight
face, Vice-President Charles G. Dawes told the senators that the
outlawry of war and the measure to build fifteen new cruisers con-
cordantly formed the current American foreign policy. And so the
Senate consented to the Pact, eighty-five yeas to a single nay, and
promptly turned to the next item of business—an appropriation
of $270 million to build fighting ships destined to sail the most
war-plagued seas in human history.

The Pact of Paris, as everyone knows, completely failed in its
original purpose. Nonetheless, its effects are measurable enough to
warrant attention. Henceforth, aggression was outlawed, and the
future would soon reveal the difficulty of maintaining neutrality
between a law-breaking attacker and his innocent victim. Hence,
the Pact provided an arsenal of arguments for the interventionists
of the New Deal Era, the ultimate victors in the battle over nonentanglement. After World War II the outlawry agreement was
taken from the wastebasket of forgotten treaties to sanction the
punishment of the Axis leaders who had planned war with malice
aforethought. Finally, the Pact was the litmus test which disproved

the theory that international promises, devoid of enforcement machinery, could deter aggression.

The bargaining surrounding this toothless Pact coincided with Herbert Hoover's landslide victory over Alfred E. Smith. And so it was that a fresh administration proclaimed the Pact in force in the fateful summer of 1929. Within three months the Stock Market Crash was to set off a chain reaction that ended the short-lived global truce of the late 1920's. However, this venture upon President Hoover's sea of troubles must await a review of inter-American relations, an area in which the Republicans made considerable progress.

CHAPTER V

The Hemisphere:
Versailles to Pearl Harbor

Shortly before the turn of the century, a veteran naval officer emerged as the oracle for a cult of young expansionists. Captain Alfred T. Mahan, preacher of geopolitics before the word had been coined, outlined a threefold formula for American foreign policy. Toward Europe his devotees (with the notable exception of Theodore Roosevelt) advised continued abstention; in the Far East they called for cooperation with other powers; in the Western Hemisphere they demanded American hegemony.

Consciously or not, postwar Republican statesmen drifted back to a rough parallel of this blueprint. They tried to break the links Wilson had forged with Europe and, at the 1921–1922 Washington Conference, they urged collective action in maintaining Far Eastern stability. In regard to the New World, however, they slowly retreated from Mahan's concept of domination and paved the way for the diplomatic revolution which we call the Good Neighbor Policy. This relaxation of control over hemispheric affairs resulted from some interconnected causes that merit thorough exploration.

In 1921 Latin Americans were entitled to grave apprehension concerning the map of the Western Hemisphere. The prewar Panama policy of the United States, designed to envelop all sea approaches to the Canal, regarded the Caribbean as an American lake, forming, as it were, part of our own shore line. In an attempt to insure the security of the American-built canal, we acquired Puerto Rico from Spain as a spoil of war and lined the Atlantic passageways to the Panamanian isthmus with protectorates, which eventually included Cuba, Panama, Nicaragua, Santo Domingo, and Haiti. Falling under the spell of this Caribbean policy, President Wilson abandoned his original anti-imperialist bias. During his incumbency came the addition of two marine-guarded protectorates and the purchase of the Virgin Islands from Denmark, a burdensome possession acquired to complete the American circle around the eastern flank of the Canal. The Wilsonians also forced Latin American governments to pass a test of constitutional legitimacy as a condition precedent to recognition by Washington. Furthermore, Wilson aroused the animosity of our nearest southern neighbor by deploying force to counter certain affronts stemming from turbulent Mexico.

Upon entering the White House, Wilson found in full panoply the Theodore Roosevelt Corollary to the Monroe Doctrine. Under the terms of this dictum, dating from 1904, the United States assumed responsibility for curbing hemispheric disorders arising from "chronic wrongdoing" or persistent impotence on the part of unruly Latin American republics. Uncle Sam was to act as an international policeman who, by wielding his "Big Stick," would maintain law and order in countries where stable government was threatened. Despite some pious words uttered early in his presidential career, Wilson used this Republican artifice to widen Washington's sphere of influence. By 1921 Latin Americans were entitled to their belief that this policy which offended their national dignity and seemingly threatened their independence had the blessing of bipartisan support in the United States.

The rejection by the Senate of the League Covenant further strained inter-American relations. Southward, the 1920 GOP triumph seemed tantamount to a reaffirmation of the meddlesome Corollary. Indeed, some of Wilson's opponents had argued that the very existence of the League was a threat to our influence over countries located on this side of the ocean. To be sure, President Wilson's deeds had belied his own benevolent words concerning Latin America. Nevertheless, he regarded the League as an expanded Monroe Doctrine—a globe-wide effort to protect all nations, great and small, from all schemes of aggression. His Republican successors rejected this generous concept, for even the most moderate amongst them originally maintained that the United States alone must be the sole guardian of hemispheric security.

This insistence resulted in a sharp division of opinion in New World circles over the League's function and future. Latin American countries hopefully believed that Geneva would act as a brake upon Washington's imperious behavior. While the Anglo-French diplomats who wielded authority in Geneva were overcautious lest they offend the United States by an interposition into Western Hemisphere disputes, the American fear remained that this hesitancy might end when the League outgrew its swaddling clothes. Actually, Secretary Hughes's ambivalence toward the League and his studied hostility to the strengthening of its peace machinery were grounded in this distrust. GOP statesmen of the 1920's were not genuinely apprehensive that a successful system of collective security might disturb the territorial status quo on this side of the Atlantic, but they dreaded the thought of European interference in New World diplomatic disputes. Therefore, they hedged against this possibility by aggrandizing the Monroe Doctrine.

The 1923 centennial of Mr. Monroe's pronouncement was proclaimed with much éclat. In honor of the occasion, Senator Henry Cabot Lodge pontificated that while this venerated shield "is not international law . . . [it] is no more to be disturbed or questioned or interpreted by other nations than [is] the independence of the United States." A metropolitan daily approved of Mary Baker Eddy's creed for red-blooded Americans: "I believe in the Monroe Doctrine, in our Constitution, and in the laws of God." The cool-headed Hughes used far more temperate language, but at the outset he was determined to enforce a *Pax Americana* by unilateral action.

Economic penetration from the North, stepped up as a result of the war, aggravated existing Yankeephobia. Our first export capital had gravitated to Latin America, and after 1914 Wall Street often replaced the European bankers who normally served that area. In the post-armistice decade, American investments south of the Rio Grande grew to almost six billion dollars. "In the lush 1920's," reports Professor Arthur J. May, "banking houses in the United States floated Latin bonds with the abandon of sailors on a drunken spree." Some of this money financed shaky dictatorships while the rest increased American control over extractive industries and corporations which handled tropical food products. Latin America offered the most immediate opportunity for economic expansion, and after 1920 war-swollen corporations branched southward. In many respects this burgeoning of trade was mutually advantageous because our surplus of manufactured hard goods (especially automobiles) was sorely needed by underdeveloped countries anxious to dispose of excess coffee, rubber, tin, copper, nitrates, oil, mahogany, sugar, and bananas.

Brisk trade and investments, however, did little to quiet fears of Yankee economic imperialism. Latin American businessmen craved economic self-sufficiency, resented tying their single-crop economies to the fluctuating world demand for staple raw materials, and felt caught in an American vise that squeezed both their imports and exports. Moreover, one-sided commercial treaties negotiated with Washington impeded the redredging of prewar channels of trade with European markets. Such business connections had long reinforced the cultural ties of these Latin nations to their sister countries of the Old World.

Reports of these resentments were not lost upon business-hungry Americans anxious to ease diplomatic friction with their New World customers and suppliers. Moreover, the current world situation warranted a relaxation of the Big Stick policy. In 1921 no naval power threatened the safety of the Canal and none contemplated defying Washington by a renewal of turn-of-the-century gunboat diplomacy on our side of the water. At home the war virtually had ended the American taste for imperial power, and a dispassionate public soon wearied of our self-imposed task of policing the Western Hemisphere.

Latin America offered a splendid opportunity to those Republicans who, in 1920, had criticized Wilson's repeated interventions southward. At the height of the imperial impulse, the United States had acquired "insular possessions," a euphemism used for colonies, since the latter were thought unbecoming to a democratic republic. By Harding's day, however, reaction set in even against this subterfuge. The thrill of conquest was gone and our wearisome experience in the Philippines and Puerto Rico had demonstrated the difficulties of coming to terms with an alien culture. Nor had our dollars always followed our flag, for Wall Street's heaviest capital outlays had gone to nearby countries independent of American control. With the urge for political domination spent, the anti-imperialists (one of the few reformist groups of the Progressive Era to survive the war) aimed their salvos at economic imperialistic ventures in Latin America. Backed by the La Follette Progressives, the liberal intelligentsia demanded an outright repudiation of the Roosevelt Corollary, and a transformation of the Monroe Doctrine into a safeguard against New World imperialistic exploitation. Journalists trained in the muckraking school wrote exaggerated but shocking exposures of Dollar Diplomacy in general and of conditions in our Caribbean protectorates in particular. How, asked these critics, could our State Department deny the Japanese demand for extra-legal rights in their sphere of influence if Washington demanded special privileges in its own? Secretary Hughes grasped the imperative need for reparative work in Hispanic America. Here was a chance to make friends by substituting for force or global collective security a GOP model of peace machinery designed to meet our own hemispheric needs.

The Republican retreat which followed had been anticipated in the lame-duck days of the Wilson regime. Recent investigation has shown that Hughes's immediate predecessor, Secretary Bainbridge Colby, had won his chief's consent for a belated inter-American rapprochement. Colby made a good-will tour to South America, prepared to liberate Santo Domingo and Haiti from occupation, refrained from the customary interference in a Guatemalan brawl, and sought to narrow the interventionist interpretation of the Monroe Doctrine.[1]

[1] Daniel M. Smith, "Bainbridge Colby and the Good Neighbor Policy, 1920–1921," *Mississippi Valley Historical Review*, L (June, 1963), 56–78.

Secretary Hughes implemented some of these efforts. While cautiously upholding the legality of intervention, he used this power sparingly and went out of his way to reassure and appease the sensitive Latins. The first step in this process was to heal Colombian wounds dating from our 1903 Panama coup. Presidents Taft and Wilson had tried to come to terms with Bogotá but the negotiations made little progress as long as Theodore Roosevelt was alive to block any agreement that might cast doubt upon the legality or sagacity of his Canal diplomacy. When the Colonel passed from the scene, his bosom friend, Senator Lodge, reported out of committee an altered version of a 1914 Colombian treaty of conciliation. It has been argued that Roosevelt's death was in itself enough to insure Senate consent. Be that as it may, it is also true that pressure from American oil companies anxious to secure concessions in newly found Colombian oil fields played a part in helping some senators forget their allegiance to the departed Rough Rider. Furthermore, President Harding showed unusual vigor in prodding the Senate to action. On March 1, 1922, the treaty was proclaimed in force. Although our "sincere regret" for precipitate action in Panama was stricken from the final agreement, the payment of twenty-five million dollars "heart-balm" to Colombia was, in the words of Thomas A. Bailey, "in itself an eloquent apology." This belated American repentance was accepted and our Colombian investments rapidly multiplied sixtyfold.

Meanwhile Hughes was engaged in allaying Latin irritations over other matters. When Brazil celebrated the centennial anniversary of her independence, the Secretary sailed for Rio de Janeiro, where he categorically denied imputations of "Yanqui imperialism."[2] Secretary Hughes also labored to breathe new life

[2] A few months earlier the Secretary had presided over a Washington conference where the five Central American republics pledged noninterference in each other's unruly politics. Although the Great Seal of the United States was not affixed to this document, it was understood that our State Department would abide by its terms. This conference reaffirmed and strengthened a 1907 treaty in which the Central American states had agreed not to recognize any new government which gained power through nonconstitutional means. Although this agreement sometimes resulted in perpetuating oppressive dictatorships, Washington continued to respect the agreement until it was abrogated in 1934 by action of the five signatory powers.

into the Pan American Union. Formed in 1889, this association included all New World nations save Canada. Its first four meetings had not fulfilled the hopes of its founders, who sought to foster closer cultural and commercial relations among its twenty members. The fifth Pan American meeting, scheduled for 1914, was postponed until 1923 because of the disruptions of war. When it finally assembled in Santiago, Chile, Hughes determined to show such evidences of good faith on the part of the United States as would lessen Latin American hostility. He saw to it that the United States did not dominate the proceedings, and he tried to settle some of the grievances that had made previous conferences sounding boards for Yankeephobia. The most important result of the Santiago meeting was the Gondra Treaty (eventually accepted by eight nations, including the United States), which required that all disputes not settled by diplomacy or arbitration be placed before a commission of inquiry prior to a resort to force. This was, at best, a minimal achievement, so Hughes turned once more to oratory in order to redress residual complaints. In a radio broadcast of 1925, the Secretary once more denied American imperialistic intentions. "Instead of encouraging the exploitation of other peoples," he explained, "we are constantly by word and deed diminishing the opportunities for it."

When Hughes retired from office six weeks later, he was at least able to count one concrete deed to match his professed intentions. American troops had been removed from Santo Domingo. This island protectorate, which had chafed for eight years under stern naval rule, was once more self-governing. The initial step had been taken in the liquidation of our five Caribbean satrapies, and the completion of this policy of withdrawal removed a perilous roadblock to inter-American concord.[3]

Secretary Kellogg, who succeeded Hughes in 1925, originally intended to implement his predecessor's policy in Latin America. However, an unexpected turn of events in Nicaragua and Mexico led to actions which undermined Hughes's missionary work.

[3] A native regime had resumed control of the Dominican Republic, and following elections, our troops were withdrawn in 1924. We continued, however, to supervise the country's finances until 1941.

The Nicaraguan protectorate dated from 1912, when President Taft, at the behest of local authorities, stationed a small "legation guard" in Managua as a deterrent to revolution in a country of special strategic and economic interest to the United States. These same considerations impelled the Wilsonian Democrats to even stronger measures. In 1916 the protectorate was formalized in a treaty which, in return for three million dollars, secured American canal rights in Nicaragua and provided for the right to construct naval bases on both coasts of that narrow country.

Nine years later the Nicaraguan situation had stabilized to the point where Coolidge and Kellogg felt the time had come to recall our small military detachment. This action proved to be premature, for old political rivalries flared anew and four Nicaraguan Presidents were sworn into office within the short period of thirteen months. Washington tried a hands-off policy in the violence accompanying these seesaw changes. Faced with danger to American investments in a country located astride the vital isthmus, Coolidge dispatched a cruiser to Nicaraguan waters, and the marines soon resumed their familiar beat. Fighting intensified as the Liberals tried to seat Juan B. Sacasa. When Mexico recognized and aided Sacasa's "Constitutional Government," Washington sent in more troops and supplied the armies of the hard-pressed Conservatives.

As the Nicaraguan situation deteriorated, the Democratic-Progressive bloc in Congress protested the administration's support of Adolfo Díaz, whom they regarded as a Wall Street lackey. The White House, in turn, reminded Congress of our Nicaraguan canal rights, our duty to protect American interests abroad, and the necessity of halting the spread of Mexican "socialistic" doctrines to adjacent countries. "We are not making war on Nicaragua," explained President Coolidge, "any more than a policeman on the streets is making war on a passerby."

Meanwhile the Nicaraguan situation reached a crisis that threatened full-scale American intervention. This was more than the wary Yankee President had bargained for, and Coolidge began looking for a face-saving device. Secretary Kellogg suggested that the Nicaraguan fracas might be mediated by sending a personal envoy armed with full powers to Managua. In March, 1927, the administration chose for this task Colonel Henry L. Stimson, veteran lawyer and public servant trained in the "hairy-chested" school of Theodore Roosevelt.[4] Coolidge briefed Stimson in characteristically laconic manner: "If you find a way to straighten the matter out, I want you to do so."

Stimson's Rough Rider tactics resulted in an uneasy peace with a promise of a settlement if both factions were assured a fair election. When he negotiated a truce that kept Díaz in power pending a supervised election, most of the belligerents placed their weapons in American custody. The Liberals won the meticulously patrolled election of 1928 and were returned to office twice more with marines guarding the ballot boxes. This stillness was disturbed by Augusto C. Sandino, a Liberal rebel who would not give up. Finally, he was treacherously shot after he had been persuaded to surrender. The Hoover administration ordered home the last American troops in 1933, following the supervision of one final election.[5]

The Mexican tangle of the 1920's followed a similar pattern—habitual disorder that developed new complications, failure of conventional diplomacy, and ephemeral success at the hands of an envoy extraordinary. Torn by its great Revolution, Mexico constituted a chronic crisis for the United States for three decades. The political and military repercussions of the Mexican revolt that began in 1910 belong to the story of Woodrow Wilson. However, social and religious aftermaths of this upheaval vexed American-Mexican relations long after domestic political stability had been restored.

The postwar Republicans inherited from Wilson two troublesome economic problems. Prior to the 1910 revolt, 835 favored Mexican families controlled about 97 per cent of the country's cultivated land. Understandably, the watchword of the peasant revolution became *tierra y libertad*—land and freedom. Then came the Constitution of 1917, a radical document the provisions of

---

[4] Stimson had served for a time as Secretary of War under President Taft.
[5] The United States continued to act as receiver for Nicaraguan customs until 1944, when the last foreign loans secured by tariff revenues were paid off.

which constituted a hatchery for diplomatic problems. This was especially true of Article XXVII, which declared all land theoretically under state ownership, and invested the government with the power of eminent domain designed to impose limits on holdings then in effect and to expropriate and divide *haciendas* formed from one-time village lands.[6] Mexican agrarian monopolists constituted a local concern, but American holders of farming, grazing, and timber lands posed a more difficult problem. When Mexican governments sought to implement Article XXVII by creating out of these acres *ejidos* (communal farms) for landless peons, troublesome disputes arose from expropriations and inequitable indemnifications.

Secondly, Article XXVII reasserted the ancient Spanish prescript that subsoil deposits were inalienable. This meant that subsurface rights of Americans and other foreigners in oil and mining deposits were held subject to actions taken "in the public interest." Inasmuch as American companies produced over half of all Mexican oil, trouble was certain to ensue.[7] Finally, the 1917 Constitution bore strong pro-labor and anti-clerical overtones and these provisions, if enforced, were surely destined to arouse business and Catholic protests in the United States.

Were the terms of Article XXVII retroactive? Did they apply to American surface and subsoil holdings acquired under President Porfirio Díaz who, for a full generation, had traded his country's resources for foreign lucre? President Venustiano Carranza, who proclaimed the Constitution of 1917, argued affirmatively, but he was too lax to enforce this decision. Three years later Carranza, like so many of his predecessors, died in his boots. After a new flare-up, Alvaro Obregón was legally elected President. The Democrats decided to leave the problem of recognition up to their successors.

Secretary Hughes, surrogate in such matters for his supine

---

[6] According to the Constitution of 1917 there were to be indemnifications for these expropriations.

[7] American oil men were subject to a Mexican export tax on their product. If this tax was raised, they would be denied the benefit of a competitive advantage with the more expensive oil gushing from wells north of the boundary.

President, tried to barter recognition of the new government for a guarantee of respect for American interests jeopardized by Mexican constitutional law. But Obregón, in no position to rouse domestic hostility against his shaky regime, rejected a compromise interpretation of the controversial Article XXVII.[8]

The matter was not finally resolved until the Bucareli agreements of 1923. This settlement gave Mexican recognition to the pre-1917 subsoil rights of foreign investors, provided these operators, previous to the adoption of Article XXVII, had shown some positive act of good faith in their promotions. Owners of surface land subject to expropriation were to be compensated, and all American debt claims arising from the revolutionary disorders of the post-Díaz period were to be handled by a special commission.

The Harding administration accepted this executive agreement. Although there was no official promise to exchange ambassadors, the United States recognized Obregón before the negotiations were concluded. On resigning his office, Secretary Hughes was justified in his optimism that quiet had been restored south of the Rio Grande. However, in parallel fashion to the Nicaraguan story, a renewed outburst of Mexican revolutionary fervor broke the Bucareli truce.

Obregón's hand-picked successor, Plutarco Elías Calles, was intent upon implementing the 1917 decision that henceforth "Mexico was for Mexicans." The crisis mounted slowly inasmuch as Calles, while President-elect, had promised that he would welcome foreign investments provided they were not "aggressive and piratical" in nature. Furthermore, he explained to Americans that his determination to raise the standard of living of his landless peons would create a more lucrative market for foreign imports.

Once in power, Calles pushed his revolutionary aims forward in a manner certain to precipitate another diplomatic crisis. The Mexican Congress passed an Alien Land Law that forbade fresh acquisitions by foreigners unless the holders of these concessions

[8] In September, 1921, Obregón finally reached an agreement with a number of foreign investment houses represented by Thomas W. Lamont. This included an adjustment of all external debts, which were to be repaid in installment fashion, and a return to private ownership of those Mexican railroads which had been nationalized since 1910.

declared their intention to become naturalized Mexicans and concurrently renounced the protection of the countries of their original allegiance. A Petroleum Law held subsoil deposits to be "inalienable and imprescribable," limited the life of pre-1917 foreign oil acquisitions to fifty years, and ordered oil promoters to make applications for operations subject to the new law by January 1, 1927. A number of American companies met Calles's conditions but twenty-two corporations, including four of the largest American oil interests, defied the law, gambling upon the friendly protection of Coolidge's State Department.

Calles, in turn, retorted that American imperialism was about to be tried in the court of world opinion and, as already related, defied Washington by a series of laws aimed against American investors. Pressures for peace on both sides of the border militated against the chances of war. When the 1927 deadline for foreign oil companies was reached, the Mexican President hinted that he would accept arbitration of the disputes arising from his drastic policies. By a unanimous vote the United States Senate passed a resolution urging this resort to arbitration, albeit the Old Guard insisted upon a proviso demanding the protection of American lives and property. President Coolidge, who made a habit of procrastinating until political dust had settled over nettlesome issues, began to tone down his scoldings. In response to a suggestion from Calles, he decided to send a "personal representative" with full powers to break the impasse. He selected for this task Dwight W. Morrow, an Amherst College classmate and fellow lawyer who, following some years of public service, had become an associate of the House of Morgan. Morrow received a typically cropped directive from the President: "Keep us out of war with Mexico."

Arriving in Mexico City in midsummer 1927, Mr. Morrow made mockery of the widespread predictions that a corporation lawyer was the wrong man for a mission to revolutionary and leftist-minded Mexico. Consulting only infrequently with his superiors in Washington, Morrow's magnetic personality won over the battle-scarred Mexican President. Accompanied by Calles, Morrow toured the country, where he displayed a genuine interest in a revolution-inspired revival of its indigenous culture. At the ambassador's behest, Charles A. Lindbergh, fresh from his triumph over the Atlantic, made a good-will solo flight to Mexico City. Will Rogers visited Mexico, and his humorous touch poured balm on old wounds.

Perhaps all of these endeavors would have been in vain had not Calles been anxious for a *détente* to ease a temporary business recession. Morrow's sharp legal mind suggested a solution that would permit Calles to retreat in good face. Could not the Mexican Supreme Court follow precedent, asked Morrow, and declare the more objectionable parts of the Petroleum Law unconstitutional? The Court responded to executive pressure and in record time rendered a decision that, in substance, restored the terms of the Bucareli agreements. The Mexican Congress then followed suit by extending the deadline for the oil companies to comply with the law and it made certain other concessions which were accepted by the American promoters.

Ambassador Morrow was unable to do much for angry American holders of surface concessions, for the Alien Land Laws were too popular to make compromise politically feasible. President Calles, however, left office disillusioned with agrarian reform. "Happiness of the peasants," he admitted, "cannot be assured by giving them a patch of land, if they lack preparation and the necessary elements to cultivate it."

In retrospect, Morrow's work was ephemeral, for Mexican economic nationalism flared anew amidst the depression that dissipated the tolerance promoted by general prosperity. Nonetheless, his mission postponed the ultimate crisis over American-Mexican difficulties until a time when the United States was willing to sacrifice private business interests in order to insure a benevolent Mexican neutrality in the struggle against the Axis.

While President Coolidge was still in office, some progress was made in the amelioration of inter-American relations. Stimson's labors in Nicaragua and Morrow's in Mexico had reduced tension in critical areas. In 1928 Washington conceded that the Roosevelt Corollary was outmoded, an admission that proved a harbinger of a Western Hemisphere Era of Good Feelings.

Hughes's State Department had anticipated the decision to

abandon the Monroe Doctrine as a sanction for intervention. The Secretary, in countering Latin American complaints, played down the Corollary by basing our rights of interference in adjacent regions of unrest on the canons of international law and the terms of existing treaties. Although he pledged that Washington would never use intervention as an instrument for economic exploitation, he insisted that a "non-belligerent interposition" was necessary on occasion to protect American lives, rights, and property in volatile areas of the New World.

Three years after retirement from the State Department, Hughes was afforded the opportunity to make one final stand for this principle. Because Secretary Kellogg was busy in Washington with matters concerning his Peace Pact, his distinguished predecessor accompanied President Coolidge to the 1928 Pan-American Conference in Havana. After the President took ship for home, Hughes faced a difficult problem, for the impatient Latins presented a resolution providing that "no state has the right to intervene in the internal affairs of another." Unable, as in previous meetings, to strike this prickly issue from the agenda, Hughes resorted to brilliant oratory. He eventually succeeded in blocking passage of this anti-Washington resolution, but the handwriting was on the wall for the Roosevelt Corollary. Latin American protests were echoed by Coolidge's Democratic and Progressive critics, whose opposition to intervention had been whetted by the current bloodletting in Nicaragua.

Unknown to these malcontents, Kellogg had already ordered Under Secretary of State J. Reuben Clark to prepare a thoroughgoing historical exegesis of the Monroe Doctrine. Clark, a somber Mormon church leader who had worked with Morrow in Mexico, completed his task in eight weeks. In an oft-quoted but seldom read document, Clark argued that the Roosevelt Corollary was not "justified by terms of the Monroe Doctrine." Except where our own immediate security was threatened, the Doctrine bore no "relationship between the United States and other American nations" since its original intention had envisaged merely self-defense. The Clark Memorandum did not apologize for past misdeeds, nor did it relinquish the right of intervention deriving from the attributes of national sovereignty. However, inasmuch as all interventions since 1904 had been made explicitly or implicitly in the name of Theodore Roosevelt's pronouncement, the document was a tacit admission that the Corollary had led to American interference and domination. This epoch-making Memorandum, not made public until 1930, did not satisfy Latin America.[9] It did, however, remove an important irritant whose excision was essential to the development of the Good Neighbor Policy.

Some weeks before President Coolidge grudgingly initialed the Clark Memorandum, a battleship carrying President-elect Hoover weighed anchor for a good-will circuit around Latin America. Blissfully unaware of the abyss awaiting the world's economy, Hoover's roseate speeches belied a characteristic reserve. The President-elect was anxious to win friends south of the border, for as Secretary of Commerce he had come to realize how much Dollar Diplomacy injured American trade interests. Hoover managed to dispel the initial hostility of his audiences, suspicious of a long-time Cabinet official whom they held responsible for unfair Yankee trade practices. "We have a desire," the President-elect promised at Amapala, Honduras, "to maintain not only the cordial relations of governments with each other but the relations of good neighbors." Ironically, it was the dour Hoover who utilized the "good neighbor" slogan although the credit for this byword went to a successor more expert in the art of enhancing his own public image.

Perhaps the story might have been different but for complications arising from the Great Depression. Good intentions were meaningless as tropical staples piled up at dockside while the collapse of the American market reduced millions to starvation. It was all too easy, in those hungry years, for demagogues to blame

[9] According to a recent article, the officers of the State Department "quietly repudiated the repudiation" contained in the Clark Memorandum. "This reluctance to acknowledge the Clark Memorandum continued unabated into the Franklin D. Roosevelt administration." This attitude did not include Secretaries Kellogg and Stimson, "but President Hoover was uncertain." It seems that the Memorandum was released by the Government Printing Office in 1930 "in some rather odd manner." See Robert H. Ferrell, "Repudiation of a Repudiation," *The Journal of American History*, LI (March, 1965), 669–673.

Yankee business moguls for all that went wrong south of the border. Nor was this situation alleviated when Hoover signed a depression-spawned tariff bill which further jeopardized the Latin American export trade.

Nevertheless, recent investigators have re-evaluated the credit due Hoover's Latin American diplomacy. During a rash of revolutions touched off by unstable economic conditions, the new administration held firmly to a "hands-off" policy. Under President Hoover the United States returned to *de factoism*, i.e., recognition of any Latin American government in mastery of the local situation, provided that the new rulers were in firm control and would promise to fulfill their international obligations.[10] This new policy, announced on February 6, 1931, removed still another grievance.

Two months later, Secretary of State Stimson formally disclaimed an impetuous Coolidge dictum that "the person and property of a citizen are a part of the general domain of the nation even when abroad." Moreover, Hoover and Stimson matched deeds with words, for they ordered the last marines out of Nicaragua and speeded the end of the Haitian occupation. "Thus it was," writes Alexander DeConde, "that the Good Neighbor idea took root in the Hoover years."

A combination of circumstances afforded Franklin D. Roosevelt the opportunity to enlarge this policy and to link it with his own name in history. In his impressionable years Roosevelt, imitating Republican "Uncle Ted," championed a dynamic expansionism backed by the battlewagons of the American navy. As the Democratic candidate for Vice-President in 1920, FDR had brought down upon his head the wrath of the anti-imperialists by an idle boast that he had written a "pretty good" constitution for our Haitian satrapy. However, long before he entered the White House, Roosevelt became a leading critic of Republican interventionism, for he wished to form a solid Pan-American front by reversing policies unacceptable to the Latins. Searching for any remedy to cure the bottomless business slump, the new President,

[10] This policy was not applied to the Central American states, for we felt bound by previous obligations not to recognize revolutionary governments in this area. The State Department was greatly relieved when, in 1934, the Central American countries abrogated the 1923 treaty and returned to the custom of *de facto* recognition.

after considerable prodding from his Secretary of State, turned his thoughts to the improvement of New World trade relations.

When Roosevelt entered the White House, the international situation was propitious for a liquidation of the last remnants of our hemispheric imperialism. The Axis crisis had not yet ripened, and in 1933 the Caribbean was entirely safe from foreign intervention. The original reason for lacing the vital Canal Zone with protectorates had thus disappeared, and all that was left for the Democrats was to complete Republican plans for withdrawal. Moreover, Wall Street's enthusiasm for protection of its investments had cooled rapidly, for 80 per cent of all Latin American government bonds were in default. This climate of opinion offered the New Dealers, receivers in national bankruptcy for the pro-business Republicans, a splendid opportunity for an unqualified repudiation of economic imperialism.

The formal launching of Roosevelt's Good Neighbor Policy came by accident. His first inaugural, delivered in the most dire hour in the nation's economic history, was largely concerned with the domestic crisis. However, the President added a few words in order to extend an olive branch to fretful peoples: "In the field of world policy," he said, "I would dedicate this nation to the policy of the good neighbor—the neighbor who . . . respects his obligations and respects the sanctity of his agreements in and with a world of neighbors." The phrase "good neighbor" caught the imagination of Latin Americans, who interpreted it as a pledge of no more interventions. Roosevelt made capital of this misconstruction. In subsequent speeches he specifically identified good neighborism with Pan Americanism. He reassured the governing board of the Pan American Union that the Monroe Doctrine "was and is directed at the maintenance of independence by the peoples of the continent." His administration, he pledged, would cultivate closer understanding and cooperation with all New World nations and would do its best to remove existing trade barriers. At a dinner of the Woodrow Wilson Foundation eight months later, the President grew even more specific by unqualifiedly renouncing intervention.

Meanwhile the Good Neighbor Policy had almost failed its first test. Cuba, where the American rights of interposition had long been firmly secured, was in a state of terror following the fall of "Butcher" Gerardo Machado y Morales. Sumner Welles, "our man in Havana," advised his superiors in Washington to dispatch a naval armada to the Caribbean and even suggested armed intervention to insure the defeat of certain radical elements. Roosevelt sent a few naval vessels to Cuban waters, under orders not to land troops unless it was absolutely necessary for the protection of American nationals caught in the strife of the contending factions. Roosevelt's refusal to extend recognition doomed the government of the left-wing revolutionary junta headed by President Ramón Grau San Martín. "I fell," Grau said, "because Washington willed it." However, by the time the new conservative Mendieta government took control, noninterference had already been designated as the heart of the Good Neighbor approach. Therefore, on May 29, 1934, Assistant Secretary of State Welles signed a new treaty with Cuba, which abrogated by mutual consent the 1903 treaty sanctioning American intervention, but which reaffirmed American control over the Guantanamo naval base.

The liberation of Cuba from protectorate status was accompanied by a reciprocal tariff agreement and the establishment of a new Export-Import Bank to foster trade with Cuba and other Latin American countries. This bank, which loaned money to New World nations in order to stimulate the purchase of American exports, gave a new twist to Dollar Diplomacy. The Good Neighbor bandwagon now picked up speed. Before the year 1934 was out, Haiti was freed from American occupation and Latin American soil stood entirely free of Yankee troops.[11]

Panama, "born an American puppet," was the last protectorate to be freed formally, although no troops were then stationed there outside of the Canal Zone. In a 1936 treaty the United States relinquished certain long-held rights (including intervention),

[11] Roosevelt speeded the liquidation of the Haitian protectorate by means of an executive agreement. American marines were withdrawn in the summer of 1934. During the same summer FDR and President Stenio Vincent worked out an arrangement whereby the National Bank of Haiti would buy the interests held in this bank by the National Bank of New York. This transaction was completed the following year. We retained some control over Haitian customs until 1941, when the last remnants of the protectorate were liquidated.

made some necessary adjustments in rental fees for the use of the Canal Zone, and secured in return a Panamanian promise of cooperation in the task of defending the Big Ditch. Pigeonholed in the Senate for three years because of anxiety for the safety of the Canal in a decade of mounting international disorder, the treaty finally passed, and in 1939 Panama became a fully sovereign state. Now we were able to say (until the events of the 1960's) that non-interference meant refusal to "influcnce in any way the course of domestic political affairs" of any member of the family of New World nations.

Meanwhile the 1933 Pan-American Conference at Montevideo had become a milestone in history. Secretary Hull headed the American delegation, which faced an uphill fight to gain the con fidence of Latin Americans, for our last-ditch defense of intervention at Havana five years before was still fresh in the memories of veteran confcrces.[12] But Hull did yeoman work in winning over hostile delegations, and his homely Tennessee charm melted the reserve of even the Yankee-baiting Argentinians. When the touchy question of intervention arose, Hull delighted the Latins by supporting a pact which provided that "no state has the right to intervene in the internal or external affairs of another." Subject only to an innocuous reservation, the Senate approved the protocol by unanimous vote. Thenceforth, observes Jules Davids, "the 'hands-off' idea . . . became the cornerstone of the Good Neighbor Policy."[13]

[12] Sumner Welles, still in Cuba, did not accompany Hull to Montevideo. Yet in the course of many years of association with Hull in the State Department, Welles's expert knowledge of Latin American affairs was at his chief's disposal and this store of information did much to make the Good Neighbor Policy a workable experiment. For a while Hull and Welles made an excellent team, for the younger man was better informed on Latin American conditions and had a deeper grasp of the problems facing the United States while the older man had the influence in Congress necessary to implement good neighborism. As is well known, they had a parting of the ways in 1943, when Welles resigned as Under Secretary.

[13] The Montevideo Conference also tried to arrange a cease-fire between Paraguay and Bolivia, when engaged in a shooting war over a wasteland area called the Gran Chaco, which was believed to contain oil deposits. After a cost of some 100,000 lives, a truce was obtained in 1935 owing to the efforts of the United States, the ABC powers, Peru, and Uruguay. The

As time passed, President Roosevelt emerged as the champion of the underprivileged masses at home and the oppressed minorities abroad. His matchless personal charm enchanted the peoples of many lands. Alfred Kazin tells the story of a peon "who saw the crippled President hobbling down the ramp from his train [during a Mexican trip and] said that he had never realized that an American, and this the President, could be as deprived as a Mexican."

With the rapid deterioration of the international situation after Montevideo (to be treated in another context), Roosevelt and Hull became ever more anxious to secure our southern flank. As black-, green-, and brown-shirted Latins fell prey to Fascist propaganda, Washington was forced to hasten its courting of South America lest the totalitarian cancer spread across the Atlantic. Many decisions of the crisis-plagued 1930's sacrificed short-run gains and advantages with the larger aim in mind of making our own record shine in clear contrast to the dark deeds of the desperado nations of Europe and Asia.

A case in point is Philippine independence. In this area altruism and economic self-interest coincided. The depression had pointed up the competition of Philippine with home-grown products. Rural politicians, anxious to throw a sop to their hard-pressed constituents, exaggerated the menace of competing coconut oil to domestic butter, lard, and cottonseed used as shortening. Similar arguments were raised against Philippine tobacco, sugar, hemp, and cordage.[14] Congress passed a law providing for eventual freedom for the Islands, but President Hoover vetoed it on the justifiable grounds that the action was premature. The law was passed by Congress over Hoover's veto, but the Filipino legislature rejected the bill in the hope of coming to better terms with the incoming

final peace treaty, however, was not signed until three years later. Nelson M. Blake and Oscar T. Barck, Jr., *The United States in its World Relations* (New York, 1960), p. 626, fn. 7.

[14] John D. Hicks, in his *Republican Ascendancy: 1921–1933* (New York, 1960), p. 255 ff., argues that this competition was more myth than reality. Two-thirds of Philippine coconut oil went into soap making, for which our own products were not suitable; in sugar the real rivalry was between Philippine and Cuban sugar, for, states Professor Hicks, we could not supply more than one-quarter of our domestic needs.

Democrats. In 1934 President Roosevelt signed into law the slightly more generous Tydings-McDuffie Act, which provided for full independence for the Philippines in 1946, following a probationary decade in which the Islands would enjoy dominion status. Whatever our motives were, the United States became the first western country to read correctly the portents of the times and to rid itself of the bane of colonialism. Our action in the Philippines was especially important, for it testified to Latin America our unqualified endorsement of the principle of national self-determination.

The next Inter-American Conference was not scheduled to meet until 1938. Long before this date, President Roosevelt grew increasingly anxious for progress on the South American front. Reports poured into the State Department of subversive activities among the millions of nonassimilated Germans and Italians domiciled in the region. Inasmuch as we had surrendered our rights of unilateral intervention, how would we react to a Fascist-sponsored dictatorship erupting in one of our neighboring republics? If the United States could no longer guarantee hemispheric security by an untrammeled use of its own power, it needed a collective security system especially designed for New World needs. Roosevelt, therefore, sent out feelers for a special Inter-American Conference for the Maintenance of Peace. His efforts met with success and the delegates gathered at Buenos Aires on December 1, 1936. Secretary Hull again headed the American conferees but FDR himself made the long sea voyage to address the opening session of the Conference. In resonant voice he promised his hushed audience that would-be assailants of New World security "will find a Hemisphere wholly prepared to consult together for our mutual safety and our mutual good."

The President struck the keynote; it was now Hull's task to woo the Conference to his government's goals. The Secretary's principal aim was to create a hemispheric system of peace machinery, sorely needed because the United States was not a League member and the Kellogg-Briand Pact provided no solution.

Space permits mention of only the most important parts of the Conference's manifold activities. One protocol incorporated an unqualified promise of nonintervention—stronger language than the 1933 Montevideo resolution. A Convention for the Maintenance, Preservation and Reestablishment of Peace provided for consultation whenever the peace of the New World was threatened. In addition a Declaration of Solidarity[15] called for a cooperative policy in the event of danger. Although the Monroe Doctrine was not mentioned by name, the Declaration, coupled with the Convention's promise of consultation, implied "continentalization" of Monroe's celebrated dictum. While the United States did not achieve its full collective security objectives for the New World, considerable progress was made at Buenos Aires. Among its accomplishments was a Convention for the Promotion of Cultural Relations. Suggested by the United States, this agreement sought to strengthen inter-American intellectual ties by exchange professors and students and by use of other means to bridge the gap between Anglo-Saxon and Latin cultures.[16]

When, in the later 1930's, the three leading aggressor nations formed the Rome-Berlin-Tokyo Axis, their coordinated timetable for expansionism brought increased foreboding about the future of Latin America. Senator Robert R. Reynolds of North Carolina made several visits to the region and sternly warned his colleagues of the nature of New World Fascist subversion:

Those residing across the sea who are desirous of gaining a foothold [there] . . . are constantly bombarding the people . . . by radio. . . . I say to the Senate that . . . we should pay attention to American matters and nip in the bud any movements made by these foreign countries.[17]

Senator Reynolds' remarks were all the more telling because of his arch-isolationist views. Hamstrung by a militant isolationism in

15 The full name is the Declaration of Principles of Inter-American Solidarity and Cooperation.
16 To offset Axis propaganda in Latin America, Congress established in the State Department a Division of Cultural Affairs. Nelson A. Rockefeller, appointed Coordinator of Inter-American Affairs in 1940, achieved some ephemeral success in promoting cultural relationships during the critical period of World War II.
17 *Congressional Record*, 75 Cong., 3 sess., p. 376.

countering Axis *Putsches* in Europe, the Roosevelt administration was nevertheless free to safeguard hemispheric security. This task was complicated by Franco's 1939 victory in the Spanish Civil War. Would a Fascist Spain make capital of its close language, religious, and cultural ties with Latin America to foster totalitarianism in a region long accustomed to personal dictatorships?

Roosevelt and Hull did not await the final outcome of the Spanish tragedy; they seized the opportunity for action offered by the approaching Lima International Conference of American States. The opening of this parley on December 1, 1938, came less than a month after Hitler's renewed fury against German Jewry had made a mockery of appeasement at Munich. With Europe hovering on the brink of war, the American delegation at Lima was charged with devising some method of consultation in the event of danger to New World security.

At Buenos Aires in 1936, Argentinian opposition had blocked implementation of the resolution calling for mutual consultation. Hull found the Argentines even more adamant two years later. Deep-seated anti-Yankee prejudices made Buenos Aires the *bête noire* of Washington. Argentines resented our predominant position in the Pan American Union. The economies of the two countries competed rather than meshed and they frowned upon our close relations with their traditional rival, Brazil. Fascist influence was particularly strong in a country where unstable governments had to pay heed to large blocs of German and Italian hyphenates. Yankees and Argentines, Professor Thomas F. McCann has observed, bore strong similarities "in the pride, optimism, aggressive independence . . . [and] regard for material achievement and its reward." As the weaker contender, the Argentine diplomats were more arrogant and unyielding than the Americans, who were now ready to bend over backward in order to achieve New World solidarity before the Axis crisis became full blown.

Even as Hull spoke in the Peruvian capital in December, 1938, Nazi agents tried to disrupt the proceedings. Finally, however, the Secretary won a partial victory with the Christmas Eve passage of the Declaration of Lima. In lieu of a permanent committee, Hull accepted the idea of consultation through the twenty-one foreign ministers, who were to meet at the call of any member of the group. The Declaration also pledged all signatories to joint action in the event of danger common to all, including peril resulting from either internal subversion or external invasion.

The Declaration of Lima completed the prewar concert of Pan-American states. However, Canadian relations belong to a separate category because this close neighbor was not a member of the Pan American Union.[18] Nevertheless, the New Deal extended the Good Neighbor Policy northward. To be successful, this action required the solution of problems essentially different from those resolved with the twenty southern republics. Eventually, writes Professor DeConde, Canada "enjoyed the protection of the enlarged Monroe Doctrine and Good Neighbor policy without being a part of the Pan-American machinery."

However, Canada hesitated in accepting the outstretched hand of inter-American fellowship. Following 1914, Canadian chauvinism grew apace as the one-time colony achieved full self-determination. Ministers were exchanged between Ottawa and Washington in 1927. However, until the repeal of prohibition, their major efforts were devoted to minor disputes of a rum-running nature. It was not until the 1931 Statute of Westminster that Canada assumed complete control of her foreign relations. The healing effect of time was required to reduce a residual bitterness stemming from the Kaiser War, a conflict in which the Canadians held that they counted their dead while Wall Street calculated its profits. Moreover, Canadians resented our rejection of the League, for like South Americans, they hoped that our membership would curb Washington's proconsular attitude toward other New World nations.

During the era of "Republican Ascendancy," Canadian relations involved no malice but were lacking in genuine cordiality. President Harding gave his blessing for a proposed Saint Lawrence Seaway designed to improve navigation from Montreal to the Great Lakes and to exploit the electric power resources of the

18 Originally Canada was excluded because it was part of the British Empire. With the evolution of self-government, Canada was eligible for membership but chose not to join.

river. When a treaty for that purpose was negotiated a decade later, it was blocked by the Senate and the undertaking was not begun until the Eisenhower Era.

There were other difficulties. American isolationism was mirrored across the border in French-speaking Quebec and in the landlocked prairie provinces. But as the Axis menace grew, it served as an antidote for Canadian national aloofness. Governments on both sides of the 3,000-mile frontier became ever more interested in a hemispheric plan for self-defense. William Lyon Mackenzie King, a Harvard-trained doctor of philosophy who led the Liberals to an unprecedented tenure of power beginning in 1935, made an Ottawa-Washington entente a cardinal goal of his policy, for he shared, to some extent, Roosevelt's distrust of London's policy of appeasement. An historic milestone was laid in 1938, when at Kingston, Ontario, President Roosevelt promised: "I give to you assurance that the people of the United States will not stand idly by if domination of Canadian soil is threatened by any other Empire." After the shooting began in Europe, relations between the two major North American countries reached new and unprecedented cordiality.[19]

It is safe to assume that Roosevelt's courting of Canada would have failed without the settlement of tariff rivalry. Subsequent to the unexpected collapse of the reciprocity arrangement promoted by President Taft, the Canadians turned to steep protectionism. By 1930, trade between the two countries was curtailed by formidable tariff barriers on both sides of the border. Reprisal followed reprisal until 1932, when Canada joined other members of the British Commonwealth of Nations in a system of imperial preference which discriminated against imports from countries outside of this *Zollverein*. This situation impeded recovery from the depression in both countries, whose economies were closely inter-

[19] In August, 1940, Roosevelt invited Prime Minister King to Ogdensburg, New York, for army maneuvers. At this colloquy they made an executive agreement (the first defense commitment ever made by Canada outside of the British Commonwealth of Nations). A Permanent Joint Board on Defense was created for the northern segment of the Western Hemisphere. Shortly thereafter the economies of the two countries were closely meshed to further the common war effort.

locked. The United States was the chief export outlet of Canada while American investors, in an attempt to escape tariff restrictions, had established numerous Canadian branches and had bought heavily into the industries of that country.[20]

This trade impasse was eased by the epoch-making Reciprocal Trade Agreements Act of 1934, a far-reaching congressional action of complex origins. Secretary of State Hull, a veteran critic of Republican protectionism, put relentless pressure on his President for tariff reform in the interest of world recovery. Hull realized that an across-the-board reduction of rates was impossible because it would play into the hands of European dictators who stockpiled exports in order to dump them on foreign markets for gold. However, he insisted that some tariff relaxation was necessary in the New World lest the Good Neighbor policy founder on the rocks of trade barriers.[21] In contrast to Roosevelt's Kitchen Cabinet, consisting of avid New Dealers who wished to speed recovery through a selfish economic nationalism, Hull believed that more lasting benefits would result from the restoration of foreign trade to its pre-1929 volume. He sought this goal through a threefold plan of tariff reform: first, by granting special tariff concessions to countries in need of our own surplus goods; secondly, by lowering the 1930 rates on imported products necessary to our own economy; and finally, by implementing these goals in such a way that our own farmers and manufacturers would not be unduly injured by the boons offered to other countries. To achieve his objectives, Hull revived the reciprocity plan long before outlined by James G. Blaine and William McKinley. This proposal sought to remove the tariff from the quagmire of congressional logrolling and lobbying by permitting the President to make barter agreements with other countries not subject to the Senate's consent. Originally Roosevelt turned a deaf ear to Hull's demands but he was later influenced by Henry A. Wallace's *America Must Choose*. This influential pamphlet argued the logic of "a middle way between

[20] As early as 1918 it was estimated that American investors owned 30 per cent of Canadian industry.
[21] During the depth of the depression our trade with Latin America dwindled to one-tenth of its 1924 volume.

total self-sufficiency and internationalism."[22] When a group of Republican internationalists supported Wallace, the President overcame his initial hesitation and asked Congress for the power to make reciprocal tariff agreements.

This proposal encountered stiff congressional opposition, for it threatened business interests with increased competition and would transfer to the White House a cherished prerogative of Capitol Hill. In testimony at hearings on the bill, Hull stressed the long-run advantages of freeing trade channels of obstacles to world economic recovery. After three months of heated debate, the Democratic majority leaders yielded sufficient ground to get a compromise measure through Congress. The Reciprocal Trade Agreements Act of 1934 permitted the President to negotiate bilateral treaties raising or lowering existing rates up to 50 per cent, providing other parties to the agreement made reciprocal concessions to our own products. These agreements would apply to all countries whose commercial treaties with the United States incorporated "most-favored-nation clauses," albeit the President was empowered to suspend this benefit to governments discriminating against our own goods. Prior to each negotiation, domestic producers might voice their opinions in hearings conducted by a special interdepartmental committee, and advice on each agreement was to be sought by State Department officials from certain other specified government agencies. Inasmuch as the life of the act was limited to three years, agreements made were eventually subject to the will of Congress.

"The passage of the act," observes William E. Leuchtenburg, "instead of resolving conflicts over trade policies within the administration, merely shifted the scene of battle." Resulting arguments revolved around the interpretation of the "most-favored-nation clause," with nationalistic New Dealers insisting that this boon not be extended automatically but only in return for specific concessions on the part of the countries affected. Characteristically, Roosevelt let his underlings fight it out for over a year until he decided in favor of Hull, a decision which meant that the uncon-

---

[22] William E. Leuchtenburg, *Franklin D. Roosevelt and the New Deal, 1932–1940* (New York, 1963), p. 204.

ditional interpretation of the "most-favored-nation" principle would eventually reduce our entire tariff structure.[23]

Of sixteen trade agreements negotiated during the original life of the 1934 act, ten were hemispheric in nature. The first, with Cuba, placed that nation in a special category and lifted the depressed economy of that island. Similar negotiations with Haiti resulted in a brisk exchange of tropical products for American hard goods. Although each separate Latin American treaty enlivened a two-way trade, some of the republics were not enthusiastic. Originally they rightly speculated whether Washington's purpose was to increase the volume of world business or to expand our own trade in exportable items.[24] Hull had inexhaustible patience, however, and he waged a stirring campaign of education in the interest of world commercial cooperation. It is fair to say that this economic arm of the Good Neighbor policy won some good will in Latin America, helped counteract enticements offered to potential commercial allies by the Axis powers, and substantially lowered our tariff boom.[25] In the fall of 1937 the onrushing course

[23] Until a caustic letter from the President resulted in the resignation of Special Adviser on Foreign Trade George N. Peek, in November, 1935, the imposition of quotas against countries with "most-favored-nation" clauses checked the lowering of tariff rates except with those countries with whom reciprocal trade agreements were negotiated.

[24] Hull met delay and hesitation in Brazil, domestic political opposition in Colombia, argument from Guatemala that its economy could not afford even temporary sacrifices, and he had to counteract a Nicaraguan move for a new tariff that would have jeopardized his program. Nevertheless, by 1940 Hull could state that American trade with the twenty-two countries with which we had reciprocal tariff agreements had increased 61 per cent since 1934, compared to 38 per cent with countries with which we had made no agreements. These figures and many other facts are based on Julius W. Pratt's *Cordell Hull* [*The American Secretaries of State and Their Diplomacy*, Vols. XII–XIII] (New York, 1964), XIII, 107–138.

[25] When the Trade Agreements Act was renewed by Congress in 1937, prior to the outbreak of war in Europe, there was less talk of domestic recovery and more of winning friends. When the Second World War erupted, FDR used his powers under the act for good-will purposes. This policy was continued by his successors after 1945 in order to restore liberal trade policies among nations outside of the Iron Curtain. The 1934 act was renewed by Congress, often in the face of opposition, until its provisions were replaced by the Trade Expansion Act of 1962. Prior to the passage of this far-reaching measure, our average rates on dutiable goods had fallen from 36.7 per cent in 1934 to 12.5 per cent in 1951.

of aggression forced an open break between Roosevelt and the isolationist segment of the New Deal coalition. By that date all save one of the Good Neighbor policy's major objectives had been accomplished. The United States had accepted wholeheartedly the principle of nonintervention; the last marine had long since departed the soil of our erstwhile protectorates, and hemispheric tariff barriers had been lowered.

The final step in this program of reconciliation, a demonstration of tolerance toward unorthodox Latin American economic policies, came at a time when Washington was determined to settle remaining New World problems prior to the anticipated outbreak of general war. When Bolivia and Mexico seriously threatened legitimate American investments, Washington set a new precedent for international tolerance toward confiscation of privately owned foreign property. We had originally expected, in return for the renunciation of armed intervention, a fair treatment of the capital of our citizens. We hoped that when confiscatory disputes arose, our "good neighbors" would submit their cases to peaceful arbitral or judicial settlement congruent to existing treaty obligations. To offset the Fascist peril in Latin America, our State Department gradually abandoned an insistence upon juridical means to settle disputes arising from American capital investments in Latin America. Washington, after 1938, used a light-handed diplomacy that, Professor Julius W. Pratt maintains, sacrificed the private for the national interest.[26]

The Mexican crisis of the later 1930's is particularly significant, for its solution marked the culmination of the Good Neighbor policy of the pre-Pearl Harbor era. Dwight Morrow's mission to Mexico had relaxed tensions with our nearest Hispanic-American neighbor. However, fundamental issues between the two countries were moderated rather than resolved. They were bound to rise again as the protracted depression increased economic unrest

[26] When Bolivia sequestered the holdings of the Standard Oil Company and Venezuela demanded higher royalties from American oil promoters, "the United States wisely exerted economic and diplomatic pressures to gain fairly equitable settlements without evoking too many new blatant cries of 'Yankee Imperialism.'" Rayford W. Logan, review article in *American Historical Review*, LXVII (July, 1962), 1078–1079.

south of the Rio Grande. In 1936 leftist-minded President Lázaro Cárdenas launched a Six-Year Reform Plan which destroyed the existing *modus vivendi* between Mexico and her foreign investors. Cárdenas divided up forty-seven million acres of land among one million peasants during his term of office. This and similar actions jeopardized American holdings in Mexican land, subsurface deposits, and public utilities. Even more ominous was the formation of the Confederacion de Trâbajadores Mexicanos (CTM), a government-fostered militant labor syndicate which melded into a powerful industrial union all of the country's oil workers.

These measures created a new crisis just at a time when the Axis Juggernaut was rolling in high gear over Central Europe and China. For obvious reasons Hull had to move cautiously but his patience wore thin as our socialist-oriented neighbor flouted vested rights in defiance of international law and treaty obligations. In retaliation Hull persuaded the Treasury Department to boycott the purchase of Mexican silver and to undermine the value of the peso on the global money market. "Poor Mexico!" complained the weekly magazine, *Hoy:* "So far from God, and so close to the United States."[27]

The world situation, however, did not permit Hull the luxury of forcing a Mexican retreat. The Secretary was subordinate to a President insensitive to Wall Street pressure and prone to hearken to the admonitions of our Ambassador to Mexico, Josephus Daniels. Roosevelt's chief during his service as Assistant Secretary of the Navy, Daniels was a black-string-tie newspaper editor of Bryanite persuasions who sympathized with Mexico's need for land and oil reform. Owing in part to his influence, we accepted a Mexican offer to pay one million dollars per year on all post-1917 land confiscations pending a general settlement of all claims. Our troubles with Cárdenas did not end with this halfway measure. Mexico continued to wage a tariff war against the United States while at the same time supplying one third of the oil for Hitler's war machine.

American-Mexican relations reached crisis proportions when, in 1937, the CTM ordered a general strike of all Mexican oil workers.

27 Quoted in Leuchtenburg, *op. cit.,* p. 209.

American promoters were willing to yield some ground, but refused to make any concessions when contronted by an arbitral decree which favored the workers. In March, 1938, Cárdenas ordered the nationalization of oil lands owned by American, British, and Dutch companies. These properties, so at least their owners claimed, were valued at about a half-billion dollars.[28]

The dispute dragged on until the fateful year of 1940. Hull originally insisted upon arbitration but he turned to political settlement in the face of the European War. Opportunity for agreement arose when Sinclair broke the united front of the American oil companies by reaching a separate understanding with Cárdenas. This breakthrough, coinciding with the cataclysmic fall of France, spurred Washington's efforts to come to terms with Mexico City. There was no time to spare, for final negotiations were concluded just eighteen days before Japanese bombs fell from the December Hawaiian sky.

Under the terms of this bloc settlement, an American and a Mexican specialist were to appraise the claims and decide upon a "just compensation" for the American oil men. These experts decided upon a twenty four million-dollar settlement, a disappointing figure for the American investors since it approximated the Mexican estimate.[29] The State Department adopted a take-it-or-leave-it attitude, so the American companies were forced to concede. This 1941 agreement also settled general claims against Mexico for forty million dollars, which included the liquidation of agrarian expropriations and other confiscations.

Perhaps the outstanding feature of this timely *détente* was the aid the United States gave Mexico to fulfill its obligations. The government of President Avila Camacho (who succeeded Cárdenas in 1940) was granted a long-term loan from the Export-Import Bank, the dollar-peso ratio of exchange was stabilized, a

[28] The foreign oil companies, represented by Donald Richberg, failed to reach a private agreement with Cárdenas.
[29] The experts worked on the basis of actual American investments in Mexico, excluding claims arising from undrilled oil. This figure contrasted sharply with the 1939 American claim of $260 million. Including the settlement made with Sinclair and some smaller companies, United States companies received about $42 million in principal and interest.

reciprocal trade agreement was negotiated, and we resumed our heavy purchases of Mexican silver. These transactions, writes Professor DeConde, revealed to Latin America that Washington "placed such importance on the Good Neighbor policy that it was willing to sacrifice the economic claims of some of its citizens to maintain it, and in effect to furnish funds for Mexico to pay for property it had expropriated."

"The outstanding success of Mr. Roosevelt's foreign policy," commented *The New Republic* in 1940, "has undoubtedly been in this hemisphere." In seven short years the second Roosevelt had undone the work of the first by transforming the Pan American Union into an organization reflecting genuine hemispheric solidarity.

The diplomatic labors of 1933–1941 were well rewarded during World War II, when most of our Latin American neighbors aided the Allied task of saving western civilization from the Fascist dictators who sought to destroy it. Time was to create new problems and tensions, but the Good Neighbor policy of the 1930's yielded, at the very least, a welcome moratorium on hemispheric disputes.

The demands of organization necessitated the fusing of the annals of New World diplomacy into a single chapter. It is now necessary to reverse the hand of time and return to that milestone of our troubled century, the Great Depression.

CHAPTER VI

The Ordeal of Herbert Hoover

The cherub faced President who entered the White House on March 4, 1929, amidst great expectations, symbolized the typical American success story. Born on an Iowa farm, orphaned at a tender age, Herbert Hoover amassed a considerable fortune as a mining engineer in partnership with some British financiers who utilized his talent for discovering unworked mining deposits in remote portions of the globe. The First World War subsequently made his name a synonym for planned thrift and quiet efficiency. Although the Wilsonian Democrats had discovered and advertised his turn for administration, Hoover cast his lot with the renascent Republicans. A prominent member of the Harding-Coolidge cabinets, he lent a certain prestige to that uninspiring era of public service.

Herbert Hoover's apprenticeship in international negotiations was served amidst the havoc of the Kaiser War and the tensions of peace-making which followed that global upheaval. Firsthand experience with foreign diplomats cooled his original enthusiasm for a grand design to preserve world peace. Greatly shocked by the wanton loss of life and property resulting from a war of European origin, he returned from the Versailles Peace Conference disgusted with continental "paternalism and state socialism," and he spoke of getting out of the Old World "lock, stock and barrel." In the decade that followed, this war-hating Quaker shared the conventional Republican conviction that the United States must stand aloof from an overseas complex of military build-ups and rival imperialisms "infested with age-old hate and fears."

Nonetheless, Secretary Hoover was not an unqualified isolationist and he stoutly championed cordial cooperation with Geneva's nonpolitical activities. "When I took office [in 1929]," Hoover recalled in his *Memoirs,* "America was so isolationist that our proper responsibilities were neglected." The new President sought to redress this imbalance by accentuating America's partnership in the League's nonforce goals—international supervision of the narcotics trade, global radio and aeronautic regulations, provisions for safety at sea, security against counterfeiting and trademark violations, and ridding the world of black and white slavery. President Hoover pursued these laudable objectives with grim determination, but he coupled them with a stern resolve to limit his country's peace-preserving activities to moral suasion. In strict accord with the tenets of neo-isolationism, Hoover believed that the United States could best serve humanity by confronting foreign troublemakers with an aroused world opinion mobilized through American efforts. Ultimately the pace of events forced Hoover to modify this stand, but he always stood firm against participation in economic sanctions or other collective action that might culminate in a shooting war. Lukewarm on the World Court issue, Hoover insisted that the formula proposed by Elihu Root to break the impasse on the Hague question was not "the slightest step toward entry in the League of Nations."

A recent monograph argues that Hoover "suffered from an inability to see beyond the range of American interests, frequently ignoring diplomatic considerations for the narrow aims of economic nationalism."[1] Even more than his friend and colleague Charles Evans Hughes, Hoover was purblind to the ultimate consequences of an unlimited American economic thrust, artificially stimulated by subsidies, one-sided tariffs, and a planned promotion of exports.

[1] See Joseph Brandes, *Herbert Hoover and Economic Diplomacy: Department of Commerce Policy* (Pittsburgh, 1962), p. 218.

Strangely enough, this circumspect President chose as Secretary of State a champion of the Rough Rider tradition of statecraft. Henry L. Stimson, a stately New York City lawyer, took exaggerated pride in the colonelcy that he had won during brief service in the recent war. As an advocate of Theodore Roosevelt's spread-eagle nationalism, the irascible and determined Stimson stood in sharp contrast to his more cautious chief. "Mr. Hoover," notes McGeorge Bundy, "liked to calculate his moves as he would the building of a bridge, while Stimson preferred to choose his main objective and then charge ahead without worrying, confident that aggressive executive leadership would win followers."

As long as the Versailles order stood intact, no serious differences of opinion arose between the two men. Stimson took office as a firm believer in the efficacy of a moral suasion to be exercised by invoking the terms of the ink-fresh Kellogg-Briand Pact. Only when this toothless treaty failed in its purpose to deter aggression did Stimson contemplate sterner measures. Even then, in soldierly fashion, he abided by President Hoover's decision for restraint.

At the outset of the Hoover administration, no serious international issues challenged the validity of existing GOP diplomatic axioms. On the contrary, the pervading calm led to an unwarranted faith in these policies, for the postwar balance of power seemed in equipoise. Following the 1925 Pact of Locarno, all was quiet along the Rhine. Mussolini's bellicose fulminations were rationalized as prods designed to excite the national consciousness of his easy-going Italians. To the east, Stalin had ousted the Trotsky faction dedicated to universal revolution, and the new Soviet dictator was busying himself with an intensive domestic program to make Communism work in Russia. In the Far East, the recent victory of Chiang Kai-shek's Kuomintang aroused cheery hopes for Chinese stabilization. To be sure, the Japanese warlords had already given the world a brief preview of their ambitions, but the moderates soon regained power in Tokyo and were expected to abide by the terms of the postwar settlement. On March 4, 1929, the world still appeared to be under the rule of law.

Seven months later came the Wall Street collapse, a catastrophe which marks the watershed between the postwar and prewar dec-

ades. Meanwhile Hoover had expressed his complete confidence in
the future of world stability in these words to Stimson: "It seems
to me that there is the most profound outlook for peace today that
we have had any time in the last century." Time was to make a
cruel mockery of this placebo, but when it was written, even the
most seasoned commentators on world affairs saw a bright horizon
on the international skies. "Nothing seems more assured today," the
veteran correspondent Frank H. Simonds assured his readers, "than
two decades of freedom from any general European conflict."

Tolerance, a luxury of the new abundance, saturated the atmosphere. Lincoln Steffens, disillusioned muckraker who had soured
on free enterprise, conceded that Big Business had cut the ground
from under the unflinching Marxists by providing "food, shelter
and clothing for all." "You will see it," he promised in a moment of
recklessness, "during the Hoover administration." The American
people had apparently reached a consensus favoring limited cooperation with the League, a state of agreement now judged to
be as useful as it seemed safe. Rare indeed was a voice of consequence lifted against the new President's promise to lend Geneva
every assistance, provided always that our aid did not involve us in
political wrangles or commit us to measures of coercion, military or
otherwise.

In the waning days of prosperity, President Hoover labored to
fulfill his inaugural promise of further progress on naval disarmament. Anglo-American naval tensions eased when J. Ramsay Mac-
Donald became Prime Minister following the June, 1929, victory
of the Labour party. A handsome Scotsman of humble origins,
MacDonald shared Hoover's twin desires for peace and a sharp
curtailment of defense budgets. After the two countries reached an
understanding in unofficial talks on an ambassadorial level in London, MacDonald announced the willingness of His Majesty's Government to accept naval parity with the United States in all categories of fighting craft.[2]

[2] Before these talks with Ambassador Charles G. Dawes had taken place, a
way out of the Anglo-American impasse on the question of cruiser limitation had been suggested by Hugh Gibson, who represented the United States
at the Geneva Preparatory Commission, then working on disarmament prob-

Following this concession, MacDonald visited Hoover's camp in Virginia. Sitting on a "log by the Rapidan," the two statesmen ironed out remaining difficulties. On October 7, 1929, invitations were issued to the leading naval powers to meet at London to establish quotas on smaller vessels not covered by the Five-Power Washington ratio on battleship strength.

Coolidge's failure to do preliminary spade-work had helped doom to failure the Geneva Conference of 1927. To guarantee success in the new effort, Hoover worked diligently on the preliminaries of the London conclave. He persuaded hesitant Paris and Rome officials to send delegates and influenced the invited powers to name prominent men as their representatives. Hoover himself chose an able American contingent, headed by Secretary Stimson.

Nevertheless, the Anglo-American conferees faced many obstacles to their plans at London. Apprehensive of growing German unrest, the French delegates refused to accept further naval limitation unless the United States would pledge itself to "consult" in the event of renewed danger from the Reich or unless the Conference would grant France naval superiority over her Mediterranean rival, Italy. Either promise on the part of Washington was politically dangerous. Therefore, the French adhered only to minor clauses in the treaty, a step which made certain that Italy would not curtail her naval strength in Mussolini's *Mare Nostrum*. The net result was a complicated three-power agreement with a 10:10:6.5 ratio on cruiser strength for the United States, Great Britain, and Japan, respectively, and about 10:10:7 on destroyers.[3] All five nations agreed to extend the Washington naval moratorium on battleships pending a new conference scheduled for 1935. They also subscribed to a meaningless pledge to use submarines according to the rules of international law and the dictates of humanity.

Subsequent events were to demonstrate that Hoover and Mac-Donald had won a Pyrrhic victory for disarmament by easing

---

lems. Gibson suggested a "yardstick" policy to measure the British demand for light cruisers and the American demand for heavy cruisers needed because of the distance between our naval bases in distant waters.
[3] Japan was granted parity in submarine strength.

Anglo-American naval tensions. Owing to the actions of France and Italy, the treaty contained an "escalator clause" which allowed the signatories escape from its terms—an out promptly invoked by Britain after Hitler began to rebuild the German navy. While cruiser limitation saved the United States about five hundred million dollars during the nadir of the depression, it is arguable that this lag on cruiser construction resulted in a dangerous Japanese superiority in East Asian waters. More important, the acceptance by Premier Yuko Hamaguchi of an inferior ratio led first to his assassination and then to eventual military control in Japan, which ultimately ended both the postwar international breathing spell and its concomitant desire for naval disarmament.

While President Hoover was laying the groundwork for the London Conference, the bursting of the stock market bubble touched off a chain reaction which ended one epoch in modern history and ushered in another. The world depression destroyed the fragile truce fostered by a tinsel prosperity, engendered dangerous aggression abroad, and exacerbated isolationism at home. This new American aloofness was much more profound than the rather superficial detachment of the Golden Twenties. There were greater numbers of unswerving isolationists in the 1930's and these men were more intense in their convictions and less tolerant of rational dissent than their predecessors. Human beings react to immediate danger more violently than to conjectural threats. The localized fighting of the Prosperity Decade had never led any serious person to suggest American intervention beyond the confines of the New World. The only issue at stake was whether to join a system of collective security that someday might conceivably necessitate armed support. In the crisis-ridden years that followed 1929, isolationism became a mass movement as shortsighted men heralded it as a substitute for an effective brake upon mounting world disorder. "Keep out of war" now superseded "Keep out of the League" as the watchword of American xenophobes.

Several overriding factors precipitated this glorified isolationism. The first of these was the prolonged distress resulting from an unfathomable dip in the global business cycle. Oddly enough, the panic that intensified economic isolationism was caused in part by the reverse policy of unbridled American business expansionism abroad. Ever since the armistice, foreign economic pumps had been primed by loans from Wall Street. When the New York money market tightened, putting an end to easy lending, the golden chain of prosperity snapped at its weakest link—the constant flow of dollars abroad. Short-term European loans were called in by fear-stricken and sorely pressed bankers. Within three weeks following "Black Thursday," October 24, 1929, prices on the New York Stock Exchange tumbled to less than half their former values. As slowly but surely the pall of depression fell upon all civilized portions of the globe, the calamity revealed the dependence of the world's economy on that of the United States. Our first great adventure in foreign lending came abruptly to an end with the spread of the business paralysis.

Before the crash, virtually every American family able to obtain credit had a house, an automobile, a radio, an electric refrigerator, or any of the other numerous items whose mass production had sustained the high consumer level of the Harding-Coolidge Era. But who was there now to buy such hard goods or to consume the vast quantities of products annually put on the market by American industry and agriculture?

The United States was the first country to feel the full effects of a business panic destined to outmatch all its predecessors in length, severity, and widespread impact. Before the dismal year of 1930 had run its course, the sharp drop in consumption had thrown six million out of work while the list of new layoffs multiplied weekly. Two years later one million wage earners were unemployed in New York City alone. In Philadelphia a quarter of that number faced actual starvation. In smaller industrial centers, such as Toledo, 80 per cent of the workers were involuntarily idle. When the depression hit rock bottom, American steel plants were working at 12 per cent of capacity owing in part to an 80 per cent drop in the demand for automobiles. The output of pig iron sank to its pre-McKinley level. Gross farm income fell by more than half. Farmers were forced to keep warm in winter by burning corn for fuel in their dreary homes while awaiting eviction for nonpayment of mortgage obligations. In the last full year of the

Hoover administration, the emigrants that quit these shores (some to try their luck in Communist Russia) far outnumbered new arrivals. In Chicago homeless men raided garbage dumps for food because the Red Cross and local charity agencies were forced to cut relief allowances to below subsistence levels. Nor were those still listed on payrolls much better off, for employers cut wages and salaries drastically in an attempt to maintain minimal levels of production. The toll of human deprivation caused by the depression is almost incalculable, paralleled on the domestic scene only by the experience of the people of the Confederacy during the terminal stage of the Civil War.

These sordid facts explain the American psyche of those threadbare days. A confused, bitter, and disillusioned people found it congenial to blame foreigners for their plight. Senator George W. Norris, Nebraska Republican insurgent who had been at sword's point with the "Eastern Establishment" for two decades, justified his 1917 vote against war on the fifteenth anniversary of American intervention. Our so-called victory was a misnomer, he said, because the war had launched an unhealthy boom whose inevitable collapse brought endless suffering. "Here in Northeast Nebraska," a Norris constituent wrote, "[we] are being driven from our homes by 'Writs of Assistance' in the hands of our sheriffs. It is the tragic heritage that has come down to us from this so-called 'war to end wars.' " "We were fools to be sucked in once in a European war," noted Ernest Hemingway in a celebrated article, "and we should never be sucked in again." Alfred Kazin has pointed out that the literary productions of the day were freighted down with an exaggerated nationalism. In Coolidge's time creative writers found European soil and themes congenial; a decade later novelists reclaimed the past of their country in stories filled with nostalgic longings for "the solid comfort of their grandfathers."

Popular economic policies mirrored this inward emphasis. As foreign trade declined to a fraction of its pre-crash volume, men came to regard overseas commerce and investments as hazardous, undependable, and unnecessary for domestic recovery. To confirm these prejudices, America saw the two and a quarter billion gambled on the future of German stability dwindling to almost nothing. In neo-mercantilist fashion, nations sought a favorable balance of trade by using foreign markets as dumping grounds for surpluses, and by manipulating their currencies to gain selfish advantages. National recovery plans based on these programs destroyed the last remaining vestiges of an erstwhile international community of interests. It was every country for itself in those hard-scrabble times.

The business panic was less than a year old when Congress raised the tariff wall to new heights. President Hoover had asked for a limited revision of rates in the illusory hope of providing additional protection for the hard-pressed American farmer. However, true to long custom, lobbying and logrolling on Capitol Hill produced the Smoot-Hawley Bill, designed chiefly to repress all types of foreign competition. In an unprecedented display of unity, 1,038 professional economists reminded the White House that "countries cannot permanently buy from us unless they are permitted to sell to us" and they foresaw inerrantly the unfortunate outcome of the measure in costly retaliations, embittered foreign relations, and further jeopardy to our overseas investments. Nonetheless, the President signed this out-of-date protectionist bill into law with six gold pens which were then dutifully handed to prominent spectators as souvenirs.

When the protests of twenty-three nations went unheeded, a new round in the tariff battle began. France and three New World nations raised their rates against our goods. Sweden created a wheat monopoly which shut out foreign exports, while other European countries specified certain articles which henceforth could be imported only on a quota system.

Europe felt the full effects of the widening slump in 1931. The new downward trend began in Austria when that country's predominant bank, the Credit-Anstalt, faced bankruptcy. The government, which guaranteed the bank's deposits, refused aid from Paris because it was coupled with a demand that Austria drop pending negotiations for a customs union with Germany. The financial emergency spread from Vienna to Berlin, where French pressure for the collection of short-term loans wrought havoc with the Reich's financial system. This collapse, in turn, was felt in England where the Labour government was maintaining an expensive welfare dole which drained the Exchequer's gold reserves. Bowing to pressure from financial interests and King George V, Prime Minister MacDonald formed a National Coalition government which provided a convenient front for the Tory opposition. The new government abandoned both the gold standard and free trade, substituting for the latter a system of imperial preference which further cut down the volume of American exports. The British dominions then raised their tariff barriers in order to place themselves in a better bargaining position with the mother country. To meet the new crisis, European nations withdrew their gold deposits from American banks and unloaded securities on the swamped New York Stock Exchange. Pessimism, hunger, debt repudiation, and a return to the law of the jungle lurked around that proverbial corner President Hoover promised so often to turn. A series of interlocking events, crowded into a few months, made Americans more distrustful than ever of European satanic chicanery.

Perhaps no other single result of the depression bred more isolationists than the Allied repudiation of their war debts. After being warned of an imminent German economic collapse, President Hoover (June 2, 1931) proposed a one-year moratorium on both reparations and war debts. Wedded to the idea that the fundamental causes of the depression were of foreign origin, Hoover favored international action as a spur to domestic recovery. Possibly the President had a more specific purpose in mind. Had Hoover not called a temporary halt on reparations, Berlin then and there might have forbidden payments on American private loans. Two immediate results of the Hoover Moratorium are deserving of mention. First, the French delayed their acceptance of the proposal for three critical weeks during which time nearly all banks in Germany and Austria closed their doors. Secondly, our debtors used the moratorium to weld more firmly the link that they had already forged between reparation payments from Berlin and war debt installments to Washington. Henceforth, they were fully resolved to pay the United States no more than they could collect from the Reich.

When the twelve-month moratorium was about to expire, Germany met with her creditors at Lausanne, Switzerland, and made a settlement that freed her from nine-tenths of her remaining reparations. Ratification of this Lausanne agreement was understood to be subject to the action of the United States in granting some forgiveness to its debtors.[4] In other words, the United States was invited to bear the chief burden of a mutual cancellation. In December, 1932, a little more than half of our debtors paid their semiannual installments, but thereafter only Finland (with a modest debt and a favorable balance of trade) paid in full. Meanwhile most of the rest sent token payments but even these bagatelles ceased after the Attorney General ruled that countries not paying in full would still be held in default. Hoover urged Congress to recreate the War Debt Commission in the hope of negotiating a fresh settlement with Europe, but Capitol Hill was fed to the gills with "welchers" and "fair-weather friends."

The virtual repudiation of nearly twelve billion dollars in debts and back interest gave waxing isolationist sentiment a gigantic fillip. William G. McAdoo, now a Democratic senator from California, reflected this sentiment:

Far from appreciating our unparalleled generosity in reducing debts . . . the debtor nations have repudiated their obligations without a semblance of justification, and with an utter disregard of every honorable consideration.[5]

Taken alone, these economic repercussions might have created the profound anti-foreign sentiment of the Hoover-Roosevelt Era. Historical trends, however, are always interrelated. The Great Depression brought into power or whetted the expansionist appetites of three regimes whose reckless lunges ultimately precipitated a Second World War. Although Japan was the first of these outlaw governments to take to the warpath, it was the deterioration of the European situation which created the opportunity for Tokyo's dangerous gamble.

Europe's inhabitants had doubled in number within the course

[4] The Lausanne agreement was never ratified because the United States never agreed to forgive or drastically cut the war debts. Within seven months Hitler was in power and the question of reparations became academic.
[5] Quoted in the New York *Times*, September 5, 1934.

of a century—a population explosion that created a restless proletariat. This city-bred class, dependent upon wages, was unusually
sensitive to the gyrations of the modern business cycle. Any downward swing meant wholesale unemployment. Prior to 1914 a sturdy
middle class had acted as a stabilizing influence amongst the urban
masses, but in Germany war and inflation ruined white-collar
workers, small businessmen, professionals, and pensioned people.
The resultant loss of bank savings, insurance policies, and investments loosened faith in the sure and trusted values of olden days.
Such was also the case with needy veterans, displaced peasants,
and idle university graduates unable to gain a foothold in their
chosen professions even amidst the frantic and uneven prosperity
of the 1920's.[6] All of these groups lent a willing ear to the siren
call of unscrupulous demagogues who pledged the use of radical
means to gain national access to raw materials and world markets.
Understandably, the number of their followers increased with the
coming of hard times.

This revolt of the "have-not" nations was complicated by chronic
ideological warfare between the rival totalitarian systems of Fascism and Communism. Warranted and exaggerated fears of Marx-
ism helped win over to the new order certain conservative elements
anxious to protect their economic position from social upheaval.
In Weimar Germany the imperial mentality had lingered among
civil service and army careerists. If the old Wilhelmenian order
could not be restored, might not an authoritarian government
prove more congenial than an unstable and supine parliamentary
regime? Moreover, economic considerations bore heavy weight.
The rearmament and expansionism promised by upstart leaders
would reduce unemployment, increase purchasing power, and promote business recovery. If the game of international blackmail
paid off, then expanded markets and sources of raw materials
would be forthcoming; if it led us to war (which most assumed
would be successful) new spheres of influence would provide fruitful fields for exploitation. H. Stuart Hughes notes that pioneer

[6] For this account of European economic and social conditions, I have
drawn heavily upon Geoffrey Bruun, *The World in the Twentieth Century*
(Boston, 1957), pp. 423–427.

recruits to this radicalism of the right were frequently younger men who "identified the national humiliation" of Germany with their own failure to find a place for themselves in the impersonal and chaotic society of postwar Central Europe. "The national defeat and the Treaty of Versailles," Erich Fromm has observed, "became symbols to which the actual frustration—the social one—was shifted." The situation in Italy was somewhat different, for that country had won a nominal victory in 1918, but the results were much the same. Here, Benito Mussolini's tenure in power after 1922 was characterized by an insistence that only a drastic revision of the Treaty of Versailles would compensate his country for its wartime sacrifices. While Italian Fascism was still a nuisance rather than a danger, Great Britain tried appeasement with some worthless African lands, but *Il Duce* told London acidly that he did not include the collection of deserts among his hobbies!

In certain respects totalitarianism was the analogue to isolationism in countries where liberal traditions were not sufficiently rooted to withstand the strains and stresses of prolonged economic depression. More favored nations with a firmly established democratic tradition tried to overcome business paralysis by fostering recovery programs grounded in national self-sufficiency. Elsewhere men turned to unscrupulous charismatic leaders who denounced international law and comity and who promised to disregard morality in decisions involving reasons of state. Americans found Fascism difficult to understand, for, unlike Marxian socialism, its goals were not clear; nor had its incredible tenets been purveyed to the outside world by seminal books or a propaganda build-up. Only slowly did the free nations grasp the true significance of a movement characterized by deliberate irrationality, "frenzied enthusiasm, state nationalism, and . . . a mechanism of terror that defied counter-revolution." Moreover, the totalitarianism of the right seemed to contain a bundle of paradoxes. Extremists of the right often spoke like Socialists. Once in ascendancy, however, they were abetted by business and military reactionaries. Upon gaining power, Fascist leaders promptly turned their backs upon their original revolutionary social and economic preachments to turn the clock of progress backward. Confusion was confounded by the fact that Fascism differed within each country that fell victim to its baneful influence. Political success, however, was always followed by the same unhappy results—a national consciousness inflated to dangerous proportions, a weird economy directed by and in the interest of a single party which enjoyed a monopoly of power, plus full control of the mass media of communications and all means of effective resistance. Dissenters who questioned a domestic Reign of Terror or dangerous adventures abroad were invariably crushed without mercy.

These outrages against decency soon revealed to outsiders a warped ideology, marked by abrupt changes and subject only to the dictates of opportunity. Americans of those years had to reconcile themselves to some unpleasant facts. Scientific and technological progress had put a premium upon the use of modernized force, a force able to subdue smaller neighbors at will and to hold subject peoples captive by streamlined methods of physical and psychological coercion. Slowly but surely men of good will learned that peace in their time was only that strange interlude which separated one drummed-up war scare from another. Perhaps the vicious cycle could have been broken if the peace-loving nations had been willing to make immediate sacrifices to uphold the principle of collective security. A risk of general war, it must be emphasized, entailed less peril before the nuclear revolution in weaponry. However, the United States and the balance of the western world refused to take this risk on time, owing to a constellation of factors neatly summarized by Professor Robert H. Ferrell. First, the economic nightmare of depression "palsied the hands of . . . statesmen." Secondly, the ultimate decision for preventive measures rested with men dedicated to the proposition that moral suasion, without the use of force, would hold in balance the existing international equilibrium. Thirdly, insufficient attention was paid to the imponderables of human behavior on the part of dictators whose capacity for evil appalled the modern mind. Finally, a rapidly accelerated pace of events baffled lethargic western diplomats, rendering them incapable of farsighted judgments.[7]

[7] Robert H. Ferrell, *American Diplomacy in the Great Depression: Hoover-Stimson Foreign Policy, 1929–1933* (New Haven, 1957), pp. 278–280.

Americans reacted to this renewed foreign turmoil in characteristic fashion—"Deal us out." They soon discovered that their country held no patent rights on a selfish isolationism, for the western Europeans were equally unwilling to crush the desperado nations until such time as their own vital interests were directly affected. Until Hitler's legions goose-stepped into Poland the illusion lingered on both sides of the Atlantic that somehow Berlin and Moscow could be maneuvered into a war whose fires would consume Europe's chief trouble-breeders. Depression, aggression, and a conniving national selfishness had all proven to be highly contagious.

While Hindenburg's Germany and Mussolini's Italy were as yet quiescent, Japan broke the post-armistice truce. In contrast to future territorial seizures of the Axis Era, this initial thrust was not simply unprovoked aggression. The 1931 Japanese Manchurian push stemmed from an involved set of remote and immediate causes.

Underlying this complex was the Chinese convulsion which began in 1911 with the fall of the decadent Manchu dynasty. The strongest revolutionary force to emerge from that crucible was Sun Yat-sen's Kuomintang party. For a decade and a half China was torn asunder by incessant civil war, and later by political vacillations arising from the Kuomintang's complicated relationship with Soviet and Chinese Communism. Red infiltration into the Kuomintang reached a high point in the mid-twenties, but this united front was broken in 1927 by Sun's successor, Chiang Kai-shek, who purged the party of Russian influence and expelled the native Communists. In command of an army modernized by foreign experts, Chiang captured Nanking and pushed northward to seize the old imperial capital of Peking, a feat accomplished on June 8, 1928. To outside observers, the unification of strife-torn China finally seemed at hand.

Chiang's attempt to solidify his gains brought him into conflict with the two powers possessing separate spheres of influence in semi-autonomous Manchuria. His first confrontation came with Moscow over control of the Chinese Eastern Railroad. This precipitated a short-lived conflict settled by direct negotiations which restored the *status quo ante bellum*.[8] Undaunted by a setback which frustrated his aims in northern Manchuria, Chiang tried to loosen Japanese control in the southern part of that outlying Chinese province. He paralleled the trackage of the Japanese-controlled South Manchurian Railway, encouraged the flow of Chinese immigrants into the disputed territory, and engineered a boycott of Japanese goods. In addition, he planned harbor improvements which, if completed, would draw business from Japanese ports located on the Liaotung Peninsula. Meanwhile the anti-Japanese warlord of Manchuria had been assassinated, only to be succeeded by the "Young Marshal," Chang Hsüeh-liang, whom Tokyo regarded as a Kuomintang puppet. As the Japanese activists viewed the situation, a dangerous rival would be crippled if Chiang's northward penetration could be halted, and Manchuria's soybeans would be secured to feed Japan's exploding population. Moreover, the promised campaign might prove the springboard for further leaps toward a Far Eastern empire governed from Tokyo. Manchuria, nine times the size of Ohio, and rich in coal, iron, and timber resources, loomed as a bridge that must be crossed before Japan could march to full imperial glory.

The chronic Manchurian crisis became acute just when Japanese foreign exports were sharply curtailed by the expanding depression. The sudden collapse of the American outlet for silk and the Chinese boycott on cotton goods injured peasants and city workers alike. About 90 per cent of all Japanese foreign investments were in nearby Manchuria and trade with this province remained brisk. Too much was at stake to risk further economic pressure on the part of Chiang. Moreover, the time for bold action seemed most propitious. A renewal of civil strife had diverted Chiang Kai-shek's attention to a degree which would limit his assistance to the Manchurian warlord. Stalin, busy with his Second Five-Year Plan, could be expected to remain neutral. England was beset by financial turmoil, and neither the United States nor the League had the hardihood or the striking power to hold in check the restless Japa-

[8] Secretary of State Stimson twice reminded the powers of the newly signed Kellogg-Briand Pact, but the fighting was ended without formal invocation of the Pact.

nese Kwantung army stationed in Manchuria. Nipponese activists were correct in their assumption that the world would not unite to stop them.

Japanese expansionists also guessed correctly that they would not be halted by civilian officials in Tokyo. We know today that the rape of Manchuria was not planned by constituted governmental authorities, consisting of members of the Minseito party who looked forward to commercial rather than military dominion in the Far East. The fuse of war was lighted by a cadre of fidgety younger officers anxious to launch a so-called Showa Restoration which, it was hoped, would revitalize the primitive Bushido spirit of classical Japan. Conquest of Manchuria would be followed by an internal political upheaval which would oust western-style bureaucrats, politicians, and industrialists, the coalition of interests which had ruled Japan for almost three generations.

The brains of the Kwantung rebels was Colonel Sheishoro Itagaki, a disciple of Kodo, or the imperial way that would herald the Showa Restoration. Because the Japanese system of government did not mandate full civilian authority over military actions, army officers were able to start shooting without a clearance from Tokyo. The army clique formulated its plans just as the conservative Minseito cabinet was at the point of settling some ugly border clashes with China. Faced with the possibility of a right-wing revolution in the event that the Manchurian army was ordered to retreat, the War Office capitulated to subordinates who had taken matters into their own hands.

So it was that the first shots of a new series of wars were fired on the wind-swept plains of Manchuria. The initial clash came on the evening of September 18, 1931, a few miles north of Mukden along the lines of the South Manchurian Railway. The Japanese told the world that their troops acted in retaliation for a Chinese-engineered explosion on the main track, but they refused to reveal the location of the damage for five days. To add to the world's suspicion of a fabricated accident, a southbound express was known to have crossed the gap in the rails a few minutes after the line was allegedly severed. Moreover, the speed and precision with which the Kwantung army (consisting of 10,400 men, half of whom were railway guards) moved made it clear that the campaign to seize Manchuria had been carefully planned beforehand. Mukden fell, and within three days Japanese forces drove seventy miles east and west of the railroad, dispersing before them the numerically superior but disorganized forces of the local warlord. In less than a month it was obvious that Tokyo's object was the complete occupation of Manchuria and that Chiang was in no position to halt the seizure.

This Japanese lunge provided a litmus test for a batch of complementary diplomatic compromises and assumptions. Included among them were the stability of the world order established at Versailles, the worth of the Four- and Nine-Power Pacts arranged at Washington, the efficacy of the treaty outlawing offensive warfare, the drive for disarmament, and the ability of a mobilized world opinion to counter force with verbal arguments. Most important, in blatant violation of the Covenant, one League member state had made war upon another. Could Geneva alone, or in cooperation with the United States, halt the drift toward international anarchy?

The first of a succession of tests of this question came in September, 1931. This initial Japanese coup came as a surprise, for our lackadaisical intelligence system provided no warning. So certain was the American ambassador to Tokyo that nothing of a serious nature was in the making that he ignored friendly warnings from some apprehensive Japanese industrialists and took ship for home on the very day of the Manchurian outbreak. Hoover and Stimson were dismayed at the news from Manchuria but regained their aplomb when Japanese ambassador Katsuji Debuchi promised that the Kwantung mavericks would soon reach the end of their tether; official Washington believed that they would then crawl "back into their dens." Hence, ominous warnings from our minister to China were ignored and Stimson urged caution upon the Geneva Secretariat after Chiang invoked the guarantee of the Covenant against external aggression.

This hopefulness was dispelled on October 8, when Nipponese planes bombed the Manchurian warlord's sanctuary at Chinchow, far removed from the scene of the railroad explosion. American confidence in Tokyo's word was now badly shaken, for the skirmish had turned into a full-scale campaign for the occupation of Manchuria. The fate of the League experiment, the Far Eastern settlement of 1921–1922, and the international outlawry of aggressive war now hung in the balance. "Civilization," writes Professor Julius W. Pratt of the decision facing the major powers, "had reached a turning point."

By generally accepted interpretation of the Covenant, other League members were obliged to come to the help of China. But Europe had become indifferent to collective action just at the time when the United States, for reasons of self-interest, was particularly anxious to maintain the status quo in the eastern Pacific. So the League's Council adjourned on September 30 after demanding a cease-fire. When the bombing of Chinchow demonstrated the futility of this admonition, the Hoover administration allowed the American Consul in Geneva, Prentiss B. Gilbert, to sit with the Council when it acted in matters relating to the violation of the Kellogg-Briand Pact. At its October session, the Council insisted that Japan evacuate the occupied territory by November 16, the date set for its next meeting.

However, President Hoover had already set definite bounds to American aid in resolving the crisis. Promising complete cooperation in methods short of sanctions, he pointedly added: "But that is the limit. We shall not go along on war or any of the sanctions either economic or military for those are the roads to war."

The League Council reconvened at Paris on November 16. Charles G. Dawes, appointed to replace Gilbert, refused to meet with the Council while caring for American interests from the privacy of his hotel suite. After three weeks of debate, the Council decided on a neutral fact-finding body to visit Manchuria, a commission of five men which included General Frank R. McCoy as the unofficial representative of the United States. The Minseito government in Tokyo accepted this Lytton Commission as its last official act, for on December 10, 1931, the activist opposition, the Seiyukai party, assumed control of Japan's destiny. The Lytton Commission arrived in the Far East in April, 1932, just when the Japanese had obtained their chief military objectives.

Meanwhile the United States decided on an independent but parallel course of action when it became apparent that the Kwantung army had almost all of Manchuria within its grasp. On January 7, Secretary Stimson dispatched identical notes to Nanking and Tokyo stating that his government would refuse to recognize any territorial or other changes in the Far East brought about in violation of the Open Door policy or the Kellogg-Briand Pact. Stimson was not taken aback by Europe's lukewarm reaction to this move, for both London and Paris had rebuffed his request for a multilateral declaration on nonrecognition. Three weeks later Downing Street's attitude hardened when a new round of Sino-Japanese hostilities erupted in Shanghai. Here, 700 miles south of the Manchurian trouble spot, new turmoil jeopardized immediate British interests.[9] Men less immune to wholesale bloodletting than our own crisis-hardened generation were profoundly shocked by the strafing of the defenseless Chinese sector of Shanghai. In the Cabinet meeting of January 29, the cautious Quaker President and his undaunted Secretary of State aired their differences. The former still placed reliance upon conciliation; the latter felt that further risks were justified in the hope of restraining Tokyo. Disillusioned with the vacillations of Geneva and London, Stimson obtained Hoover's permission for a still sharper warning to Japan.[10] This step was in direct response to Japan's actions in the Shanghai sector. Further, subsequent to Stimson's note of January 7, Tokyo had declared the Nine-Power Pact outmoded, another way of saying that no legal barriers remained to shield China, for the moment the victim of a two-pronged Japanese attack.

Mr. Stimson couched his new message to Tokyo in an open letter to the Chairman of the Senate Committee on Foreign Relations, William E. Borah. This device gave no opportunity for di-

[9] This attack was ordered by the local Japanese commander because of a Chinese boycott on Japanese goods and mob violence against Japanese nationals. After brisk fighting, which involved the International Settlement of Shanghai, this incident was settled with the help of on-the-spot neutrals, and the Japanese began to withdraw on May 5, 1932.
[10] Stimson was particularly perturbed because England refused to join the United States in invoking the Nine-Power Treaty, a step which he hoped might prod the League into using economic sanctions against Japan.

rect reply. The Secretary carefully refrained from committing the United States to a defense by arms of the Open Door principle. However, with the recent creation of the puppet state of Manchukuo in mind, he upbraided Japan for violating the Nine-Power Pact, restated his government's insistence upon its lawful treaty rights, and invited the world to join in a refusal of recognition to recent territorial changes in the eastern Pacific. Although the United States was never to carry out the threat, Stimson warned that violation by Japan of one of the treaties released all signatories from the terms of the other Washington agreements of 1921-1922.

This blistering letter was only partially effective. The British Foreign Secretary, Sir John Simon, persuaded the League to join in the doctrine of nonrecognition. A stand was thus taken by the concert of peace-loving nations that would provide a partial precedent for dealing with future aggressions. On the other hand, this Stimson Doctrine[11] had no immediate effects. Armin Rappaport has noted that Stimson "elected to give vent to his ire by brandishing the pistol, which, unhappily, was not loaded, thereby transgressing the cardinal maxim of the statesman."[12] Neither the League nor any major power was willing to change war by using anything more than words to halt Japan. "The American people," noted the Philadelphia *Record*, "don't give a hoot in a rain barrel who controls North China." Europe, especially Britain, was more

[11] Historians are not agreed on whether Hoover or Stimson should receive major credit for the doctrine of nonrecognition. The President first recalled that in 1915 Secretary of State William J. Bryan had suggested nonrecognition in response to Japan's Twenty-One Demands on China. Then Stimson made the plan a corollary of the 1921–1922 Washington treaties on the Far East and the Pact of Paris. Professor Richard N. Current in "The Stimson Doctrine and the Hoover Doctrine," *American Historical Review*, LIX (April, 1954), 513–542, holds that in reality there were two doctrines. Hoover relied solely on moral suasion while Stimson looked to enforcement through collective economic and even military pressure. Other authorities assert that Current overemphasizes the differences between the two men in 1931–1933 and maintain that they drew apart only after the close of the Hoover administration. While some historians still use the term "Stimson Doctrine," many prefer to call it the "Hoover-Stimson Doctrine."
[12] *Henry L. Stimson and Japan, 1931–1933* (Chicago, 1963), p. 203.

concerned with the Shanghai thrust, but here Tokyo decided on a withdrawal before learning of the letter to Borah.

The Hoover administration set an all-time record for close coordination with the League in the Manchurian dispute, but this concord meant little because the President adamantly refused to approve any risks of war. Nor were the depression-weary European powers ready to make the sacrifices necessary to uphold the principle of collective security. The Lytton Commission's report, adopted by the League in 1933, condemned Japanese aggression in Manchuria, but conceded that Tokyo had acted under severe provocation. The compromise suggested by the Commission was not accepted by Japan. That country withdrew from the Covenant, "taking as a souvenir," notes one authority, "the Pacific islands held under League mandate." Certainly the affair destroyed much of the remaining American faith in the efficacy of collective action, for the League did enough to make Japan quit the organization while failing to save Manchuria. Indeed, Geneva's blunders had encouraged other would-be plotters against the peace. A splendid opportunity to uphold firmly the inviolability of territorial integrity had been lost.

By the time Japanese war planes soared over Manchuria, the European skies had already darkened. Gustav Stresemann was dead, and the sun of Locarno set over his grave. The German tragedy that followed must be explained in the light of both remote and immediate circumstances. For well over a century, a segment of Teutonic thought, dominated by aberrant philosophers, chauvinistic historians, extravagant romanticists, and scheming militarists, had prepared the way for totalitarianism. Then the bitterness of national defeat, a ruinous inflation, and the ravages of depression invited mass consumption of Hitler's warped gospel. This unreason included anti-Semitism, unquestioned obedience to a self-appointed leader, and an unbridled taste for predatory expansionism. Robert L. Koehl has demonstrated that the exigencies of World War I helped make some of these notions endemic in Germany. A grandiose scheme for making nearby neighbors subjects of Berlin was frustrated by military collapse, but the cry of *Lebensraum* would rise again when the time for action appeared opportune.[13] Hitler, it has been said, charged these old imperial aims "with a neurotic emotional exaltation and fury."

As long as prosperity endured, the Nazis made only fitful progress. The party had suffered a severe setback after the failure of its comic-opera *Putsch* in 1923. Following his release from Landsberg prison, Hitler created "a completely new and independent party devoted to legality and propaganda, to politics rather than revolution."[14] "Effective propaganda," Hitler explained in *Mein Kampf*, "must keep to a very few points, and be used like slogans till the very last man comprehends its import."

This perverted genius combined in his untoward ideology two regnant strains of modern thought—nationalism and socialism. To all with grievances against Weimar, save the minorities he vowed to destroy, he promised something. Revenge for defeat appealed to unregenerate Junkers, relief from reparations was attractive to taxpayers, full employment gave new hope to idle millions. These promises were all the more alluring because the Reich's production had fallen to 39 per cent of its pre-depression volume by the end of 1932 and that year found roughly half of the country's population in desperation and want. The German Communists, acting under orders from Moscow, foolishly helped the Nazis undermine faith in German republicanism. "The road to Soviet Germany," a Russian official in Berlin reported, "lay through Hitler."

The German conservative party leaders also played into the hands of the radical right. Ruling by emergency decree, after 1930 Chancellor Heinrich Brüning was unable to stimulate economic recovery or to arrest the forces of internal subversion. In 1932 President Paul von Hindenburg won re-election over Hitler because the powerful Social Democratic Party supported him as the choice of the lesser evil. A few months later a nationalist-Nazi bloc controlled the Reichstag and began to upset ministries in kaleidoscopic fashion. When parliamentary government failed to bring stability, key industrialists, large landowners, and influential army spokesmen decided to come to terms with Hitler. On January 30,

[13] "A Prelude to Hitler's Greater Germany," *American Historical Review*, LIX (October, 1953), 43–65.
[14] Earl R. Beck, review article, *ibid.*, LXVIII (October, 1962), 217–218.

1933, the grizzled old President invited Hitler to become Chancellor of a coalition cabinet. Between that date and August 2, 1934, *Der Führer* liquidated all domestic opposition, instituted unprecedented regimentation, withdrew Germany from the League of Nations, and declared himself to be the supreme ruler of what was potentially the strongest country in Europe. Another first-class power, headed by a frenzied dictator with a ready-made chart for international piracy, had hoisted the Jolly Roger. All this came as Hitler's Italian counterpart, Mussolini, was watching from the side lines, awaiting the first opportunity for territorial seizure.

These ominous rumblings across the waters intensified American isolationism. Veteran Wilson-baiters and erstwhile proponents of collective security now began to speak the same "keep-out-of-war" language. By the election year of 1932 this sentiment was strong enough to break the ranks of the liberal internationalists.

On February 2, 1932, Democratic front-runner, Franklin D. Roosevelt, announced his surrender to the victorious isolationists. As Governor of New York, FDR had carefully dodged questions on foreign policy issues. This reticence, however, made him all the more suspect in the eyes of the patrioteers. William Randolph Hearst, returning for the nonce to the Democratic fold, told the country that he would never support a candidate for the prized nomination who did not hoist the ensign of "America first." Hearst was in Speaker John N. Garner's camp, but Roosevelt's supporters were anxious to have the tycoon on their side "just in case." Colonel Edward M. House and Joseph P. Kennedy gave Hearst verbal assurance that FDR was no longer an internationalist, but he demanded a public disavowal. Anxious for the nomination in a most promising Democratic year, Roosevelt yielded.

The governor made his shrift before a meeting of the New York Grange. The League, he explained disarmingly, had not lived up to Woodrow Wilson's expectations and therefore America had no place in it. He also repeated his conviction that the war debts were obligations of honor which must be paid in full.

At the Democratic national convention in Chicago, a deadlock threatened between Roosevelt and Alfred E. Smith. For victory over Smith, James A. Farley needed the sizable California and

Texas blocs of votes for Roosevelt. At a strategic moment, William G. McAdoo switched the California delegation into the Roosevelt column and Garner, pressured by Hearst's personal representative at Chicago, withdrew from the presidential race in favor of the New York governor. In return, Speaker Garner received the vice-presidential nomination.

Hearst disliked President Hoover and threw the full weight of his influence behind Governor Roosevelt. Neither candidate said much about foreign affairs in a year when domestic issues were of paramount interest. Nonetheless, it is fair to say that during the course of this one-sided contest, FDR appeared more attractive to the ultra-isolationists than did Hoover. Roosevelt's nomination in 1932 was tantamount to election, all the more so because he had reached a proper understanding with the hypernationalists. This meant that as President, Roosevelt was compelled to liquidate this political mortgage at a time when the payment would jeopardize the cause of world peace.

CHAPTER VII

The Great Isolationist Aberration

Franklin Delano Roosevelt was the last President to be sworn into office on the historic fourth of March. Following this inauguration, FDR moved with unprecedented alacrity to lift the paralysis that gripped the nation's economy. At first this task absorbed most of his ebullient energy. Circumstances forced him to give top priority to promoting domestic programs of recovery, and this precedence received hearty popular approval.

In 1933, John M. Blum reminds us, two nineteenth-century illusions still lingered in America—that our traditional detachment would shut out foreign turmoil; and that peace, or the absence of war, was the expected conduct of mankind. Although Roosevelt was, by inclination, a theoretical internationalist, he had customarily temporized with politicians holding a more provincial outlook. An opportunist by nature, the President thoroughly understood that too much attention to the unhappy course of events abroad would alienate the bipartisan progressive isolationist combine in Congress on which he relied to sustain his ambitious legislative program. Even so forceful a leader as FDR was compelled to defer to the current mood of withdrawal. "It's a terrible thing," he once complained to a friend, "to look over your shoulder when you are trying to lead—and to find no one there."

The pattern for early New Deal diplomacy was set during an

international conclave to which the Republicans had committed their successors. The World Disarmament Conference had assembled on February 2, 1932, under the worst possible conditions. A League-sponsored commission had diligently prepared a comprehensive disarmament blueprint only to have it promptly scrapped by the Conference. The Japanese were then running loose in Manchuria and Shanghai, and the major powers were loath to weaken their own military striking power. Popular pressure and demands for action from the faltering republican regime at Berlin made postponement impossible. Nevertheless, the delegates were deadlocked within a month, for France refused to cut back her armaments without additional guarantees of security against a resurgent Germany.[1] A recess was called to spar for time, but when the conferees returned to Geneva in 1933, the situation was even more precarious. Japan had just walked out of the League and the German Chancellor was now Adolf Hitler.

President Roosevelt made one final attempt to save the day. Norman H. Davis, a soft-spoken businessman who had made a fortune in Cuban banking, acted as FDR's trouble shooter and proposed a package deal on May 22, 1933. In return for a mutual pledge against aggression and an over-all reduction in arms, the United States would consult with other powers in the event of crisis. If it concurred on the identity of the aggressor, Washington would refrain from interference with sanctions imposed by the League on a Covenant-breaking state. In view of the American political climate, these promises were as far as the administration could safely go. The venerable dean of international lawyers, John Bassett Moore, called even this modest proposal "a danger involving our very independence." At all events, it was too little and too late to help the cause of global disarmament. The death knell for the World Disarmament Conference tolled on October 14, 1933, when Hitler ordered his delegates home and a few hours later announced that the Reich was withdrawing from the League of

---

[1] Assuming that the acceptance of the Kellogg-Briand Pact outlawed all but defensive wars, President Hoover had proposed a one-third across-the-board cut in arms. Made without proper evaluation of the existing European situation, this proposal failed when it was seconded by Weimar Germany.

Nations. The President lamented this new blow to world organization, but he recognized the strength of his isolationist tether. In consequence, Mr. Davis stated bluntly that the United States would make no "commitment whatever to use its armed forces for the settlement of any dispute anywhere."

Roosevelt's attitude toward the London World Economic Conference of 1933, a plan which he also inherited from the Republicans, informed foreign observers that the New Deal was to be geared to economic as well as political nationalism. A multipower meeting had been convoked in order to find a way to pull the world out of the quagmire of depression. President Hoover had refused to place on the agenda the reparations-war-debts tangle, but he had conceded privately that some compromise might be reached as part of a general agreement. But FDR, taking his cue from congressional sentiment, flatly ruled out any discussion of the vexing issue of intergovernmental debts. Nevertheless, British Prime Minister MacDonald tactlessly reintroduced the war debt question in his opening speech to the Conference.

One of the principal problems to be discussed was the achievement of a "greater freedom of international trade." Secretary of State Cordell Hull, head of the American delegation, strongly favored accomplishing this purpose through reciprocal tariff reductions. Hull had sailed for England after the President had promised he would ask Congress for such action. But FDR revoked this pledge by cable. Secretary Hull later wrote that this restriction left him "with empty hands" in London.

The question of currency stabilization also provided a troublesome issue for the Conference. At that time it was hoped that devaluation of our currency would stimulate our sagging economy. In line with this thinking, Roosevelt had taken the United States off the gold standard on April 20, 1933, a step certain to hinder solution of the international monetary muddle. At London the gold bloc countries, led by France, demanded currency stabilization in terms of gold. Under heavy pressure from avid New Dealers, Roosevelt decided, after Hull's departure, against any commitment which would prevent him from manipulating the national currency in the interest of raising price levels. Blissfully unaware of the

President's reversal, the Conference delegates worked out a program that pledged Washington to an eventual return to the gold standard and, in the interim, to the avoidance of unnecessary speculative fluctuations in national currencies.

While enjoying the ocean breezes aboard the *Indianapolis* off the Maine coast, Roosevelt unexpectedly sent the Conference his famous "bombshell" message. FDR rejected the proposed plan for stabilization, scolded the delegates for giving currency matters priority at the expense of other "fundamental ills," and announced his faith in planned national currencies as a substitute for the "old fetishes of the so-called international bankers." All hope for a concerted move to lift the globe-wide depression now vanished, for the President had aligned himself behind the isolationist-minded economic theoreticians who preferred a controlled currency to a multilateral monetary agreement.

Roosevelt has been sharply censured for this headlong act. Many authorities insist that it retarded world recovery, sharpened international rivalries at a moment when joint action was clearly indicated, and weakened the democracies by denying them a last opportunity to wage general war on a world-wide depression. The Nazi financial wizard, Hjalmar Schacht, remarked that FDR now held with the Fascist principle of taking "your economic fate in your own hands." But could the nations have agreed upon an effective course of action in any event? Much can be said, William E. Leuchtenburg points out, for the President's view "that stabilization at a low level of prices would have been an error." The celebrated British economist, John Maynard Keynes, proclaimed Roosevelt "magnificently right." No nation was really ready to make tariff sacrifices on the altar of general recovery, and if the dollar had been tied tightly to world exchange, it well might have impeded the New Deal's efforts to bring immediate relief to American debtors. In retrospect, the tragedy lay not in the Roosevelt message which undermined the Conference, but in an all-pervading selfish nationalism which ruled a mutual recovery program out of the realm of political possibilities.

The New Deal's first noteworthy diplomatic departure was the recognition of Communist Russia. Lenin had died in 1924, leaving no designated heir. After a lengthy party duel, the stolid but aggressive Joseph V. Stalin emerged victorious over the brilliant, sophisticated, and intellectual Leon Trotsky. To the non-Communist world, Stalin appeared the less dangerous of the rivals, inasmuch as his immediate aim was limited to "Socialism in One Country." Stalin implemented his blueprint by a forced industrialization of the USSR, an act which made Moscow a prized customer of nations burdened with stockpiles of heavy goods. Millions of dollars in equipment had been sold to the Communists by General Electric even before the Great Depression whetted the appetite of American industrialists for Russian business. Ford alone planned a Russian unit to produce 100,000 cars a year. Our capital and supplies had been used in the construction of the colossal Dneprostroi Dam. Following the Great Slump, sorely pressed midwestern farmers eyed the Russian market greedily. Many were oversanguine concerning the possibility of trade with the Kremlin, but such roseate prophecies were made at a time when exports to Russia were especially heavy.[2]

In 1931 Senator Borah promised that a tamed USSR, no longer bereft of legal recognition, would aid our quest for disarmament and global stability. He thought it highly unrealistic to put a prime world power in the category of a perpetual outlaw. The Idahoan's pleas went unheeded until the party revolution of 1932. Thereafter, Roosevelt proved receptive to such arguments, albeit he was probably less moved by the allurements of trade or the belief in the possibility of Soviet regeneration than by the hope that Russia might prove a bulwark against Germany and Japan.

The Kremlin took the initiative when Maxim Litvinov established rapport with the American delegates attending the London Economic Conference. Following some additional Russian overtures, Roosevelt wrote a warm letter on October 10, 1933, to

[2] William White, the New York *Times* Moscow reporter, who made one of the cheeriest estimates, overlooked the fact that we needed no Russian products in exchange for our goods and that the USSR lacked both the gold and established credit to balance a two-way trade.

President Mikhail Kalinin, titular head of the Soviet government, suggesting "frank, friendly conversations." The next month, Litvinov, now Commissar for Foreign Affairs, arrived in Washington to consummate the negotiations.

Nine days of diplomatic give-and-take yielded a bundle of agreements and understandings. Litvinov promised that his government would "refrain from interfering in any manner in the internal affairs of the United States," would hold in check subversive organizations operating within our borders, and would assure the enjoyment of religious liberty and civil rights to Americans domiciled in the Soviet Union. Financial claims and counterclaims were postponed until such time when "a speedy and satisfactory solution" could be arranged. On November 16, 1933, President Roosevelt announced our intention to resume normal diplomatic relations with Russia.

Roosevelt's move was widely acclaimed. Before returning to Russia, Commissar Litvinov was feted by some New York City business moguls at the newly opened Waldorf-Astoria Hotel. But the cheery hopes expressed at this gala dinner were speedily doomed to disappointment. Trade results were negligible, for the 1934 Johnson Act forbade new credits to proven defaulters. The following year negotiations of debt settlements were stalemated when Stalin gave second thoughts to payments that might lead to demands from his other creditors. When we woke up to the fact that the Comintern was operating as usual, Moscow brazenly explained that Litvinov could never have promised to curtail propaganda in the United States since the Kremlin exercised no control over foreign Communist parties. Our first ambassador to Soviet Russia, William C. Bullitt, labored heroically to persuade the Kremlin to abide by the Roosevelt-Litvinov agreements. This veteran friend of Soviet Russia became completely disillusioned. In 1935 he uncannily predicted that Stalin would await an American-Japanese war and, at its close, "acquire Manchuria and Sovietize China." Much was expected from the 1933 rapprochement between Washington and Moscow; all that was gained was a belated diplomatic recognition and the creation of an American listening-post in a capital destined to play a stellar role in the complicated events of the future.[3]

The Russian frustration constituted but one of a series of diplomatic setbacks during the earlier Roosevelt years. Despite the President's absorption with the domestic economy, he was not impervious to the war clouds gathering on the foreign horizon. A few days before he took office, Yosuke Matsuoka led the Nipponese delegates out of the League of Nations. On the very morrow of his inauguration, the Reichstag invested Adolf Hitler with the unbridled power he was to use to such malevolent purpose. In all probability Roosevelt's broad cosmopolitanism made him secretly agree with the Wilsonians that only collective action could stabilize the international situation. But the President refused to court political disaster by defying the powerful isolationist front in Congress. A man who could never be forced to reveal the impolitic, FDR was prone to keep his innermost thoughts to himself.

Scholars have indicted Roosevelt for abdicating diplomatic leadership at a time when bold action might have averted global disaster. There is merit to this criticism, but it is salutary to recall that the President faced difficult political obstacles. Beset by countless personal crises arising from the protracted depression, the American people chose to ignore the mounting perils overseas. Some even argued that the best way to avoid war was to let "the sharecroppers of world politics," the "have-not" nations, force such adjustments to the Treaty of Versailles as would balance the scales in their favor.

The new Secretary of State, Cordell Hull, was even more politically circumspect than his chief. This veteran of congressional battles lisped a hill-country drawl that masked an iron will and

[3] Some American mistakes account in part for Russia's actions after 1933. It is possible, as William A. Williams argues, that Stalin might have made special concessions on the American debt (Roosevelt apparently was willing to settle for $150 million) if Washington had not spurned Litvinov's offer of a bilateral pact aimed against Japan. Moreover, whereas the Roosevelt-Litvinov correspondence of 1933 spoke of a "loan," we subsequently offered only a "credit." William A. Williams, ed., *The Shaping of American Diplomacy* (Chicago, 1956), pp. 729, 764; Julius W. Pratt, *Cordell Hull [The American Secretaries of State and Their Diplomacy*, Vols. XII–XIII] (New York, 1964), XIII, 598 ff.

determination. A southern Democrat inspired by Wilsonian international idealism, Hull was nonetheless overfearful of senatorial wrath on Capitol Hill. He maintained a cordial relationship with the isolationist kingpins he had known in the Senate and was disposed to handle them with kid gloves.

The possibility of breaking the isolationist shackles was further diminished because Key Pittman was Chairman of the Senate Foreign Relations Committee from 1933 until his death seven years later. This tall, sinewy, short-tempered, hard-drinking Nevadan lacked the endowments of his immediate predecessors, Lodge and Borah. In many respects a capable politician, Senator Pittman devoted too much time to western silver interests and evinced little sense of urgency in diplomatic matters. On occasion he used considerable skill in pacifying the outspoken isolationists who freighted down his committee. Chairman Pittman was not a back-to-Jefferson isolationist, but his lack of a strong commitment on foreign policy issues meant that the Borah-Johnson view usually prevailed in committee decisions. It is too bad that in those critical years the Roosevelt administration had to depend upon so limited a person as its official senatorial spokesman in the area of international affairs.

One of the first triumphs of the ultra-isolationists in Congress was the passage of the Johnson Act in 1934. This act forbade American citizens to lend money to, or buy the securities of, foreign governments in default to the United States. The ultimate results of this law were unfortunate, for it prevented credits that might have revived our export trade, and it deprived the Treasury of the token payments on war debts made by some debtor countries up to this time. No nation was induced by this law to resume its biannual obligations, but European sneers of "Uncle Shylock" increased apace.

The President became even more wary of the isolationist phalanx in Congress after it showed unexpected strength in a 1935 encounter. Nine years before, the Senate had deadlocked the World Court question by imposing reservations unacceptable to the other signatory powers. In 1929 the eighty-four-year-old Elihu Root went to Geneva in response to an invitation from the

League's Council. The upshot of these efforts was the "Root Formula" dealing with the nettled problem of advisory opinions. It was proposed that the United States be granted equal opportunity with the League states to object to the rendering of such opinions, and, in the event that our refusal was denied, we could then withdraw from the Court without imputations of ill will.

President Hoover, bedeviled by other problems, delayed in submitting the plan to the Senate. Thereafter it languished on Capitol Hill for four years as the isolationists used their well-perfected tactics of procrastination. By the time Roosevelt and Hull were prepared to press for a decision, the issue had grown stale and distasteful. In the interim the Court lost much good will in the United States when it ruled illegal a proposed customs union between Austria and Germany. This decision was fully exploited by the Nazis in the undermining of the Weimar Republic.

President Roosevelt sent the Root proposal to the Senate on January 16, 1935, with the reminder that adherence offered the United States one final chance to "throw its weight into the scale in favor of peace." The administration seemed confident of winning a two-thirds margin in the top-heavy Democratic Senate, for informal newspaper polls predicted a White House victory. Had the votes been taken on Friday, January 25, it is possible that the judgment of these polls would have been vindicated. During the weekend, however, wavering senators were bombarded with messages, telegrams, and letters that arrived in such heaps that they had to be delivered by wheelbarrow! This mass protest against the World Court was engineered by the Detroit "radio priest," Father Charles E. Coughlin, and by the press czar, William R. Hearst.

Coughlin's broadcasting career had begun in 1926 with an attack on the Ku Klux Klan. Before long he shifted to politics, making studied use of the radio to popularize his "rolling brogue and vivid rhetoric." In 1932 Coughlin supported the Democrats with the hyperbolic slogan of "Roosevelt or Ruin." As late as the spring of 1934, he hailed the New Deal as "Christ's Deal." But Coughlin was rapidly veering toward a type of Christian Socialism which conflicted with the President's pragmatic approach to politics, and his gratuitous advice was studiedly ignored by the White House.

Moreover, an exaggerated isolationism constituted a vital ingredient of Coughlin's general outlook. So the radio charmer of the hour urged millions of listeners to exhort their senators to "keep America safe for Americans . . . and not [make it] the hunting ground of international plutocrats."

William Randolph Hearst had entertained Father Coughlin at San Simeon in 1932, and the alliance between the two men was sealed when both came to reject the New Deal. Hearst, who had a phobia about a Leviathan State, feared that Roosevelt's policies were leading to that end. The press magnate's differences with the President were advertised when he visited Germany in 1934 and was escorted to *Der Führer* accompanied by four Storm Troopers. Hearst was certain that someday Fascism and Communism would collide in war, and he feared that the American way of life would be destroyed unless we kept entirely clear of the conflict. In far-flung editorials he advised: "The way to keep America out of the League of Nations trap . . . is to keep America out of the League Court. Telegraph your senators . . . today." When the votes were tallied, the resolution for adherence to the World Court protocol fell short of the required two-thirds majority by seven votes. And this in a Senate with sixty-eight Democratic members!

The President might have turned the scales in his favor by using an executive squeeze play upon some fidgety senators or by resorting to one of his mesmerizing fireside chats, but the timing was late for such tactics. It is also possible that Roosevelt did not think the Court protocol, watered down as it was by reservations old and new, worth an all-out White House offensive. Even if the United States had joined the Court in 1935, it is doubtful that this tardy action would have had any measurable effects. The Senate's action, however, proclaimed to the world that we would not make even one single gesture to save the faltering Versailles peace structure. FDR's sharp rebuff had special symbolic significance, for every President since Taft had favored adherence to the protocol. While the President had not used all his influence to win, he had done enough to demonstrate that he was still basically a champion of world organization and hence an object of suspicion on the part of the senatorial chauvinists.

The time was now ripe for the supreme triumph of the isolationist concept—the inflexible neutrality legislation of the middle thirties. Six years of sharp depression and successive aggression had intensified introversive thinking. To understand this frame of reference it is necessary to untangle certain strands of thought which had come to dominate the American mind.

In 1925 *The Big Parade* began a spate of literary and cinema indictments against war. Four years later Erich Maria Remarque's *All Quiet on the Western Front* pressed home the charge. Similar stirring books and movies, including Hemingway's *A Farewell to Arms,* aroused the American people against wanton bloodshed just as *Uncle Tom's Cabin* four score years before had indoctrinated the people of the free states against human slavery. Stuart Chase, a popularizer of social and economic trends, warned of a lightning-bolt war in which "not even a rat, not even an ant, not even a roach can survive." Mr. Chase's extreme pessimism was a bit premature, but the outlook was grim enough even at a time when nuclear fission was still a figment of the scientific mind.

War, as General William Tecumseh Sherman had said and proven long ago, was Hell. Having been persuaded of this fact, Americans began to search for the devils responsible for this scourge, only to discover that they were the same irresponsible covey of industrialists and bankers upon whom the New Dealers pinned the blame for the depression. The theory that Wall Street's satanic network had beguiled the country into war dates back to Wilson's day. Its greatest popularity, however, came at a time when Big Business had been convicted at the bar of public opinion for that most heinous of crimes—the ruination of prosperity.

A series of writings published in 1934 made vivid once more the trials of American neutrality. Helmuth C. Englebrecht was the chief author of a book bearing the catchy title *Merchants of Death.* *Fortune's* lead article "Arms and the Men" made easy reading, while George Seldes's sensational work *Iron, Blood and Profits* accused the munition-makers of thriving on "bloodshed for profits." This new literature of exposure assumed the existence of a sinister world-wide conspiracy of arms manufacturers operating continuously "at the two axioms of their trade—[to] prolong wars, [to]disturb peace."[4]

Ever since the German surrender, the pacifist lobby had demanded federal control over the munitions industry. Coincidence now strengthened such plans. Arms control as part of the anti-Big Business prejudice of the day was linked to a plan to remove the profits from war. So all-pervading was the notion that pressure from the economic royalists had propelled the country into the Kaiser War that even the American Legion wanted to harness the munitions tycoons. Furthermore, there was a good deal of deserved resentment against brazen lobbying on the part of the munitions manufacturers who had their front men both in Congress and in influential governmental agencies.

These considerations motivated the Senate to investigate the "Merchants of Death." A leading role in this decision was played by Dorothy Detzer, a professionally trained social worker. A lobbyist for the Women's International League for Peace and Freedom, she was trying to implement her sponsor's demand for arms control. The counsel of Senator George W. Norris helped her select the proper man to push the investigation. The aging Nebraskan suggested Senator Gerald P. Nye, who was particularly eligible inasmuch as he was a left-of-center Republican from North Dakota, an ultrarural state devoid of defense industries. On February 8, 1934, Nye introduced his momentous resolution for investigation. This proposal was subsequently combined with Senator Arthur H. Vandenberg's move to end, once and for all, war profiteering. On April 12, the Senate adopted the Nye resolution without dissent and empowered Vice-President John N. Garner to appoint a special committee of seven to handle the assignment.

The administration supported the resolution halfheartedly. Ultimately, however, Roosevelt and Hull bowed to the force of public opinion, hoping that the Nye investigation would lead to governmental control over the manufacture of arms. The President

---

[4] "Arms and the Men," *Fortune*, IX (March, 1934), 53–57 ff. Alfred Kazin has noted the recent irony that while a previous generation sought to curb the arms traffic, their children, facing a weaponry of unlimited destructive power, petition the federal government when the shutdown or dismantling of a neighboring war plant threatens the prosperity of a single congressional district!

endorsed the proposal on May 18 and vainly suggested that the committee search for a solution to the problem along international lines.

The group of men who began their labors in the fall of 1934 left an unexpected imprint upon the course of American history.[5] Vice-President Garner allowed them to select their own chairman, and they promptly chose Nye. The Senator, a lean, rough-hewn Solon from the North Dakota hinterland, had the advantages of a high school education and journalistic experience on several back-country papers. In leaving the editorship of a county-seat weekly, notes Jeannette P. Nichols, Nye jumped "from the narrow confines of an every-Thursday deadline to the broad arena of the world's most powerful legislative body."

Senator Nye's first nine years on Capitol Hill were largely devoted to domestic affairs. Sincere, humorless, and overzealous, he was prone to blow every crisis out of proportion. Although the editorials of Nye's youth had defended Wilson and the League, he had long since replaced such views with an agrarian isolationism more congenial to the prejudices of his region. With almost 90 per cent of its scattered population located on farms or in small towns, North Dakota formed a rural prototype. The state was a hothouse for all major seeds of isolationist thought, for here were combined geographical insularity, Republican politics tinged with a Non-Partisan League flavor, German and Scandinavian island ethnic groups, and a proclivity to pacifism stemming from Old World religious commitments. Senator Nye began his work of uncovering the malicious machinations of the "down east" war-breeding interests with his customary vigor and gusto.

The Munitions Investigating Committee was provided with plenty of assistance. Its secretary and chief investigator was a crusading lawyer, Stephen Raushenbush, son of the famous Christian Socialist and pacifist, Professor Walter Rauschenbusch. Joseph C. Green, expert on munitions traffic, represented the State Depart-

[5] In this committee rural isolationist sections of the country were heavily overrepresented. Only Senator James P. Pope of Idaho voiced the opinion of the nonisolationists. See Robert A. Divine, *The Illusion of Neutrality* (Chicago, 1962), p. 66.

ment's interests and, for a few months, Alger Hiss was given leave from another government agency in order to lend additional legal advice.

As its work progressed, the committee released preliminary reports digested for the public by headline-hungry reporters. These press reports reinforced the conviction that our 1917 intervention grew out of a well-planned conspiracy of munitions makers. Before long the committee widened its scope of investigation to include the part played in this plot by Wall Street's international bankers and the White House. To determine the extent of these influences, the committee ransacked company records and the files of the State and Treasury departments, much to the discomfiture of responsible statesmen who feared that some of the muck raked would hamper the conduct of our foreign relations.[6] The seven reports of the Munitions Investigating Committee amounted to some 1,400 pages, and 44,000 copies of each were run off and distributed under Senate authorization. It is a safe guess that only those select readers inured to punishment read all these documents in raw form; the rest absorbed the information after it had been parboiled, garnished, and pointed up to teach certain lessons. Unquestionably, many of these exposures were both true and shocking. The munitions magnates ran an effective Washington lobby. They had made colossal profits from the last war. Their business techniques often fell in the twilight zone of legality, and their overseas sales staff wished to promote business in explosives rather than to ease global tensions. Moreover, the web of the industry spun far enough to justify suspicions of the existence of an international cartel. Certain it was that the armament companies welcomed world disarmament as much as bootleggers had welcomed the end of prohibition. Still, to deduce from these facts that the munitions people and the Wall Street bankers who financed their foreign sales had, as Senator Nye charged, "made our going to war inevitable," was a dangerous oversimplifi-

[6] Some of the committee's early revelations had complicated our Latin American relations to the point where Secretary Hull thought that Nye and his associates were endangering the Good Neighbor policy. Pratt, *op. cit.*, XII, 192.

cation. No writer has unearthed a single shred of telling documentary evidence to prove the charge that President Wilson had been unduly influenced by greedy industrialists and financial "war mongers." Besides, Nye's committee stubbornly ignored the obvious fact that the effective cause of American intervention had been Emperor William's deliberate gamble on the unrestricted use of U-boats, a gamble made, as we now know, to starve Britain rather than to retaliate against American lapses from an impartial neutrality.

The depression generation, however, had been conditioned to accept Nye's glib historical doctrine. Another European holocaust was in the making, and the pro-Ally influence of a previous era became a lucid commentary on current events.[7] The lesson seemed clear—the country needed a fixed neutrality policy *before* the outbreak of a new Armageddon. Legislation must embargo arms and loans to warring countries while at the same time protecting the country from the baneful pressure of self-seeking economic groups. The net result was a "Maginot Line" neutrality policy which, in practice, was to be as easily turned by the course of events as the vaunted French fortifications were to be flanked by Nazi Panzer divisions.

The Nye investigation transformed the "revisionist" interpretation of American entrance into World War I into a popular orthodoxy. It became highly fashionable to argue that a reluctant

[7] Senator Nye and his committee colleague, B. Champ Clark of Missouri, were in constant demand as speakers. Larding their talks with hyperbole and occasional distortion, they toured the lecture circuit, gladly granting interlocutory interviews to local reporters. The war guilt subject formed a welcome distraction from the tedium of the depression, and news hawks did full justice to these firsthand accounts of the current inquest. The view that the Nye Committee had preponderant influence in shaping American thought on foreign policy is challenged in John E. Wiltz, *In Search of Peace: The Senate Munitions Inquiry, 1934–6* (Baton Rouge, 1963). The author argues that the Committee had no *direct* influence on the passage of the prewar Neutrality Acts. He also feels that by failing to prove its case on the munition-makers-bankers theory of our 1917 intervention, the Committee's findings led eventually to a loss of popular confidence in this thesis. Wiltz also points out the considerable contribution of other members besides Nye to the Committee's work, i.e., of Senators Arthur H. Vandenberg, B. Champ Clark, Homer T. Bone, and James P. Pope.

country had been tricked into a European war "by the twin forces
of profiteering and Allied propaganda."[8] Revisionists dodged the
all-important proposition: What would have happened had America chosen to sit out the War of 1914–1918? How comfortable
would the United States have been in the event of a German
victory? Certainly, the Junkers had portended enough Nazi tactics
to justify some of the worst suspicions of the Kaiser's foes.[9]

The Nye inquest freshened the wellsprings of revisionist source
material. Resulting effusions preached a doctrine congenial to the
prevailing desire of the moment, for if the causes of our former
intervention could be clearly identified, we could then control
these entangling forces by proper legislative action.

The first important work of this new genre of history came from
the gifted pen of Walter Millis, a *Herald Tribune* editorialist
already famous as the debunker of our 1898 clash with Spain.
Road to War, insured wide distribution as a Book-of-the-Month
selection, was written in a fascinating style which more restrained
professional historians were unable to match. Millis's readers could
hardly escape the conclusion that a combination of rashness,
hyperemotionalism, and desire for profits had lured the country
into a war that succeeded only in creating what Dexter Perkins
had aptly termed "a muddle of majestic proportions."[10]

The country still awaited a specialized synthesis that would
place the stamp of professional approval upon the revisionist
hypothesis. It came with the publication of Charles C. Tansill's

8 William F. Leuchtenburg, *Franklin D. Roosevelt and the New Deal, 1932–
1940* (New York, 1963), p. 198.
9 Recent research reveals that as early as 1914 German war aims included
a European "empire of grandiose dimensions." There is now ample evidence
that these ambitions were not confined to an extremist minority. See review
by Hans W. Gatzke of Fritz Fischer, *Griff nach der Weltmacht: Die
Kriegszielpolitik des kaiserlichen Deutschland 1914/18* (Düsseldorf, 1961)
in *American Historical Review*, LXVIII (January, 1963), 443–445.
10 Millis soon began to explain away the thesis expounded in his book. See
"Will We Stay Out of the Next War?" *New Republic*, LXXXIII (July 31,
1935), 323–327. Before the onset of World War II he had joined the ranks
of the so-called "interventionists." However, in *Road to War*, he actually
suggested that an arms embargo in 1914–1917 might have kept the United
States out of the European war.

America Goes to War. This book implied that intervention grew out of a lax neutrality, that it was a mistake to have helped the Allies, and that the results of our involvement were more disastrous than the possible consequences of an Imperial German victory.

The most assiduous and thought-provoking elaborations of the munition-makers-bankers-propaganda thesis were formulated by the prolific senior historian, Charles A. Beard. This sensitive and dauntless scholar had been deeply moved by the plight of the depression. About the time of the Nye Committee's inquiries, he became obsessed with the fear that Roosevelt would yield to the temptation to use an activist foreign policy as an instrument of economic recovery. To avert this catastrophe, Beard proposed in a seminal book, *The Open Door at Home*, to widen the New Deal type of national planning to the point where a western hemisphere economy could flourish independent of the vicissitudes of trade with war-prone foreign nations.[11] While, in the words of Cushing Strout, Beard was "an uneasy guest . . . [in] the company of xenophobes," the celebrated historian later elaborated upon the Nye findings, for they buttressed his own conviction that the United States ought to abandon "moneylending and huckstering abroad."

Historical revisionism engendered a climate of opinion that made congressional neutrality legislation all but inevitable. Past diplomatic errors were belabored while contemporary aggressors were allowed to prepare for the spoliation of the world. Seldom in the annals of the United States had a popular misreading of history been so fraught with danger for the future. Men had come to believe that it made no difference whether our potential friends or enemies controlled the seas, possessed the sources of raw materials essential to modern warfare, or occupied strategic outposts that held the keys to the occupation of continents. There was heavy public demand to "get the profits out of war" and to "let Congress keep us out."

The attempt to embargo arms to warring countries dates from

[11] Charles A. Beard (with the collaboration of G.H.E. Smith), *The Open Door at Home* (New York, 1934).

the later 1920's, when several bills looking to this end were blocked in Congress because one group of sponsors wished to levy an arms embargo solely against identified aggressors while another insisted on a nondiscriminatory ban against all belligerents.[12] At the same time, the successful negotiation of the Kellogg-Briand Pact widened the cleavage between segments seeking American arms embargo for entirely different purposes. A pro-League faction argued that the acceptance of the outlawry of war meant the end of old-fashioned neutrality in any offensive war waged by a treaty-breaker. This school demanded a flexible arms embargo which, subject to the discretion of the President, could be used to complement League sanctions against an outlaw power. Such convictions ran counter to the hyperisolationist trend of the Depression Era. Although President Hoover and Secretary Stimson favored a discretionary embargo, they were forced to retreat in the face of congressional resistance.[13] During the shakedown period of the new administration, Roosevelt and Hull prodded Congress for an arms embargo which could be used to uphold international stability, but they dropped their demands when the Senate Foreign Relations Committee amended the proposal in such a way as to thwart their purpose.

Another factor which eased the passage of neutrality legislation was the overriding fear of involvement in a new European war, a conflict seemingly made inevitable by the new pattern of international banditry. Hope that Hitler's conduct would be sobered by responsibility or that he would be overthrown from within van-

12 The earliest attempt to embargo arms dates back to a 1927 bill introduced by Representative Theodore E. Burton of Ohio. The idea was revived two years later by Senator Arthur Capper of Kansas. The debates over Capper's proposal foreshadowed the later cleavage between those who wished to use a discriminatory embargo to help curb aggression and those who wished an impartial ban designed to buttress American neutrality and to halt the wartime trade in munitions. See Robert A. Divine, "Franklin D. Roosevelt and Collective Security, 1933," *Mississippi Valley Historical Review*, XLVIII (June, 1961), 42–59.
13 In the Chaco War involving Bolivia and Paraguay, we imposed a non-discriminatory embargo, cooperated with twenty-seven other arms-producing countries, but not directly with the League of Nations. Roosevelt first supported the original Hoover-Stimson plan, but, to the consternation of Secretary Hull, yielded to Congress.

ished on June 30, 1934. On this "Bloody Sunday," Hitler liquidated nonconformist Nazi Party chieftains, and, following the death of President von Hindenburg five weeks later, he combined the two chief offices of state in his own person. The world had not long to await the diplomatic reverberations of these actions. In March, 1935, the Nazi dictator publicly boasted of the existence of a formidable *Luftwaffe*, restored conscription in defiance of the Treaty of Versailles, and announced plans for the largest army on the continent.[14] These steps were rashly condoned by England when its Tory government signed a treaty with Berlin agreeing to the construction of a German surface naval force equal to 35 per cent of British tonnage.

Simultaneously Hitler stepped up oppressive domestic programs destined to pour more poison into international waters. The estrangement of Germany's 500,000 Jews from their native culture was systematized in the infamous Nuremberg Laws of September, 1935. In three years the aim of this particular Nazi outrage was completed within the Reich's borders. The plight of the many pathetic refugees to the West, a large proportion of whom were highly talented professional people, brought home to the free world the meaning of Nazi *Gleichschaltung*. Of more intimate concern, because it pinched pocketbooks, was Hitler's perverted sense of economics, which called for an autarchical system purposely designed "to destroy the economic independence of victims preparatory to conquest." Although Hitler's megalomania did not include plans for the subjugation of the United States, his economic warfare, said Cordell Hull, consumed "in devilish fashion" the more than two billion dollars owed to Americans.[15]

---

[14] We now know that the Weimar Republic had successfully evaded the arms limitation clauses of Versailles by maintaining a ground force designed for easy expansion, by setting up arms factories in other countries, by maintaining close relations with the Soviet army, and by aircraft experimentation that would prove valuable in building up a future force of fighting planes.

[15] Hitler's steps against these investments came in piecemeal form. He began by paying monies due half in cash and the balance in scrip that was discounted 50 per cent even in Germany. After similar acts of financial legerdemain, Germany bought up these depressed bonds at a great loss to American investors. Pratt, *op. cit.*, XII, 184.

We know today that Washington received many acutely accurate warnings of Hitler's master plan of conquest. Our ambassador to Berlin, Professor William E. Dodd, repeatedly admonished that Hitler could not be appeased by western concessions. Because Dodd was thought too extreme by certain State Department officials, one of his subordinates in the Berlin embassy was sent to observe a Nazi party congress. Completely disillusioned, this diplomat reported German plans for military conquest and for Fascist subversion in Latin America and emphasized the Nazi desire "to spread their medieval system over the whole world."

Along with these official alarms came reports from private citizens who visited the Third Reich. Lincoln Steffens compared Germany to an oversized insane asylum where deranged patients were regarded as sane. From all sides came information that the Nazis were counting on American fears of war to keep the western colossus neutral in a new conflict to be waged for the aggrandizement of the Third Reich.

One is inclined to agree with Dwight E. Lee's observation that "intelligence was remarkably high; judgment and will extremely low." But the Roosevelt administration was forced to handle speculation about Germany's plans gingerly. These warnings were shrewd guesses rather than established facts and could not, in the nature of things, be broadcast for public consumption. In matters that would directly menace the New World, Hitler was cautious, for he realized the necessity of forestalling collective action pending the completion of his military preparations. His early speeches, designed for American ears, sounded reassuring to those well endowed with the will to believe:

Germany needs peace and desires peace . . . We recognize Poland as the home of a great and nationally conscious people . . . Germany neither intends nor wishes to interfere in the internal affairs of Austria.

President Roosevelt and Secretary Hull undoubtedly paid more attention to official intelligence than to these soporifics. However, the direct German threat was postponed by Nazi subtlety until isolationist sentiment had jelled to a point that made American participation in collective action all but impossible. Meanwhile the administration was in futile search for "a method both to preserve peace and to bolster those elements in Britain and France which were attempting to curb the fascists."[16] When it became clear that London and Paris were either unwilling or unable to stop Hitler, Roosevelt tested some new ideas. In 1935 he turned over in his mind the prospect of a "summit" meeting of leading heads of state which might restore some sense of sanity to international relations. He decided against the step, however, because he feared the accusation that he was fomenting a foreign crisis in order to draw attention away from unsolved domestic difficulties. Yet the Nazi threat refused to subside. On March 7, 1936, against the advice of his generals who felt the move too risky, Hitler reoccupied the Rhineland in violation of both the Versailles Treaty and the Locarno Pact. Secretary Hull summarily dismissed Hitler's coup as "a European development in which we were not involved." "The time was still distant," observes Professor Leopold, "when the Roosevelt administration was prepared to devise extraordinary measures to halt the spread of Naziism."

The short-lived Italo-Ethiopian war preceded Germany's more blatant violations of the peace. Hence, the new American neutrality policy came in immediate response to Italian rather than German bellicosity.

Benito Mussolini, who began his career editing a Socialist newspaper, emerged after 1918 as the would-be savior of Italy from Communism. This pioneer Fascist cleverly combined the two most appealing ideologies of the day—nationalism and socialism. In 1922 Mussolini marched on Rome, built an all-powerful superstructure over the existing monarchy, and brutally crushed all opposition. For a full decade *Il Duce* remained a potential rather than an immediate threat to world tranquillity and, during this period, was often admired in democratic countries for the spur he had given the lethargic Italians. In the beginning Mussolini was counted upon to hold in check that "mad man from the north," Adolf Hitler.

Unknown to his western admirers, Mussolini was contemplating an East African campaign against independent Ethiopia in order to

16 Leuchtenburg, *op. cit.*, p. 211.

consolidate Italian holdings south of Suez. The Italian dictator's motives were mixed: Manchuria had convinced him that he could move without interference from the League; he wished to wipe out memories of a former Italian reverse in Abyssinia; and the timing was opportune, for Paris and London were paralyzed with fear arising from the revival of Germany. Finally, a splendid little war in Africa might divert attention from some of *Il Duce's* unfulfilled domestic promises. Incidents along the Ethiopian-Somaliland border began to spell trouble in 1934. Mussolini made a pretense of arbitrating these difficulties while simultaneously completing preparations to give his Blackshirts marching orders. Emperor Haile Selassie of Ethiopia, certain of Italy's intentions, repeatedly appealed to the League for help.

The eruption of the Italo-Ethiopian volcano in the fall of 1935 brought American policy makers to the crossroads of decision and put new steam into the drive for a "foolproof" neutrality law. Eventually three distinct opinions on the subject crystallized. Advocates of collective security demanded full cooperation with Geneva in the hope that American help would put the League's creaking peace machinery in working order.[17] Only an articulate minority grasped at this hope, for it was evident that the United States would have to bear a major share of the burden in making collective security effective, since the European democracies seemed unwilling to make the sacrifices needed to hold would-be aggressors in check. Widespread faith in world organization was lacking, for the nations had a dismal record of failure in cooperat-

[17] Richard Current has pointed out that the term "collective security" had only recently come into popular usage. In 1934 a League-sponsored commission, attended by American delegates, had met in London. The conferees were searching for some formula for collective action that might be acceptable to isolationist-minded America. The following year Professor C.A.W. Manning of the University of London explained that "collective security" was a "sly" term devised to convince American public opinion that the Kellogg-Briand Pact had really meant "quasi-membership in the League." Defined as "the safety of all by all" it appealed to the veteran Wilsonians although there was no agreement even in this group as to how much involvement in League action "collective security" implied. See Richard N. Current, "The United States and 'Collective Security,'" in Alexander DeConde, ed., *Isolation and Security* (Durham, 1957), pp. 33–55.

ing either to lift the depression, or to halt the arms build-up and aggression.

On the other polar extreme stood the second group, traditionalists who argued against any departure—past, present, or future—from the strict tenets of international law. This school insisted that Wilson could have avoided war had he adhered closely to the canons of the law of nations. For men of this persuasion, the lesson had clear implications: henceforth let the government maintain an unwavering neutrality. Included in the ranks of these die-hards were such "George Washington" isolationists as Senators Borah and Johnson, who seemed impervious to the fact that nineteenth-century international law, defied and excoriated by the totalitarian brigands, had become an anachronism.[18]

Thirdly, there arose a group of neutralistic innovators of whom Charles Warren was chief. In 1934 he formulated a novel plan that seemed suitable for implementation. Warren, an international lawyer and legal historian of distinction, had served the Wilson administration as Assistant Attorney General. His blueprint for a revamped neutrality policy envisioned an impartial arms embargo, a ban on loans to belligerents, restrictions against traveling in wartime, and making all trade with combatants subject to the risk of the buyer. These suggestions fitted perfectly the popular mood of the day and found eager reception in some administration circles.[19]

As the Italian divisions prepared to storm the Ethiopian frontier, confusion surrounded the consideration of a plethora of neutrality bills. Inasmuch as Congress stubbornly refused to adjourn until it had taken some action, compromise had to be reached on how much leeway was to be left to the President in applying the law and just how much profitable trade would be sacrificed on the

[18] The most scholarly defense of the traditionalist point of view is Edwin M. Borchard and William P. Lage, *Neutrality for the United States* (2nd ed., New Haven, 1940).
[19] Warren outlined his scheme in a speech before the American Society for International Law. His remarks were published as "Troubles of a Neutral" in *Foreign Affairs*, XII (April, 1934), 377–395. Later that year, on invitation, he prepared a lengthy memorandum for the State Department.

altar of peace. The Democratic leadership was not certain just where the administration stood; the President had left Nye and other champions of "dynamic" neutrality with the impression that he favored their scheme while Secretary Hull used his usual tactics of procrastination and delay.[20] When the situation threatened to get out of bounds at midsummer, Roosevelt and Hull took a hand to insure maximum flexibility in the legislation that Congress seemed determined to enact. When the "peace bloc" in Congress threatened a filibuster against an administration-sponsored measure, Senators Pittman and Borah helped draft a substitute measure. Limited to six months' duration, this bill required the President, in event of a foreign war, to proclaim its existence and to withhold the shipment of arms to or for *all* belligerents. American vessels were prohibited from carrying all implements of war. The President might, if he deemed it necessary, warn citizens that they could travel on belligerent ships only at their own risk. To implement the work of the Nye Committee, the law provided for a National Munitions Control Board, which would place imports and exports of armaments under federal control. Realizing that a mutinous Congress might override a veto, Roosevelt reluctantly signed this joint resolution into law. The President did favor the creation of a National Munitions Control Board and, in view of Ethiopian helplessness on the seas, the embargo promised principal harm to the aggressor power, Fascist Italy. However, upon signing the bill, Roosevelt took it upon himself to warn the country that the measure might well "drag us into war instead of keeping us out."

So certain was official Washington that Mussolini was in dead earnest that, before departing for a cruise in Gulf waters, Roosevelt signed an undated proclamation invoking the Neutrality Law. Actually, Roosevelt went beyond the terms of the law, for he denied diplomatic protection to American firms intent upon selling either belligerent such nonembargoed commodities as coal, oil, scrap iron, and copper. This action, however, did not cut off American

---

[20] The Nye Committee seemed uninterested in neutrality legislation per se until March 19, 1935, when FDR gave it the impression, in an interview, that he favored such a law. Divine, *Illusion of Neutrality*, pp. 86–87.

trade with Italy in many of the basic commodities of modern warfare, for Ethiopia was in no position to interrupt the carriage of these materials to *Il Duce's* war factories. Therefore, trade with Italy mounted to a point that has led Professor Robert A. Divine to remark that "it seemed as if American businessmen were intent on proving Nye's thesis."

Contrary to expectations, the Neutrality Law injured the victim more than the aggressor, for Mussolini did not need our arms and was able to get necessary nonembargoed American shipments. To remedy this defect of the law, the President and his Secretary of State asked American concerns to observe a "moral embargo" which would cut back to normal the size of our swollen Italian exports on oil and certain other commodities. Possibly the administration realized that such a program of voluntary self-denial would meet with only partial success, but it hoped to prod the League into clamping tighter sanctions on Italy.

Meanwhile Geneva's blunders in handling the crisis upset the balance of power in Europe and undermined remaining faith in the efficacy of collective action. This disillusionment was prompted, in part, by the exposure of the unsavory Hoare-Laval negotiations. Premier Pierre Laval began the ill-fated French policy of appeasing the Fascists. He persuaded the British Foreign Secretary, Sir Samuel Hoare, to agree to a partition of Ethiopia whereby Haile Selassie would surrender about two-thirds of his empire. As part of the deal, Paris and London would restrain the League from effective action against Italy, thus allowing Mussolini to keep what he had already conquered. Some source, possibly one of Laval's political enemies, leaked the information to the French press before the details had been approved in the British Cabinet. The entire negotiations were premised on the ill-advised assumption that diplomatic adroitness could keep Mussolini out of Hitler's welcoming arms and, at the same time, turn the Fascist nations into a bulwark against the spread of Communism. However, an aroused British public opinion forced Hoare out of Prime Minister Stanley Baldwin's Cabinet. He was replaced by Anthony Eden, who opted for closer Anglo-American ties.

This British Cabinet shake-up did not retrieve the League's

record on the Ethiopian situation. The Council had earlier declared Italy an aggressor and had embargoed the shipment of arms, certain other commodities, and credit to Rome. The crucial question, however, as Mussolini made perfectly clear, was the Italian supply of foreign oil, and here the League powers hesitated to act. Geneva could not be certain of American cooperation on oil sanctions, for while Washington had placed that vital commodity under a moral embargo, Europe understood that any more stringent efforts might well be blocked by an isolationist-minded Congress.

The callous indifference of Congress to the ultimate outcome of Mussolini's Ethiopian campaign was broadcast by the terms of the Second Neutrality Law, February 29, 1936. As the six months limit of the first act drew to an end, the administration pared down its proposal of the previous summer for a flexible arms embargo and merely requested power to hold the shipment of nonembargoed goods to peacetime limits. This bill died in committee. In its place Congress sent to the White House a law more sharply isolationist than the one it replaced. This measure extended existing provisions for fourteen months and also forbade loans to belligerent powers. Thus, Congress formally recognized the Nye Committee's contention that banking loans were a lure to war.[21]

More important, this Second Neutrality Law notified the world that the United States was not only unwilling to lend a hand in halting aggression, but was also bent upon discouraging European collective security efforts. The old law had provided that if an existing war spread, the President was empowered to extend the arms embargo to new belligerents. Now, however, Congress directed him to extend the provisions of the law to all nations entering an existing conflict. In other words, if Geneva took actions stern enough to goad Mussolini into war against the League powers, the United States would automatically clamp an arms embargo against the concert attempting to halt the epidemic of lawlessness.

[21] It should be pointed out that the State Department had urged that this provision be included.

All this is not to argue that the Second Neutrality Act and a supposed American refusal to cooperate with League sanctions on oil were the fundamental reasons for Geneva's halfhearted actions against Italy. Whatever steps we might have taken, it is still doubtful if the League powers would have halted fuel for *Il Duce's* war machine. Nevertheless, the League was still talking of tightening the economic vise around Mussolini when Hitler ended the discussion by marching his troops into the Rhineland. Two months later, when Haile Selassie's capital, Addis Ababa, fell to a motorized Italian column, the question of sanctions became academic.

The faltering diplomacy of the western powers bore bitter fruit on October 25, 1936, when Germany reached an understanding with Italy, an agreement which formed the nucleus of the Rome-Berlin-Tokyo Axis. In retrospect, two cardinal errors helped precipitate this dangerous combination of aggressors. The first was the League's blunder in provoking Italy to the point where Mussolini was ready to ignore his differences with Hitler, and yet not going far enough to parry his African lunge. Secondly, London and Paris made a fatal error in allowing Hitler's Rhineland *Putsch* to go unchallenged. They passed up the last real chance to stop Hitler short of a major war. In March of 1936 the French army could have marched eastward into an unfortified Germany. It is entirely possible that the German generals might have deposed Hitler rather than face certain defeat on the battlefield. Be that as it may, Germany was now free to build her *Westwall* fortress at will, and France was cut off from the "Little Entente" allies whose territory lay to the east of the Reich. Henceforth, notes H. Stuart Hughes, "it was impossible to consider the League seriously as an instrumentality for keeping the peace."

The age of never-ending crises now began in earnest. A month after Washington lifted the embargo against Italy, the Spanish Civil War erupted. The remote origins of this sanguinary conflict are deeply rooted in Spanish history. Spain remained an anachronism—a backward country that had failed to meld its feudal past with the dynamic forces of modernism. This circumstance divided the people between activists who demanded change and a coalition of military, ecclesiastical, large land-holding and mercantile interests who were determined to resist it through the establishment of an authoritarian state. Defenders of the liberal republican government, which replaced the monarchy in 1931, consisted of a proletariat concentrated in the region of Catalonia in northern Spain, the peasants, anti-clerical elements, and radicals who wished to remold Spanish society. Yet even the republican Loyalists were divided into an assorted group of anarchists, Marxists, and liberal democratic revolutionaries. There is no convincing evidence that any outside power ignited the fuse to this political powder barrel, albeit by 1936 the country had become virtually ungovernable.[22] Then, as Hugh Thomas has said, the "wrath of generations" exploded.

This fateful uprising was triggered on July 17, 1936, by a revolt of an army garrison stationed in Spanish Morocco. Francisco Franco, under whose leadership the fighting was carried to the Spanish mainland, was catapulted into his role as a result of an airplane accident. This took the life of the designated leader of the army insurgents who planned to supplant the republic with a conventional military dictatorship. The cold-blooded Franco worshiped tradition and discipline but lacked a firm ideological commitment. A supreme opportunist by nature, he was ready to grasp any proffered hand of assistance.

Hitler and Mussolini promptly determined to use Spain's ordeal to their own advantage. The Nazi dictator, with Karl Haushofer's geopolitics in mind, wished to forestall a Communist foothold in a strategically located country producing raw materials vital for his war machine. He was also anxious to use Spain as a combat testing ground for some of his untried weaponry. Therefore, he sent Franco planes, tanks, expert personnel, and selected troop detachments. Mussolini, fresh from his Ethiopian triumph, sent the Spanish rebels greater numbers of ground forces plus seasoned Italian aviators and naval help.

Circumstances dictated that the Kremlin counter these moves

---

[22] There is a good, concise account of the Spanish Civil War in H. Stuart Hughes, *Contemporary Europe: A History* (Englewood Cliffs, N.J., 1961), pp. 285–294.

by aiding the besieged Loyalists. Probably Stalin acted from
motives which changed as the Spanish Civil War progressed. The
beginning of the conflict had coincided with the Russian drive for
a Popular Front against Fascism, and Stalin was anxious for full-
fledged western cooperation against Franco. Yet only limited help
was forthcoming, despite the fact that Stalin had partially restrained
Communist penetration of Madrid government circles in the hope
of allaying fears on the part of the democratic nations. However,
England and France showed their usual indecision, vacillation,
and perilous will to believe that it was possible to make binding
agreements with Hitler and Mussolini. Stalin came to fear "any
extensive intimacy with the liberal and socialist world of the
West," and he eventually realized that Russia was not a suitable
partner for the free world in "the cause of resistance to fascism."[23]
It has also been suggested that the Russian dictator never wanted
Communism to become deeply rooted in a country potentially
strong enough to challenge Moscow's leadership in the Marxist
world. Whatever his true reasons, in 1938 Stalin determined not
to push through to victory on the Spanish front.

Meanwhile in Paris the Popular Front coalition in control sent
some secret help to the Loyalists, but Premier Léon Blum was soon
replaced by a government overfearful of Axis reprisals. Across the
Channel in London, the Tory regime hoped for the impossible—a
Franco victory that would blot out Spanish Communism and
would not simultaneously turn Franco into an Italo-German puppet. The result was the formation of an International Nonintervention Committee in London, a group which eventually included
twenty-seven nations.

Powers interested in the outcome of the Spanish struggle gave
only lip service to the deliberations of this organization. The
European democracies, observes William E. Leuchtenburg with
justifiable cynicism, "enforced 'nonintervention' against themselves." Italian troops fought openly on Franco's side, Mussolini's
press celebrated the fall of Malaga as a national victory, and the
Nazis did not bother to explain away the fact that German planes

23 George F. Kennan, *Russia and the West under Lenin and Stalin* (London,
1961), p. 312.

had bombed Bilbao. Franco's massive offensive of December, 1938, marked the beginning of the end. The strategic Loyalist defense triangle of Madrid, Valencia, and Barcelona was punctured and on March 28, 1939, Franco entered the Spanish capital. Once again the paralyzing fear of a general war had rendered futile halfhearted western efforts to halt concerted aggression.

The bloodletting in Spain had ideological repercussions in the United States. With the exception of some extremists on the far right and left, public opinion reflected a plague-on-both-your-houses attitude. Significantly, American Communists compared the Loyalists to the embattled patriots of 1776 rather than to the Russian revolutionaries of 1917; and in the end, Franco's American friends confessed that his victory might shrink the area of human freedom. The liberals were similarly torn between a strong desire to aid the Spanish Loyalists and an equally powerful wish to keep America out of the dispute.[24]

Governmental action in the prolonged thirty-two-month Spanish crisis was determined by two factors. First of all, the administration refused to take any step that would imperil American neutrality or one which might increase the danger of a civil war becoming a major-power duel. Secondly, while official Washington was greatly relieved when it was not invited to join the London Committee, it gave full support to the Anglo-French contention that only a strict policy of nonintervention would confine the shooting to Spain. At the very outset the United States made an important decision. Instead of following our usual custom in dealing with Latin American revolutions, we treated the conflict as a war between two sovereign states. Had it been accepted for what it was, an uprising against a legitimate government, such a stand would have allowed us, under long-accepted practice, to ship arms and supplies to the Loyalists. But the administration chose otherwise. Secretary Hull pointed out that existing neutrality legislation did not apply to civil strife. Therefore, he proclaimed a moral embargo against sending arms or munitions to either side.

By the end of 1936 the efficacy of this extralegal embargo was

---

[24] For American reaction to the war, see Allen Guttman, *The Wound in the Heart; America and the Spanish Civil War* (New York, 1962).

endangered when a group of exporters sought licenses to ship planes to the Madrid government. To establish this principle in law, pursuant to a request from the President, Congress passed a joint resolution extending the Neutrality Law of 1936 to the Spanish struggle. This legal embargo on the implements of war primarily injured the Loyalists, for arsenals of the insurgents were well stocked by Germany and Italy. Franco expressed his appreciation when he called Roosevelt's action "a gesture we Nationalists will never forget."

Why did Roosevelt make a decision which impeded the containment of the Fascist menace? Some writers reason that he was anxious to please the powerful Catholic segment of his own party, but the timing of the move, coming as it did after the Presidential election of 1936, argues against a political motive. Probably the best answer to the riddle is that FDR feared that a nullification of the moral embargo would undermine the work of the London Committee. Significantly, friends of collective security did not oppose this particular extension of mandatory neutrality, for here the United States was following the lead of the League powers.

Before the Spanish tragedy had run its course, Roosevelt began to rethink his hands-off policy. The essential inconsistency of his stand was highlighted in 1938, when Senators Nye and Borah proposed the lifting of the embargo against the Madrid government. This shift of opinion on the part of these arch-isolationists caused the President considerable soul-searching. According to Secretary of the Interior Harold L. Ickes, the President admitted that the extension of the arms embargo had been "a great mistake," but added that it was too late to rectify the error, as indeed it was. Secretary Hull, influenced by reports of Ambassador Joseph P. Kennedy from London, insisted that the policy must be maintained if the fighting was to be localized to Spain. It is doubtful if any last-moment change in American policy would have tipped the scales on the side of the Loyalists. After Franco took Madrid, his government was recognized by London and Paris, and once more Washington followed their lead.

The immediate results of Allied Spanish Civil War diplomacy were unfortunate. France was now surrounded on three sides by unfriendly states which forced her to dissipate her strength by maintaining a close watch on her southern frontier as well as the others. In the war soon to come, Franco's victory complicated British patrol of the Mediterranean sea lanes and forced constant vigilance to forestall an Axis push through Spain to West Africa. Yet from our present angle of vision, would a Communist triumph have been preferable? "In the long pull of the cold war," Julius W. Pratt has observed, "better a Franco Spain than a Communist Spain."

In 1937, the first full year of the Spanish Civil War, Congress completed its neutrality policy by passing a permanent law which consolidated and augmented previous makeshift measures. It had already prohibited the export of arms to belligerents and had forbidden the granting of loans to warring nations. But as yet nothing had been done to curb trade in noncontraband goods carried in American ships. According to revisionist gospel, this traffic had been a prime cause of our 1917 intervention. The delay on the trade issue is understandable, for it was difficult to hit upon a plan that would preserve both profits and peace.

Bernard M. Baruch, of World War I mobilization fame, helped solve the dilemma when he suggested a magic formula that would not cripple trade with belligerents and yet would minimize risks of involvement. Baruch proposed that American manufacturers be allowed to sell combatants anything but the implements of war, with one special provision. All transactions must be "cash on the barrel-head" with shipments made only in foreign vessels. This suggestion appealed to the State Department, for it favored the Allied powers. Owing to the advantage of sea power, they alone could engage in a cash-and-carry wartime commerce.

Roosevelt, busy hassling with Congress over his Court-packing plan, decided to take a back seat while Capitol Hill ironed out the particulars of a permanent neutrality policy. The bill was the work of Senator Pittman, an ardent advocate of the cash-and-carry proposal. Significantly, some of the most seasoned isolationists were not swept away by the new fad. "We seek," said Senator Borah "to avoid all the risks, all danger, but we make certain to get all the profits." Senator Hiram Johnson argued vigorously against an untried experiment that would jeopardize our neutrality by favoring nations which had ready money and control of the seas. This nationalist school would have preferred to uphold our rights in wartime, by force if necessary, rather than to surrender them in advance.

The final struggle between contending interests was worked out in conference committee. The Third Neutrality Act (May 1, 1937) extended indefinitely the arms embargo and the prohibition against loans. American citizens were *forbidden* rather than *warned* against taking passage on belligerent liners. For a period of two years the President might, at his own discretion, prohibit the export to belligerents of all nonmilitary goods unless those commodities were paid for in advance and shipped out of the country aboard foreign bottoms. This particular clause expired before Hitler marched into Poland, and had to be re-enacted in somewhat different form after hostilities began. Nonetheless, its inclusion in the 1937 law is very revealing of the regnant thinking of the day. Congress wanted to avoid, in the next war, the kind of maritime incidents that had so often in the past jeopardized American neutrality. Yet only a small minority of isolationists were willing to follow the Nye theory to its logical conclusion and embargo *all* goods to warring nations. "We are still attempting," remarked Representative Everett M. Dirksen of Illinois, "to eat our cake and have it too. We say we want neutrality, but along with it we want a slice of the profitable trade of belligerent nations."

Professor Divine correctly labels the Third Neutrality Act "a curious mixture of mandatory and permissive features." The retention of the arms embargo would prove beneficial to the Axis nations whose munitions factories were working at full blast, while the cash-and-carry arrangement favored the Allied sea powers. Significantly, self-denying parts of this bill fell upon munitions-makers and big city bankers, while agriculture and mining interests would be affected to a far lesser degree by the imposed restrictions.[25]

25 This point is made by Wayne S. Cole in *Senator Gerald P. Nye and American Foreign Relations* (Minneapolis, 1962), pp. 9 ff, 97.

What is a fair over-all judgment on the neutrality laws of the 1930's? The United States was now protected, unless by its own fiat, against being drawn into a foreign war in defense of freedom of the seas. But what of the other multitudinous causes of war—aggressions, encroachments on sovereignty, wholesale outrages against human dignity, and radical shifts in the balance of power that no great country could ignore with impunity? The New York *Herald Tribune* saw the point and suggested sardonically that the enacting clause of the 1937 law read: "An Act to Preserve the United States from Intervention in the War of 1917–1918." It has been argued that Hitler took the neutrality laws as a clear indication that the United States would not intervene in the next war and advanced his timetable of aggression accordingly. But in the light of recent investigations, it is doubtful if anything that Congress did or might have done would have restrained this paranoiac dictator.

Perhaps the soundest verdict is that the neutrality fixation bound the hands of the President just at a time when he should have been granted a maximum freedom in the choice of policy. Before the summer of 1937 was out a new round of Axis aggression, this time in the Far East, demonstrated the folly of a permanent neutrality law tailored to meet any and all predicaments.

CHAPTER VIII

The Partial Eclipse

There was little in the official record of President Roosevelt's first administration to foreshadow creative diplomatic leadership. The challenges presented by the Italo-Ethiopian fray and the Spanish Civil War had not been met by vigorous American policies designed to stay the drift toward global anarchy. Until 1937 Roosevelt and Hull made only halfhearted attempts to temper the dominant mood of exultant isolationism.

If one takes them at face value, Roosevelt's public utterances reflected a cheerful confidence that the avowed American determination to avoid war would succeed in its purpose. On October 2, 1935, he promised that come what may overseas, the United States "shall and must remain . . . unentangled and free." His annual message of January, 1936 (written during the height of the Italo-Ethiopian war), conceded that he could no longer confine his observations on foreign affairs to a few sentences. But he pledged, once more, his resolve to adhere rigidly to the ancient policies of neutrality and nonentanglement. FDR, notes Robert A. Divine, had become "the prisoner of his own policies."

The Democratic platform for the presidential election of 1936 promised to avoid "being drawn, by political commitments, international banking, or private trading, into any war which may develop anywhere." When even this blanket endorsement of rigid neutrality was not sufficient to lure the progressive Republicans to the New Deal banner, Secretary of the Interior Harold L. Ickes persuaded Roosevelt that a stirring isolationist speech might win over Nye and other wavering political independents.

Roosevelt seemed to take this cue in his scheduled address at Chautauqua, New York, on August 14, 1936. Said the President:

> We are not isolationist except in so far as we seek to isolate ourselves completely from war . . . I hate war. I have passed unnumbered hours, I shall pass unnumbered hours, thinking and planning how war may be kept from the Nation.

Albeit these words and sections of the speech explicitly endorsing the neutrality legislation were later thrown back to Roosevelt by critics of his foreign policy, he had hardly given isolationism his full blessing. The President warned that so long as war exists, no nation can be entirely certain of escaping its scourge. "No matter how well we are supported by neutrality legislation," he added, "we must remember that no laws can be provided to cover every contingency, for it is impossible to imagine how every future event may shape itself." Evidently Senator Nye himself got the point, for he subsequently announced that he would support neither the President nor Governor Alfred M. Landon in the presidential race.[1]

In this "as goes Maine so goes Vermont" election, FDR carried every state in the provincially minded American heartland. A few weeks after his triumphant re-election, he chose to ignore the deteriorating international situation in his annual message to Congress. Yet the patrioteers on Capitol Hill always suspected FDR of secretly harboring a Wilsonian world outlook. This skepticism was not fully justified. Originally Roosevelt had shared with the Nye school the desire to harness the economic forces which might draw us into a new European conflict. At the same time he characteristically did not spell out all of his reservations to the basic assumptions of the extreme isolationists. Nor, as foreign skies darkened, did he immediately reveal his growing conviction that

---

[1] Wayne S. Cole, *Senator Gerald P. Nye and American Foreign Relations* (Minneapolis, 1962), pp. 136–138.

chronic global upsets mandated a sharp turnabout in the American diplomatic course.

This hands-off attitude had been possible during Roosevelt's first term, when no serious confrontation with Japan threatened immediate trouble. After the seizure of Manchuria and adjacent Jehol, Tokyo had halted military operations in northern China, signaling a truce which lasted four years. During this lull, the Nipponese tried to subvert five northern Chinese provinces by setting up puppet governments as a buffer to protect Manchukuo and as a method of forcing Chiang Kai-shek to cooperate with Tokyo against Soviet influence in the Far East.

When these fifth-column tactics failed, the Japanese grew apprehensive. A cacophony of other events also helped destroy the flimsy Asiatic armistice. On November 25, 1936, Germany and Japan signed the Anti-Comintern Pact containing a promise of mutual help against Soviet interference should the shooting resume in China. A change in the government in Tokyo also worked against continuing the peace. The moderate-minded civilians who wished to quash Chinese resistance by methods short of a shooting war were displaced by an aggressive military dictatorship.

In China, meanwhile, other forces were at work. Prior to 1936 Chiang Kai-shek had been actively engaged against the Chinese Communists, recently unified under the command of Mao Tse-tung, and Chiang had been able to uproot them from various strongholds in the provinces. Now, however, one segment was firmly entrenched in the semi-arid region of the northwest while another was organized as the Fourth Route Chinese Army south of the Yangtze River. At this same time, the Chinese Communists had become interested in joining the universal anti-Fascist Popular Front, and the Chinese assignment was an all-out effort against the Tokyo activists. In the last days of 1936, Chiang Kai-shek was mysteriously kidnaped by one of his own marshals and this precipitated negotiations leading to the formation of a Kuomintang-Communist coalition. Mao Tse-tung now placed his forces under a central national command and entered into a working agreement with the Nationalists.

Unlike the earlier Manchurian plunge, the 1937 collision resulted from accident rather than design. Neither China nor Japan desired an immediate showdown, but once the firing had begun it could not be stopped without loss of face—an oriental impossibility. The fuse was set off on July 7, 1937. Japanese forces stationed in Hopei Province clashed with units of the 29th Chinese Army near the Marco Polo Bridge, eighteen miles west of Peiping.

At first it was hoped that the affair might pass as another in a long string of minor incidents. Apparently the Japanese, alarmed at Chiang's rapprochement with Mao, thought the time opportune to settle matters once and for all in North China. Therefore, Tokyo decided to send in reinforcements. Had Chiang shown the restraint that had hitherto marked his conduct, the fighting might have been contained, but this time Nanking decided upon all-out resistance.

And so the conflict spread. Peiping soon fell to the Japanese forces. In a matter of five weeks another provocation at Shanghai precipitated a full-scale Japanese attack by air, land, and sea. In the sack of Nanking in December, 1937, some 100,000 Chinese soldiers and civilians were said to have perished. Hankow and Canton were lost and Chiang's government appeared on the verge of collapse when 1938 arrived. But the Chinese fought on, backed by Russian matériel and moral support from the United States. Chiang now moved his capital deep into the interior, to Chungking. The invaders eventually gained control of China's key cities, overran its richest and most densely populated areas, and seized its strategic ports and arterial railroads. But Chiang would not yield, and scattered Communist pockets of resistance, manned by defenders expert in guerrilla warfare, made it impossible for the Japanese to stamp out resistance in the vast hinterland.

This Chinese deadlock upset the *détente* that had existed between Tokyo and Washington since 1933. Roosevelt and Hull had continued the Republican policy of nonrecognition of Manchukuo, but there were no new protests over past wrongs. Silence to Tokyo meant consent. Prior to 1937 a number of incidents involved the Open Door in Manchuria, but none of these resulted in more than a desultory exchange of notes.

This easing of tensions under the Democrats was more superficial than real. Secretary Hull had decided from the first that a free China was essential to American interests and he was determined to keep Japan from dominating the Far East. Hull snubbed Japanese offers to divide up the Pacific into spheres of influence, and in 1934 he made it perfectly clear that America would not accept a Japanese Monroe Doctrine over East Asia. The litmus test of this decision came when the midsummer thrust of 1937 defied the Nine-Power Pact, whose signatories, including Japan, had promised to honor the territorial and administrative integrity of China. Initially, Washington hesitated to invoke the Pact lest precipitate action prevent localization of the Marco Polo incident. Similarly, no immediate decision was reached concerning the use of the Neutrality Act of 1937.

The situation remained confused until American headlines proclaimed severe fighting in China. The President then stated that our foreign policy was on "a 24-hour basis," but he took advantage of the fact that war had not been declared when he chose not to put the Neutrality Law into effect. This policy was a legal one, and was supported by a majority of the American people. Had Roosevelt followed the spirit of the law and proclaimed an arms embargo, his action might have injured a weakened China more than a fully armed Japan.[2] Further, given Tokyo's economic and maritime advantages, Japan probably would not have been seriously embarrassed by the cash-carry provisions of the 1937 act. As the President later observed, the Neutrality Law worked in the Atlantic, where our potential allies controlled the sea lanes, but did not work in the Pacific, where Japan had the cash to buy nonembargoed goods (including scrap iron and petrol) and the ships to carry their purchases home. According to Robert A. Divine, this failure of an inflexible neutrality policy to serve American interests in the Sino-Japanese War marked the beginning of the end for the "peace-at-any-price" criterion of United States diplomacy.

[2] Robert A. Divine, in *The Illusion of Neutrality* (Chicago, 1962), p. 218, argues that nonapplication of the Neutrality Act was not as favorable to China as is generally supposed. Japan had purchased a good many planes prior to the application of the moral embargo and, as some argued at the time, heavy purchases by Japan under cash-carry provisions might have severely strained the economy of that country.

When it became apparent that Japan was determined upon nothing less than the subjugation of China, Washington saw the necessity of preventing maritime incidents that might increase the clamor to invoke the Neutrality Act. The administration, therefore, forbade government-owned ships from carrying arms to either combatant and announced that privately owned vessels would sail at their owners' risk.

The question of utilizing the Neutrality Act was far less important than an effective method of halting the Sino-Japanese conflict before it became a threat to global peace. The question that had vexed Hoover and Stimson in the previous administration now arose once more. Should American diplomats abide by the isolationist axiom that a foreign conflict was none of our business, or should they take the contrary position that the maintenance of universal order was a matter of concern to all law-abiding countries? In theory Roosevelt and Hull agreed with the collective security enthusiasts, for their ringside seats had made the grim facts crystal clear. The newly formed Berlin-Tokyo Axis (soon to be joined by Rome) amounted to an organized plot against peace. Could the United States allow the civilized world to be engulfed piecemeal by nations dedicated to a militantly anti-democratic way of life? The threat was particularly startling because, unlike the Manchurian crisis of Hoover's day, there was now the distinct possibility of a European war which "might be joined with the struggle in Asia."[3]

The evidence is persuasive that high-level Washington authorities saw the possibility of this diplomatic nightmare but the weight of the isolationist albatross prohibited an effective Far Eastern policy during the opening years of the Sino-Japanese crisis. Also, the champions of collective security within the administration could not agree upon any peace machinery to be substituted for the fumbling League.

[3] Dorothy Borg, *The United States and the Far Eastern Crisis of 1933–1938* (Cambridge, 1964), pp. 533–544. The author of this impressive study feels that despite the administration's realization of the danger, its policy during the earlier part of the Sino-Japanese War was essentially timid and marked by great "passivity."

In the early months of the new Far Eastern emergency, the outstanding American spokesman was Secretary Hull, who refrained from pinpointing the aggressor and insisted that the United States was following a course of "strict impartiality." His single constructive idea was to mobilize world opinion behind a series of ethical precepts. In his slow, plodding way, Hull persisted, hoping at best that Japan could be deterred by moral suasion and at the worst that he could alert America to the perils of a stringent isolationism and Europe to the necessity of self-defense.

As the fall ripened, leadership passed from the cautious Hull to his kinetic President. This transfer came with the delivery of the famous Quarantine Speech on October 5 at Chicago in which FDR suggested that war be quarantined as an epidemic disease. Many observers jumped to the conclusion that this address marked a sudden and decisive turn in Roosevelt's thinking, but this assumption is unwarranted in the light of fresh evidence. Actually, the President had long been searching for a new peace blueprint to replace the creaking League machinery. He had made frequent private mention of the possibility of quarantining or isolating an aggressor. This scheme was only one of many feasibilities that came to his resourceful mind, as Dorothy Borg has put it, with "bewildering rapidity." When he broached the plan publicly at Chicago (to Secretary Hull's surprise and dismay), he had not worked out the details nor had he any specific plan in mind for halting aggression in China or Europe. He was merely engaging in metaphoric oratory.

However, the public took the quarantine parallelism seriously and the resulting isolationist outcry shocked the administration into overcaution. The *Wall Street Journal* warned: "Stop Foreign Meddling; America Wants Peace." Some extremist congressmen muttered impeachment, Senator Borah equated quarantine with war-breeding sanctions, while the Hearst press told its readers that Roosevelt had made a deal with Downing Street to save Great Britain's Far Eastern empire. Although the President received many commendations, so many that some authorities argue that he badly misjudged the reaction, no one questions that for once he had lost his sense of timing. In 1937 the country was in the throes of a severe business recession, irked at the New Deal's inability to bring lasting economic recovery, and sullen over the ill-fated attempt "to pack the Supreme Court." Now, said the isolationist-led Republicans, "that man" had fallen back upon the timeless ruse of all autocrats—he was rattling the saber in order to divert attention from failures on the home front.

In a private letter the President stated cheerfully that the popular reaction to his speech had not taken him by surprise, for it would take time to make the masses "realize that war will be a greater danger to us if we close all doors and windows than if we go out in the street and use our influence to curb the riot."[4] It was typical of FDR to suggest a bold project and then to backtrack. So he softened his words in a fireside chat and confounded curious reporters by stating with a straight face that the type of quarantine he had in mind might actually widen rather than contract the existing neutrality policy. The President refused to expand further on quarantine for the simple reason that he had no definite plan in mind. The Chicago speech had merely been a shot in the dark.

A dreary year of uncertainty followed, marked by fits and starts to pacify the Far East and halt the drift toward international anarchy. Roosevelt's own ambivalence mirrored a serious cleavage among his perplexed advisers. Secretary Hull felt that the situation was so hopeless that the United States had no choice but to re-arm, urge the democracies to build up their military establishments, and expound his "pillars of peace" philosophy until Europe took the cue and stopped the jingoist nations in their tracks.

Possibly the Secretary was correct in assuming that the United States had no choice but to wait until appeasement had been tried and proven futile. But a standstill policy was distasteful to a President who habitually believed trial and error preferable to no action at all. Roosevelt's agile mind was churning over a number of peace schemes. On the morrow of the Quarantine Speech, he decided to try an idea of Under Secretary Sumner Welles's. Was it not possible to negotiate a multilateral agreement with Germany

[4] Roosevelt to Colonel Edward M. House, October 19, 1937. Quoted in Lorraine L. Freeman, "Isolationist Carry-Over, 1933–1937" (M.A. Thesis, University of Buffalo, June, 1955), p. 119.

and Italy settling relatively noncontroversial interpretations of international law? This modest beginning might lead to improved relations with the prime European aggressors. Then perhaps Hitler and Mussolini might prove willing to persuade Japan to accept a Far Eastern cease-fire agreement which would not violate the fundamental terms of the Nine-Power Pact.[5] Roosevelt's enthusiasm for the plan was sparked by some vague hints from Rome and Berlin that an American overture would be well received. Possibly, as Secretary of the Treasury Henry Morgenthau, Jr., suggested, the arms race might be halted by bringing home to the other camp the economic handicaps imposed by a "guns before butter" philosophy.

The original plan called for a full-dress assembly of the Washington diplomatic corps on Armistice Day, 1937, where the President would stress common grounds for agreement on international conduct and economic cooperation. But this grand gesture was never made. Secretary Hull was able to delay it by arguing that the United States could not proceed with the plan without definite assurances of support from England and France.

So the Welles plan was shelved for the time being. Meanwhile the administration was willing to give the League of Nations a chance to halt the fighting in China. On the very day of Roosevelt's controversial Chicago speech a League Committee ruled that Japan was guilty of violating both the Kellogg-Briand and Nine-Power pacts. The next day the League Assembly suggested that all signatories to the Nine-Power Pact meet to discuss the Far Eastern crisis.[6] Washington accepted the invitation, suggested Brussels as the meeting place, and named Norman H. Davis to

---

[5] Julius W. Pratt notes that the Welles proposal was little more than what Hull wanted, but the younger man wished to advertise these moral precepts in a more dramatic and binding way. Welles himself hoped, at the very least, that his plan would warn the Axis and rally the neutral nations to a defense of world order. *Cordell Hull* [*The American Secretaries of State and Their Diplomacy*, Vols. XII–XIII] (New York, 1964), XII, 257.

[6] The Belgian Government sent out invitations to the original signatories; to Bolivia, Mexico, Denmark, Norway, and Sweden who had subsequently signed the Pact; "and, at British urging, to Germany and the Soviet Union." *Ibid.*, p. 255.

head the American delegation. While Davis was known as a friend
of collective action, Roosevelt's instructions to him, Dorothy Borg
tells us, amounted to "a powerful injunction to remain within the
bounds prescribed by isolationist sentiment."

The Conference, which opened on November 3, 1937, proved a
dismal failure. Tokyo declined to send a delegation while the Axis
permitted the Italian conferees to voice the views of the revisionist
powers. (To make matters worse, the word was flashed on the
fourth day of the meeting that Italy had joined the Anti-Comintern Pact.) The Russians did a good deal of talking but were unwilling to back their words with deeds. The British originally opposed strong measures against Japan on the grounds that such
action would endanger rather than preserve the peace. Paris favored
coercion only if the other powers would make commitments safe-
guarding French interests.

Despite these reservations, Washington was surprised when
"other large powers represented at Brussels went much further
than had been anticipated . . . in urging a consideration of the use
of coercive measures against Japan."[7] When Davis sensed this
trend, he proposed application of the nonrecognition doctrine to
the Sino-Japanese dispute, the leveling of financial sanctions
against the Tokyo aggressors, and recommended that the President
prod Congress to repeal or modify the neutrality legislation. Although these proposals were considerably more modest than
FDR's recent notion of a quarantine, Washington twice rejected
them. While Davis argued that the League Assembly had left the
question of sanctions open for action at Brussels, Hull ruled that
the Conference's action should be narrowly confined to arranging
a Far Eastern truce. The Brussels Conference ended on a note of
utter futility.

The meeting, therefore, did more harm than good. The Chinese
were greatly disillusioned while Japan became more determined
than ever to fight through to victory. Japanese documents that have
come to light since 1945 indicate that Brussels destroyed any
chance there might have been to end the Far Eastern conflict
through the good offices of the major powers.

[7] Borg, *op. cit.*, p. 540.

In the early days of 1938 the President took another hard look at the Welles Peace Plan. In doing this, FDR was not trying to cover up the Brussels fiasco; rather, the evidence suggests that he was contemplating a move to counteract recent British appeasement measures. The refurbished plan called for nine representatives of minor powers to draw up a basis of agreement that might induce the Axis to relax world tensions. Hull now agreed to the overture, providing British Prime Minister Chamberlain and the heads of other friendly nations gave their consent.

But the Prime Minister had reasons of his own for opposing the plan. Neville Chamberlain, a Birmingham industrialist, was almost fifty before he held national office. Honest, efficient labor coupled with a supreme self-confidence brought its reward and he rose in Tory circles to become Prime Minister following the retirement of Stanley Baldwin in the spring of 1937. The new Prime Minister typified the complacent British mind of the prewar era.[8] This frame of reference viewed Hitler's deeds as shocking but held that German economic stability would make the Reich a bulwark against the spread of Bolshevism and a helpful tool to British recovery from the long depression. Moreover, British Socialists preferred economic reforms to rearmament. Hitler's false promises were eagerly devoured by Little-Englanders weary of the burden of empire, and, paradoxically, by imperialists who preferred commonwealth cooperation to meddling in continental politics.

How, then, could Hitler and his Axis partners be tamed and brought into the fellowship of polite international society? Chamberlain thought that he had the answer to this question, and alas for the fate of world history, he brushed aside all opposition and tried his dangerous experiment. He would carefully cultivate personal contacts with the snarling dictators, engage them in friendly negotiations, and assuage their land hunger by legitimatizing some of their demands at the expense of their smaller neighbors. He would redress the injustices done the vanquished at Versailles, and

[8] H. Stuart Hughes, *Contemporary Europe: A History* (Englewood Cliffs, N.J.), pp. 206–207; Keith Feiling, *The Life of Neville Chamberlain* (New York, 1946), *passim*.

in the course of the process the Fascist bandwagon would join the orderly parade of western nations.

In retrospect, appeasement per se is neither necessarily foolish nor evil. But it was both when applied to a megalomaniac dictator whose political and economic aims were not limited by the ordinary bounds of reason. Each new concession only increased the appetite of the outlaw nations and weakened the will of the British people to resist.

In early 1938 Chamberlain rejected the Welles Peace Plan. He was then in the midst of trying to mend Anglo-Italian relations by recognizing the King of Italy as Emperor of Ethiopia and he stood ready to acknowledge Hitler's seizure of Austria.[9] Fundamentally, Chamberlain was against any move which might embarrass his use of studied appeasement as a prime diplomatic tactic. He therefore rejected any large-scale scheme of conciliation that would rival his personal diplomacy. Years later Winston Churchill called the Welles proposal "the last frail chance" for peace and his gifted pen severely castigated Chamberlain's obstinacy. But could the Welles Plan or any other diplomatic scheme have deterred the *Führer?* Hitler was utterly impervious to the kind of reasonable action that Welles proposed. History bears witness that he was equally insensitive to repeated appeasement. The character of Adolf Hitler made any kind of accommodation impossible.

For the most part, the American government's vacillating response to the Far Eastern menace stemmed from the current public aversion to war or coercive acts that might lead to war. This antipathy was vividly demonstrated in December, 1937, when Japanese planes attacked the gunboat *Panay* and three Standard Oil Company tankers in the Yangtze River. Three lives were lost and seventy-four men were wounded in this extraordinary provocation in which Japanese aviators strafed the struggling survivors of their attack.

A serious confrontation was avoided when Tokyo promptly

---

[9] Anthony Eden resigned as Foreign Minister on February 20, 1938, in the midst of the controversy over accepting the Welles Plan and recognizing the King of Italy as Emperor of Ethiopia. He was replaced by an outright appeaser, Lord Halifax.

promised to pay full indemnity, and pledged itself to prevent similar incidents. Significantly, the nonbelligerent mood of the day
prevented any "Remember the Maine" demonstrations. With the
exception of a few hardheaded admirals, no demands were heard
for a "get-tough-with-Japan" ultimatum and even the so-called internationalists willingly accepted Japan's profound apology. Instead, public opinion questioned what our boats were doing in
such obviously dangerous waters.

A month after the 1938 appeasement at Munich the Japanese
Foreign Office boldly proclaimed a "New Order" in the Far East.
This sought to establish a "tripartite relationship of mutual aid and
coordination between Japan, Manchukuo and China." This step
was the logical culmination of Tokyo's repeated insistence that
changed circumstances had rendered existing treaties obsolete,
that Japan was fighting a war of self-defense in China, and that the
exigencies which grew out of this local dispute were the proper
concern of no outside nation. In other words, Japan had her own
Asiatic blueprint—unity against Soviet influence, economic and
cultural advance under Nipponese generalship, and a bid for
Chinese acquiescence in the program through an appeal to Mon-
golian racial pride.

The United States rejected the "New Order" forthwith. Washington was willing to parley over obsolete parts of the existing
treaty structure but would not accept the dubious assertion that
any country could force hegemony over territory outside of its
legal control.

In the twenty-one-month span between the *Panay* attack and
the eruption of hot war in Europe, American policy toward Japan
remained essentially unchanged despite a succession of bombings
in China, all the more irritating because the Nipponese targets
seemed frequently to be churches, missionary schools, and hos-
pitals. Simultaneously the Japanese stepped up their restrictions
on foreign business firms within their Chinese orbit to the point
where the Open Door Policy became a farce.[10] Herbert Feis sums

[10] Sadao Asada in "Japan's 'Special Interests' and the Washington Conference, 1921–1922," *American Historical Review* LXVII (October, 1961),
62–70, argues on the basis of Japanese archival material that the Open

up all American peace efforts in the Orient with the curt comment
that "the only concurrent action taken was to do nothing."

The United States and Japan reached a deadlock over the
"China Incident" just when the international spotlight shifted from
the Yangtze to the Danube. As the European situation steadily
deteriorated, the Japanese became progressively more intransigent.
The net result merged the menace of Germany with that of Japan.

During these perturbed years of the later 1930's, public opinion,
hitherto overawed by the neutrality obsession, returned once more
to its normal bifurcated streams. In a democracy public opinion
is almost invariably divided and confused on the eve of a crisis involving peace or war. In a country such as the United States,
wedded to the tradition that the enemy must fire the first shot, a
consensus for military action comes only after an electrifying
shock. Until the crisis is full-blown, the same news portending
danger creates massive blocs of public opinion with opposing
views on how best to avert hostilities.

One group was composed of people loosely called interventionists. While, for the most part, they refrained from demanding advance commitments to foreign countries, they urged parallel action
with the Atlantic democracies in meeting each new Axis thrust
and they wanted more help for beleaguered China. Endemic
among this group was the conviction that we could not escape involvement in general war. They demanded speedy rearmament
of the United States on the grounds that such a build-up might
possibly give the aggressor nations pause. It would be easier to
avert this calamity, according to this reasoning, if Congress would
unshackle the President's hands by relaxing the rigid provisions of
the Neutrality Law.

One factor in the revival of a vigorous internationalist segment
of opinion was a new tack on the part of Moscow which, for a season, turned Communists and fellow travelers into ardent advo-

---

Door meant different things in Tokyo and Washington. The Japanese based
their interpretation upon some tactless assurances of Elihu Root to Shidehara
that the Open Door parts of the Nine-Power Pact would not be applied to
Manchuria and Inner Mongolia. Asada insists that Tokyo never meant to
promise to maintain the Open Door in those regions.

cates of a system of general security. The idea of a Popular Front consisting of global anti-Fascist elements stemmed from French and Italian Communist circles and was accepted by the Communist International at Moscow in 1935. In the United States the New Deal political climate nurtured its growth. Moreover, Russia recently had been admitted to the League of Nations and Dictator Stalin embraced collective security with apparent zeal. The USSR's image in American eyes sharply improved, for Fascism seemed the more immediate threat. In 1936 the Soviets proclaimed a new constitution which some innocents hailed as "the most democratic in the world." Moscow, for the nonce, played down the long-run revolutionary aims of international Communism and stressed domestic reform, nationalism, and anti-totalitarianism. Americans of the depression generation, to whom the issue of economic inequality was a matter of intimate concern, took a fresh look at the Red experiment. The many Communist-front organizations of the day infiltrated liberal organizations, preaching the message that "Communism is twentieth-century Americanism."

Meanwhile Adolf Hitler's deeds spoke louder than any words mustered by the internationalist pressure groups; German ruthlessness reawakened the American conscience. The veteran cosmopolites were steadily reinforced by recruits from labor organizations, Jewish ranks, devotees of civil rights, and other segments kindred to the German groups whom Hitler tortured and liquidated. Many Americans hitherto relatively indifferent to the Nazi terror were shocked into action against the new barbarism as they read John Gunther's best seller of 1936, *Inside Europe*. Before Hitler had set foot upon one square inch of foreign soil, an articulate fragment of American opinion was convinced that the Nazi leader, if unchecked, would devour western civilization.

When the perennial Axis raids began, not all Americans were equally perturbed, although even the insensate could hardly shut their ears to the blow-by-blow descriptions of these forays that came through the loud-speakers. Never before had the Old World seemed so close as in the critical days of the later 1930's, when people sat hushed in their living rooms to listen to crisp summaries of the latest news. They eagerly awaited shrewd guesses from observers in London, Paris, Prague, and Berlin as to whether the tribute demanded would be paid or the bombs would begin to fall. Hitler's hysterical rantings, translated phrase by phrase over the air waves, bestirred millions of Americans. It slowly dawned on more and more men and women that modern technology had all but caused space to disappear. Many such listeners began to fear the spread of the totalitarian cancer more than the surgeon's knife of war.

A goodly number of Americans generally called isolationists listened to this same grim news from overseas and thanked God for our oceans and the Neutrality Law. This school insisted that the United States meet all crises singlehandedly, regardless of the effect of our aloofness upon the fortunes of our potential allies. Many of these people still nursed grievances against Britain and France for the repudiation of their war debts and harbored some measure of sympathy for a Germany which allegedly was trying to unshackle itself from the chains of Versailles. The argument was also heard in the land that patience would be rewarded when Fascist dictators fell of their own weight without the impetus of war. Isolationist views were most popular in true-blue Republican bailiwicks, parts of New England heavily penetrated by French-Canadians, eastern urban centers filled with "Anglophobic Irish Catholics," and the northern midwestern states, where the GOP tradition and the influence of German and Scandinavian enclaves prevailed.[11] However, a country-wide 1937 public opinion poll reported that 71 per cent of all those questioned replied that our intervention in World War I had been a grievous error. Taken for what such samplings are worth, this poll indicated that isolationism was by no means entirely a regional prejudice.

As President Roosevelt began his campaign of education to dispel the neutrality fixation, the isolationist backlash was extremely forceful. His opponents usually captured the headlines. Brazen-faced young men, calling themselves "Veterans of Future Wars," demanded government benefits *before* death.

These arch-isolationists of the appeasement era found their

[11] Cushing Strout, *The American Image of the Old World* (New York, 1963), p. 204.

natural leader in Father Charles E. Coughlin. Subsequent to his
disenchantment with FDR, the radio priest founded the National
Union for Social Justice. This organization, boasting a membership
of nine million in 1935, was a weird combination of anti-New
Deal extremists resembling the radical right of the 1960's.[12] A
coalition of such extremists formed the Union Party and put up
a presidential ticket in the 1936 election. Coughlin, in a reckless
moment, promised that if the new party failed to poll a minimum
of ten million votes, he would retire from the air. Inasmuch as
William Lemke of North Dakota, the Union's choice for President,
received less than a thinly scattered million popular votes (derived
mostly from German and Irish hyphenate pockets), Coughlin
temporarily halted his tirades. When Coughlin broke his pledge
and resumed his weekly broadcasts, millions who tuned in on
his speeches found him more than ever an apologist for the Fascist
brand of racism. So far did Coughlin go in excusing Hitler's giddy
ventures that he even explained away the 1939 Nazi-Soviet deal.
Until finally silenced by church authorities after the onset of the
Second World War, Coughlin's broadcasts and his widely distributed weekly, *Social Justice*, voiced the harebrained gospel of
the bitter-enders.

The mass strength of the ultra-isolationists was dramatically
revealed in January, 1938. The administration was forced to play
all trumps in hand to halt a drive to amend the Constitution so as
to make war, except in event of actual invasion, subject to a
popular referendum. This Ludlow Amendment dated back to
Wilsonian days, when it had stemmed from opposition to American intervention in the First World War. Revived sporadically in
the intervening years, it failed to compel serious attention until it
was picked up by Representative Louis Ludlow, an Indiana anti-
war Democrat. Ludlow's efforts were supported by Senator Nye,
who added the amendment to his five-point neutrality program.
Church and pacifist groups also hailed the referendum idea.

[12] Coughlin hoped to form a nucleus from followers of Senator Huey Long's
"Share-Our-Wealth" faction, devotees of Dr. Francis Townsend who had a
weird plan for liberal old-age pensions, and other nonconventional opponents
of Roosevelt.

Nevertheless, the plan seemed safely pigeonholed in the House Judiciary Committee until the *Panay* war scare of December, 1937, suddenly revived interest in this "foolproof" peace plan. The Indiana congressman secured sufficient signatures on a petition to force a vote on discharging the measure from committee so that it might be considered on the floor of the House.

The administration went to extraordinary lengths to block Ludlow's maneuver. Speaker William B. Bankhead left the chair to read a warning from FDR that the amendment "would cripple any President in his conduct of foreign relations and . . . would encourage other nations to believe that they could violate American rights with impunity." Supporters of the referendum plan fought back vigorously against this executive interference. "It may be true," said Congressman Hamilton Fish, Jr., New York Republican who represented Roosevelt's own Hyde Park district in the House, "that Mussolini, Hitler, and Stalin sneer at the very idea of permitting the American people to vote on the question of foreign wars. If, however, we set such an example, the people of Italy, Germany, and Soviet Russia would eventually clamor for the same privilege, because they have far more to fear from the horrors of war than we." The peace bloc seemed entirely oblivious to the effects that this handcuffing amendment would have upon the future conduct of foreign affairs. Fish insisted that "we could do nothing better or greater for world peace than to give the American people the right to vote to stay out of war."[13]

Fortunately for their country, 44 Democrats who signed the discharge petition yielded to White House pressure and voted against bringing the amendment to the House floor, so that it failed, by a margin of 21 votes, to get the required two-thirds. However, the bloc of 188 House votes that supported Ludlow, notes William E. Leuchtenburg, suggests "a measure both of the President's tenuous control of foreign policy, and as late as 1938, of the hardrock strength of isolationist sentiment in America."

The battle over the Ludlow Amendment foreshadowed the difficulties the administration would face in requesting authorization

[13] Radio address of January 14, 1938, printed in *Congressional Record*, 73 Cong., 3 sess., pp. 923–924.

for extensive military preparedness. President Roosevelt found it much easier to change his own mind than to win over Congress and public opinion. Although he moved cautiously in suggesting revisions of the existing neutrality legislation, he was determined to match the perils of the world situation by an adequate armament build-up.

In 1920 Congress had set the maximum strength of ground forces at 280,000 enlisted men, but even this goal was never reached in the interwar years. In 1934 Congress rejected a recommendation to increase the enlisted personnel of the regular army to 165,000 and the National Guard reserves to 210,000. This request from General Douglas MacArthur, coupled with a demand for modernized fighting equipment, failed because depression-spawned relief and recovery measures were given priority in budget considerations. Congress alone was not entirely to blame; most army bigwigs of the day were ready to write off the Philippine Islands as a military liability and thought mainly in terms of shielding the mainland through naval protection.

Europe was far ahead of the United States in grasping the significance of the airplane. The stern warnings of General "Billy" Mitchell that the airplane had outmoded the dreadnought went unheeded and Mitchell's ultimate vindication had to await another war. However, Lindbergh's 1927 solo Atlantic crossing sparked a new interest in the military use of aviation. Late in the following decade the development of the B-17 bomber prototype marked a major breakthrough in the flying range of fighter craft, their carrying capacity, and their striking power. Nevertheless, a request for long-range bombers by the Army Air Corps was refused on the grounds that "our national policy contemplates preparation for defense, not aggression."

The Navy Department was less isolationist-minded and somewhat more generously treated by Congress because its big battle-wagons were needed to stand guard over our vaunted ocean moats. While the army refused to take seriously the possibilities of a foreign war, naval planners designated Japan as the most probable enemy and planned accordingly.

However, as a result of parsimonious appropriations, complacent public opinion, and the current disarmament mood, when Roosevelt took office our naval strength stood far below treaty limits in virtually all categories of craft. The new President, who understood naval matters from long administrative and dilettante experience, promptly diverted $238 million from make-work recovery funds to shipbuilding. Congress passed the Vinson-Trammell Act, which empowered the President to bring the fleet to full treaty strength by 1942, but failed to make the necessary appropriations. The anti-preparedness spirit of the day is illustrated by the suggestion of one wit that J. P. Morgan build his own navy to protect his own far-flung investments! The voice of the pacifist lobby, a combine of some forty organizations, was echoed by a midwestern congressman who declared it a crime "to spend all this money while our people here are starving to death."[14]

In 1935 a treaty crisis with Japan developed and this converted Roosevelt and Hull to outright champions of naval rearmament. Another naval conference was scheduled to be held as called for by existing agreement. Before the preliminary differences on future ratios could be ironed out, Japan filed notice of her intention of withdrawing from the existing treaty structure. This meant that all curbs on Japan, including the cruiser ratio of 1930, would expire automatically on the last day of 1936.

The Japanese demand for naval parity with the United States and Great Britain foredoomed the 1935 London Naval Conference to failure. Some minor limitations on ships and guns were agreed upon, but even these innocuous restraints were abandoned when Japanese naval activity forced the invocation of escape clauses. Peace on the basis of disarmament had once more been proven an impossibility. By 1938 the Roosevelt administration was resolved to construct a two-ocean fleet strong enough to match the combined naval power of the three Axis nations. The President's special message to Congress on rearmament (January 28, 1938) followed hard on the heels of the Brussels fiasco and the refusal of Great Britain to support the Welles Peace Plan. Roosevelt asked for 46 new ships and 950 additional fighter planes, pointing out

14 *Ibid.,* 73 Cong., 2 sess., p. 1632. The remark was made by Representative Francis H. Shoemaker of Minnesota.

that the global armament race involved "a threat to world peace and security."

The forthcoming bill encountered heavy opposition. Charles A. Beard condemned it before the House Committee on Naval Affairs while Representative George H. Tinkham and Senator Hiram Johnson were certain that Roosevelt's plans included a secret Anglo-American alliance. This charge stemmed from the disclosure that, following the sinking of the *Panay*, Captain Royal E. Ingersoll of the War Plans Division had been dispatched to London for staff talks designed to explore possibilities of cooperation with Great Britain in the event of a Pacific war.[15] Why all this money in battleships, demanded Representative Maury Maverick of Texas? "You can as surely sink . . . a battleship," he replied to his rhetorical question, "as small boys can hit a barn with a rock." But neither Maverick nor his sympathizers were willing to follow this point to its logical conclusion by proposing an air force large enough to reflect the revolution they sensed in modern warfare. Rather, the isolationists argued that if we divested ourselves of all responsibility for the Philippines, a moderate increase in appropriations would suffice to defend our New World ramparts. Wayne S. Cole has clarified one aspect of the regional opposition to heavy rearmament by pointing out that the program would have cost certain rural taxpayers money while northern industrial centers and western mineral areas and southern states with climates suitable for army camps would have been given a welcome boost out of the prolonged depression.

After four months of rancor, Congress passed the Vinson Naval Expansion Act calling for twenty-four new battleships, corresponding additions in lighter craft, and a lesser increase in army and air strength. The administration's victory was aided by the logical vulnerability of the isolationist position. The majority realized that the die-hards were equally opposed to international cooperation that might halt aggression and to a rearmament that would allow the United States to uphold its interests without the help of world

15 We know today that these talks were regarded from the first as "a modest undertaking" which produced few significant results. See Borg, *op. cit.*, p. 542.

organization. Furthermore, the isolationists themselves were divided on the bill, for many in their ranks were hemispherists who wanted a two-ocean navy to shield Hawaii, Alaska, the Panama Canal, and Latin America without reliance upon the British fleet. Fortunately this determination to defend the western hemisphere prevailed in time, for without the ships planned under the Vinson Act, the United States would have been virtually helpless following December 7, 1941, when Japanese bombers put out of commission so many units of the older fleet.

Naval officials were still not satisfied and urged appropriations to fortify and develop twelve outlying bases. The most important of these was Guam, an island which assumed new strategic importance because of the anticipated independence of the Philippines. When the 1922 Washington treaties lapsed, a board recommended the construction of a fully equipped fleet base, but the administration was willing to settle for improvements that would make it possible for long-range planes to operate out of Apra harbor. The issue was sharply debated early in 1939, but the House, in fear of aggravating Japanese relations, struck out a five-million-dollar item for the development of Guam. When war came, the island was defended by only 605 marines and six light machine guns.

The Guam episode has often been cited as an example of isolationist shortsightedness. However, it is only fair to remember that the Philippines, Wake, and Midway had been reinforced and they too fell into Japanese hands. Only the erection of a "Pacific Gibraltar" might have averted the military calamities that followed Pearl Harbor, but this naval dream was beyond the purview of prewar political realities.

The Vinson Act was only one step in the administration's new preparedness campaign. The President was authorized to stockpile essential raw materials and the entire defense budget was substantially increased. Congress heeded most of Roosevelt's admonitions primarily because Germany began to scramble the map of central Europe. The first country marked for absorption into the Third Reich was Hitler's native Austria. Four years earlier the *Führer* had prepared to move against Vienna following the

murder of Chancellor Engelbert Dollfuss by some local Nazis
but Mussolini had prevented this *Anschluss*. In the face of *Il
Duce's* interposition, Hitler promised to respect Austrian independence and so he marked time until he could be sure of Rome's
acquiescence.

On February 4, 1938, Hitler dismissed some unsubmissive
generals who argued that the *Reichswehr* was unprepared to make
good a reckless lunge. "As of now," he proclaimed, "I am personally assuming direct command of the entire Wehrmacht." A
week later, he summoned to his presence Austrian Chancellor
Kurt Schuschnigg, who headed a coalition Fatherland Front that
was determined to uphold the sovereignty of its landlocked
country. Hitler stated his terms in a no-nonsense manner; Schuschnigg was ordered to grant immediate amnesty to imprisoned
Austrian Nazis and to appoint a member of that fifth-column
party to the key position of Minister of Interior. On his return
to Vienna, the Austrian Chancellor stiffened his resistance and
precipitated an immediate crisis by calling for a national plebiscite
on the question of union with Germany. Hitler then ordered invasion. Schuschnigg was succeeded by a Nazi puppet who invited
the Germans into Vienna. On March 12, 1938, Hitler told the
world that his native country had been absorbed into the Third
Reich.

The Austrian coup vindicated Hitler's remarkable sense of timing. Paris, hamstrung by one of its seriatim changes of ministries,
failed to take effective action. Mussolini was annoyed at not having
been informed beforehand of the deed, but Hitler came to Rome
and soothed his feelings with a promise to respect Italy's control
of the Brenner Pass and assurances of support for some of *Il Duce's*
own projected land thefts. Austria lent Prime Minister Chamberlain a rationalization for appeasement. Would not Hitler now be
tamed after having consolidated eighty million German-speaking
people into one nation? Chamberlain thought so. *Anschluss* was
an old question and much could be said for it had it not been
consummated at gun-point by a paranoid dictator.

Anxious statesmen might well have surmised Germany's next
lunge; the addition of Austria had half encircled cigar-shaped

Czechoslovakia. Hitler's propaganda machine, now working at full blast, blew out of all proportions some usual minority complaints. The Versailles peacemakers had awarded to Czechoslovakia a mountain rim containing some three million German *Ausländer*. These Sudeten Germans, as they were called, were whipped into a state of frenzy by Nazi agitators. The task of Konrad Henlein, Hitler's chief Sudeten minion, was aided by mass unemployment in the glass and pottery works which dotted the region. True to his policy of one swallow at a time, Hitler waited until after he had devoured Austria before promising the German minority in Czechoslovakia that he would free them from "torture and oppression." As a sign to London and Paris that he meant business, *Der Führer* placed twelve divisions along the frontier and speeded the completion of the fortifications guarding Germany's western boundary. A secret directive ordered the army readied for a fall attack against the Prague government.

Peace became more precarious with each passing month. Austria had no choice but to submit, but Czechoslovakia had a reliable army and air force, some of the best armament works in Europe, a system of alliances with France and Russia plus a well-defended frontier. Without consulting its major allies or England, Prague ordered partial mobilization.

The chances of the powers coming to the armed assistance of Prague were very slim. There was mutual distrust between Russia and the West. Stalin was apparently ready to fight if France would honor her pledges, but he had no land frontier with Czechoslovakia and so would be forced to march his troops through Poland and Rumania. He was justified in doubting that France could arrange peaceful transit. The small states which separated Russia from Germany, instead of forming a common front against Hitler, manipulated things in the hope of picking up detached parts of their unfortunate neighbor. Furthermore, Paris was tied to London but the British had given Prague no guarantees. Chamberlain was dubious of Russian help in view of recent Soviet army purges and feared that Stalin wished to foment a war with Germany only to pull out and sit on the side lines. In turn, the Soviet dictator realized that some hyper-Tories were hoping for a diplomatic finesse whereby the Brown and Red terrors would consume each other in the fires of war. Chamberlain argued that justice based upon self-determination would demand the assignment of the Sudetenland to the Reich even after a successful war to maintain the territorial integrity of Czechoslovakia. As Gerhard L. Weinberg has put Chamberlain's case, why "be dragged into a war in which a doubtful victory would lead only to acceptance of what appeared to be the enemy's main demand? . . . To avoid war, he [Chamberlain] would go to great, in fact to almost any length, on an assumption that proved erroneous: that others, including Hitler, shared his aversion to war." Therein lay the Prime Minister's egregious miscalculation. In this as in other great crises of the 1930's England, the power with the least continental stakes, pointed the way and that direction always led to appeasement.

The crisis ripened in September when Hitler ordered army maneuvers and told the Nazi Party Congress that he would settle for nothing short of full self-determination for the Sudetens. Chamberlain, who had dispatched a pro-German mediator to soften Prague, now asked Hitler for a conference. Two days later, September 15, the two men met at Berchtesgaden. Chamberlain returned to London from his maiden flight with a "self-determination" formula which he forced his own Cabinet as well as Paris and Prague to accept. The Czechs were to cede to the Reich all areas more than 50 per cent German in population in return for international guarantees to uphold the territorial integrity of the rump of Czechoslovakia.

When Prague grudgingly accepted these harsh terms, Chamberlain flew to Godesberg on the Rhine for another parley with Hitler. To the Prime Minister's utter amazement, Hitler now increased his demands. No longer interested in negotiations, he insisted upon immediate military occupation of the disputed areas. The chagrined Chamberlain refused and left for home. Apparently there were limitations to the points on which even he was willing to yield.

Europe now stood on the very brink of war. France started to mobilize, while England made hurried preparations for civil defense. Prague, now backed by her allies, threw down the gantlet to Germany and readied the country for invasion. But the caprice of events decreed that the dogs of war were not to be unleashed for another year. Roosevelt cabled two anxious appeals to Hitler, and along with Chamberlain urged Mussolini to use his influence for peace. The latter's subsequent action probably owed less to the prodding of these messages than to *Il Duce's* own concern over the grave possibility of an immediate war. The Italian dictator therefore telephoned Hitler renewing his suggestion of a four-power meeting. Hitler may have reconsidered the proposal because he too wanted to buy time and the obvious anxiety of the democracies boded well for German bargaining power.

The forthcoming "summit" meeting was held in the Nazi stronghold of Munich. This city's name was destined to be linked in history with the appeasement that it housed. Hitler won his maximum demands; the West gained only a postponement of war plus some meaningless face-saving devices. To Neville Chamberlain, Munich meant "peace in our time." Winston Churchill's comment was much nearer the truth—"We have sustained a total and unmitigated defeat." Probably the Germans themselves were surprised at the loot gained by their bloodless victory. Particularly appreciated were the Skoda and Bruenn armament works, which exceeded German expectations and helped them perfect the blitzkrieg that was to play havoc in Europe within a year. After Munich, army opposition to Hitler's indomitable will all but disappeared, for had not the Allied capitulation proven beyond all doubt the wisdom of Hitler's intuition?[16]

The Reich had now taken the first step toward the old imperial goal of controlling *Mitteleuropa*. Would Hitler be satisfied with an economic hegemony over a region which, in all probability, he could gain without war? Could he, without bloodletting, transform his war-geared economy to peaceful purposes and calm the German public which he had prepared for battlefield victories? The

[16] At the Nuremberg War Trials in 1946, Field Marshal Wilhelm von Keitel argued that Germany was bluffing in 1938. "The object of Munich was to get Russia out of Europe, to gain time, and to complete the German armaments." Quoted in Kenneth S. Davis, *The Hero: Charles A. Lindbergh and the American Dream* (Garden City, 1959), p. 377, fn. 1.

evidence indicates that Hitler did not wax euphoric over his triumph at Munich. According to his twisted logic, had he refused all concessions, he could have marched into Prague and taken the entire country with no interference. "He felt," suggests Gerhard Weinberg, "that Chamberlain had bluffed him . . . in August 1939 . . . the only thing he feared was that at the last minute some *Schweinehund* would offer a mediation proposal." Next time no one would cheat him out of his war. The peace-loving statesmen of the world, were, of course, not privy to Hitler's private reasoning, so for a few weeks men breathed easier.

Although President Roosevelt had played an inconsequential role in the events of Munich, the record suggests that he was willing to give appeasement one last try. However, his sense of relief lasted less than six weeks. A young Jewish refugee from Poland shot and killed the third secretary of the German legation at Paris. Hitler's vengeance against the German-Jewish community included the burning of virtually all synagogues on the infamous *Kristallnacht*, the temporary incarceration of adult male Jews in concentration camps, the despoliation of remaining Jewish businesses within the Reich, and the levying of a one-billion-mark fine on the entire community. In a supreme act of defiance of decent opinion, the Nazi government collected the insurance for the damage thus done to Jewish property. Roosevelt was thoroughly shocked. "I myself," he stated, "could scarcely believe that such things could occur in a twentieth century civilization." Our ambassador to Berlin was recalled for "consultation," and the German ambassador to Washington was summoned home in retaliation. Neither official ever returned to his post.

At this time, Roosevelt was operating under some severe domestic handicaps. Within less than two years he had received a number of political rebuffs—the collapse of his "court-packing" plan, a sharp business recession which the Republicans pinned on New Deal economics, and the boomerang of his campaign to "purge" Congress of Democratic stand-patters. Most important, the GOP had made a noteworthy comeback in the recent congressional elections and the President was now confronted on Capitol Hill with a working coalition of southern conservative Democrats and anti-New Deal Republicans.[17] The vicissitudes of politics demanded that Roosevelt muster support for his foreign policy by assurances that he would call a halt to radical domestic reform. His annual message made it perfectly clear that he would welcome a truce with the business-minded conservative Solons.

President Roosevelt spoke some somber truth to the newly elected Congress which met in January of the foredoomed year of 1939. The European situation had taken a decided turn for the worse, for Hitler had quickened his military build-up a few days after Munich, with the flimsy excuse that Chamberlain might be replaced by a Prime Minister who would threaten German security. Moreover, it was already freely predicted that Germany would soon seize the remainder of truncated Czechoslovakia. The burden of Roosevelt's address dealt with the delicate foreign situation. No nation was safe, said the President, in a world in which three major powers would not sit down and reason across the council table. Conceding that the country was not ready to insure peace through armed police action, he suggested that "there are many methods short of war, but stronger and more effective than mere words, of bringing home to aggressor governments the aggregate sentiments of our own people." It was typical of FDR not to spell out what he meant by measures "short of war," but he made it perfectly clear that he wanted Congress to repeal or revise the existing neutrality statute. Would Congress act before a *declared* European war would compel enforcement of the arms embargo regardless of the consequences? The President's logic seems obvious today, but his arguments were by no means persuasive to the host of arch-isolationists who bristled at his words.

Roosevelt's message touched off still another six-month debate on neutrality. His opponents, regardless of party affiliation, denounced his request as "inflammatory and provocative," "dangerous to the peace of the world," a "red herring" aimed to divert public attention from the political bankruptcy of the New Deal. The isolationists tartly reminded the President that Switzerland and other neutralist European countries who minded their own

[17] Milton Plesur, "The Republican Comeback of 1938," *Review of Politics*, XXIV (October, 1962), 525–562.

business felt no sense of insecurity or impending danger. Senator Robert A. Taft explained that the United States was absolutely safe, for the war, if it came, would be a "protracted" one in which combined Allied power would crush the Fascist upstarts. Therefore, our sole task was simply to raise rather than lower our neutrality dikes.

While Congress was debating the issue, the Axis began its 1939 season of aggression. Under the pretext of ending incessant quarrels between the Czechs and the Slovaks, Hitler occupied the balance of Czechoslovakia in mid-March. Mussolini celebrated Good Friday by ordering the invasion of Albania. While world attention was centered on Europe, Japan seized some island stepping-stones to French Indochina, British Malaya, the Philippines, and the Dutch East Indies. Once more land grabbing had proven to be an endless chain reaction.

The occupation of Prague was a milestone in prewar diplomacy. Appeasement hinged on the assumption that Hitler's ultimate aim was only to gather within the borders of the Reich all people of German blood. "We want no Czechs," he had shouted to the world barely six months earlier. Now in one fell stroke he proved the utter worthlessness of his plighted word and destroyed the logic of appeasement by seizing non-German territory. This flash of diplomatic lightning revealed him as the would-be conqueror of Europe. As Nazi propaganda began to clamor incessantly for the reannexation of Danzig and the Polish Corridor, men (certain members of Congress excepted) no longer asked *if* there would be war but rather *when* it would begin.

During this gloomy spring of 1939, the Roosevelt administration spared no efforts to prod Congress into repealing the ban on the export of arms. These efforts yielded a category of blunders. The administration first erred in bowing to the insistence of Key Pittman that it leave the matter in the hands of his Senate Foreign Relations Committee. The Nevada senator, a self-styled political realist, told Roosevelt and Hull that all they could get from Congress was repeal of the arms embargo and legislation placing *all* commodities, including weapons of war, on a cash-carry basis.

Pittman received reluctant consent to this proposal. Then, two unexpected developments played into the hands of the ultra-isolationists. When an army bomber on a test flight crashed in California, a French air officer was pulled out of the burning wreckage. Congress thus learned that the President was permitting foreign military personnel to study our secret equipment and fly our newest army planes. This in itself was enough to stiffen congressional resistance, but while the fur was flying it was reported that the President had told members of the Senate Committee on Military Affairs that the "frontier of America is on the Rhine." FDR publicly labeled the story "a deliberate lie" and unequivocally denied a military alliance with France. Nonetheless, these episodes impeded Pittman's efforts in the Senate.

After Hitler's march into Prague, the administration determined upon bolder tactics. Secretary Hull, using the salty language that he could command, called the arms embargo "a wretched little bob-tailed, sawed-off domestic statute." In the privacy of his suite at the Carlton Hotel, he warned some senators that the coming conflict would not be "another goddam piddling dispute over a boundary line" but an assault on the peace of the world by "powerful nations, armed to the tooth, preaching the doctrine of naked force and practicing a philosophy of barbarism."[18]

Moving with new alacrity, Pittman introduced "The Peace Act of 1939." This bill, drafted with the help of the State Department, provided for the repeal of the arms embargo and the placing of all categories of goods on a cash-carry basis. It also empowered the President to designate "combat zones" in order to keep American vessels out of hostile waters. The isolationists opened fire while the bill was still in committee. Representative Hamilton Fish, Jr., predicted that the United States would become "a slaughterhouse" for the benefit of preserving the British Empire. Appearing before the Senate Foreign Relations Committee, a Dartmouth professor decried the alarmists and promised that "whatever happens in Europe or in Asia, the United States is as safe as a kitten in its basket."

Key Pittman, resorting more and more "to alcohol as a daily companion," proved unable to get the bill out of committee. In desperation, the administration turned to the House for action. At a White House Conference, which Professor Divine contends

18 Pratt, *op. cit.*, XII, 311.

marked a turning point in Roosevelt's campaign to unfasten
the neutrality strait jacket, the President told the congressional
leadership some blunt truths. The repeal of the arms embargo, he
said, at best *might* deter the Axis from war; at the very least, such
action would pose obstacles in the coming conflict for the potential
enemies of the United States. But the President's pleas went unheeded. After much time-consuming debate, the House passed a
bewildering measure which continued the embargo on "arms and
ammunitions" but permitted the exportation of "implements of
war."

Rebuffed by the House, the perplexed administration turned
once more to the deadlocked Senate. From Hyde Park, on Independence Day, Roosevelt tried to prod the senators by promising
to keep Congress in session until he got favorable action. But a
floor vote was scarcely possible as long as the bill was bottled up
in Committee. The crisis was reached a week later when the
Senate Foreign Relations Committee met for a fifteen-minute session. Senator Clark of Missouri, an uncompromising isolationist, saw
an opportunity for mischief. Two Democrats who were expected to
support the bill were nursing grievances against Roosevelt because he had tried to deny them renomination for their posts.
Clark cleverly reopened these political wounds and the two
helped form a majority of one which voted to postpone revision
of the neutrality statute until the January session of Congress.

The administration's sense of urgency was intensified by advance
knowledge of a possible Soviet-Nazi deal. At a White House conference on July 18, however, Roosevelt confessed: "I've fired my
last shot. I think that I ought to have another round in my belt."
Then Senator Borah, recklessly using a tidbit from a tawdry London magazine, blandly stated that he had better sources of information than did the State Department, which convinced him
that Europe was in no danger of war. Thereupon, Vice-President
Garner turned his weather-beaten face to Roosevelt and said:
"Well, Captain, we may as well face the facts. You haven't got
the votes and that's all there is to it." The isolationists had won
what proved to be their last major triumph. Congress adjourned
on August 5, but FDR released Borah's prediction that there would

be no war and this bad guess helped discredit the extremists when the events of that tragic summer unfolded. Secretary Hull was so certain that the sands of peace were running out that he went on vacation to replenish his energy for the trials ahead. While he was gone, his staff drew up the proclamations and executive orders that would be needed when Hitler took his supreme gamble.

It is doubtful if any action on the part of Congress could have stayed Hitler's hands. He was determined to round out his eastern boundary in highhanded fashion. Thus he forced Lithuania to surrender Memel and, despite a nonaggression pact of his own making with Poland, he gruffly demanded the seaport of Danzig (a free state administered by the League of Nations) and the retrocession of the Polish Corridor. These claims involved London and Paris, for both of these capitals had given absolute assurances of help to Warsaw. The fate of Czechoslovakia had revealed the folly of making partial concessions to Hitler so the Poles remained adamant against a one-sided territorial surrender.

Inasmuch as the Atlantic democracies were unable, by reasons of geography, to help Poland without Russian assistance, the fate of that country depended upon whether London and Paris could meet Stalin's terms. Instead of immediately flying their most skilled negotiators to Moscow, the British sent some second-rate diplomats who preferred to go by boat in order that they might enjoy the summer sea breezes. There ensued a long period of bargaining, with Stalin continuously raising the price for Soviet cooperation. Negotiations broke down when the Russian dictator made it plain that in order to risk war against Germany he would have to strengthen his defenses by occupying the Baltic states including southeastern Finland. Consent for this was almost out of the question. Neither the British nor the French paid enough attention to the grim fact that a Nazi drive into Poland could be thwarted only by a vigorous Russian counteroffensive. On the other hand, a firm western alliance with Russia might goad Hitler into a push toward the English Channel. Impaled on the horns of an ugly dilemma, the Allies hesitated and sparred for time.

Meanwhile Russia and Germany were secretly negotiating "the greatest diplomatic bombshell of the century." Viewed in full context, this Nazi-Soviet Pact of August 23, 1939, is not entirely amazing. Relations between Soviet Russia and Weimar Germany had been marked by close military cooperation, a political understanding, and a common interest in a fourth partition of unhappy Poland. In the 1920's Russo-German trade was so brisk that the Kremlin put pragmatic considerations ahead of fomenting a proletarian revolution in republican Germany. After 1933 Hitler posed as the savior against Communism but even he once noted that "there is more that binds us to Bolshevism than separates us from it." Moreover, many Aryan German Reds had been absorbed into the Nazi party and their influence lingered.

Some harbingers of the electric events which followed came in the spring of 1939. The West speculated on a long speech by Stalin, the barbs of which were aimed at London rather than Berlin. Seven weeks later Hitler delivered one of his customary harangues without once castigating Bolshevism. Then Litvinov, a Jew by birth and an ardent friend of collective security, was replaced as Commissar for Foreign Affairs by the flinty Molotov.

Thanks to post-1945 archival disclosures, it is possible to follow the course of this fateful haggling. Berlin, recognizing the dismissal of Litvinov as a meaningful gesture, renewed some interrupted trade talks with Moscow. Hitler tread cautiously at first, but he knew that Stalin had a hundred divisions ready for action and he realized that he could not attack Poland until this Soviet force had been neutralized.

As the summer dragged on there was a new sense of urgency in Berlin. The Nazi ambassador to Russia made it plain to the Kremlin that his government desired a mutual understanding on the future of the independent Baltic states and promised Stalin that Germany would pressure her Japanese ally for an easing of tensions in Asia. Some time in August Stalin decided to accept the immediate fruits of an understanding with the Nazis. The Allies had offered nothing in the Pacific and they were unwilling to assure him "natural ramparts" in eastern Europe. If he joined the democracies in a war against the Reich, he would have to bear the initial burden of the fighting; if he agreed with Germany to remain neutral, the resultant war might end in a stalemate that could redound to Russian benefit. Furthermore, he would buy time to prepare against future trouble with Hitler, would be repaid in territory for his patience, and could gamble on precipitating the Armageddon of capitalism that Marx had foretold.

Hence, Stalin notified Berlin that he was ready to come to terms. Foreign Minister Joachim von Ribbentrop sped to Moscow and in two days negotiated the pact that shook the world. The terms that were released to the public at the time were simple: no attack by one party against the other for a decade, and neither side would join a bloc of nations against the other party. Also included was a commercial treaty designed to help Hitler withstand a British naval blockade. Most important was a secret protocol which delineated spheres of influence "in the event of a territorial and political rearrangement." This agreement would allow Stalin to occupy most of the Baltic states, eastern Poland, and Bessarabia. Stalin and Hitler had gambled on the short run; both men were to rue their lack of foresight.

The Nazi-Soviet Pact, by protecting Hitler's eastern flank, made war inevitable. "Operation White," the Nazi code name for the despoliation of Poland, was promptly put into operation. On August 29 Berlin demanded that London force Warsaw immediately to dispatch an envoy empowered to make the demanded concessions. Sir Neville Henderson, the appeasement-minded British ambassador, suggested that the dispute be handled through the usual diplomatic channels. Ribbentrop then read "at top speed" a sixteen-point ultimatum. Not until these demands were broadcast over the radio did Henderson grasp their full meaning. When the Polish envoy failed to arrive within twenty-four hours, the Germans held that their terms had been rejected, although not until that selfsame day had London a chance to see a full text of the Reich's demands.

On the night of August 31–September 1, spearheaded by mechanized divisions and an air armada, the Nazi legions swept across the pillboxes which defended the Polish border. Two days later, when the Germans refused to withdraw, England and France declared war. For the second time within twenty-five years, American neutrality faced the supreme test.

CHAPTER IX

The Convulsion of Europe

In the wee hours of "Gray Friday," September 1, 1939, the telephone rang in a White House bedroom. Ambassador Bullitt was calling from Paris to tell the President that Hitler's *Panzer* divisions were storming across the Polish border. That day in Washington a war map was hung in the executive offices of the White House in order to keep Roosevelt abreast of hourly developments on the eastern front. Across the broad Atlantic in Holland former German Emperor William II led his household entourage in prayer. Then, acting entirely in character, he unfolded a dog-eared map of Poland and, with an experienced hand, placed rainbow-colored pins in the positions marking the Nazi advance.

William Hohenzollern was probably more startled by the news than Franklin Roosevelt. Studied government planning to meet the crisis indicated an American realization that the hours of peace were numbered. Washington's warnings that trouble would break out during the long Labor Day weekend were so stringent that twenty-two Atlantic liners, jampacked with homeward-bound tourists, had left Europe before the Polish invasion began. Now a navy squadron of overage destroyers lay at anchor in a French port ready to carry stranded Americans to ports of embarkation for New York.

Sobered by the grim news from overseas, a good many Americans canceled their holiday jaunts and remained glued to their radios. Even the carefree who could not resist the temptation of a last summer outing, managed to locate a radio where they could hear the President's fireside chat of Sunday evening. Roosevelt's words were unusually solemn. He was mindful of the fact that President Wilson had faced similar conditions a quarter-century before. Wilson had called for neutrality in thought as well as action, but to little purpose. Roosevelt chose to face reality. "Even a neutral," he said, "has a right to take account of facts. Even a neutral cannot be asked to close his mind or his conscience." He went on to assure his audience that as long as he could prevent it there would be "no black-out of peace" in the United States. But, he added, we must realize from the outset that "when peace has been broken anywhere, the peace of all countries is in danger."

Two days later Roosevelt issued the routine proclamation of neutrality, and also proclaimed the Neutrality Law of 1937 in force. This latter action injured the Allies, for under its terms they could not use their command of the sea to carry American-made war materials to replenish their arsenals. However, the President had already announced his decision to summon Congress in special session for the express purpose of lifting the arms embargo.

This act touched off the Great Debate over neutrality destined to last until the isolationists were silenced by the bombs that fell over Pearl Harbor twenty-seven months later. During this prolonged ordeal, American foreign policy was to shift from formal neutrality to material aid for England and finally to an undeclared naval war with Germany. The extended controversy was the logical result of a twenty-year schism over the feasibility of American neutrality in any war that might reverse the world balance of power.

Nevertheless, the lines of debate were not always sharply drawn. As a matter of convenience, Roosevelt's opponents are generally called "isolationists." However, many of the President's critics were veteran theoretical internationalists who, for one reason or another, opposed intervention in the present European war. In no other sense were they isolationists. On the other hand, to dub Roosevelt's supporters "internationalists" or "interventionists" is equally misleading. As Wayne S. Cole reminds us, a powerful segment within the group stoutly opposed any action that would go beyond "methods short of war." Moreover, included among the "interventionists" were some fiery nationalists who displayed only contempt for the concept of world organization. Also, one must never forget that a goodly majority held to a middle ground during most of the long debate. This influential body, always foremost in Roosevelt's mind, recognized the peril and wanted to build up national defense, but only slowly moved to a position where it shrank at the prospect of an uneasy coexistence with the triumphant Fascist dictators. In the long months ahead, Roosevelt was to gain most of his points, thanks to the support of these middle-of-the-roaders.

American thought in the fall of 1939 was permeated by two conflicting aims. The overwhelming majority fervently hoped that the Allies would prove victorious, but this wish was coupled with an equally strong desire to keep the United States out of the war. Roosevelt had paid heed to this split thinking in his speech of September 3. However, as Time noted, FDR had, by implication, "invited Americans to condemn Hitler as loudly as they liked, possibly a first step to fighting him with arms." In addition, the President had thrown down the gantlet to the peace bloc by calling for reconsideration of the "no-war insurance" neutrality program.

The isolationists accepted the challenge with alacrity. Never must we forget, admonished the Chicago Tribune, our bitter 1917 lesson in "false friendship, broken faith, entrapment, disparagement and repudiation." The isolationist assumption that America had a destiny all its own was forcefully restated. The staid Saturday Evening Post queried:

When shall we learn that Europe is Europe, America is America, and these are two worlds? When shall we believe again that our destiny is unique, parallel to nothing? . . . Where is the America that saw only the star of its singular destiny and pursued it?[1]

Less restrained sources spoke in more incisive terms—"At least one nation should be left to pick up the pieces"; "Let us sit out this

[1] Editorial, "That of Our Own," CCXII (March 23, 1940), 26.

dance of death." This point of view had wide appeal. And as long as Hitler was caged behind the Maginot Wall, Roosevelt's foes held many other trumps. They had able and experienced leaders, adequate financial resources with which to advertise their cause, and ultimately they were to perfect a national organization. Isolationists could tax their opponents with warmongering, thus putting them on the defensive. They could rally to their standard war-hating liberals, business elements irreconcilably opposed to "that man" Roosevelt, potential draftees and their anxious parents. In addition the Republican leadership in Congress was more than willing to plead the isolationist cause. The GOP, its appetite for victory whetted by repeated defeats, found the "no-foreign-war" theme politically appealing. But the cleavage did not adhere strictly to party lines. Some of the most articulate congressional isolationists were Democrats, while a fair-sized group of Republicans gallantly supported the President.

The isolationists soon discovered that the Chief Executive had lost none of his cunning. FDR realized that if he was to give the democracies substantial help, he would have to muster majority votes in Congress on key measures. Therefore, he cleverly combined the "keep-out-of-war" theme of the isolationists with the "prevent-war" insistence of the internationalists.[2] There was a certain logic to this union of ideas. FDR argued that by helping the Allies we would avoid war. If the Allies collapsed we would ultimately have to settle scores with Hitler.

It soon became obvious that FDR's policies involved a calculated risk of war, although for political reasons he was prone to minimize such speculation. In all probability, he was entirely sincere in saying that he wanted to keep the United States at peace. But when it became apparent that Hitler could be defeated only by increasing the chances of American involvement, Roosevelt chose the possibility of war as the lesser evil.

Because the President did not present the issue to the American people as he himself saw it, he laid himself open to charges of prevarication and guile. "He lied the American people into war,"

[2] Richard N. Current, "The United States and 'Collective Security,'" in Alexander DeConde, ed., *Isolation and Security* (Durham, 1957), pp. 33–55.

Clare Boothe Luce has charged, "because he could not lead them into it." This is, at best, a half-truth. To be sure, he did not always take the country into his confidence. He often larded his proposals with promises of peace while he gradually took actions necessary to defeat the Nazis. When the prospects of success on Capitol Hill seemed promising, he submitted vital issues to Congress. When the risk was great that some "irrevocable act" of Congress might dishearten the nations fighting the Axis, he skirted Congress by negotiating executive agreements or by extending his powers as commander in chief. Admittedly, he was often disingenuous, but it is salutary to remember that some of the most crucial American decisions of the day, such as the Lend-Lease Bill, were passed by Congress after full and fair debate. It is not difficult to explain why Roosevelt sometimes dissimulated. Both Capitol Hill and the country were badly divided. National unity, so necessary in time of crisis, would have been further jeopardized by absolute frankness.

Roosevelt succeeded in his ultimate objectives primarily because Hitler's deeds justified the President's counteractions. However, FDR's victories in many closely contested bouts with the isolationists were also due to his brilliant use of the media of mass communications. A sixth sense seemed to tell him just when the country was in the mood for another folksy fireside chat. Avoiding drab statistics or complicated idiom, he hammered home his points in short pithy sentences laced with simple concrete examples. Frequently flashes of delightful humor lightened his unlabored but carefully planned remarks. No one who heard him could ever doubt that he spoke in deadly earnest.

The initial brush between the President and the isolationists, destined to set the pattern for more than two years of polemics, involved the hackneyed issue of relaxing the Neutrality Law. The President took no chances; this time from the outset he assumed personal command of the campaign. But he found it necessary to proceed with caution. A preliminary public opinion poll had shown the country sharply split on the question of repealing the arms embargo.

On September 20, he met with congressional leaders. Admitting that "we are all for cash-and-carry neutrality," Roosevelt urged bipartisan support for the administration. The next day the President laid before Congress a package plan designed to secure majority consent. He requested a repeal of the embargo on arms, the placing of all commodities on a cash-carry basis, and the designation of combat zones where American vessels could not travel. For political reasons he neglected to reveal his deep concern for the fate of the Allies. Instead he argued that the embargo was a hindrance to genuine American neutrality. Further, he predicted that its repeal would stimulate both American business and the production of defense necessities. Secretary Hull, in a public statement, explained that it was fair to change the rules during wartime, for the United States was entitled to protect its own "interests and safety." As Frieda Kirchwey put it, the American people wanted "to be as unneutral as possible without getting into war."[9]

Key Pittman shepherded the administration's bill in the Senate, where seventy senators spoke more than a million words for or against the measure. Both sides organized to prod hesitant legislators by nurturing a nation-wide ground swell of opinion. Pittman was reinforced by incessant White House efforts. Influential Republicans were carefully wooed—Alf Landon, Henry L. Stimson, Frank Knox came out for the bill, and temporarily Senator Taft deserted the GOP regulars and voted for it. William Allen White, the widely known Kansas pundit, defied the prejudices of his region and organized national leaders of civic thought in defense of the administration's stand. Meanwhile the President won over to his side the Bourbon bloc of southern senators. Possibly all of these tactics might have failed without Hitler's blitz. The brutal crushing of Poland had powerful reverberations in the United States. A majority swung over to the view that the United States ought not deny weapons to the nations in array against Berlin.

Still the isolationists put up stiff resistance, sustained by formidable backing outside of Congress. An unusually heavy barrage of mail descended upon the capital, a woman aviator dropped

3 Quoted in Robert A. Divine, *The Illusion of Neutrality* (Chicago, 1962), p. 312.

peace leaflets over the White House, and radio loud-speakers bristled with isolationist oratory. Senator Borah, old and failing, led the attack. A revision of the Neutrality Law in favor of England and France, he warned, would tell the world that America had taken sides. "You will," he prophesied, "send munitions without pay and you will send your boys back to the slaughter pens of Europe." It would prove impossible, Senator Vandenberg noted, to "become an arsenal for one belligerent without becoming a target for another." Wisely the Democratic leadership, under the mentorship of Vice-President Garner, let the isolationists talk themselves out.

At last, the Senate passed the Pittman bill by a substantial majority. The proposal then went to the House, which tacked on a few amendments acceptable to the administration forces. It was signed by Roosevelt on November 4. From the domestic point of view, it is significant that only 6 Republicans in the Senate and 19 in the House voted "aye" in the final countdown. Roughly one-third of the membership of both houses, including a preponderant majority of Republicans, were unwilling to accept any compromise on neutrality. This determined opposition, which was to retain its numerical strength throughout the long trial ahead, compelled Roosevelt to move cautiously lest he alienate his marginal supporters in Congress.

True to the spirit of American politics, this Fourth Neutrality Law was a compromise measure. While the President gained the repeal of the arms embargo, the new law contained strong isolationist overtones. It was enacted while the Maginot Line still shielded the New World by confining Hitler's legions to central Europe. All exports for belligerents, whether implements of war or other goods, could leave the United States only if paid for and transported in foreign bottoms. The President was also empowered to delimit combat zones prohibited to American craft. The new law mirrored the schizoid state of American opinion, which demanded an Allied victory but not at the cost of involvement in the war.

The combat zones which Roosevelt promptly marked off forced the withdrawal of some ninety American ships from the Atlantic run, thus placing an increased burden on Allied shipping. A contemporary noted that closing the North Atlantic to American vessels strengthened the German submarine blockade as effectively "as if all our ships had been torpedoed." To make matters worse, England and France, clutching their dollar reserves in anticipation of a long war, failed to make heavy purchases after the lifting of the arms embargo. Contrary to all the well advertised warnings of the isolationists, the American war spirit was not whipped up by the sale of munitions, foreign propaganda, or Wall Street's machinations.

While the war in the West remained at a standstill, Stalin created a temporary diversion. First Poland was wiped off the map when the Soviets, according to previous arrangement, moved in from the east and met the German advance columns. After confirming the partition of Poland with the Nazis, Stalin forced the three Baltic countries to allow Russian bases on their soil. When Finland refused similar concessions, Russia attacked without bothering to declare war. To everyone's surprise, three thrusts of the Red army were blocked by unfavorable terrain and unexpectedly stiff resistance. When it became apparent that the Russian troops were not equipped for ski warfare, the democracies hoped that the Finnish lines would hold.

The attack on Finland, coming only three months after the execrable Nazi-Soviet Pact, excited American public opinion against Russia. But official Washington moved cautiously despite the frenzied pleas for aid to heroic Finland. The President and the Secretary of State guessed correctly that Stalin's main objective was to improve his defensive position by creating a protective buffer around the metropolis of Leningrad, which lay only thirty miles inside the border. Hull later explained that the administration was unwilling to take any steps that would drive the Soviets "further into the arms of Germany." Hence, the Neutrality Law of 1939 was not invoked in this Winter War and only token aid was extended to Finland.[4] The administration was saved from mount-

---

[4] The Export-Import Bank extended a credit to Finland of ten million dollars, with the proviso attached that the funds not be used for weapons. The administration allowed Helsinki to buy a few war planes in the United

ing pressure in Congress when, with the waning of the cold northern winter, the Russians crushed Finnish resistance.

This "war within a war" was only a side show. The main theater was still the western front and here an uneasy quiet prevailed. Hitler declared that no further disputes with the Allies existed now that the Polish question had been settled, and he called upon them to make peace. London and Paris refused, but they showed no serious intentions of preparing to break the deadlock by a spring offensive. Skeptics like Senator Borah called the whole affair a "phony war"; others, annoyed with the tedium, spoke disgruntledly of the "Great Boer War." This winter calm generated a malignant optimism on the part of the Allies and their American well-wishers. The Germans cleverly disguised their preparations and encouraged wishful thinking on the part of their foes. For the first seven months of the war, the western situation seemed firm. The French were certain that Hitler could never crack their "impregnable" Maginot fortress. Britain relied on the Royal Navy to crush Germany in the jaws of an economic vise, while the United States felt no acute sense of urgency, shielded as it was by the great Atlantic moat. In which direction could Hitler possibly move, asked the optimists? The Germans, argued these Pollyannas, faced another 1914–1918 stalemate, during the course of which they would be slowly choked to death by an Allied sea blockade.

President Roosevelt understood that the ocean was a highway as well as a barrier and that the strategic bridgeheads to the New World would be uncovered by a successful German push to the Atlantic Ocean. Why not gamble on one last attempt to bring peace in Europe before the Nazi terror struck again? Hence, he acquiesced in Sumner Welles's suggestion that he be sent to explore the European situation. Welles visited three war capitals and Rome, which was still officially at peace. He found Mussolini anxious to end the conflict, but a trip to Berlin convinced him that *Il Duce* had correctly assumed Hitler would lay down arms only on his own terms. Welles found London equally committed to vic-

---

States and instituted a "moral embargo" against the sale of airplanes to Russia. Julius W. Pratt, *Cordell Hull* [*The American Secretaries of State and Their Diplomacy*, Vols. XII–XIII] (New York, 1964) XII, 332–333.

tory. After another stop at Rome, where he made futile efforts to teach Mussolini the advantages of neutrality, Welles took ship for home on March 20, 1940. As Secretary Hull had predicted, Welles returned with no information that could be translated into policy. Washington could do nothing but watch and wait until one side or the other ended the wearisome "*Sitzkrieg.*"

Hitler soon demonstrated to the anxious world the increased tempo of modern warfare. The Germans had perfected their war-making techniques to the point where major countries could be conquered in weeks while smaller neighbors could be subdued in days or even hours. This revamped military strategy usually began with surprise mass air raids on the victim's cities, ammunition depots, and communication centers. Following this softening process, tanks and armored columns would pierce defenses, cut supply lines, and spread terror and confusion in the front and rear of the baffled defenders. Then the Nazi infantry would move in to clean up pockets of resistance. In the tempestuous spring of 1940, this revolutionary pattern of warfare was to play havoc with the map of western Europe.

Shortly before sunrise on the morning of April 9, the Danish government received a curt note from Berlin stating that the Germans had "indubitable evidence" that the Allies intended to turn Scandinavia into a military base. Copenhagen was told that all resistance would be crushed by overwhelming power; this force began to be applied even before the startled Danes could muster an answer to the German charge. Although Nazi preparation for this "Operation Weser" had been going on for three months, it was set in operation following an Allied announcement that they were mining the territorial waters of Norway. Denmark was occupied for its own "protection"; Norway tried to resist but Allied counter-moves were, in the idiom of the day, "too little and too late." Within six weeks, Norway became another German satrapy. Hitler had gained a strategic base from which he could step up air and submarine attacks on England, and his bottled surface fleet secured a wider base of operations. Americans, glued to their radios in those exciting days, found it difficult to believe that two proverbially neutralist Scandinavian countries had fallen prey to the Nazi vulture.

Men had hardly recovered their sense of balance before the scourge struck once more. Hitler's sledge hammer against Holland, Luxembourg, Belgium, and France fell on Friday, May 10. Holland fought for a hundred hours. The Belgian fortifications upon which France counted so heavily to stall the Nazi mechanized divisions, failed in their purpose. Within a week a *Panzer* outfit raced to the sea, cutting French communications and isolating the bulk of the French army from Anglo-French units fighting in Belgium. After King Leopold of Belgium surrendered, the ingenious British evacuated some 338,000 troops from Dunkirk, but their equipment was not salvaged. Had Hitler not been so insistent upon an immediate march into Paris, he might have pinned these troops against the sea. Dunkirk was a feat that aroused the admiration of the free world but as the new Prime Minister, Winston Churchill, realistically remarked, "wars are not won by evacuations."

The first days of June proved crucial for France. Could the Boche be stopped in a repetition of the 1917 miracle of the Marne? For a moment, the French put their faith in the aged General Maxime Weygand, who had been recalled from the Middle East to take command. But he, no more than his predecessor, was able to overcome the German superiority in planes, mechanized power, and superb military coordination. The government of Premier Paul Reynaud fled to Bordeaux, whence Reynaud hoped to cross over to Algiers and continue resistance with the help of the French navy. "Can you," Reynaud asked Roosevelt in a public message, "stretch your hand across the ocean to help us save civilization?" The demand that "this very day the weight of American power" be placed behind faltering France was politically and militarily impossible. No answer that it was in Roosevelt's power to give would have satisfied the defeatist French politicians who surrounded Reynaud. The Premier resigned to President Albert Lebrun, who, using his emergency powers, named Marshal Henri-Philippe Pétain to head a new government. This octogenarian, a pessimist by nature and a semi-Fascist by inclination, immediately sued for peace. Five days later, June 22, 1940, an elated *Führer* clicked his heels in unrestrained ecstasy as he accepted the French surrender in the same *wagon-lit*, in the same forest of Compiègne, where the Germans had capitulated twenty-two years before. Under the terms of the surrender, the Nazis occupied about half of France including Paris and a strip of the Atlantic coastline reaching down to the Spanish border. Following demobilization, Pétain was permitted to form a government for the unoccupied rump of his country. As all parties understood, this regime, with its capital at the spa resort of Vichy, was to exist at the fiat of Hitler. France, the second military power in Europe with the fourth largest navy in the world, had been reduced to vassalage in six weeks of actual combat. This cataclysm left England and the United States in a state of bewildered frustration.

In the feverish summer of 1940 the administration in Washington began to ponder the problem of dealing with Vichy France. A few weeks after the French defeat both houses of Parliament empowered the authoritarian-minded Marshal Pétain to draw up a new constitution. He chose to delay such action, and in dictatorial fashion gradually abolished parliamentary government. The distinct danger existed that France would re-enter the war on the side of Germany, for Vichy had broken relations with London when the British crippled main units of the French fleet to keep these ships out of Hitler's clutches. The German ambassador to Vichy, Otto Abetz, was an old Nazi hand who tried to win Pétain over to closer union with the Axis. The upshot was a secret agreement between Hitler and Pétain which left the door open for Vichy to find a preferred place in the new European order. Recognizing that Pétain was surrounded by outright Nazi collaborationists, Washington feared that remaining segments of the French fleet might be put at Germany's disposal and that the French African colonies could become Nazi Atlantic outposts.

Roosevelt and Hull had three alternatives. They could have broken relations with Vichy and ignored internal French problems; they might have recognized Charles de Gaulle, who was mustering Frenchmen who lay outside the Nazi orbit to continue resistance from his base in England, or they could decide to court Pétain's good will. The administration chose the latter course in the hope of minimizing Hitler's influence over Pétain and neutralizing the remaining French naval and colonial assets. London, though unable to repair the break with France, wanted the United States to keep an eye on Axis intrigues through the Vichy peephole.

Roosevelt determined to establish rapport with old soldier Pétain by appointing a military man to the key Vichy post. He chose retired Admiral William D. Leahy, who was ordered to cultivate personal ties with the marshal and to warn him that a surrender of French ships or bases to Hitler would cost him American friendship. The Admiral was also to offer Red Cross relief to the sorely pressed French colonies, always providing that such supplies would not be used to impede the British war effort.

During the sixteen months that Leahy spent in France he tried to check collusion with Germany, dispel Axis propaganda which foretold the coming doom of Britain, and take the measure of men in control. His greatest accomplishments stemmed from the work of Robert D. Murphy, a shrewd but unpretentious diplomat who had trekked with the French government from Paris to Vichy. Assigned to North Africa just before Leahy's arrival, Murphy arranged with General Weygand, the local French commander, for American officials stationed at strategic control points to supervise the distribution of fuel and other supplies to insure that nothing passed into hostile hands. "The result," writes Professor Pratt, "was a psychological and informational beachhead in North Africa for the future."

Historians are not agreed on the balance sheet of our controversial Vichy policy. Some authorities argue that we encouraged Pétain to resist German pressure, thereby withholding from Hitler's clutches French Africa and the remainder of the once proud French fleet. Viewed in this light, the labors of Leahy and Murphy helped make possible the 1942 "Torch" landings in North Africa. On the other hand, there is some merit to the opinion that our opportunism damaged our ideological image more than it helped our cause. Certain it is, however, that Hitler blundered badly in believing that unoccupied France would enlist in the Nazi cause. His failure to take all that belonged to defeated France in June, 1940, proved to be a colossal error.

In the meanwhile, a stunned America anxiously watched the majestic Churchill rally his people. They soon found that the new leader "possessed in supreme degree the qualities needed for the hour: vigilance, drive, joy of battle, love of responsibility, resounding eloquence, and above all courage and faith." His stentorian voice commanded the attention of the war-swollen radio audiences in the free countries. Can any American who heard Churchill's maiden broadcast as Prime Minister ever forget his sublime words?

I have nothing to offer but blood, toil, tears, and sweat. . . . You ask what is our policy? I will say: It is to wage war by sea, by land and air with all our might . to wage war against a monstrous tyranny never surpassed in the dark, lamentable catalogue of human crime.

This was no idle boast. Following the collapse of France, the intrepid war chieftain exploited to the full his country's remaining assets. He could count upon the tremendous exertions and courage of the British people, the support of the Dominions, the help of the Free French and other exiled groups, and above all the benevolent neutrality of the United States. Churchill's grasp of Roosevelt's political predicament was masterful. He prodded slowly but firmly, timing his moves with remarkable precision. With a candor that he failed to reveal while the issue was still pending, he later confessed that from the first his goal was full American participation in the war against Hitler.

Churchill's mettle was promptly put to the test. Hard on the heels of the French capitulation, the Germans launched an all-out air assault on the British Isles. Goering's *Luftwaffe* had a numerical superiority over the Royal Air Force. Yet, owing to the unexpected developments that so often determine the gambles of war, the Nazis lost this Battle of Britain. The British fighter planes were newer and better than the Nazi aircraft. The recent invention of radar made it possible for the defenders to anticipate enemy attacks, and the RAF was better organized and directed than its German counterpart. Hitler, inflated by his easy French victory, made some reckless miscalculations. When the British bombed

Berlin, he chose immediate retaliation in kind rather than the long-run objective of destroying RAF air fields and radar stations. The *Luftwaffe's* fury was met with the quiet and efficient civilian defense that formed part of Britain's "finest hour." Moreover, persistent rain and fog denied the "Jerries" the spell of clear weather so sorely needed by Goering's flyers. By the end of September it was evident that Britain could not be conquered by bombs. Two weeks later the planned invasion of Britain, code named "Operation Sea Lion," was permanently abandoned. Uncertain and vacillating in naval matters, Hitler had neglected to iron out serious interservice wranglings and this failure helped make "Sea Lion" an unthinkable military risk.[5] With Britain intact and growing in strength, thanks to American aid, Hitler would have to turn eastward for further battlefield glory. One is tempted to wonder if the Nazi leader, before he made his fatal decision to attack Russia, pondered Napoleon Bonaparte's cardinal error when he faced a similar situation.

The fall of France and the ensuing German air assault on Britain had aroused great concern for the security of the United States. Gamesters willing to wager on the future of humanity offered odds that the swastika would fly over Westminster before winter whipped up the waves of the Channel. What of the Atlantic moat if England decided to scuttle the fleet or if Churchill were to be replaced by a defeatist who would advise the King to surrender the Royal Navy? In the excitement of the hour, the actual threat to American safety was frequently overstated. At the same time, it was apparent that we had too long taken for granted the existence of a friendly British fleet on the Atlantic to help guard the western hemisphere.

Churchill made certain that Americans grasped the full implications of a Hitlerian victory. On May 15, even before the French breakdown, he warned Roosevelt that procrastination on his part might leave the United States with "a completely subjugated Nazified Europe established with astonishing swiftness." To prevent this tragedy, he asked the President to "proclaim non-belligerency which would mean that you would help us with everything short

[5] Walter Ansel, *Hitler Confronts England* (Durham, 1960), pp. 256–302.

of actually engaging armed forces."[6] FDR pointed out that he could hardly go so far without Congress, but he did promise to do what he could within the range of his constitutional authority. Clever legal legerdemain opened the way for the War Department to turn over to the British outmoded or surplus planes, rifles and artillery which helped compensate for the equipment lost in the hurried exit from Dunkirk.

This token gesture was just the beginning. The French surrender meant that the national interest had to be equated with future security. What of the Monroe Doctrine if the well-oiled Nazi propaganda machine in Latin America were to make malignant the conventional dictatorships that flanked our southern border? Hitler had exposed the Atlantic islands that formed the stepping stones to the New World. Only a short blue ocean space on the map separated Dakar, where French West Africa bulges out into the Atlantic, from the hump of Brazil that projects eastward toward it. If Hitler failed to subdue Britain with air power, it seemed likely that he would move southward through Spain into Africa. This was certainly a strong possibility and one that almost came to pass.

The specter of a Nazi victory also possessed a perplexing economic dilemma. Could we really do business with Hitler? A handful of last-ditch isolationists said yes, but the Nazi concept of foreign commerce was just as totalitarian as their notion of government. They regarded trade, not as a mutually beneficial exchange of goods, but as another tool that could be used to achieve diplomatic aims. The triumph of such a nation, linked by alliance to rapacious Japan and by diplomatic understanding with Communist Russia, boded ill for the future of our cherished free enterprise philosophy.

Granted, for the moment, that we could defend ourselves without Britain, and that a victorious *Führer* would heed his business-minded industrialists by making a satisfactory commercial treaty with us, there still remained the threat to our prized political beliefs. Did we want to try a hermit existence in a totalitarian world where England would be reduced to Vichy-like vassalage and where the congenial little European democracies would be con-

6 Quoted in Nelson M. Blake and Oscar T. Barck, Jr., *The United States in its World Relations* (New York, 1960), p. 652.

verted into German satellites? Few Americans relished the thought. While the Battle of France was still in doubt, the President asked Congress for appropriations to enable production of 50,000 planes a year, a huge increase in all categories of armaments, and enough additional tonnage to create a genuine two-ocean navy at the earliest possible moment. Congress responded by breaking all peacetime records for defense spending. Significantly, the bill which provided for the first peacetime draft in American history was sponsored by an anti-New Deal Democrat in the Senate and a Republican in the House. Roosevelt tried to further this bipartisan spirit by appointing Henry L. Stimson, who had served in two Republican cabinets, as Secretary of War, and Frank Knox, the defeated vice-presidential candidate in the 1936 election, as Secretary of the Navy. GOP stalwarts accused the President of playing politics on the eve of a presidential election, but the gesture was applauded by many in the opposition who argued that the world crisis must take precedence over the welfare of the Republican party.

There was virtually unanimous agreement that the European upheaval compelled an overhaul and enormous increase in our defense system. No one in a position of influence questioned the necessity of guarding the western hemisphere from all possible assaults. However, a corollary to this axiom divided the country. One group said that if we remained fully armed, at best the eventual outcome in Europe would not affect us and, at worst, if we had to fight for our liberty, then let it be in our own "back yard." The President, supported by majority opinion, as it turned out, insisted that we could best guarantee our own security by supplying liberal aid to those nations still standing up to Hitler.

The move toward this latter position began early. Shortly before France fell, FDR took a long step away from old-fashioned neutrality toward the nonbelligerency requested by Churchill. The day was June 10, 1940; the place was the old university town of Charlottesville, Virginia. The President was deeply disturbed, for he had just learned that Mussolini had fallen upon prostrate France. In a fiery speech Roosevelt pledged that the United States would extend material aid to countries resisting aggression and simultaneously would hurry up production so that "we ourselves in the Americas may have equipment and training equal to the task of any emergency and every defense. . . . Signs and signals call for speed—full speed ahead."

While the administration was trying to scour up large-scale aid for Britain, it was forced to meet several diplomatic problems posed by the European upset. Would Hitler, as conqueror of Holland and France, claim title to their "orphaned" New World colonies? Historically, the risk of such action appears negligible, but when Congress recapitulated the ancient American contention that no European power might transfer its western hemisphere holdings to another country, defiance from Berlin excited alarm. Washington was stirred to action on the Latin American diplomatic front for additional reasons. German salesmen and commercial attachés were writing orders for future delivery under threats that the Reich would retaliate against countries which refused to do business. Furthermore, wartime dislocations had upset Latin American economies and the State Department feared lest hard times pave the way for Fascist subversion.

Consequently, Secretary Hull rushed plans for another meeting of New World foreign ministers. It convened in Havana on July 21, 1940.[7] The Washington delegation secured the adoption of the Act of Havana providing for joint action in the event of violation of the "no-transfer" principle. In urgent cases one power was authorized to act alone, and inasmuch as this would probably involve only the United States, the provision tokened faith in the Good Neighbor policy. Political understanding was matched by American economic concessions and loans from the Export Import Bank to Latin American nations in order to offset the lures of Axis agents. Acting together, the New World nations were able to coordinate their defenses and mobilize their national resources.

In the meantime the United States began to sustain in earnest

---

[7] The first such wartime meeting had been held in Panama in the fall of 1939. The assemblage adopted the Declaration of Panama, which established a "safety-belt" of about 300 miles along the Atlantic south of Canada. This action was violated by both sets of belligerent powers and is important only in the context of future American actions to be explained in the following chapter.

the British cause. Churchill had no sooner taken office than he asked Roosevelt for a flotilla of overaged destroyers to help in convoy duty and in the defense of Channel waters. By midsummer, 1940, British naval needs were acute. Churchill had to prepare for possible invasion, and the submarine menace had increased as U-boats nested in French coastal ports. "Mr. President," the Prime Minister said bluntly, "I must tell you that in the long history of the world this is a thing to do *now*."

Roosevelt could readily spare the ships, for many of them had been decommissioned for years. But the President hesitated. What if our own destroyers should be lost to the Nazis with the balance of the Royal Navy? Was it possible to surmount the legal obstacles involved in a transfer that, by all existing standards, disregarded both domestic and international law? Moreover, the country was in the midst of a presidential campaign, and politics made bipartisan support for bold action in Congress unlikely.

A way out of Roosevelt's perplexity came from an unexpected quarter. A handful of internationally minded New York lawyers suggested that the destroyers could be exchanged under existing law for bases located on British New World possessions. Such a barter, they thought, would silence legal quibbles. Further, it would allay the isolationist protest that we were weakening our own defenses, for the bases would more than compensate for the loss of our superannuated ships.

Roosevelt eagerly picked up the proposal after making certain that the transfer would not evoke complete repudiation from the GOP presidential candidate, Wendell L. Willkie. There followed some haggling with Churchill. The doughty Englishman thought the swap a "sordid deal" and felt it beneath his dignity to promise that the King would never surrender the royal fleet. However, Churchill understood that Roosevelt needed legal justification for his action and so he agreed to compromise. An exchange of letters between Secretary Hull and the British ambassador worked out the details. This executive agreement (not requiring approval by the Senate) provided that in exchange for fifty overage destroyers the United States would receive rent free for ninety-nine years naval and air bases in six southern British possessions. To assuage

Churchill's pride, the two most important concessions, located in Newfoundland and Bermuda, were given "freely and without consideration." As to the future of the Royal Navy, Churchill gave informal assurances that it would be the Nazi fleet that would be destroyed, scuttled, or surrendered.

In announcing the deal, the President explained to the press that the eight bases had cost us only the value of the old ships in scrap –about a quarter of a million dollars. He called the transaction the greatest "reinforcement of our national defense that has been taken since the Louisiana Purchase." Perhaps this was an exaggeration, but with possible Nazi outposts only ten flying hours away from New World shores, the bases provided an excellent air screen guarding the approaches to the United States and the Caribbean. Moreover, the harbors they provided well suited the needs of light auxiliary craft pressed into use to guard the Panama Canal.

Constitutionally speaking, Roosevelt stood on vulnerable ground. Never before had a chief executive made so sweeping an arrangement by his own action, and it was obvious that he had not consulted Congress because he feared the results. Attorney General Robert H Jackson's opinion, which found warrant for the transaction under a forgotten domestic statute, split hairs to the point where a misplaced comma was pressed into service! The violation of international law was beyond question. Yet it seems fair to say that this destroyer-bases deal pleased most of the American people. Some, including Mr. Willkie, winced at the methods used to bring it about, but the majority were ready to overlook the means if they could achieve the goal of buttressing national security.

Great reluctance against the final plunge into war still existed. Nevertheless, a powerful segment of opinion was willing to sanction unusual risks to keep England in the field against Hitler. If necessary, this group would go even further, for it believed that the security of Great Britain was vital to the United States, Veteran internationalists, educators, Protestant and Jewish clergymen, eastern businessmen, and journalists were willing to devote time and money to the cause. Their initial intent had been to press for the repeal of the arms embargo. When the war burst into full fury with the Nazi offensives of 1940, Roosevelt appealed to William

Allen White to organize a nation-wide pressure group "to get the American people to think of conceivable consequences [of the war in Europe and Asia] without scaring the people into thinking that they are going to be dragged into this war."[8] The Committee to Defend America by Aiding the Allies, with White as national chairman, had as its original purpose the promotion of sentiment for halting the Axis by means "short of war." From its New York City headquarters, the outfit established regional offices which in turn sponsored the organization of hundreds of local chapters. Within less than six months, 733 units scattered throughout the country mustered some 10,000 active workers. Rallies were held, paid advertisements dotted the pages of influential dailies, countless leaflets were distributed, and a crescendo of pro-Ally letters were dispatched to members of Congress.

When it became apparent in December, 1940 that British pluck and grit might ward off but not subdue the Nazi terror, opinion within White's committee split sharply. The Kansas editor, a self-styled "abstentionist," demanded that a distinct line be drawn between material aid for England and action that would make American intervention inevitable. A more militant element, including President James B. Conant of Harvard University, formed the Century Group in New York City to preach that the survival of Great Britain was paramount to the preservation of peace.

The formation of a national pro-Ally group necessitated the creation of a corresponding isolationist organization. On September 4, 1940, just two days after the consummation of the destroyer-bases exchange, the America First Committee came into existence. The most formidable isolationist coalition in American history, it evolved from a Yale University student group led by R. Douglas Stuart, Jr. This twenty-four-year-old law student was the son of the first vice-president of the Quaker Oats Company in Chicago. These valuable contacts helped the younger Stuart gain the ear of some important midwesterners eager to weld the various isolationist elements into one national front. Suitably enough, the

[8] Quoted in Wayne S. Cole, *Senator Gerald P. Nye and American Foreign Relations* (Minneapolis, 1962), p. 177.

headquarters of America First was placed in Chicago, where General Robert E. Wood, chairman of the board of Sears, Roebuck and Company, presided as national chairman.[9]

America First chapters sprouted quickly throughout the country. Within six months, it boasted 450 groups and a roster of 800,000. Although the bulk of this support centered in the region dominated by metropolitan Chicago, about a quarter of the membership resided in northeastern urban areas. The list of prominent personalities who at one time or another rallied to its banner is imposing: Kathleen Norris, Irvin S. Cobb, Henry Ford, General Hugh S. Johnson, Chester Bowles, Amos Pinchot, Mrs. Nicholas Longworth, and, of course, Charles A. Lindbergh. Although the organization welcomed the help of all truly patriotic opponents of American intervention, its stewardship and financial backing rested upon conservative business elements irreconcilably opposed to Roosevelt's New Deal. The recognized authority on America First, Wayne S. Cole, has neatly summarized the aims of its responsible leadership:

Like all noninterventionists . . . [they] believed it was more important for the United States to stay out of the European war than to assure a British victory . . . They feared that the administration's moves to aid Britain short of war would lead to war itself. It was not a pacifist organization and it advocated construction of an "impregnable defense for America." The committee was charged with harboring pro-Fascists, but its leaders made earnest efforts to bar such persons from its ranks.[10]

America First was constantly embarrased by unwelcome fellow travelers. Until Hitler swung eastward against Russia, the Chicago outfit had to ward off Communists who would have liked to take over the organization. And Marxists aside, it was not always easy to be certain where the wearer of an America First button stood. Was he a rabid anti-New Dealer outraged at FDR as much for his encroachment on private enterprise as for his warmongering? An old-fashioned progressive who thought the President's foreign policy a Wall Street conspiracy to save its British investments? An

[9] *Ibid.*, pp. 177–178.
[10] *Ibid.*, p. 179.

uncompromising pacifist dedicated to the tenets of nonresistance? A German- or Italian-American loath to fight his Old World kinsmen? A father or mother more interested in the safety of a son than in the future of humanity? Or a disciple of Father Coughlin with pronounced pro-Nazi or anti-Semitic prejudices? Try as it would to shake off unwanted supporters, every pro-Fascist in the country was attracted to the orbit of America First. The organization's top echelon discovered that groups fighting for the same immediate purpose are held together by a magnetic force generated in the heat of the struggle. Although America First did not will it, circumstances dictated that it share a major objective with the Nazi Foreign Office—keeping the United States out of the war.

Some America First orators were prone to use excessively harsh language and to make nasty insinuations. Senator Nye, for instance, was coauthor of a resolution to investigate the warmongering propaganda of the motion-picture and radio-broadcasting industries, a move supported by America First. When Nye spelled out his complaints to the nation, he read off a list of Hollywood names that were distinctly Jewish. Charged with parroting the Nazi line, the Senator's answer was not too convincing: "as yet at least . . . [he was] bitterly opposed to the injection of anti-Semitism as a cause or issue in our American thinking and acting."[11] America First also suffered from the overzealousness of its other chief senatorial ally, Burton K. Wheeler. The Montana senator had championed liberal causes for a quarter of a century. Few men in Congress had supported the New Deal more vigorously although later he became the mastermind of the opposition to Roosevelt's "court-packing" plan. As a Democrat estranged from the administration, he found the America First lecture circuit a congenial outlet for his vitriolic platform language, albeit foreign policy issues had hitherto not engaged his interest. Wheeler still retained the old Populist-Progressive phobia that wars stemmed from an unholy alliance of international bankers, influential Jews, and greedy munition-makers. His biting stump oratory, intended for the listening ear rather than the reading eye, frequently boomeranged to discredit the isolationist cause.

11 *Ibid.*, pp. 186–189.

The noninterventionist crusade of Charles A. Lindbergh merits special attention. During his self-imposed exile in England, following the brutal murder of his infant son, Lindbergh paid several visits to Germany, where he was cordially received by Nazi kingpins. Originally he had pursued these contacts at the behest of an American military attaché at Berlin, but eventually he was overawed by what he saw. A 1938 inspection tour of the air might of leading European powers convinced Lindbergh of Nazi invincibility. He returned home persuaded that it was futile for the West to fight a Germany arrayed in full panoply.

With the isolationist-minded radio commentator, Fulton Lewis, Jr., as his sponsor, Lindbergh began his broadcasting career during the 1939 Polish blitz. From the beginning, he stressed that our bond with Europe was a racial one and he ignored or discounted conflicting ideologies which, *Time* observed accurately, "were not his meat." Competent observers began to note a sharp reversal in Lindbergh's logic. Originally he had maintained that the strength of the *Luftwaffe* left us no choice but to accept a Nazi victory with complacency; after the cataclysm of 1940, when men feared for the security of America, he underplayed air power and insisted that the spacious oceans made any attack on our shores all but impossible. He undoubtedly shared the views of his wife, Anne Morrow Lindbergh, whose book, *The Wave of the Future*, was a best seller in 1940. In some mystical fashion, the "Forces of the Past" were struggling with the "Forces of the Future," and that which other people considered totalitarian outrages against human decency, Mrs. Lindbergh explained away as evanescent "scum on the wave of the future."

Colonel Lindbergh did not join America First until April, 1941. In his first speech on behalf of the organization, he predicted that Britain would lose the war and opposed aid to prevent that eventuality. He claimed there was no way of launching a successful invasion against Nazi-held Europe or any hope of matching the striking power of the German Air Force. Sensitive by nature, unused to the rough and tumble game of politics, the Colonel became increasingly rash and bitter. When the President returned blow for blow, and implied that Lindbergh was a modern-day "Copperhead," Lindbergh resigned his commission in the air force. He became more and more of a loner. Slowly losing his sense of perspective, he was, as his biographer puts it, "driven step by step toward an at least tacit acceptance of those elements of Nazism which were most distasteful to him."[12]

Some Nazi-like racial slurs in his Des Moines speech in the fall of 1941 turned Lindbergh into a liability to the America First Committee. These remarks came at a time when responsible isolationists were trying to disassociate their movement from the unsavory racism of Father Coughlin and his copartner Gerald L. K. Smith. Lindbergh spoke of a small minority of "war agitators" whom he identified as the Anglophiles, the Roosevelt clique, and the Jews. He stated that he did not condone Hitler's anti-Semitism but added that, owing to their great influence over the mass media of communications, American-Jewish interventionist activities presented a danger "both for us and for them." Habitually purblind to the chemistry of human emotions, Lindbergh advised Jews to oppose war. He warned that they would be the first to feel the consequences of American involvement.

The colonel had pointed up the affinity that existed between the current variety of noninterventionism and a pernicious foreign ideology. The high command of America First refused to reprimand him, but they did state that they deplored "the injection of the race issue into the discussion of war or peace." Many outspoken isolationists tried to undo the damage, but Lindbergh made matters worse by questioning whether he would be denied the right of free speech and hinting that the administration might call off the next scheduled national elections.

It would be unfair to place all of the blame for the reversal of the fortunes of America First upon Lindbergh and its other protagonists. Regardless of the type of case they could have formulated, they could not have assured the majority that an Axis victory would not prove detrimental to the security, to the business interests, and to the most cherished political beliefs of their

---

[12] Kenneth S. Davis, *The Hero: Charles A. Lindbergh and the American Dream* (Garden City, 1959), p. 410. Mr. Davis's work contains the fullest account of Lindbergh's association with the America First Committee.

country. As Dexter Perkins has observed, "Time has placed their arguments in perspective, revealing that they were largely unsound." They predicted that involvement in war would destroy civil liberties at home, but instead the conflict engendered a broader conception of democracy. The isolationist leaders proposed a negotiated peace to end the conflict, but in the light of Hitler's frenzied zeal and Churchill's dogged resistance, a negotiated peace was out of the question. Probably America First was correct in assuming that in 1940 Hitler had formulated no war plans against the United States, but, as Professor Perkins concludes, "what he would have done after a decisive victory is a totally different matter."[13]

It is impossible to gauge accurately the influence of either the White Committee or America First at the height of their struggle to control public opinion. Contemporary observers may have overestimated the possibilities of organized propaganda and undervalued the impact on public thought of the onrushing pace of events. Time and again, Axis lunges and outrages came unwittingly to the aid of Roosevelt's supporters. Further, the America First combination had been welded just two months prior to the 1940 presidential election. By this time it was evident that the turn of events had prevented the isolationists from full exploitation of the issue of nonintervention. Before the fall of France, it seemed certain that the Republicans would nominate Senator Arthur H. Vandenberg, Senator Robert A. Taft, or the rising young GOP star, Thomas E. Dewey. All of these men, in 1940, tended toward isolationism and could have run on an appealing "no-foreign-war" platform.

But the Republican convention met just two days after the French surrender. The situation was further complicated by the eleventh-hour entry into the race of Wendell Willkie, a former pro-League Democrat whose candidacy was sponsored by eastern seaboard business, finance, and newspaper interests. Thanks to the mood of apprehension over the critical foreign situation and superb political timing and organization, the "Eastern Establishment" won

[13] Dexter Perkins and Glyndon G. Van Deusen, *The United States of America: A History*, 2 vols. (New York, 1962), II, 603–604.

a twin victory. First, the platform adopted called for "prompt" and "realistic" defense coupled with a promise of such aid to the victims of aggression as would not violate international law. Secondly, Willkie's supporters waged a blitz campaign which resulted in a victory for their candidate. The Republicans had nominated the most alluring personality to head a GOP ticket since the days of Theodore Roosevelt and one who, as far as circumstances permitted, would take a bipartisan approach to the crucial question of war or peace.

In all probability, President Roosevelt had decided in May to scrap precedent and run for a third term, but he carefully guarded his secret. Not until after the Republican convention did his Cabinet associates learn officially of his decision. The Democratic platform had to make certain concessions to the party isolationists, including Senator Wheeler, who helped draft it. The platform promise of aid to Britain was stronger than the Republican pledge, but it made a similar commitment against waging war "except in case of attack." Secretary Hull complained to the President of isolationist leanings in the platform, but the latter assured him that "he intended to state that there would be no change in our foreign policy."[14]

Roosevelt accepted the nomination in a radio broadcast, but then made no professed campaign speech until the middle of September. While the President kept busy with pressing affairs of state, interrupted only by occasional "nonpolitical" inspection tours of defense centers, Willkie spoke incessantly, exhausting his own fund of energy and the public's store of patience. During the summer the Republican nominee seemed a candidate in search of an issue, for he had previously endorsed many of the New Deal's domestic and foreign objectives. Moreover, the "no-third-term" exhortation failed to strike fire, and prosperity was returning as the preparedness effort poured money into many pockets. Willkie spared no effort to win, for it was not in his nature to reconcile himself to the inevitable. Republican professional politicians implored him "to abandon this nonsense about a bipartisan foreign

14 Pratt, *op. cit.*, XII, 351.

policy—to attack Roosevelt as a warmonger—to scare the American people with warnings that votes for Roosevelt meant wooden crosses for their sons and brothers and sweethearts."[15]

Frustrated and desperate, Willkie put the foreign policy issue back into his lagging campaign. He made a series of charges that the "third-term candidate" was secretly plotting war. Willkie himself promised that he would "never send an American boy to fight in any European war" and he flatly predicted that if the Republicans lost, American transports would be loading up with troops by April, 1941. This was, as Willkie disarmingly explained after the election, just "a bit of campaign oratory," but coming when it did, it forced Roosevelt to out-promise his plucky opponent. Letters from anxious parents demanding reassurances of peace flooded White House mail bags. The public wanted a false optimism about the future and so was given it.

Roosevelt was at his very best at a Madison Square Garden rally in New York City. He ridiculed the defense record of the GOP congressional leaders and set off the famous audience chorus of "Martin, Barton, and Fish." The President had already repeated the platform pledge that there would be no war except to repel attack, but while on the New England hustings he was inundated with telegrams predicting a Democratic defeat unless he spoke out in even more specific terms. Yielding to terrific pressure, he decided to include in his Boston address a few sentences that would rebound to plague him in the stormy months ahead:

While I am talking to you mothers and fathers, I give you one more assurance. I have said this before, but I shall say it again and again and again: Your boys are not going to be sent into any foreign wars.

Three days later in Buffalo he reiterated: "Your President says this country is not going to war."

And then, in a hotly contested election, Roosevelt won by a large electoral majority and a margin of about five million popular votes. Freed of immediate political concerns, the President could

15 Robert E. Sherwood, *Roosevelt and Hopkins: An Intimate History* (New York, 1948), p. 187.

now tackle the problem of stepping up help to Great Britain to the point where Churchill could hope to break the stalemated war with Germany.

The supreme crisis in the long foreign policy debate was precipitated shortly after the American electorate had returned FDR to the White House for an unprecedented third term. For months, the President had been seeking to break through the obstacles that blocked his aim to see London through to complete victory. How could he, in the face of existing laws, extend gigantic credits to a besieged Britain whose dollar reserves had been exhausted by heavy cash purchases? Was there not some method of dispelling the "business as usual" proclivity in order to accelerate production in the interest of our own defense and the British war effort? As he mulled over possible answers to these questions, the military situation deteriorated. A few months earlier Tokyo had negotiated a pact with her two Axis partners which looked as if it was aimed squarely at the United States. Mussolini had set the Balkans afire by invading Greece and, until the Greeks showed their mettle, few believed that *Il Duce* could be stopped. "Two worlds are in conflict," Hitler stated bluntly; "one of these two worlds must break asunder." The *Führer's* evident purpose was to crush democracy wherever it flourished. Long before Berlin hurled this latest defiance, Roosevelt had concluded that unless Churchill was reinforced sufficiently to win the war, "all of us in all the Americas would be living at the point of a gun."

This time Congress would have to be consulted. Secretary Stimson and other activists suggested outright repeal of the Neutrality Law so that American ships, freed of the combat zones restriction, could haul supplies across the Atlantic. Roosevelt, however, doubted that Congress would approve a bill that might easily provoke war by permitting our vessels to ply submarine-infested waters.

Still pondering the matter, the President left for some "mental refueling" aboard the cruiser *Tuscaloosa*. On December 9, a navy seaplane dropped alongside the ship to deliver a long letter from Churchill. The Prime Minister wrote that he took it for granted that America had decided to link its fate with Britain's. If so, then

Roosevelt was entitled to know the grim facts. The danger of England's sudden collapse had receded, but the German submarine threat remained, resulting in "the steady and increasing diminution of sea tonnage." The "crunch of the whole war," said Churchill, lay in the Battle of the Atlantic. Furthermore, England lacked the cash to pay for American orders now on file. Churchill indicated that he would leave the dollar nexus for Roosevelt to work out in his own way. Meanwhile the Prime Minister asked for three million tons of additional shipping and thousands of combat aircraft and training planes. "We ask," he added, "for an unexampled effort [on the part of the United States] believing that it can be made." With sufficient material aid forthcoming, he pledged that England, without American manpower, could put an end to the Third Reich. Aiming to influence American opinion, Churchill declared publicly: "Give us the tools, and we will finish the job."

Roosevelt studied Churchill's proposals for two days and then moved swiftly. At a press conference held the day after his ship reached port, he nonchalantly outlined his plan, characteristically concealing that he had spent many hours in lonely decision. Roosevelt's scheme was a political master-stroke, for he carefully linked the success of Great Britain's efforts with American national security. He would throw our own war production into high gear and then, if the materials that came off the assembly lines were essential to the immediate needs of Britain, we would either lease or sell some of them "to the people on the other side." To avoid a fresh snarl of war debts, he suggested that America forget that "silly, foolish, old dollar sign." In one of his most telling homespun parables, the President explained that if the house next door were on fire, one would not bother to say: "'Neighbor, my garden hose cost me $15; you have to pay me $15 for it.' You connected it up and helped put out the fire, and later you got the hose." When an insistent press hawk queried whether such an arrangement would not lead to war, FDR replied emphatically: "No, not a bit of it." Here was the nucleus of the Lend-Lease proposal.

On December 29, 1940, Roosevelt presented his plan to the country in a frank and straightforward fireside chat. He declared that the United States must become "the great arsenal of democracy." He admitted that this build-up might possibly lead to war, but he hoped that a majority would agree with him that his proposed step "involves the least risk now and the greatest hope for world peace in the future."

A week later, in his annual message to the newly elected Congress, the President presented his plan in full detail. In a spurt of idealism which invoked memories of Woodrow Wilson, he foresaw the day when the four great freedoms cherished by all popular governments would prevail throughout the world.

Meanwhile Treasury officials had been hurriedly drafting House Resolution 1776, euphemistically entitled a bill to promote the "defense of the United States." After final touches by the White House and the approval of sympathetic congressional leaders, it was introduced into the House on January 10, 1941.

It would be difficult to imagine a more radical break with either conventional neutrality or the newfangled neutrality of the 1930's than this Lend-Lease proposition. The President was authorized, under any terms that he thought proper, to lend, lease, sell, or barter arms, ammunition, food, or any "defense article" or to release any military information to "the government of any country whose defense the President deems vital to the defense of the United States." Secretary Hull explained the thinking of the administration to the nation. He said that the United States was forced to take this step lest the control of the seas pass into hostile hands. In the event of such a catastrophe, he warned that the New World would no longer be immune from attack. Here lay the gist of the controversy which was to stir Congress for two months: was the defense of Great Britain vital to the security of the United States?

The administration forces were ably led and they successfully beat down all crippling amendments. Both houses of Congress held public hearings. The case of the noninterventionists that the bill would surely lead to war was heard out, but leaders from all walks of life, including Wendell Willkie, supported the President's contention that mammoth aid to Britain short of actual war was, despite the risks entailed, the lesser evil. Senator Taft, who in 1939 had voted in favor of repealing the arms embargo, now lent his great talents to the isolationists. The Ohioan argued that, granted Roosevelt's premise that American security warranted an all-out effort to support Britain, then logic would demand that we start shooting, for the contention would have been accepted that it was *our* war. There was a good deal to be said for this point of view, but FDR was interested in immediate results, and he refused either to tackle this fundamental issue or to speculate whether we might be forced to deliver the goods produced by our "arsenal of democracy." The administration held firmly to the old adage "sufficient to the moment is the evil thereof," and allowed the bill to pass with a specific disavowal that anything in the new law permitted American convoys to carry "defense articles" across the submarine-plagued Atlantic.

The congressional debates reveal that lend-lease was opposed by two different groups for somewhat divergent reasons. The arch-isolationists held that the measure would lead to war with Germany and, while the conflict was pending, would milk the United States of resources needed for its own defense. "Kill Bill 1776, not our boys," said their sloganeers. Senator Wheeler was reported as saying that lend-lease was the New Deal's "Triple-A foreign policy to plow under every fourth American boy," Then an angry President told reporters, "Quote me on that. That really is the rottenest thing that has been said in public life in my generation."

More temperate opinion (including that of Senator Taft and his long-time mentor former President Hoover) wanted to extend a loan of two billion dollars to England instead of offering a virtually unlimited store of supplies. This group vented its anger against the provision which allowed the President to determine to which countries lend-lease was to flow. Inasmuch as rumors were already rife about an eventual day of reckoning between Germany and Russia, conservatives were loath to entrust Roosevelt with the power to put the resources of the United States at Stalin's disposal. They were unable, however, to amend the bill in such a way that would exclude shipments to Russia if the President should ever deem such aid essential to our own security.

When the votes were tallied, the administration won a clear victory in both houses. However, the final count (317 to 71 in the

House, 60 to 31 in the Senate) connoted strong dissent, especially in the Senate. This and the venomous nature of the debates gave Roosevelt pause, for still bolder proposals might well upset his margin of victory. Lend-lease went into effect with lightning speed. In less than a half hour after Congress completed its task, the bill lay on Roosevelt's desk and the formalities of signing it into law took only a matter of minutes. The next day the President asked for an initial appropriation of seven billion dollars—more than ninety times the amount of the national debt funded by Alexander Hamilton in Washington's first term! At this point the Republican leadership bowed to the administration's appeal for united action in the national interest and supported the implementation of lend-lease. The first installments of what was eventually to reach the staggering sum of fifty billion dollars in assistance went out to the British, who were holding Hitler at bay, and to the Greeks, who, to everyone's surprise, were repulsing Mussolini's invasion.

The American public was not privy to the entire extent of what Cushing Strout has aptly termed our "common-law alliance" with the anti-Axis forces. Early in 1941 military and naval officers, representing the British Chiefs of Staff, arrived in the United States to engage in long-run strategy talks with corresponding American officials. Anticipating the passage of the Lend-Lease Bill, they agreed on the most effective use of this help and laid plans for future cooperation if and when the United States became an open belligerent. Many months before Pearl Harbor it was decided that if Japan entered the conflict, the West would nevertheless concentrate first on the defeat of Hitler. To lessen the direct commitment, Roosevelt did not sign this "ABC-1 Staff Agreement," but that was only a technicality.

Even without knowledge of these top-secret arrangements, Hitler understood that the United States had halted only short of a declaration of war. American flags waved proudly in the bomb-shattered streets of London. As Prime Minister Jan Christian Smuts of the Union of South Africa put it, "Hitler has at last brought America into the war." This overstated the case, for in March, 1941, the bulk of American opinion still opposed a hot war with Germany. But events in Europe and Asia were destined to thwart their desire. The noninterventionists had correctly predicted that the adoption of lend-lease would mark a point of no return for the United States. Production of war material would mandate delivery under convoy; convoying would lead to an undeclared naval war with Germany. Meanwhile the fortunes of war took an unexpected turn when Hitler decided to add Soviet Russia to his list of enemies.

CHAPTER X

Edging Toward War

For the Axis powers it was always on Sunday! On June 22, 1941, Germany hurled a massive assault against Russia, sending the war into another tailspin. The opening of a 2,000-mile front against the Soviets proved an unexpected boon for Hitler's other enemies. Britain received a reprieve from aerial pounding; the United States gained precious time for military preparations. On the other hand, Russia's plight goaded Japan into the southward advance that finally precipitated war with the United States.

For once, in the case of Russia, the West was not caught by surprise, for intelligence reports had confidently forecast the invasion. Russo-German relations had been deteriorating for many months. Stalin was determined to collect immediate spoils in the Balkans rather than accept Hitler's cynical invitation to expand southward "in the direction of the Indian Ocean." Yet, even had the Russian dictator been more accommodating, it is probable that Hitler eventually would have made war upon him. The subjection of the Soviet state was integral to Hitler's master plan of conquest.[1] The *Führer* thought the Soviet empire a jerry-built structure sure to collapse with one "kick in the door." Late in 1940 Hitler ordered the implementation of "Barbarossa," the code name

[1] See Gerhard Weinberg, "Hitler's Image of the United States," *American Historical Review*, LXIX (July, 1964), 1006–1021.

for the Russian offensive. He expected a speedy victory, after which he would use Russia's immense resources to bring Great Britain to her knees. Meanwhile, freed from fear of the Soviets, Japan might step up her timetable in the Far East enough to keep the United States so busy that further help to England would be unthinkable.

Unfortunately for the Germans, Hitler's schedule was upset by Mussolini's impetuous invasion of Greece. Hitler was forced to secure his Balkan flank before he marched against Russia. Shielding the entrance to Greece from the north stood the heroic Yugoslavs who held the Nazis at bay long enough so that Hitler lost five weeks of good weather before he was free to launch "Barbarossa." Had the offensive been started at the appointed date, it is entirely possible that the Nazis might have broken the back of Soviet resistance before the onset of the harsh Russian winter.

The bomb-ridden British enthusiastically welcomed their newly found ally. "I have only one purpose," Prime Minister Churchill commented, "the destruction of Hitler." And he added, "If Hitler invaded Hell, I would make at least a favorable reference to the Devil in the House of Commons." Words of conciliation were followed by the delivery of generous British supplies to Stalin. Inasmuch as the bulk of this matériel was sent by the long oceanic route around North Cape, Nazi aircraft from Norwegian bases preyed heavily on convoys bound for Russia's Arctic ports. One result of the Russian invasion was to place an additional burden upon British sea power. Now the Royal Navy had to keep the sea lanes open as far east as Murmansk and Archangel.

Roosevelt's task in buttressing Russian resistance was far more delicate than Churchill's. For the moment, the Russo-German war seemed to bolster the arguments of America First. The isolationists now demanded that the Red and Brown terrors be allowed to destroy each other in mortal combat. From their angle of vision, Providence had afforded humanity a supreme opportunity for the mutual destruction of two evil ideologies. "The war party," stated an isolationist broadside, "can hardly ask the people of America to take up arms behind the red flag of Stalin." Fifteen top Republican leaders, including Herbert Hoover, Alfred M. Landon, and

Charles G. Dawes, jointly declared that the Anglo-Russian alliance had turned the war into a power struggle utterly unrelated to the preservation of global liberty and democracy. Catholic journals with Coughlinite leanings warned of the moral ruin that would result from any *mésalliance* with the "Godless Soviets." Yet liberal Catholic organs such as *America* and *Commonweal* overcame their repugnance to Communism to agree in substance with Walter Lippmann that the United States and the Soviet Union were "separated by an ideological gulf and joined by the bridge of national interest."

While the Nazi *Panzer* divisions were pinning the Russian defenders back toward Moscow, the isolationists on Capitol Hill showed a sudden splurge of voting power. A plague-on-both-their-houses sentiment swept Congress as the terms of 900,000 draftees, mustered into service under the 1940 law, were about to expire. The War Department's request for an extension of these terms of duty led to acrimonious debate as Republicans insisted that the government was under contract to these men to release them at the expiration of their year of service. The publicized remark of a British general that "we certainly are going to need American manpower" forced the administration to deny plans for a new AEF and to base the extension of the draft on hemispheric security needs. After a protracted debate, a bill to extend the term of service by six months passed the Senate. On August 12, 1941, the House concurred by the paper-thin margin of 203 yeas to 202 nays.

The ultimate Russian triumph over Germany, made possible by generous American help, eventually substituted one totalitarian threat for another. When this misfortune became apparent, it brought to mind Senator Robert A. Taft's prediction that Stalin would prove to be a greater menace to the freedom-loving world than Hitler. Even if one grants this questionable conclusion, such a concession does not in any way minimize the dire Nazi peril of 1941. If Hitler had conquered Russia, he might well have joined Japan in a successful attempt to impose the new European and Asiatic orders upon the balance of the world. It *might* not have happened, but it was a risk that no responsible American statesman could have taken.

Although Roosevelt had promised Churchill aid for Russia in the event of a German invasion, the President moved cautiously. At first, he only freed forty million dollars in frozen Soviet funds and refrained from invoking the Neutrality Law against her. However, he made it perfectly clear that the United States stood ready to help Stalin if the Red army was able to stabilize a front against Hitler. Almost to a man, the President's military advisers placed no faith in Russian survival, and the force of the initial German thrust seemed to bear out their pessimism. But Roosevelt and Hull were more sanguine and future events vindicated their judgment. While the Nazi armies were pushing steadily eastward, Roosevelt sent his closest confidant, Harry L. Hopkins, to Moscow to determine Stalin's most pressing needs. As a consequence of this visit, the United States pledged Russia massive economic assistance. Upon returning from his August, 1941, rendezvous with Churchill, Roosevelt told congressional leaders that the survival of Russia was absolutely essential to victory over Hitler, and he indicated that aid to the sorely pressed Soviets would have to be on a long-term basis. Nonetheless, he prudently waited until Congress approved a new lend-lease appropriation before he declared Russia eligible for such assistance.

Roosevelt also faced a growing problem in the delivery of lend-lease shipments. In the spring of 1941 Germany augmented her Atlantic submarine drive. U-boats now combed the sea lanes in "wolf packs." In order to increase the range of its striking power, Berlin stretched the war zone westward to the mid-Atlantic. Nazi surface raiders ventured out of their lairs to aid the submarine offensive while part of the *Luftwaffe* was assigned to scout the seas for enemy vessels. As a result of these new methods, over half a million tons of shipping were destroyed in each of three successive months. It seemed foolhardy to strain the American economy to produce myriads of defense articles only to allow Nazi U-boats to send so many precious cargoes to the bottom of the Atlantic.

The President was fully aware of the critical situation but his spokesmen in Congress, during the debate over the Lend-Lease Bill, had created the impression that no need would arise for American delivery of supplies to England. Roosevelt therefore avoided blanket action. Slowly he used his powers as commander-in-chief to increase American commitments in the naval war. He authorized naval yards to repair damaged British vessels, he put Coast Guard cutters at the service of the British anti-submarine patrol, and he seized for American use some forty interned ships of Danish registry.

These measures were not sufficient to check the submarine peril. Members of his Cabinet, particularly Secretaries Ickes, Knox, and Stimson, wanted him to throw caution to the winds and authorize the delivery of American goods by American naval power. But Roosevelt hesitated because he did not think that public opinion was prepared to accept outright convoying. Refusing to outrun the possibilities of domestic politics, the President preferred to play the game by ear, gauging each new step by his own estimate of its probable public reception.

Although he withstood the pressure for a faster pace toward full belligerency against Germany, Roosevelt did make several far-reaching decisions in the spring of 1941. He pushed the hemispheric neutrality zone (proclaimed by the 1939 Conference of American Foreign Ministers but subsequently violated by both belligerents) far out into the Atlantic. This American decree incorporated Greenland into the limits of the western hemisphere. It also meant that henceforth the American navy would patrol the waters of the western Atlantic for U-boats and inform nearby British ships and planes of their position. Moreover, in April, 1941, the administration concluded an arrangement with the anti-Nazi Danish minister in Washington providing for American occupation of Greenland, where the Germans had set up concealed weather stations. This irregular agreement, repudiated by the captive Danish government, provided the American navy with useful bases from which it could effectively patrol the western sector of the North Atlantic. Further, the President struck the Red Sea region from the list of combat zones prohibited to American craft, thus making possible direct shipment of goods to the British forces guarding the vital Suez waterway.

The month of May, 1941, was particularly grave for the anti-Nazi cause. The war was going badly on all fronts—on the barren stretches of Africa, where the able General Erwin Rommel turned an Italian rout into a successful Axis counteroffensive; in the Balkans, where Hitler was mopping up pockets of organized resistance; and in the Atlantic, where the submarine toll was staggering. Nazi concentrations on the Norwegian coast facing Iceland loomed ominously as an additional threat to the North Atlantic convoys. In desperation, Churchill asked for an American declaration of war as a "decisive counterweight" to the Nazi advance. Roosevelt shrank from this drastic request, but he tried to alert the country to its peril by proclaiming an "unlimited national emergency." "Our patrols," he admitted in an unusually frank fireside chat, "are helping now to insure delivery of the needed supplies to Britain. All additional measures necessary to deliver the goods will be taken. We will not accept a Hitler-dominated world."

With each passing month, the United States drew nearer to actual participation in the Atlantic war. On July 1, we negotiated an agreement with Iceland (which had declared its independence from Denmark) permitting American troops to replace British and Canadian garrisons stationed on that island country. Inasmuch as the 4,000 American troops in Iceland had to be supplied, our own naval escorts began to protect American and Icelandic ships as far as Reykjavik. These convoys were given secret orders not only to "patrol" the seas as far as Iceland, but also to destroy any hostile force that challenged their passage. This decision greatly eased the strain on Britain. Now the Royal Navy had to protect only the short leg of the North Atlantic crossing from Iceland to the northern Scottish ports. Thereafter, it was only a matter of time before Roosevelt would sanction the convoying of all friendly shipping to Iceland, more than three-quarters of the way across the ocean.

Before this decision was reached, Roosevelt met Churchill for a shipboard conference off Argentia, Newfoundland. This long overdue conference of August 9 to 12, 1941, came at a critical juncture in the war. The Nazis were pushing toward Moscow while the restless Japanese were edging slowly toward the strategic Allied possessions which lay south of the Chinese mainland. Therefore, high on the informal agenda at this "summit" meeting was the bolstering of Russian might and morale as well as plans for checking Tokyo's advance in southeast Asia. This was a unique colloquy, unprecedented in history, for Roosevelt represented a country which still professed technical neutrality. Further, top-level diplomatic discussions were paralleled by strategy talks between high-ranking British and American military and naval officers.

The personal encounter between President and Prime Minister proved more important than any specific decisions reached at the Atlantic Conference. However, the flow of lend-lease supplies was speeded up and special consideration was given to Russian needs. Churchill argued vigorously for a stern warning to deter Japan from attacking British Malaya or the Dutch East Indies. Roosevelt tentatively promised a strong statement, but its teeth were subsequently drawn by the State Department.

The most publicized by-product of Argentia was a press release which embodied the terms of the so-called Atlantic Charter. This eight-point declaration provided a prospectus for the postwar world. Recalling all too vividly the fate of the Fourteen Points, Roosevelt hesitated to limit his freedom of action at any future peace conference, albeit he was anxious to put Churchill on record as to the purity of his war aims. The Charter disavowed Anglo-American territorial ambitions; both parties promised to be guided by the yardstick of self-determination in making the peace and pledged themselves to promote a fair distribution of raw materials so that in the future "all men in all lands may live out their lives in freedom from fear and want." In addition, at the war's end, the two countries would disarm all aggressors "pending the establishment of a wider and permanent system of general security." Ultimately the Atlantic Charter was to join the Fourteen Points on the scrap heap of forgotten pledges, but it succeeded in its immediate purpose of lifting the hopes and strengthening the will of those people trying to hold in check the Axis Juggernaut.

"Perhaps it was at Argentia," Dexter Perkins has speculated, "that the President came to the conclusion that sooner or later the United States would have to enter the war." This might very well be the case, but such a secret determination did not solve the

President's dilemma. His chief military advisers, still underestimating Russian powers of resistance, told him that Hitler could not be stopped short of full American participation in the war. Yet FDR knew that even if he pried a declaration of war out of a reluctant Congress, he would badly divide the country. It is doubtful if the President spent much time contemplating his predicament, for he faced an immediate task that required his entire attention. At Argentia he had agreed to permit all friendly vessels to join the American convoys bound for Iceland. He was pondering the problem of how to inform the country of his commitment when a suitable opportunity presented itself.

On September 4, 1941, a German U-boat fired on the American destroyer *Greer* while she was on patrol duty southwest of Iceland. The *Greer* had veered from her course to trail the submarine and was signaling a nearby British patrol plane when the German torpedoes were launched. Without disclosing all the facts, Roosevelt delivered a history-making fireside chat. He accused the U-boat of "piracy, legally and morally," and revealed that he had ordered the navy to exterminate these "rattlesnakes of the Atlantic" now poaching on our defensive waters. Here was the disclosure that the United States was guarding all shipments from the American mainland to Iceland.

No matter how reckless Hitler was on other occasions, he wanted to avoid the kind of naval incidents which would give Roosevelt an excuse for all-out war. The German dictator was anxious to finish with Russia; then there would be time to settle other scores. Yet the Nazis could not allow the frustration of their U-boat efforts. On the night of October 16–17, the destroyer *Kearney* was torpedoed while doing convoy duty on the Iceland run. Eleven members of the crew perished in the attack, but the destroyer managed to make port. "We have wished to avoid shooting," the President stated, "but the shooting has started. And history has recorded who fired the first shot." Four days after this broadcast, the *Reuben James* became the first American warship sunk in World War II. The undeclared naval war against Germany was now in full swing.

The President asked Congress to repeal that section of the

Neutrality Law which forbade the arming of merchant carriers engaged in foreign commerce. This self-imposed handicap made no sense at a time when the navy was guarding cargo ships en route to Iceland. The President also hinted that Congress might wish to reconsider that part of the 1939 law which set up war zones prohibited to American craft. We should, he insisted, "deliver American goods under the American flag." Yet, even at this late date, Roosevelt assured Congress that his goal was not war. It was, he suggested, a return to the time-honored American principle of maintaining the freedom of the seas.

The prewar isolationists made their final stand in the six-week debate which ensued, but they were doomed to one final defeat. Congress repealed the most important sections of the 1939 law. Still, the end results were disquieting. The administration forces had carried the House in the final tally by the slender margin of eighteen votes. Reports from the country at large were similarly disturbing to those advisers of the President who felt that we must make war for the sake of our own ultimate security. Although public opinion polls disclosed that a majority approved of stop-Hitler measures that involved a clear risk of war, the same samplings showed that a majority opposed an outright declaration of war. Regardless of this schizoid reaction, a slim majority in Congress had removed all effectual neutrality safeguards. American vessels were now free to sail into the fiercely contested sea zones which washed the British Isles. In the nature of things, maritime incidents were certain to become more frequent and more serious.

Could the tension have continued indefinitely without a formal declaration of war on the part of an irate *Führer* or an exasperated Congress? It is idle to speculate on this riddle in view of the fact that eight days after the President approved the law abolishing combat zones, a Japanese task force sailed for its surprise visit to Hawaii. The bombs that it dropped over Pearl Harbor were lethal, but some of Roosevelt's most perplexing problems vanished with the smoke which they generated. Impelled by the deterioration of the Atlantic situation, Japan advanced in the Pacific. On December 7, 1941, the two crises merged to become the greatest war in modern history.

Although American-Japanese relations had been severely strained in the later 1930's, there was, until after the fall of France, little danger of an open rupture. American eyes were focused on the Nazis while Japanese activities were temporarily halted when Hitler made his 1939 pact with their ancient enemy, Soviet Russia. Japanese pride was deeply hurt by Hitler's double-dealing. The Anti-Comintern Pact of 1936 had excluded separate political treaties with the USSR unless there was prior consultation with other signatories. The episode illustrates Paul W. Schroeder's cogent observation that Germany and Japan were "faithless allies who exploited each other whenever possible and betrayed each other when necessary." The Nazi-Soviet Pact was further disturbing to the Japanese because they had hoped, after securing their objectives in China, to attack Siberia.

On July 26, 1939, the United States had delivered a sharp warning to Japan. Washington gave Tokyo the required six months' notice of termination of the 1911 commercial treaty between the two countries. This action informed Japan that the United States stood ready to use strong economic retaliation against any further upset of the Far Eastern status quo.[2] After January 26, 1940, the United States would be free to deny to the Japanese war machine essential American imports of iron, steel, and oil.

In the initial stage of the European war, the Roosevelt administration moved warily against the Japanese in the hope of driving a wedge into the Axis coalition. Washington merely repeated its opposition to the "new order" in Asia and sent some reinforcements to its Pearl Harbor bastion in the Pacific. Prior to the Nazi military breakthrough of 1940, the Japanese showed similar restraint. Tokyo ended its border clashes with Russia, tried once more to liquidate the "China Incident," and made overtures to Washington designed to forestall an embargo when the commercial treaty expired. Albeit opposing American views on China made a new commercial

[2] The immediate reason for Washington's action was the fact that Japan had, a few days before, forced the British to recognize the "special requirements" of the Japanese army in China. Abrogation of the treaty was meant to be "a gesture of disapproval." Julius W. Pratt, *Cordell Hull* [*The American Secretaries of State and Their Diplomacy*, Vols. XII–XIII] (New York, 1964), XIII, 458.

agreement impossible, the Roosevelt administration paid little heed to popular demands for strong economic sanctions against Japan. When the treaty of 1911 finally lapsed, action was confined to making slight additions to the category of commodities falling under the existing voluntary embargo. The balance of traffic with Japan was placed on a day-to-day basis in the hope of deterring Tokyo from strengthening its ties with Berlin and from pushing toward strategic Allied holdings in the South Pacific.

As long as the western European front remained stabilized, Japan was careful not to defy the West by deepening her Axis entanglements. This policy of caution became manifest when, in January, 1940, a Cabinet shake-up brought to power Admiral Mitsumasa Yonai and a ministry of moderates. The new Japanese leaders seemed anxious to steer clear of the European conflict and they tried to attest their friendliness to the democracies by making a fresh effort to end the fighting in China. For the time being, the Roosevelt-Hull policy of putting Japan on her good behavior subject to economic retaliation looked promising. This maneuver might have worked but for the dazzling German military victories of 1940. The power upheaval that followed the fall of France bolstered the arguments of the Japanese activists. The distress of the West afforded an opportunity to divert attention from the bogdown in China and to focus it upon the lush Anglo-French-Dutch Pacific possessions that seemed ripe for the picking. This glance southward would heighten American-Japanese tensions. Washington dared not allow these territories, with resources vital to continued British resistance, to fall into Japanese hands. On the other hand, Japan could not resist the temptation to turn from the deadlocked war with Chiang toward the plentiful rice fields, productive rubber plantations, and rich oil fields that beckoned from the south.

The discreet Yonai Cabinet dragged its heels until France had actually surrendered. It then secured some concessions from the bewildered West, but these did not satisfy the expansionist appetite of the army. Yonai resigned in July, 1940, and was succeeded by Prince Fumimaro Konoye as Premier, with Yosuke Matsuoka as Foreign Minister and General Hideki Tojo in the War Office.

The accession of this triumvirate boded ill for the future of American-Japanese relations. Konoye had been the chief architect of the "new order"; Matsuoka was a boastful, garrulous individual who had led the Japanese walkout from the League of Nations, while Tojo was known to sympathize with the extremists. The American ambassador to Japan bluntly warned his superiors that these men would pay scant attention to western rights and interests.

The Konoye government promptly increased the pressure on the helpless French regime in Vichy for the privileges of constructing air fields and stationing troops in the northern sector of Indochina while demanding additional allotments of crude oil from the Dutch East Indies. The French reluctantly acquiesced. The Dutch, backed by the United States, managed to keep their concessions to a minimum.

In September, 1940, the Konoye regime sketched a bold plan of future acquisitions. The backbone of the new Japanese Empire was to be the home islands, Manchuria, and China. From this nucleus Nipponese control would spread to "the former German islands under mandate, French Indo-China and Pacific Islands, Thailand, British Malaya, British Borneo, Dutch East Indies, Burma, Australia, New Zealand, India, etc." The Philippines were by-passed for the moment, but the "etc." was a clear hint that the list of places earmarked for conquest could be easily expanded.[3]

This voracious territorial appetite could be satisfied only if Hitler approved and if the United States refrained from interference—a brace of diplomatic aims which were mutually exclusive. Upon the arrival of a new German ambassador in Tokyo on September 7, 1940, the Japanese began to sound out the Reich. Hitherto the *Führer* had been somewhat cool to grandiose Japanese plans for expansion, but conditions now compelled him to second thoughts on the subject. The United States had just concluded the destroyer-bases exchange with Britain. Perhaps a new wave of aggression in the Far East could keep Washington from further help to London. Besides, Japan's ambitions might lead her into war against Britain, and if Singapore fell in the course of the

[3] Richard W. Leopold, *The Growth of American Foreign Policy* (New York, 1962), p. 584.

fighting, this loss might force the capitulation of stubborn England. Hitler had nothing to lose by tightening the chains of his alliance with Japan.

On September 27, 1940, Germany, Italy, and Japan concluded a Tripartite Pact. Tokyo recognized the leadership of her Axis partners in Europe and they blessed the "new order" in Asia. The core of the agreement was Article III. This promised mutual assistance "if one of the three Contracting Powers is attacked by a Power at present not involved in the European War or in the Chinese-Japanese conflict." To dispel all doubt that this provision was aimed at the United States, a subsequent provision specifically excluded Russia. One of three secret understandings stipulated that questions concerning the obligations for assistance under the terms of Article III were to be decided by consultation. The Pact was probably taken less seriously by Japan than by the United States, but unfortunately the Japanese never made it entirely clear that their promises to the Reich were something less than appeared on parchment. From the American point of view, Japan was now part of a global Fascist challenge. The alliance seemed of no benefit to Japan unless Tokyo was determined to push southward. It could be of little assistance in crushing Chiang's annoying resistance or in attacking Stalin, who in 1940 was believed to be aligned with Hitler. The negotiation of the Pact was followed by a distinct hardening of the American attitude toward Japan.

At first Roosevelt and Hull had merely desired to deter Tokyo from a thrust into the South Pacific. In the perilous months following the fall of France, Washington's attention was fixed on the desperate plight of England and its own preparedness campaign. Nevertheless, in the summer of 1940, after the British ambassador pointed out that American exports were fueling the Japanese war machine, the President embargoed aviation gasoline, lubricating oil, and top-grade qualities of ferrous scrap. This order was only a minor annoyance to the Japanese. They converted low-octane gasoline into aviation fuel and made good use of inferior scrap.

But even before the conclusion of the Tripartite Pact, the administration began to clamp down on Japan. The American Ambassador to Japan, Joseph C. Grew, had hitherto advised restraint, but he now changed his mind. He reminded his superiors in Washington that a "soft" policy toward Japan also involved a risk of war. When Japan bullied Vichy into turning certain key positions in northern Indochina over to her, Roosevelt retaliated by embargoing all grades of iron and steel scrap and by granting Chiang a new loan. Further, Washington persuaded London to reopen the Burma Road, Chungking's principal supply route. Japan protested, but to no avail. This firm stand, coinciding with rumors of Anglo-American military coordination in the Pacific, forced a temporary retreat on the part of Tokyo.

The closing weeks of 1940 witnessed a momentary relaxation of American tensions with Japan. The Roosevelt administration reckoned that its diplomacy had kept the Japanese from making full capital of the European power vacuum that followed the collapse of France. Hopes for a definitive Japanese settlement rose with the appointment of a new Ambassador to the United States, Admiral Kichisaburo Nomura. He was known to share the Japanese navy's aversion to war with the United States. Moreover, he had accepted the assignment to Washington only after the naval high command had assured him that a diplomatic *détente* rather than war was the serious intent of the Konoye Cabinet. However, Nomura's delicate task required more diplomatic finesse than could be expected from a man of such limited experience and modest talents. Much of the good will surrounding his appointment evaporated when, at a farewell luncheon in the admiral's honor, Matsuoka delivered a harangue calling for Axis unity.

Nomura faced obstacles that would have dismayed even a seasoned diplomat. Such halting progress as he made with Hull was invariably dissipated by Matsuoka. Even the Japanese moderates, who could be expected to support Nomura's efforts, would accept nothing less than a free hand in China. In return, they were willing to promise a token withdrawal from territories already seized and a disavowal of new expansionist lunges. This meant that the maximum concession that Nomura was prepared to make was less than the United States was willing to accept.

Unfortunately Nomura took ship for San Francisco without being briefed on one of the strangest episodes of the time. This involved an American Catholic bishop and a priest in Japan on business connected with the Maryknoll Mission. They had met with some high-ranking Tokyo officials, including Foreign Minister Matsuoka. As an upshot of these talks, the two clerics were asked to convey a personal message to President Roosevelt. At a White House interview following their return to the United States, they intimated that Japan was willing to water down her obligations to Germany and Italy under the 1940 pact, was contemplating withdrawal from China, and stood ready to reaffirm the Open Door Policy. In return, so the priests reported, Konoye asked only a permanent settlement with the United States broad enough to include means of alleviating Japan's severe economic difficulties. No duly accredited Japanese spokesman ever repeated or confirmed the purported offer in the course of lengthy negotiations. Meanwhile the priests had been told to work through official channels in the Japanese embassy. In due time Nomura was informed of the pending negotiations. After weeks of diplomatic palaver, the Japanese handed Hull a specific offer on April 9, 1941. The terms of this proposal were eagerly awaited on the American side. Here at last was the official version of the proposition conveyed by the Maryknoll Fathers.

In short, this "Draft Understanding" (actually formulated by a Japanese colonel on duty in Washington) proposed peace for China without annexations or indemnities, and reaffirmation of the Open Door Policy with specific interpretations to be spelled out in the future. In addition, Japan promised to pursue only peaceful activities in the southwest Pacific, provided that the United States helped her obtain essential supplies from that region. Hull was understandably taken aback by the offer. The wording seemed to imply that the United States would have to force Chiang to make peace on Japanese terms. Furthermore, the document's phrasing on the relationship of both countries to the European war appeared intentionally "tricky."[4]

Secretary Hull avoided outright rejection of the Japanese bid. Instead, he countered with a four-point platform which restated traditional American moralistic principles of international conduct, in-

[4] Pratt, *op. cit.*, XIII, 480–482.

cluding a repudiation of territorial expansion through the use of force. At this juncture, the inexperienced Nomura blundered badly. He forwarded the Japanese proposal of April 9 to Tokyo, permitting his superiors to believe that these terms, actually formulated by his own embassy, represented an official offer from Washington. Little wonder that when Tokyo later learned of Hull's four-point proposal, it was thought that the United States had suddenly upped its demands.[5]

Foreign Minister Matsuoka had been out of the country when Nomura's "Draft Understanding" arrived, and the cabinet awaited his return before replying. Matsuoka had visited Berlin, where Hitler urged that the Japanese strike at Singapore as soon as possible. Then, if the Soviets attacked their exposed Manchurian flank in the course of the ensuing Anglo-Japanese war, the Reich would invade Russia. Although strong hints were forthcoming that a Russo-German war was not inconceivable, the dull-witted visitor to Berlin did not seem to grasp the Nazi intent. To the consternation of the Germans, the Foreign Minister next visited Moscow. Here, on April 13, 1941, he signed a Neutrality Pact which provided that Russia and Japan would remain neutral if either country was attacked by a third party. This agreement certainly violated the spirit of the 1940 Tripartite Pact with Germany and Italy, but Matsuoka was determined to protect Japan's exposed northern border in the event that a southward thrust led to war with the Anglo-American combination.

On his return to Tokyo, Matsuoka dealt with the proposal of April 9. It is a salutary corrective to writers who insist that a more flexible American diplomacy might have avoided a collision with Japan to point out that Matsuoka was not willing to accept even the terms formulated by his own diplomats in Washington! Acting under orders, Nomura handed Hull an even less satisfactory note than the original proposal. Although Hull tried to keep the talks going in the hope that a cabinet shake-up would drive the unruly Matsuoka from power, his negotiations with Nomura soon became deadlocked.

[5] Robert J. C. Butow, "The Hull-Nomura Conversations: A Fundamental Misconception," *American Historical Review*, LXV (July, 1960), 822–836.

Then came the German invasion of Russia on June 22, 1941. One of its results was to embolden the Japanese. Now they had absolute assurance that Stalin would not strike at Manchuria should their march southward embroil them in war with England and the United States. On the other side, the Russian invasion caused America to stiffen her position vis-à-vis Japan. With Britain granted a temporary relief, Washington could afford to take longer risks in the Far East.

At all events, one American wish was granted. Matsuoka, who apparently wanted to attack Siberia while Hitler was pounding the Soviets from the west, lost his post to Admiral Teijiro Toyoda in the cabinet upheaval of July 16, 1941. On the other hand, owing to the fact that the United States Army and Navy Intelligence Services had cracked the top-secret Japanese diplomatic code, Washington soon learned that Tokyo's expansionist designs had not ended with the fall of Matsuoka.

On July 2, 1941, Tokyo formulated plans which rendered a war with the United States all but inevitable. The setting was a full-dress Imperial Conference. Here the highest-ranking Japanese officials agreed to avoid war with Russia for the time being by resisting the temptation to invade Siberia. They would make still another effort to bring China to terms. But, in all events, they would fulfill the aim of a Greater East Asia Sphere of Co-Prosperity by an "advance into the southern regions," even at a risk of war with Great Britain and the United States.

Ten days later, as a preliminary step in the implementation of this expansionist blueprint, Japan demanded from Vichy land, air, and naval bases in southern Indochina. This action alarmed Washington. In contrast to the occupation of the northern half of the French possession, control of the south bore no relationship to the war effort against Chiang. Only one interpretation made sense: Japan had determined to push southward in the direction of the Anglo-French-Dutch Pacific possessions. The newly occupied bases also put the Japanese army within easy striking distance of the Philippines.

The President spoke frankly to Ambassador Nomura. Hitherto, said Roosevelt, he had hesitated to levy a total oil embargo against

Japan lest this step lend "incentive or pretext" for designs against the oil-rich Dutch East Indies. But now American supplies could be used to fuel a military campaign that would jeopardize American interests. If Japan would keep hands off southern Indochina, the President promised, he would try to get this region neutralized and would help Nomura's government obtain raw materials from other sources. Evidently the admiral thought little of the President's proposal, for he failed to stress it in his dispatches to Tokyo.[6]

The administration now applied undisguised economic sanctions against Japan. That country's funds in the United States were impounded, thus placing a virtual interdict on normal trade between the two countries. The Panama Canal was closed to Japanese shipping. In view of the threat against the Philippines, General Douglas MacArthur was recalled to active American service and was placed at the head of all United States and Philippine forces in the Far East. Oil exports to Japan were drastically reduced in a series of gradual steps, culminating in a complete ban on the export of oil to Japan. The final step was taken after Tokyo made demands upon Thailand. This oil embargo was all the more effective because the British and the Dutch paralleled American action.

Japan had only eighteen months of fuel reserves. Therefore, notes Herbert Feis, the effect of our embargo was "to force Japan to choose between making terms with us or making war against us." Yet the evidence suggests that neither side wanted war. Roosevelt preferred "to baby" the Japanese rather than dissipate in a Far Eastern war American military strength which he was prepared to use against Germany. The President complained to those who demanded stronger actions against Japan that he just did not have enough navy to go around. Still, FDR was not prepared to make the kind of concessions that possibly might have strengthened the hands of the Japanese moderates. It is entirely probable that Roosevelt and Hull sincerely believed that a firm rather than a wobbling stand against Japan was the best guarantee of peace. Similarly, top Japanese civilian and business spokesmen clung tenaciously to the hope of a diplomatic settlement with the United

[6] Pratt, *op. cit.*, XIII, 491.

States. Until they became alarmed at the rapid depletion of their oil reserves, Japanese naval officers also wished to avoid an American war. Caught between the moderates and the activists, official Tokyo hoped for a diplomatic miracle whereby peace with America could be preserved with a minimum of concessions. In this spirit, Prince Konoye played his last diplomatic trump.

Roosevelt was en route to his rendezvous with Churchill at Argentia when Nomura broached the possibility of a "summit" conference to resolve outstanding difficulties. Hull seems not to have grasped the significance of the proposal immediately, but the Japanese kept pressing for a top-level conference.[7] Upon Roosevelt's return to the White House, he favored the proposal for he had a flair for personal diplomacy. But Hull was skeptical of the value of the meeting unless the Japanese would first agree in principle to the main American contentions, including a solution to the ticklish Chinese problem. Konoye's invitation was bandied back and forth for several months until Hull, with the President's consent, politely but firmly refused.

We will never know whether the President and the Premier could have reached a satisfactory agreement. Roosevelt's champions point out that the administration understood, from decoded dispatches, that Konoye was the prisoner of the militarists and therefore had little new to offer. Those who are always ready to believe the worst of Franklin Roosevelt insist that he did not confer with Konoye because his goal was really war with Japan, not peaceful settlement. But it is possible to argue, without seconding the proposition of these extreme revisionists, that the administration blundered in not accepting the invitation. Roosevelt and Hull, it has been contended, should have realized that war with Nazi Germany was inevitable. It was, therefore, their obligation to avoid a two-front war by relaxing economic sanctions against Japan and striking a bargain with Konoye whereby Japan would refrain from

[7] At Argentia "the British gained additional hope of American armed support, though the United States again refused to make a definite commitment." Raymond A. Esthus, "President Roosevelt's Commitment to Britain to Intervene in a Pacific War," *Mississippi Valley Historical Review*, L (June, 1963), 28–38.

further aggression in Southeast Asia in return for a moratorium on the Chinese settlement. Such a policy, it has been suggested, might well have strengthened the hand of the Japanese moderates and have postponed a Far Eastern showdown until after the European conflict ended.[8]

However, the "ifs" of history are incapable of proof. Ambassador Grew, a seasoned and trustworthy diplomat, argued then and later that Konoye was in earnest and that, backed by the Emperor and the moderates, he would have honored the commitments he was prepared to make. The evidence is convincing that Roosevelt and Hull *did not* want war with Japan. Their error lay in clinging doggedly to the belief that a rigid American stand would eventually force a Japanese diplomatic retreat.

How wrong they were is apparent from the proceedings of a secret Japanese Imperial Conference held on September 6, 1941. Here the Japanese formulated the minimum terms that they would accept from the United States. They were ready to promise that they would not use Indochina as a base for further aggression and that they would withdraw from all of that region after "a just peace" had been arranged in the Pacific. These concessions were predicated on the conditions that the United States restore normal trade relations with Japan and cut off help to Chiang. On the crucial question of the Tripartite Pact, all that the Imperial Conference was ready to promise was that, in the event of an American-German war, Japan would construe the alliance in the light of her own interests. "If by the early part of October," the Conference concluded, "there is no reasonable hope of having our demands

[8] Paul W. Schroeder, *The Axis Alliance and Japanese-American Relations, 1941* (Ithaca, 1958), pp. 200–216, criticizes the administration's strong measures of July, 1941. He feels that until that time American goals to drive a wedge between Japan and the rest of the Axis powers and to halt the drive southward were "reasonable" and "attainable." Then Washington added a third goal—to force the Japanese to retreat in China, a goal which the author thinks could not have been obtained without war. Schroeder holds that the American diplomats of 1941 should not have considered China as within our strategic interests. It was adherence to this illusory goal in China which forfeited for the United States "the diplomatic victory which she had already won."

agreed to . . . we will immediately make up our minds for war against America."

These resolves indicate that the gap between Japanese and American thinking was wide and deep. Yet Tokyo was willing to give diplomacy one last try to bridge the chasm. At the same time, the Japanese military establishment was feverishly preparing for war.

As Ambassador Grew had predicted, the Konoye government could not survive Roosevelt's rebuff in refusing a personal conference. The Premier resigned on October 16, 1941. In his place, the Emperor appointed General Tojo, subject to a promise that the new government would continue negotiations looking to a peaceful settlement with the United States. Under such conditions, the final tedious weeks of negotiations began. These efforts were undertaken at a time when decision-making in Japan was vested in the army and navy general staffs which, in turn, were strongly influenced "by radical elements both within and without the armed services." Tojo would have found it difficult, if not impossible, to take the path of conciliation rather than war.[9] Nonetheless, optimists on both sides of the Pacific clung to the hope that the new Premier, as an army careerist, could hold the extremists in check. The anti-war group in Tokyo had persuaded the army fire-eaters to push one final peace offensive.

Still another Imperial Conference, held on November 5, reviewed Japanese basic strategy. This gathering handed Ambassador Nomura two propositions for American consideration. Plan A contained a broad settlement of outstanding differences; Plan B was designed merely as a temporary expedient. If the Roosevelt administration still remained adamant, the Imperial Conference decided to make war on the United States, with or without the support of its Axis allies. The deadline was set for November 25.

Time was running out on the Japanese moderates. The Japanese had to press for an immediate diplomatic decision lest the coming of heavy winter foil their military plans. Because their oil reserves were running dangerously low, they could not afford to call a halt

[9] Pratt, *op. cit.*, XIII, 501.

until spring. However, Tokyo did extend the deadline for a diplomatic agreement to November 29. Thanks to "Magic," the code name for the operation decoding Japanese diplomatic dispatches, Hull knew of this extension. "After that," warned the intercepted dispatches, "things are automatically going to happen." The United States had everything to gain by prolonging the discussions. Washington wanted time for more B-17 bombers and other reinforcements to reach the Far East.

At Nomura's request, Tokyo sent an experienced diplomat to assist in rendering Japan's ultimate offer. Saburo Kurusu was a competent strategist with an American wife. Familiar with the American turn of expression, he remarked that his chances of success rested on going "through the line for a touchdown." But Kurusu had helped affix Japan's signature to the Tripartite Pact, a deed which did not endear him to Secretary Hull.

Kurusu arrived in Washington in mid-November. It soon became apparent to him that Plan A was unacceptable to Hull, for its terms were less satisfactory than previous offers turned down by the United States. Therefore, under orders from Tokyo, the Japanese negotiators presented Plan B as their "absolutely final proposal." To Hull's keen disappointment, Kurusu had brought with him no new concessions, although the Japanese offer reiterated several shopworn proposals. There would be no further armed advance by either party south of the Chinese border. Japan would be willing to withdraw immediately from southern Indochina and would evacuate all of that French province upon the restoration of general peace. Commercial intercourse between the two nations was to be restored. The United States would give Japan "a required quantity of oil" and the two countries would cooperate to obtain additional resources from the Dutch East Indies. Then came the joker in the pack—the United States was, in effect "to cease giving aid and comfort to the Chinese Government of Chiang Kai-shek, leaving China the choice of fighting on alone or making peace on Japan's terms."[10]

[10] *Ibid.*, XIII, 507. Kurusu told Hull privately that Japan would interpret the Tripartite Pact "freely and independently" and "would never project the people of Japan into war at the behest of any foreign power."

Of course, Hull found these conditions "utterly unacceptable." As he later explained in his *Memoirs*, our acceptance would have involved the betrayal of China plus the abandonment of American moral principles, while a strengthened Japan might well have become a still greater menace to American security. From today's perspective, this reaction appears exaggerated. A double-front war seems too high a price for the questionable benefit of exchanging a Communist-ridden for a Japanese-dominated China. But as Professor Pratt reminds us, Mr. Hull was not clairvoyant. He equated "an independent and integral" China with a "friendly and democratic China" and he thought that the United States could leave Chiang to his fate "only at the cost of moral bankruptcy." Even had Hull been so minded, it is doubtful if American public opinion would have sanctioned the concessions demanded by Japan. Acceptance of Plan B would have been labeled appeasement and that word had a particularly ugly connotation in 1941.

American statesmen tried to work out a *modus vivendi* of their own which they planned to submit to Nomura and Kurusu in lieu of an outright rejection of Plan B. This abortive American counter-offer called for a three months' truce during which time both parties would refrain from military action in the South Pacific. It further stipulated immediate Japanese withdrawal from southern Indochina as well as a limited restoration of trade with Japan, including the grant of oil supplies earmarked for civilian use. However, this plan was never submitted. It was dropped on November 25, when the administration learned of a concentration of Japanese troopships off Formosa, a military move which cast doubt on Japan's good faith in the pending negotiations. Besides, Roosevelt and Hull now realized that news of a possible temporary truce with Japan had caused consternation in London and Chungking. Chiang's reaction had particularly ominous overtones. He hinted that such an American-Japanese deal might mean the collapse of Chinese resistance. In any case, the American *modus vivendi* probably would have been rejected by the Japanese inasmuch as they had previously refused similar offers.

The morning after the truce plan was shelved, Hull took the most controversial step of his official career. Strangely enough, the habitually prudent Secretary consulted only the President and failed to inform either the American defense chiefs or friendly governments of his contemplated action. On Wednesday, November 26, Hull handed Nomura and Kurusu so stringent a reply to their previous offer that the two men hesitated to relay it to Tokyo. Japan, according to Hull's ten-point manifesto, was to withdraw its troops from China *as well as* Indochina and to support the Nationalist regime in Chungking against which they had been making war for over four years. As a token of good faith, Tokyo was invited to join a multilateral nonaggression pact designed to preserve the peace of the Far East. All that Hull offered in return for these sweeping demands was a favorable trade agreement, the unfreezing of Japanese assets, and a promise to stabilize the dollar-yen ratio.

Secretary Hull must have realized that to reply to "Japan's minimum terms by a statement of America's maximum demands" would precipitate a shooting war.[11] The Japanese government, as then constituted, would most certainly prefer war to an ignominious retreat in the face of American exactions. Why did a diplomat with a reputation for circumspection wax impatient and take such a dangerous gamble? It has been suggested that Mr. Hull had lost all confidence in Japan's good faith and therefore reasoned that any further American concessions would not be worth a short delay in the outbreak of war. This argument is given weight by the postwar observation of Tojo's Foreign Minister that war would have come regardless of any American course. If Secretary Hull reached a similar conclusion, then it made sense to place the final statement of Washington's aims on high moral grounds. Or perhaps, as his biographer suggests, the fateful decision "was a petulant one" made "by a tired and angry man." At all events, it is certain that Hull's intransigent stand of November 26 convinced remaining doubters in Tokyo that war was the only alternative to a slow economic strangulation that would eventually remove Japan from the category of stellar world powers.

Would a more flexible American diplomacy have avoided a

11 William L. Langer and S. Everett Gleason, *The Undeclared War, 1940–1941* (New York, 1953), p. 898.

double-front war? It is fashionable among certain writers to censor Hull's rigidity and to lament the fact that the more pliable Roosevelt did not take personal charge of last-minute negotiations with Japan. Such historians hold that it was a cardinal American error to insist, as we did after July, 1941, that Japan pull back from China as well as from Indochina. Instead of trying to settle all scores with Japan, Hull should have focused his attention on those disputes where agreement was within the realm of possibility. Had the Chinese problem been postponed for later settlement, then a workable compromise could have been reached on other points at issue. But these arguments are vulnerable because their proponents take at full value glib proposals made by a government whose diplomatic record was studded with broken pledges and unfulfilled treaty obligations. Moreover, it is doubtful if any pre-Pearl Harbor Japanese cabinet could have survived a workable compromise with the United States.

While the diplomats were parleying in Washington, the general staffs in Tokyo were perfecting their plan of sudden attack. As far back as January, 1941, the Commander in Chief of the Japanese Combined Fleet had begun to display serious interest in the possibility of a raid on the great American naval base at Pearl Harbor. Preparations for this campaign were to be one of modern history's most carefully guarded secrets. In September the plan was disclosed to the Naval War College in Tokyo in the presence of top-brass naval officials. Implementation was now speeded up, but Tojo promised no hostile move until it was certain that there could be no meeting of minds with the United States.

It seems remarkable that Japanese military planners contemplated a madcap attack on a nation possessing ten times the industrial potential of their own country. Louis Morton has pointed out that the Japanese decision-makers realized that they could not win a protracted war with the United States. Hence, they hoped that the immobilization of the American Pacific fleet would make Washington so desperately anxious to insure Hitler's defeat that the United States would negotiate a Far Eastern settlement permitting Japan to consolidate its power in Southeast Asia. If this be true, then Tokyo planned to desert Germany by making a separate peace with the United States.

An influential sector of Japanese opinion, including Emperor Hirohito, looked askance at this harebrained gamble. However, the skeptics were muted by Hull's stiff note of November 26 and by momentarily favorable Axis prospects in Europe. On November 29 Hirohito consented to war. Two days later an Imperial Conference ratified his decision and the carrier task force heading for Hawaii was ordered to attack on the first Sunday in December.

The Japanese armada, assembled behind an imperceptible screen in the Kurile Islands, had sailed on November 25, subject to recall orders. Its progress was shielded by heavy seas, foggy weather, and the stratagem of radio silence. The mission of this task force was, of course, unknown to the Americans. Nonetheless, official Washington was aware that a Japanese strike was imminent. But intelligence reports based on the known locations of Japanese troop convoys and military concentrations all pointed to Siam, Burma, British Malaya, or the Dutch East Indies as possible targets. American Intelligence Services had flirted with thoughts of a possible attack on the Philippines or Guam, but such notions were dismissed because it did not seem logical that the Japanese would fuse American opinion by a direct attack on United States territory. It seemed much more reasonable to believe that Tokyo would strike at British, Dutch, or neutral targets in the South Pacific so as to confront the White House with the problem of asking Congress to make war either to preserve the vestiges of European colonialism or to uphold the independence of far-off Siam. No American in a position of authority had sufficient imagination to conceive of a coordinated Japanese assault on objectives stretching from Singapore to Hawaii. From time to time there had been vague hints of an attack on Pearl Harbor, but such reports had been discounted as bordering on the fantastic. So, in the critical week that preceded the attack, American attention was centered on what to do if and when the Japanese fell upon British or Dutch possessions.

Certain in their own minds that the blow would fall in Southeast Asia, American statesmen deliberated countermoves to the anticipated Japanese aggression. Army and navy officials advised a declaration of war. They argued that American security would be jeopardized should the Japanese march on strategic Allied Pacific territory. Secretary of War Stimson was even more impatient. He wanted the American B-17 bombers based on the Philippines to halt the Japanese convoys as they steamed into the South China Sea. Roosevelt and his war council vetoed this precautionary measure, for they were addicted to the American shibboleth that the enemy must fire the first shot. Finally, the President decided to send Emperor Hirohito a personal appeal for peace. If this message failed in its purpose, he would then lay his quandary before Congress. This action would be followed by a request for a declaration of war against Japan in response to the attack on friendly Asiatic territory. With this piecemeal strategy, administration circles hoped that Congress and the public would be prepared for the shock of war and that the President would be able to time his steps by the sense of popular reaction.

The administration deliberated a full week on the precise wording of the dramatic appeal to the Emperor. On the very day before Pearl Harbor, it was hurriedly dispatched as the news flashed across the wires that a powerful Japanese armada was rounding the tip of Indochina and apparently heading for Siam. The note to Hirohito, sent too late to have any impact on the course of events, called attention to the historic friendship that existed between the two nations. Present tensions, said the President, were reaching a breaking point that could only be avoided by swift imperial intervention. Significantly, Roosevelt stressed the problem of Indochina as a stumbling block to peace but failed to make mention of China itself.

So far Washington had received no answer to Hull's note of November 26. Saturday afternoon, December 6, American monitors began picking up the reply. Decoding was slow. Not until the next morning did Hull have positive knowledge that Tokyo was about to end negotiations. The Japanese envoys were ordered to present their reply at precisely 1:00 P.M., Washington time. In the excitement of the moment, no one in authority grasped that this hour coincided with daybreak in distant Hawaii.

Because it has long been common knowledge that our crypt-analysts had cracked the Japanese diplomatic code, many have questioned why the raid on Pearl Harbor was not anticipated and adequate steps taken to repulse the attack. Some Roosevelt-baiting historians assume that the White House knew what was about to happen but purposely failed to warn the field commanders. They claim the President and his military chiefs did not wish to forfeit an attack that would facilitate a "backdoor" entry for the United States into World War II. Complete lack of evidence, direct or circumstantial, makes it possible to dismiss this fanciful assumption.

More responsible writers have raised legitimate questions about the lack of communications, gross miscalculations, and regrettable misfortunes that surrounded the Pearl Harbor debacle. Many different answers, all of them related to human frailty, explain these errors in judgment. Neither the field commanders nor their Washington superiors foresaw the possibility of a massive, carrier-based attack on American territory. Both groups, with the white man's characteristic disdain for the abilities of other races, thought the Japanese incapable of taking great risks or striking simultaneously at both Hawaii and the South Pacific. The intelligence intercepts seemed to point in every direction but Pearl Harbor. All indications apparently confirmed the prevalent notion that the Japanese were going to advance in the area where we expected them to go. It was a case of what psychologists call selective perception, "the very human tendency to pay attention to the signals that support current expectations about enemy behavior."[12]

Operation "Magic" never gave absolute indication of the Japanese plans. Intelligence reports were clouded because many "spoofs" aiming to throw us off the track were interspersed with germane information. Only after the event was it simple to separate the wheat from the tares. Picking up intercepts from many monitors, one of which was located in Hawaii, a central

[12] This discussion of the intelligence aspects of Pearl Harbor and the confusion in the vast governmental bureaucratic organizations is based largely on Roberta Wohlstetter, *Pearl Harbor: Warning and Decision* (Stanford, 1962), *passim*. The quotation cited is on p. 392.

control station put the information together after comparing it with conventional intelligence reports. But there were some serious drawbacks to the system. The items sent on to the field commanders were brief in nature so as not to overtax communications. Moreover, it was imperative not to spell out all details lest Tokyo deduce that we had broken its diplomatic code. Not all of the material intercepted by "Magic" was properly evaluated. For instance, the significance of the Japanese curiosity about ships berthed at Pearl Harbor was overlooked. Nomura and Kurusu were not informed of the imminent attack on Pearl Harbor, and hence we could not know more than was relayed from Tokyo to these and other Japanese diplomats stationed elsewhere. Finally, there is no persuasive evidence that the "winds" messages, which actually signified war, were received before the bombs began to fall. The most that the decoded intercepts seemed to say was that negotiations were to be ended. Some signals were scattered, some were never decoded, some were passed on to the policy-makers while others "never reached a center of decision." The main weakness in the American system, according to a competent authority, was that "no single person or agency ever had at any given moment all the existing signals in this vast information network."[13]

Inasmuch as the Hawaiian field commanders, Lieutenant General Walter C. Short and Admiral Husband E. Kimmel, did not fully utilize even the information which they did have, it is doubtful that they would have acted much differently had they known everything contained in the government's secret files. Short and Kimmel had received routine warnings of war from Washington. They were told that negotiations with Japan had collapsed, and that an attack somewhere in the South Pacific seemed imminent. The field commanders had not read all of "Magic's" revelations. Fearing internal subversion rather than external attack, their main preoccupation was to prevent sabotage. This led them to anti-sabotage measures which eased the Japanese errand at Pearl Harbor. General Short lined up his planes on Wheeler Field nose to

[13] *Ibid.*, p. 385.

tail, with the result that they could not be sent into the air during the attack. Anti-aircraft ammunition was stowed away to guard against would-be saboteurs. Kimmel moored his ships along Battleship Row on the southeastern shore of Ford Island. These precautions were reported to their superiors, who did not dissent. Therefore, the blame rests also on top-ranking army and navy officials. In addition, there was a good deal of misunderstanding all along the line of communications. Washington assumed that a joint defense plan was in operation and that it provided for a continuous air search, especially in the sector north by west. This security safeguard, which might have taken the edge off the Japanese surprise, was abandoned because the Pearl Harbor base was short of men, aircraft, and fuel oil. Radar, then still something of a novelty, was working only on a part-time practice basis. Moreover, espionage had been unusually efficient. A Japanese vice-consul in Honolulu, aided by a naval officer disguised as a steward on a commercial liner, supplied enough precise information so that each Japanese aviator could be given a specific assignment.

A number of preliminary incidents, had their importance been comprehended, might have given the American ships and planes a brief time to prepare for action. Early on that historic morning, a mine sweeper sighted a periscope two miles off the entrance to the harbor and patrol craft destroyed a midget submarine. However, owing to downright stupidity and inexcusable delay, the information did not reach headquarters in time to be of help. Army radar installations indicated the approach of aircraft, but it was thought that the blips on the screen signaled the arrival of some B-17 bombers from the United States. Almost an hour before the attack, a civilian American aviator reported the presence of several warplanes, but the military refused to believe his story. Negligence and lack of foresight extended down the line of command from the White House to the lowliest privates and seamen guarding the approaches to the Pearl Harbor post.

And so the attack on Pearl Harbor fulfilled Japanese expectations. The campaign was, writes Professor Leopold, skillfully planned, superbly executed, and accompanied by "unbelievable good luck." The carrier task force was not sighted as it approached to the northwest of Hawaii. The first planes arrived over their targets at 7:55 A.M., just as battleship crews were assembling on deck for Sunday morning services. Another wave of bombers followed an hour later to complete the demolition of air fields and ships hawsered at mooring quays. By the time the last Japanese planes stopped strafing and veered back toward their carriers, Pearl Harbor was a smoking shambles. The enemy left over 2,300 dead, destroyed or disabled almost every plane on Oahu, and sank or put out of commission eight battleships, three cruisers, and three destroyers. But for some fortunate circumstances, the disaster might have been complete enough to force the Pacific fleet to retreat to the west coast. A fully modernized American task force, commanded by Admiral William F. Halsey, managed to escape because it was at sea on a special mission. Moreover, the raiders did not tarry long enough to demolish installations, fuel tanks, and repair ships. The Japanese also overlooked one army air squadron stationed at an auxiliary air field. Its planes, a few anti-aircraft units, and a handful of minor naval craft managed to get into action and fired the only American shots at the invaders. Nevertheless, the cost to the enemy was negligible—5 midget subs, 1 fleet submarine, and 27 planes.

The catalogue of events in Washington on that bleak Sunday is intriguing. At mid-morning, but still prior to dawn in Hawaii, the State Department received the decoded message which ordered the Japanese envoys to burn all codes and records and to present their answer to Hull at 1:00 P.M. When General George C. Marshall, Chief of Staff, returned from his famous horseback ride about 11:00 A.M., he telephoned Chief of Naval Operations Harold R. Stark to discuss any possible new warning in view of the latest information garnered from "Magic." Stark hesitated to consent to another alert to the field commanders lest confusion be confounded. However, another caution was sent to the Pacific outposts. Because the transoceanic telephone was never used for classified messages, this media of instant communication was not employed. To avoid possible interception by the Japanese, the warning was sent by commercial cable. Ironically, the messenger boy who delivered the wire to Pearl Harbor had to dodge Japanese fire while completing his errand.

Shortly after lunchtime, Admiral Kimmel's curt message came over the wires: "AIR RAID ON PEARL HARBOR. THIS IS NOT DRILL." Actually, the Japanese Foreign Office had wanted Nomura and Kurusu to present Hull with the declination of his ten-point demands before the attack began. But there were decoding difficulties at the embassy and the envoys did not reach the State Department until after Hull had learned of the assault. The Secretary kept Nomura and Kurusu waiting for a quarter of an hour before showing them into his office. Without asking them to be seated, he glanced cursorily at their note, the contents of which he already knew. Contrary to legend, he did not "cuss them out" in rich mountain language. Instead, he declared in grave, measured tones:

In all my fifty years of public service I have never seen a document that was more crowded with infamous falsehoods and distortions . . . on a scale so huge that I never imagined until today that any Government on this planet was capable of uttering them.

Without giving the two downcast envoys a chance to reply, Hull motioned them out of his office.

Bad news kept pouring into Washington on that frantic Sunday afternoon. Additional alarms told of the Japanese declaration of war and attacks on Hong Kong, Wake, and Midway Islands, the Philippines, Siam, and Malaya. The Roosevelt administration sprang into action with hurriedly summoned cabinet meetings and a conference with congressional leaders of both parties. The following day, speaking to a joint session of Congress, the President asked legal recognition of the state of war which had been forced on the United States. This request was granted with but a single dissenting vote. Pearl Harbor, like Lexington and Fort Sumter before it, galvanized public enthusiasm for war.

The President's message to Congress had purposely omitted mention of Japan's Axis partners, for Roosevelt wished to toss the decision for general war into Hitler's lap. It is tantalizing to speculate on what might have happened had Hitler betrayed Japan and opted for neutrality. The Nazi chieftain was perfectly capable of such wholesale treachery, but for once he kept his plighted word. Four days after Pearl Harbor, Germany and Italy declared war on the United States. Hitler had no prior knowledge of the Pearl Harbor plan, but he had shortly before given Tokyo a blank check promising support should the Japanese decide to attack the western powers. Still, Hitler must have been tempted to permit Japan and the United States to fight it out between themselves. He may have hoped that, once in the war, the Japanese would give Russia the *coup de grâce* by invading Siberia. Or he may have reasoned that the United States was already so involved in the European conflict that the formality of war would make no appreciable difference. Certainly it was something else besides a sense of honor that led him to fulfill his obligations to Tokyo. Whatever his motives, Hitler's decision to unite the fate of the Atlantic and the Pacific wars provided great relief for Franklin D. Roosevelt. The United States was now engaged, to the utmost limits of its manpower and resources, in a struggle that the President regarded as "The War for Survival."

Twenty-three years and twenty-six days elapsed between the close of hostilities in the First World War and the formal American entry into the second great ordeal of our century. Americans spent most of this interim period searching for a talisman that would shield their country from the *bête noire* of war. For a brief spell the League of Nations was equated with the magic formula for peace. However, ere Woodrow Wilson left the White House in 1921, the short-lived enthusiasm for world organization had cooled.

Throughout the balance of the flush 1920's, Republican statesmen toyed with surrogate blueprints for peace which excluded full-fledged American association with the League. Aided by an ubiquitous prosperity, a new global equilibrium emerged but soon collapsed with the coming of hard times and the concomitant emergence of war-hungry dictatorships. Once more American public opinion was transformed, this time into an inflexible and intolerant variant of isolationism. During the Depression Decade, the vast majority believed that the elusive elixir of peace had been found in the keep-out-of-war legislation of that era.

Slowly but surely the rapid pace of world events undermined this new panacea, yet when war came to Europe in 1939, the entrenched isolationists fought a stubborn rear-guard action. However, remaining vestiges of this mood of withdrawal all but vanished with the sudden descent of unlimited war from the December skies.

At the time of Pearl Harbor, the dedicated internationalists still formed a small segment of popular opinion. Events had seemingly confirmed their foreboding that only an effective world organization could abort war and thus remove the possibility of American involvement. The ideological wheel had turned full circle. Soon after 1941 the country at large fell once more under a new spell of international idealism.

This vein of wartime thought, like that of Wilson's day, was soon to be dissipated by the harsh realities of international existence. In the nuclear age, idealism was to give way to realism as the regnant principle in the conduct of foreign relations. Nonetheless, the interwar experience left a deep imprint on the American psyche. Gone, probably forever, was the unfounded notion that Providence had blessed the New World with a unique destiny unrelated to the fortunes and misfortunes of other nations and continents. The irruption at Pearl Harbor was an omen that the future would be crowded with the stirrings of non-Caucasian peoples determined to redress the handicap of centuries.

Further Reading

GENERAL WORKS

This bibliography is designed to guide the undergraduate, his instructors, and the general reader to the more significant writings on American diplomatic history during the interwar decades.

Leading bibliographical guides are cited for the benefit of those who consult these pages for research purposes. Oscar Handlin *et al.* (eds.), *Harvard Guide to American History* (Cambridge, 1954), while general in scope, includes many valuable particulars on twentieth-century foreign relations. More specialized entries are presented in the four volumes of *Foreign Affairs Bibliography* (New York, 1933–1955; 1964), sponsored by the Council on Foreign Relations. These master compilations provide complete bibliographical information on American interwar diplomacy. The following briefer guides evaluate the most pertinent literature: Alexander DeConde, *New Interpretations in American Foreign Policy* [pamphlet, Service Center for Teachers of History: A Service of the American Historical Association] (Washington, 1957); and sections by Richard Lowitt and Wayne S. Cole in William H. Cartwright and Richard L. Watson, Jr. (eds.), *Interpreting and Teaching American History* (Washington, 1961), pp. 242–247; 282–295.

Advanced students should also consult certain collections indispensable for a detailed chronicle of events. Since 1938, *Documents on American Foreign Relations* has appeared annually. Although these volumes were sponsored originally by the World Peace Foundation, responsibility for them was later assumed by the Council on Foreign Relations. Another annual series on foreign policy began in 1928 as *Survey of American*

Foreign Relations. After three years the title was changed to *The United States in World Affairs* and its volumes have been published since 1931 in New York under the auspices of the Council on Foreign Relations. *Foreign Relations of the United States* is an official governmental project dating from Civil War days. These volumes incorporate selections from American diplomatic correspondence and, for the more recent period, frequently group together specialized material pertaining to important persons, controversies and events. Taken together, the above-mentioned three sets of publications re-create a comprehensive year-by-year portrayal of diplomatic developments.

Standard textbooks on American diplomatic history devote liberal coverage to the period between Versailles and Pearl Harbor. Samuel F. Bemis, *A Diplomatic History of the United States* (5th ed., New York, 1965) is the pioneer modern work of its kind and is based upon a lifetime of multi-archival research on the part of its distinguished author. Thomas A. Bailey, *A Diplomatic History of the American People* (7th ed., New York, 1964) is written in a lighter vein and emphasizes the role of public opinion in the formation of policy. The student will find Bailey's digest of recent research findings, listed as "Appendix F," most helpful. Julius W. Pratt's outstanding survey, *A History of United States Foreign Policy* (2nd ed., Englewood Cliffs, N.J., 1965), has been updated recently by incorporation of the latest research in the field. Nelson M. Blake and Oscar T. Barck, Jr., *The United States in its World Relations* (New York, 1960) is an able treatment which effectively highlights unfamiliar details. Richard W. Leopold's *The Growth of American Foreign Policy: A History* (New York, 1962) is particularly valuable for its focus on twentieth-century global developments. Leopold explores with a certain hand the foreign upheavals which so largely shaped the course of post-1914 American diplomacy. New points of view in diplomatic history are deftly woven into the narrative of Alexander DeConde's *A History of American Foreign Policy* (New York, 1963).

There are also some able texts which cover the field in briefer compass. Robert H. Ferrell, *American Diplomacy: A History* (New York, 1959) is highly interpretative and stimulating. Samuel F. Bemis, *A Short History of American Policy and Diplomacy* (New York, 1959) is a skillful condensation. L. Ethan Ellis, *A Short History of American Diplomacy* (New York, 1951) is a handy book of reference emphasizing broad principles and their development.

A monograph rather than a text, Foster R. Dulles's *America's Rise to World Power, 1898–1954* (New York, 1955) traces the evolution of the United States to world power and, in the course of this task, conveys keen insights into many of the problems of the recent past. Jules Davids's *America and the World of Our Time: United States Diplomacy in the Twentieth Century* (New York, 1960) richly details those world politics of the past half century which so often determined Washington's cardinal decisions.

The student will benefit from the following collections of important documents, other contemporary material, and sections of monographs and articles deemed worthy of reprint: Ruhl J. Bartlett (ed.), *The Record of American Diplomacy: Documents and Readings in the History of American Foreign Relations* (4th ed., New York, 1964); Dorothy B. Goebel (ed.), *American Foreign Policy: A Documentary Survey, 1776–1960* (New York, 1961); William A. Williams (ed.), *The Shaping of American Diplomacy: Readings and Documents in American Foreign Relations, 1750–1955* (Chicago, 1956); Robert A. Divine (ed.), *American Foreign Policy* (New York, 1960); Norman A. Graebner (ed.), *Ideas and Diplomacy: Readings in the Intellectual Tradition of American Foreign Policy* (New York, 1964) and Daniel M. Smith (ed.), *Major Problems in American Diplomatic History: Documents and Readings* (Boston, 1964).

Viewing the past from the pitiless perspective of the Nuclear Age, an influential school of writers severely condemns the "legalistic-moralistic" approach of bygone American policy makers. This critical view is stressed by the scholar-diplomat, George F. Kennan, in his spirited essays, *American Diplomacy, 1900–1950* (New York, 1951). Hans J. Morgenthau, *In Defense of the National Interest: A Critical Examination of American Foreign Policy* (New York, 1951) and Ernest W. Lefever, *Ethics and United States Foreign Policy* (New York, 1957) embellish the arguments of the realists.

The time-honored axioms of American diplomacy are defended in the following works: Dexter Perkins, *The American Approach to Foreign Policy* (Cambridge, 1952); Thomas I. Cook and Malcolm Moos, *Power Through Purpose: The Realism of Idealism as a Basis for Foreign Policy* (Baltimore, 1954) and Frank Tannenbaum, *The American Tradition in Foreign Policy* (Norman, Okla., 1955). The historical conflict in diplomatic aims is brilliantly surveyed by Robert E. Osgood in *Ideals and Self-Interest in America's Foreign Relations: The Great Transformation of the Twentieth Century* (Chicago, 1953). This pathbreaking study contains many acute observations on topics covered throughout this present volume. Ruhl J. Bartlett, *Policy and Power: Two Centuries of American Foreign Relations* (New York, 1963) is particularly strong on the interwar period and offers many fruitful observations.

CHAPTER 1: THE TOTTERING OF IDEALISM

The fullest treatment of the postwar years is Frederic L. Paxson, *Postwar Years: Normalcy, 1918–1923* (Berkeley, 1948). In more dramatic fashion Thomas A. Bailey describes the reaction against Wilsonian idealism in *Wilson and the Peacemakers* (New York, 1947). This book, a combination of two of Professor Bailey's earlier monographs, is sympathetic to liberal internationalism but places much of the blame for the failure of the treaty in the United States on the shoulders of the half-sick Wilson. For a recent and illuminating article on a brace of bitter-end opponents of the League, consult Ralph A. Stone, "Two Illinois Senators Among the Irreconcilables," *Mississippi Valley Historical Review*, L, 443–465 (December, 1963).

Samuel H. Adams's *Incredible Era: The Life and Times of Warren Gamaliel Harding* (Boston, 1939) is a colorful rather than scholarly piece of work. Certain aspects of Harding's essential weaknesses are well treated in Francis Russell, "The Four Mysteries of Warren Harding," *American Heritage*, XIV, 5 ff. (April, 1963). But see also Andrew Sinclair, *The Available Man: The Life Behind the Masks of Warren Gamaliel Harding* (New York, 1965); a recent study which partially re habilitates Harding's reputation.

The flavor of the postwar reaction is captured by a number of books which bear only indirectly on foreign affairs. Robert K. Murray, *Red Scare: A Study in National Hysteria, 1919–1920* (Minneapolis, 1955) is a sound monograph. The xenophobic trends detected by Murray are skillfully portrayed in William E. Leuchtenburg, *The Perils of Prosperity, 1914–1932* (Chicago, 1958), a book marked by shrewd and penetrating insights into the growing indifference to overseas events. Karl Schriftgiesser, *This Was Normalcy: An Account of Party Politics During Twelve Republican Years, 1920–1932* (Boston, 1948) is hyperbolic in tone but does serve as an interesting primer on the politics of this era of rising isolationism. Frederick L. Allen's *Only Yesterday: An Informal History of the Nineteen-Twenties* (2nd ed., New York, 1957), although devoted mainly to social history, tells much of the general disillusionment which so rapidly outdated Wilson's dream of a new world order. See also Edmund Traverso, *The 1920's: Rhetoric and Reality* (Boston, 1964). John Higham, *Strangers in the Land: Patterns of American Nativism, 1860–1925* (New Brunswick, 1955) is the best account of the postwar wave of anti-immigrant prejudice which crested with the restrictions imposed by Congress in 1924.

The best account of the Ku Klux Klan of the 1920's forms part of David M. Chalmers's recent study, *Hooded Americanism* (New York, 1965). See also the contemporary but shrewd analysis of John M. Mecklin, *The Ku Klux Klan: A Study of the American Mind* (New York, 1924). Some idea of the wide range of the Klan's influence can be gained from reading Emma Lou Thornbrough, "Segregation in Indiana during the Klan Era of the 1920's," *Mississippi Valley Historical Review,* XLVII, 594–618 (March, 1961). A recent survey of the political operations of the KKK in certain southern states during this period is found in Arnold S. Rice, *The Ku Klux Klan in American Politics* (Washington, 1962). This selective history is especially penetrating when it deals with the various state conventions of the Klan during the presidential election of 1924.

Harding's election has only recently come under full-scale historical investigation. It is explored by Wesley M. Bagby in *The Road to Normalcy: The Presidential Campaign and Election of 1920* (Baltimore, 1962). Indispensable reading on the period must include the initial installments of two multivolumed biographies of FDR, still in the process of completion: Frank Freidel's *Franklin D. Roosevelt: The Apprenticeship* (Boston, 1952) should be used to supplement Bagby on the 1920 campaign, and for an understanding of how the Democrats subsequently tried to cast off the League albatross. Arthur M. Schlesinger, Jr.'s parallel work, *The Age of Roosevelt: The Crisis of the Old Order, 1919–1933* [I] (Boston, 1957), while devoted almost entirely to domestic developments, vividly recalls many episodes directly or indirectly related to the conduct of foreign affairs. The material covered in this chapter is presented in greater detail in Selig Adler, *The Isolationist Impulse: Its Twentieth-Century Reaction* (New York, 1957), Chapters III–V. Conflicting American opinions on the Wilsonian plan for collective security are emphasized in John Chalmers Vinson, *Referendum for Isolation: Defeat of Article X of the League of Nations Covenant* (Athens, Ga., 1961).

CHAPTER 2: BLUEPRINTS FOR PEACE

In recent years much deserved attention has been paid to the role of public opinion in the shaping of foreign policy. Thomas A. Bailey, a pioneer historian in this area, found popular attitudes influential but "also ignorant and fickle" in *The Man in the Street: The Impact of American Public Opinion on Foreign Policy* (New York, 1948). One group of political scientists, viewing the matter from a different perspective, has investigated the problem with somewhat divergent results. See Gabriel A. Almond's behavioral study, *The American People and Foreign Policy* (New York, 1950), and Robert A. Dahl, *Congress and Foreign Policy* (New York, 1950). Indispensable to the student of foreign affairs are the annual records of diplomatic developments listed in the "General Works" section of this bibliography.

Thoughtful reflections concerning the impact of public opinion upon diplomatic decisions may be found in Elihu Root, "A Requisite for the Success of Popular Diplomacy," *Foreign Affairs*, I, 3–10 (September 15, 1922). Appropriately enough, this penetrating analysis by a renowned older statesman ornamented the very first issue of a journal whose contents have shed so much light on the course of American foreign policy. Noteworthy among these contributions are the vivid recollections of a prime mover in the popularization of the workings of diplomacy, Hamilton Fish Armstrong. See his arresting article, "Last Time," *ibid.*, XXIII, 349–377 (April, 1945).

A number of writers have concentrated upon the resurgence of isolationism following the American rejection of the Treaty of Versailles. In addition to Adler, *The Isolationist Impulse*, consult the sections by DeConde and Kenneth W. Thompson in Alexander DeConde (ed.), *Isolation and Security: Ideas and Security in Twentieth-Century American Foreign Policy* (Durham, 1957), pp. 3–32, 159–183. Many articles deal with specific phases of recent isolationism. See Selig Adler, "The War-Guilt Question and American Disillusionment, 1918–1928," *Journal of Modern History*, XXIII, 1–28 (March, 1951) and William G. Carleton, "Isolationism and the Middle West," *Mississippi Valley Historical Review*, XXXIII, 377–390 (December, 1946). Carleton argues that the wave of midwestern isolationism did not crest until the 1930's. His views invite comparison with Ralph H. Smuckler's "The Region of Isolationism," *American Political Science Review*, XLVII, 386–401 (June, 1953) and Ray A. Billington's "The Origins of Middle Western Isolationism," *Political Science Quarterly*, LX, 44–64 (March, 1945). Billington stresses sectional and ethnic factors. These points are emphasized to the exclusion of other basic causes in the ephemeral writings of Samuel Lubell and in his lively book, *The Future of American Politics* (New York, 1952). In "The South and Isolationism," *Journal of Southern History*, XXIV, 332–346 (August, 1958) Alexander

DeConde explains why Dixie, traditionally provincial in outlook, was attracted to the internationalist goals of Wilson and the second Roosevelt. In numerous writings, especially "The Legend of Isolationism in the 1920's," *Science and Society*, XVIII, 1–20 (Winter, 1954), William A. Williams has maintained that the United States never reverted to a species of isolationism after the First World War. While some of Williams's arguments modify previous interpretations, he overstates his case.

Two recent studies synthesize the numerous factors which gave rise to interwar isolationism. There is a well-balanced analysis of this causation in Wayne S. Cole, *Senator Gerald P. Nye and American Foreign Relations* (Minneapolis, 1962), pp. 4 ff. But see also the contrasting approach of Leroy N. Rieselbach, "The Basis of Isolationist Behavior," *Public Opinion Quarterly*, XXIV, 645–657 (Winter, 1960). The political background of the influential farm bloc is fully explored in Russel B. Nye, *Midwestern Progressive Politics: A Historical Study of its Origins and Development, 1870–1958* (2nd rev. ed., East Lansing, Mich., 1963).

After 1919 the flag-waving nationalists were often confused with the continental-minded isolationists. The former group actually wanted their country to play a leading but unilateral role in the game of world politics, and this desire made them champions of national power. Their reliance upon force is illustrated by a contemporary article: William L. Rodgers, "Can Courts and Tribunals Maintain World Peace?", *The Annals*, CXX, 69–76 (July, 1925). Public support for strident militarism is carefully weighed in Robert D. Ward, "The Origins and Activities of the National Security League, 1914–1919," *Mississippi Valley Historical Review*, XLVII, 51–65 (June, 1960). Armin Rappaport has skillfully deflated the importance of the organized navalists in *The Navy League of the United States* (Detroit, 1962).

Historians have given less heed to the persistent Wilsonians than to the activities of their isolationist counterparts. Pending monographic treatment of the subject, the trials and tribulations of the internationalists must be followed in Frank Freidel, *Franklin D. Roosevelt: The Ordeal* (Boston, 1954); relevant parts of Eric F. Goldman, *Rendezvous With Destiny: A History of Modern American Reform* (New York, 1952) and Chapters Six and Nine of Adler, *The Isolationist Impulse*. Insight into how the internationally minded viewed contemporary problems can be gained by reading the essays in Esther E. Lape (ed.), *Ways to Peace* (New York, 1924). The activities of a foremost proponent of world organization, former Supreme Court Justice John H. Clarke, are related in the following studies: Hoyt L. Warner, *The Life of Mr. Justice Clarke: A Testament to the Power of Liberal Dissent in America* (Cleveland, 1959) and Carl F. Wittke, "Mr. Justice Clarke— A Supreme Court Judge in Retirement," *Mississippi Valley Historical Review*, XXXVI, 27–50 (June, 1949).

A good understanding of the press's attitude toward foreign affairs in Coolidge's day can be found in Silas Bent, "International Window-Smashing: The Role of Our Newspapers in Foreign Affairs," *Harper's*, CLVII, 421–428 (September, 1928). This subject is also treated in Charles Fisher, *The Columnists* (New York, 1944) and William A. Swanberg, *Citizen Hearst: A Biography of William Randolph Hearst* (New York, 1961).

By all odds the most penetrating account of the peace movements of the 1920's is Robert H. Ferrell's superb monograph, *Peace in Their Time: The Origins of the Kellogg-Briand Pact* (New Haven, 1952). America's search for a substitute for the League's pattern of collective action is neatly summarized by the same author in DeConde (ed.), *Isolation and Security*, pp. 82–106. The grip of international law upon the American mind and the limitations of this legal approach are weighed by Gunnar Myrdal in Harold K. Jacobson (ed.), *America's Foreign Policy* (New York, 1960), pp. 188–212. Percy E. Corbett, *Law in Diplomacy* (Princeton, 1959) measures the long run relationship of legalism and foreign policy by means of case studies pertaining particularly to diplomatic controversies involving the United States, Great Britain, and Russia. This erudite study concludes: "Law fares rather badly in diplomacy. It seeks to correct human weaknesses: diplomacy accommodates them. Between the two there is an invisible strain, and at a certain tension the law breaks."

CHAPTER 3: MIDSTREAM DIPLOMACY

No specialized work treats in detail all aspects of the diplomacy of the Republican Restoration. A sagacious but brief interpretation by an outstanding historian, Allan Nevins, *The United States in a Chaotic World: A Chronicle of International Affairs, 1918–1933* (New Haven, 1950), constitutes a profitable supplement to this and the ensuing chapter. The most recent scholarly survey which incorporates many particulars on foreign affairs is John D. Hicks, *Republican Ascendancy,*

1921–1933 (New York, 1960). As customary in all volumes of *The New American Nation Series,* Hicks's book includes a comprehensive "Bibliographical Essay."

Existing biographies of Harding and Coolidge are relatively thin on foreign affairs. However, Claude M. Fuess, *Calvin Coolidge: The Man from Vermont* (Boston, 1940) is a fine piece of work and provides a sympathetic understanding of its prosaic subject. William Allen White, *A Puritan in Babylon: The Story of Calvin Coolidge* (New York, 1938) is more impressionistic but a masterpiece of style. The gap in the diplomatic history of the 1920's is partially filled by some superior work on the career of Secretary of State Hughes. Merlo J. Pusey, *Charles Evans Hughes,* 2 vols. (2nd ed. New York, 1963) is a detailed semiofficial work based in part on information supplied by Hughes to the author. While this biography won a Pulitzer Prize, Pusey's approach was fairly uncritical and he assumed that Secretary Hughes accomplished as much as could be expected, given the circumstances under which he labored. More interpretative, concise, and perceptive, yet still generally favorable to Hughes is Dexter Perkins, *Charles Evans Hughes and American Democratic Statesmanship* (Boston, 1956). Two studies concentrate on Hughes's Cabinet career. Charles Cheney Hyde, an outstanding authority on international law associated with Hughes in the State Department, wrote the section on "Charles Evans Hughes" in Samuel F. Bemis (ed.), *The American Secretaries of State and Their Diplomacy,* Vol. X (New York, 1929), pp. 219–401. A briefer sketch, based upon more recent material, is that by John Chalmers Vinson in Norman A. Graebner (ed.), *An Uncertain Tradition: American Secretaries of State in the Twentieth Century* (New York, 1961), pp. 128–148. John F. Bass and Harold G. Moulton, *America and the Balance Sheet of Europe* (New York, 1921) is a detailed description of the European economic havoc which prevailed at the time the Republicans returned to power.

Early American relations with the Soviet Union have yielded a plethora of literature. The interested student should begin with the authoritative writings of George F. Kennan, who is completing a trilogy entitled *Soviet-America Relations, 1917–1920.* Thus far he has published *Russia Leaves the War* (Princeton, 1956), a Pulitzer Prize winner which carries the story from the November, 1917, revolution to March, 1918. It was followed by *The Decision to Intervene* (Princeton, 1958), which probes in depth Wilson's motives in landing American troops on Soviet soil. Kennan has also written a less detailed work, *Russia and the West under Lenin and Stalin* (Boston, 1961); a book which abounds with the interesting judgments of a highly informed observer and a first-rate scholar. Contrasting reasons for American wartime military intervention in Soviet Russia's Pacific region are ably presented in Betty M. Unterberger, *America's Siberian Expedition, 1918–1920: A Study of National Policy* (Durham, 1956). The commanding general of the American expedition, William S. Graves, explains the reasons for the Siberian venture and overemphasizes his noninterference in the Soviet revolutionary caldron in *America's Siberian Adventure, 1918–1920* (New York, 1931).

For the views of an American historian who tries to penetrate and understand the wiles of Soviet diplomacy, consult William A. Williams, *American-Russian Relations, 1781–1947* (New York, 1952). A more conventional and spirited account is Thomas A. Bailey, *America Faces Russia: Russian-American Relations from Early Times to Our Day* (Ithaca, 1950). James W. Morley, *The Japanese Thrust into Siberia, 1918* (2nd ed., New York, 1957) is a penetrating analysis of Tokyo's motives in the light of Japanese archival material. Leonid I. Strakhovsky, *American Opinion about Russia, 1917–1920* (Toronto, 1961) illustrates how popular opinions about the USSR were based upon wholesale ignorance and unfounded rumors. The cleavage in American liberal ranks precipitated by the Soviet takeover is fully explored in Christopher Lasch, *The American Liberals and the Russian Revolution* (New York, 1962). Russian misunderstandings and distortions about the actions of the United States during the early Bolshevist period are described in George F. Kennan, "Soviet Historiography and America's Role in the Intervention," *American Historical Review*, LXV, 302–322 (January, 1960). Herbert Hoover, *An American Epic; Famine in Forty Five Nations: The Battle on the Front Line, 1914–1923*, [III] (Chicago, 1961) contains valuable but biased information on the author's relief efforts in Russia during the famine years of the early 1920's.

A fresh survey of relations between the United States and the League of Nations would be welcome. Meanwhile the best work on the subject remains that of Donna F. Fleming, *The United States and the League of Nations, 1918–1920* (New York, 1932) and *The United States and World Organization, 1920–1933* (New York, 1938). These comprehensive and splendidly organized books set a pro-League pattern of interpretation which widely influenced subsequent writers. Dexter Perkins's discerning essay, "The Department of State and American Public Opinion," in Gordon A. Craig and Felix Gilbert (eds.), *The Diplomats: 1919–1939* (Princeton, 1953), pp. 282–308, contains many fruitful observations on earlier American relations with the Geneva organization. See also the masterly article by David D. Burks, "The United States and the Geneva Protocol of 1924: 'A New Holy Alliance?' ", *American Historical Review*, LXIV, 891–905 (July, 1959). John S. Bassett, *The League of Nations: A Chapter in World Politics* (New York, 1928) is dated but still worthy of consultation. Charles A. Beard, "Prospects for Peace," *Harper's*, CLVIII, 320–330 (February, 1929) strongly reflects the positive reactions toward the League which prevailed in the United States on the eve of the Great Depression. The definitive work on the total accomplishments and failures of the League is Francis P. Walters, *A History of the League of Nations*, 2 vols. (London, 1952). William W. Kaufmann, "The Organization of Responsibility," *World Politics*, I, 511–532 (July, 1949) incisively evaluates the causes of the League's nonfeasance. European developments in the postwar decade which so often determined American diplomatic decisions are conveniently summarized in H. Stuart Hughes, *Contemporary Europe: A History* (Englewood Cliffs, N.J., 1961).

The standard work on disarmament projects and their execution during the period prior to 1947 is Merze Tate, *The United States and Armaments* (Cambridge, 1948). No up-to-date monograph covers all features of the numerous agreements reached at the Washington Naval Arms Conference of 1921–1922. For an on-the-spot but still valuable account consult Raymond L. Buell, *The Washington Conference* (New York, 1922). The mounting public demand for armament reduction is well measured in C. Leonard Hoag, *Preface to Preparedness: The Washington Disarmament Conference and Public Opinion* (Washington, 1941). The naval issues facing the American conferees are meticulously explained in Harold and Margaret Sprout, *Toward a New Order of Sea Power: American Naval Policy and the World Scene, 1918–1922* (Princeton, 1940). Intimate details of attempts to arrive at a formula for naval cutbacks in 1929 are described in Raymond G. O'Connor, "The 'Yardstick' and Naval Disarmament in the 1920's," *Mississippi Valley Historical Review*, XLV, 441–463 (December, 1958). From the very beginning Tokyo took a different interpretation of the Nine-Power Pact from that of Washington, according to Sadao Asada, "Japan's 'Special Interests' and the Washington Conference, 1921–22," *American Historical Review*, LXVII, 62–70 (October, 1961). It has been popular knowledge for over a generation that United States intelligence forces broke the Japanese military code and, in so doing, supplied Secretary Hughes with a trump card at the Washington Conference. This exciting story is told in Herbert O. Yardley, *The American Black Chamber* (Indianapolis, 1931).

Although superseded in some details by recent disclosures, A. Whitney Griswold, *The Far Eastern Policy of the United States* (New York, 1938) contains an outstanding analysis of the Washington meeting. See also Yamato Ichihashi, *The Washington Conference and After: A Historical Study* (Stanford, 1928). Charles N. Spinks, "The Termination of the Anglo-Japanese Alliance," *Pacific Historical Review*, IV, 321–340 (December, 1937) traces the course of this association and explains its dissolution. John Chalmers Vinson, *The Parchment Peace: The United States Senate and the Washington Conference, 1921–1922* (Athens, Ga., 1955) is a splendid description of the Senate's reluctant but final consent to the Four-Power Pact. Some inkling of how Americans of the 1930's came to believe that the Japanese had gained a major diplomatic victory at the Washington Conference can be gained from reading George T. Davis, *A Navy Second to None: The Development of Modern American Naval Policy* (New York, 1940). This book also expertly analyzes American naval problems between the World Wars.

CHAPTER 4: MAKESHIFT PEACE AND PROSPERITY

A clear and readable account of shifting American economic policies related to foreign affairs may be found in Hicks, *Republican Ascendancy*. Other analyses of the switch from debtor to world creditor status include John T. Madden *et al.*, *America's Experience as a Creditor Nation* (New York, 1937); Cleona Lewis, *America's Stake in International Investments* (Washington, 1938) and Muriel F. Jolliffe, *The United States as a Financial Centre, 1919–1933* (Cardiff, Wales, 1935). Herbert Feis, *The Diplomacy of the Dollar: First Era, 1919–1932* (Baltimore, 1950) is a particularly excellent overview by a scholar who served as adviser on economic affairs to the State Department in the early 1930's. Its conclusions have strongly influenced the views of subsequent writers. But see also Duncan M. McDougall's recent survey, *World Power and New Problems, 1914–1930* (New York, 1964). A judicious account which skillfully scrutinizes the relationship between American business needs and subsequent policies is Raymond F. Mikesell, *United States Economic Policy and International Relations* (New York, 1952).

Published before the Great Depression but still affording useful information is the pioneer study by Benjamin H. Williams, *The Economic Foreign Policy of the United States* (New York, 1929). The veteran journalist Frank H. Simonds recorded some seasoned judgments on the economic phase of diplomacy in *American Foreign Policy in the Post-War Years* (Baltimore, 1935). A foremost authority on international affairs, George H. Blakeslee, viewed matters from the vantage of Coolidge's day in *The Recent Foreign Policy of the United States: Problems in American Cooperation With Other Powers* (New York, 1925). There are also some rewarding comments on the foreign impact on the domestic economy in Simon S. Kuznets, *Economic Change: Selected Essays in Business Cycles, National Income and Economic Growth* (New York, 1953). The tenuous control of the State Department over private bankers who floated international loans in the 1920's is pointed up in James W. Angell's booklet, *Financial Foreign Policy of the United States* (New York, 1933). Economic determinism in the shaping of Republican diplomacy, 1921–1933, is overstressed by William A. Williams in *The Tragedy of American Diplomacy* (Cleveland, 1959). Two helpful articles illustrating American business expansionism subsequent to the First World War are John A. DeNovo, "The Movement for an Aggressive American Oil Policy Abroad, 1918–1920," *American Historical Review*, LXI, 854–876 (July, 1956) and John B. Hutchins, "The American Shipping Industry Since 1914," *Business History Review*, XXVIII, 105–127 (June, 1954).

The delicate interwar relationship between global prosperity, reparations, and war debts has never been subjected to full-scale analysis. Harold G. Moulton and Leo Pasvolsky, *World Debts and World Prosperity* (Washington, 1932) is a careful but technical study which needs revision in the light of lengthened historical perspective and the availability of additional sources. Bascom N. Timmons, *Portrait of an American: Charles G. Dawes* (New York, 1953) is an interesting biography covering a long and varied career which included the formulation of the Dawes Plan. Dawes published his diary entries for the first half of 1924 as *A Journal of Reparations* (New York, 1939), but no startling disclosures are found in it. For information on the origins of active American participation in the reparations-war debt tangle, consult the listings on Secretary Hughes cited in the bibliography for Chapter 3. The defiant attitude of the French toward their American war debt is described in Donald C. McKay, *The United States and France* (Cambridge, 1951). The most discerning account of American financial involvement in the Weimar Republic following the adoption of the Dawes Plan remains Feis, *The Diplomacy of the Dollar*. Further information on the Reich's monetary obligations is available through the assistance of the Royal Institute of Economic Affairs in Charles R. S.

Harris's *Germany's Foreign Indebtedness* (London, 1935) and in W. M. Jordan's *Great Britain, France and the German Problem, 1918–1939* (London, 1943). Dexter Perkins's essay, "The Department of State and American Public Opinion," in Craig and Gilbert (eds.), *The Diplomats,* pp. 282–308, has pointed comments on the State Department's dim-sighted view of global economic realities.

The standard biographies of President Coolidge have been previously cited. Authentic glimpses of the man may also be caught in the perceptive portrait sketched by Gamaliel Bradford, "The Genius of the Average: Calvin Coolidge," *Atlantic Monthly,* CXLV, 1–13 (January, 1930). It is indicative of the Yankee President's disdain of foreign affairs that the bibliography for his second Secretary of State is richer than his own. L. Ethan Ellis's manuscript-based account, *Frank B. Kellogg and American Foreign Relations, 1925–1929* (New Brunswick, 1961) is a restrained and judicious treatment. Ellis has also been responsible for the section on Kellogg in Graebner (ed.), *An Uncertain Tradition,* pp. 149–167. In addition, the diplomacy of the second Coolidge administration has been thoroughly analyzed in "Frank B. Kellogg, 1925–1929," by Robert H. Ferrell, in Ferrell and Bemis (eds.) *The American Secretaries of State and Their Diplomacy,* Vol. XI (New York, 1963), pp. 1–135. Ferrell's outstanding bibliographical notes on the period merit the attention of all future investigators.

There are two biographies of Senator William E. Borah who, as chairman of the Senate Foreign Relations Committee during the Coolidge-Hoover Era, helped tunnel the vision of the State Department. Claudius O. Johnson, in *Borah of Idaho* (New York, 1936) used his subject's personal papers, but he had to be cautious since he wrote during the Senator's lifetime, Marian C. McKenna, *Borah* (Ann Arbor, 1961) is more illuminating and rests upon some hitherto untapped sources. The dean of American diplomatic historians, Samuel F. Bemis, makes some astute observations on interwar foreign relations in "The Shifting Strategy of American Defense and Diplomacy," *Virginia Quarterly Review,* XXIV, 321–335 (Summer, 1948).

The sole monograph tracing the protracted campaign for American adherence to the World Court is Donna F. Fleming, *The United States and the World Court* (Garden City, 1945). Additional information and fresher insights into the problem may be found in the following: John Chalmers Vinson, "Military Force and American Policy, 1919–1939," in DeConde (ed.), *Isolation and Security,* pp. 56–81; the competent but brief biography by Richard W. Leopold, *Elihu Root and the Conservative Tradition* (Boston, 1954) and relevant parts of Robert H. Ferrell's stimulating text, *American Diplomacy*. See also the bibliographical items listed for Secretary Hughes, who formulated the original American reservations to the World Court Protocol, and for Secretary Kellogg under whose incumbency the Senate consented to the entry of the United States, subject to stipulations which proved unacceptable. The rancor engendered by the World Court battle in select journalistic circles is reflected in William Hard's writings, "The New World Court," *Nation*, CXXII, 6–7 (January 6, 1926); 30–31 (January 13, 1926); 58–60 (January 20, 1926).

Much literary attention has been focused on the story of the Kellogg-Briand Pact. The basic work on the subject is Ferrell, *Peace in Their Time*. How a private citizen can at times influence the course of world action is well portrayed in John E. Stoner, *S. O. Levinson and the Pact of Paris* (Chicago, 1943). Also noteworthy in this regard is Nicholas M. Butler's autobiography, *Across the Busy Years: Recollections and Reflections*, 2 vols. (New York, 1939–1940). President Butler of Columbia ridiculed Levinson's plan of outlawry until his own interest in the fight was sparked by the events of 1927. He then almost singlehandedly aroused enough public commotion to force the lethargic Coolidge administration into action. A leading historian who prompted Briand's suggestion for a no-war agreement with the United States tediously tells his story in James T. Shotwell, *War as an Instrument of National Policy and its Renunciation in the Pact of Paris* (New York, 1929). In contrast to some more recent investigators, Shotwell vindicated Briand of hidden motives in proposing a bilateral agreement with Washington. John Chalmers Vinson, *William E. Borah and the Outlawry of War* (Athens, Ga., 1957) assigns the Idaho senator a substantial part in the conclusion of the Pact and views charitably Borah's professed concern for American responsibility in the promotion of world peace. There is also some valuable information in an older account by Russell M. Cooper, *American Consultation in World Affairs for the Preservation of Peace* (New York, 1934).

It is a rewarding experience to read John Dewey, "If War Were Outlawed," *New Republic*, XXXIV, 234–235 (April 25, 1923), in order to understand the hold of Levinson's idea in rarified intellectual circles. Another important proponent of the cause, Charles C. Morrison, argues his case in *The Outlawry of War: A Constructive Policy for World Peace* (Chicago, 1927), a book which scarcely disguises the author's dislike of the League of Nations. On the basis of the above-cited readings, it is apparent that the outlawry camp included both ardent champions and severe critics of the League Covenant, each side hoping to gain specific objectives from the triumph of the plan. The end results of their joint efforts are cogently evaluated by Richard N. Current, "Consequences of the Kellogg Pact," in George L. Anderson (ed.), *Issues and Conflicts: Studies in Twentieth Century American Diplomacy* (Lawrence, Kans., 1959) pp. 210–229.

CHAPTER 5: THE HEMISPHERE: VERSAILLES TO PEARL HARBOR

The American Diplomatic History textbooks listed under "General Works" include separate sections which supplement the material covered in this chapter.

Latin American relations have attracted a great deal of specialized attention. The most comprehensive treatments of the general subject are Samuel F. Bemis, *The Latin American Policy of the United States: An Historical Interpretation* (New York, 1943) and Graham H. Stuart, *Latin America and the United States* (5th ed., New York, 1955). Bemis ordinarily defends Washington's actions and his comments are often tinged with a nationalist flavor. The book contains an excellent description of the GOP retreat from the imperious Big Stick policy. While some of his interpretations must be viewed in the light of more recent investigations, Bemis's survey remains the most important reference on the subject. Stuart's book is an adequate summary which has been periodically revised.

Dexter Perkins, *A History of the Monroe Doctrine* (2nd ed., Boston, 1955) is a distillation of a lifetime of research on the subject. See also Perkins's stimulating lectures published as *The United States and Latin America* (Baton Rouge, 1961). Arthur P. Whitaker, *The Western Hemisphere Idea: Its Rise and Decline* (Ithaca, 1954) is a penetrating piece of scholarship dealing with a broad sweep of time. The essential work on the wane of the expansionist impulse in the United States and the consequent liquidation of imperial responsibilities is Julius W. Pratt, *America's Colonial Experiment* (New York, 1950). Other books which touch, in part, on Pan-American affairs include Hicks, *Republican Ascendancy* and the sketches of Secretaries of State in Graebner (ed.), *An Uncertain Tradition*, pp. 128–209.

The southward economic thrust of the United States during the Prosperity Decade is measured in Max Winkler, *Investments of United States Capital in Latin America* (Boston, 1928) and Margaret C. Marsh, *The Bankers in Bolivia: A Study in American Foreign Investment* (New

York, 1928). Volume XCVI, pp. 31–44, of *The Annals* (July, 1921) embodies articles by three prominent Americans who feared for the Monroe Doctrine should the newly founded League of Nations prove successful. This worship at the shrine of the Doctrine also pervades Henry C. Lodge's complacent piece, "One Hundred Years of the Monroe Doctrine," *Scribner's*, LXXIV, 413–423 (October, 1923).

Doris A. Graber, *Crisis Diplomacy: A History of U.S. Intervention Policies and Practices* (Washington, 1959) is a useful synthesis tying together the American diplomatic actions which gave rise to so much foreign apprehension. Miss Graber argues convincingly that Washington's policies conformed to conceptions of the national interest and were seldom based on rigid adherence to doctrinal positions or legal standards. Big Stick diplomacy is caustically but recklessly assailed in Scott Nearing and Joseph Freeman, *Dollar Diplomacy: A Study in American Imperialism* (New York, 1925).

The Latin American point of view is examined in Clarence H. Haring, *South America Looks at the United States* (New York, 1928). The case for a union of southern republics to offset Yankee domination is forcefully presented by an Argentine intellectual, Manuel Ugarte, in *The Destiny of a Continent* [with an introduction and bibliography by J. Fred Rippy] (New York, 1925). This book invites comparison with an exposition by an eminent Mexican diplomat written at the height of the Good Neighbor rapprochement. See Luis Quintanilla, *A Latin American Speaks* (New York, 1943).

Daniel M. Smith, "Bainbridge Colby and the Good Neighbor Policy, 1920–1921," *Mississippi Valley Historical Review*, L, 56–78 (June, 1963) is a recent contribution illustrating the possibilities of archival research. Smith demonstrates that the campaign to reach a more cordial understanding with Latin America, pursued by Republican statesmen of the 1920's, was launched by Wilson's last Secretary of State. Secretary Hughes made a number of speeches defending his concept of New World diplomacy and rationalizing his reaction to Latin American demands. These addresses are published as *Our Relations to the Nations of the Western Hemisphere* (Princeton, 1928) and *Pan American Peace Plans* (New Haven, 1929).

A goodly number of studies survey the relations of the United States with individual Latin American countries. On Nicaraguan tensions, consult the old but reliable treatment by Isaac J. Cox, *Nicaragua and the United States, 1909–1927* (Boston, 1927). L. Ethan Ellis sheds new light on the disputes of the 1920's in Chapter Three of his *Frank B. Kellogg and American Foreign Relations*. Henry L. Stimson defends his own strong-handed methods in Managua in his *American Policy in Nicaragua* (New York, 1927). For the firsthand observations of a competent New York *Times* reporter, consult Harold N. Denny, *Dollars for Bullets: The Story of American Rule in Nicaragua* (New York, 1929). There are also two general accounts embracing American relations with this Latin American region: Dexter Perkins, *The United States and the Caribbean* (Cambridge, 1947) and J. Fred Rippy, *The Caribbean Danger Zone* (New York, 1940).

Supplementary material on twentieth-century relations with Mexico is plentiful. Charles W. Hackett, *The Mexican Revolution and the United States, 1910–1926* [World Peace Foundation Pamphlets, No. IX] (Boston, 1926) is an older work of merit. The most up-to-date general survey in Howard F. Cline, *The United States and Mexico* (2nd rev. ed., New York, 1963). The story of Morrow's mission to Mexico is well told in Harold G. Nicholson's excellent biography, *Dwight Morrow* (New York, 1935). But see also the more recent inquiries of Stanley R. Ross in "Dwight Morrow and the Mexican Revolution," *Hispanic American Historical Review*, XXXVIII, 506–528 (November, 1958) and L. Ethan Ellis in "Dwight Morrow and the Church-State Controversy in Mexico," *ibid.*, pp. 482–505. Ellis also has much to say about Mexican relations under Coolidge in Chapter Two of his *Frank B. Kellogg and American Foreign Relations*. The mission of Josephus Daniels during the 1930's is splendidly set forth in E. David Cronon, *Josephus Daniels in Mexico* (Madison, 1960). Daniels tells his own story with the gusto of a small-town newspaper editor in *Shirt-sleeves Diplomat* (Chapel Hill, 1947). There is an excellent summary of American-Mexican relations during FDR's day in Julius W. Pratt, *Cordell Hull, 1933–1944* (Robert H. Ferrell and Samuel F. Bemis, [eds.]), *The American Secretaries of State and Their Diplomacy*, Vols. XII–XIII, (New York, 1964).

Thomas F. McGann, *Argentina, the United States, and the Inter-American System, 1880–1914* (Cambridge, 1957) concentrates on an earlier period, but this basic work explains the origins of tensions which later grew bothersome. For a recent detailed treatment with a main focus on post-1914 relations, consult Harold F. Peterson, *Argentina and the United States, 1810–1960* (Albany, 1964).

The technical reasons for the abandonment of the Roosevelt Corollary to the Monroe Doctrine are fully outlined in the historical exegesis upon which this decision rested. See J. Reuben Clark, *Memorandum on the Monroe Doctrine* (Washington, 1930). The story is told in less technical fashion in Gaston Nerval, *An Autopsy on the Monroe Doctrine*

(Washington, 1930) and with keener perspective in Perkins, *A History of the Monroe Doctrine*. The impact of new currents of thought on the matter is reflected in Robert H. Ferrell, "Repudiation of a Repudiation," *The Journal of American History*, LI, 669–673 (March, 1965). Ferrell stresses President Hoover's initial vacillations on the Clark Memorandum and reveals that even after the document became official policy it was disowned in high State Department circles.

Latin American relations during the initial stages of the Great Depression are surveyed in Alexander DeConde, *Herbert Hoover's Latin American Policy* (Stanford, 1951). This well-researched monograph explains the shift in Latin American relations which began under Hoover and awards much credit to the latter in launching the Good Neighbor policy. A different point of view is suggested in Bryce Wood, *The Making of the Good Neighbor Policy* (New York, 1961). Wood maintains that the New Deal's liberal domestic orientation won over the hesitant Latins, and he stresses the importance of giving priority to national interests rather than to the claims of the private investor. Under Hoover and Stimson the United States returned to the practice of *de facto* recognition of revolutionary regimes, thereby removing one source of irritation with Latin America. On this topic consult Henry L. Stimson, "The United States and Other American Republics," *Foreign Affairs*, IX, No. 3, i–xiv (Special Supplement, 1931).

The following books are helpful in understanding the course of Latin American affairs in the New Deal years: Edward O. Guerrant, *Roosevelt's Good Neighbor Policy* (New York, 1950) and Donald M. Dozer, *Are We Good Neighbors? Three Decades of Inter-American Relations, 1930–1960* (Gainesville, Fla., 1961). Both authors laud FDR's efforts. However, it should be pointed out that part of the President's success is attributable to the cordial relationship which he cultivated with some depression-spawned dictatorships. The Good Neighbor policy was promptly put to test by the Cuban upheavals of 1933. E. David Cronon, "Interpreting the New Good Neighbor Policy: The Cuban Crisis of 1933," *Hispanic American Historical Review*, XXXIX, 538–567 (November, 1959) is an illuminating article which explains the President's moderation as due in part to the temperate counsel of his old chief in the Navy Department, Josephus Daniels. The details of the epoch-making inter-American conferences of the Roosevelt Era are fully described in J. Lloyd Mecham, *The United States and Inter-American Security, 1889–1960* (Austin, 1961), Chapters Five, Seven, and Eight.

The best general survey of Canadian-American relations is Hugh L. Keenlyside and Gerald S. Brown, *Canada and the United States: Some*

Aspects of Their Historical Relations (2nd rev. ed., New York, 1952). See also in this regard Carl F. Wittke, *A History of Canada* (2nd ed., New York, 1952). James M. Callahan, *American Foreign Policy in Canadian Relations* (New York, 1937), though old, is still functional. Canada is regarded as the diplomatic "coupling-pin" that linked Washington and London, in Harry C. Allen, *Great Britain and the United States: A History of Anglo-American Relations, 1783–1952* (London, 1954). Richard N. Kottman, "Volstead Violated: Prohibition as a factor in Canadian-American Relations," *Canadian Historical Review*, XLIII, 106–126 (June, 1962) points out the farcical importance of rumrunning during our earliest individual diplomatic dealings with Ottawa.

The background of Philippine independence is ably sketched in Gerald E. Wheeler, "Republican Philippine Policy, 1921–1933," *Pacific Historical Review*, XXVIII, 377–390 (November, 1959). A longer span of time is covered in Garel A. Grunder and William E. Livezey, *The Philippines and the United States* (Norman, Okla., 1951). Theodore Friend's seminal work, *Between Two Empires: The Ordeal of the Philippines, 1929–1946* (New Haven, 1965) supersedes all existing accounts of the separation of the Islands from the United States.

Chapter Five of Pratt's *Cordell Hull* is a fresh and lucid investigation of the Reciprocal Trade Agreements program, which constituted the economic arm of the Good Neighbor policy. This subject is also dealt with in masterly fashion by Arthur M. Schlesinger, Jr., in Chapter Fifteen of *The Age of Roosevelt: The Coming of the New Deal* [II] (Boston, 1959). Standard older monographs on the subject, still useful for details, include: Henry J. Tasca, *The Reciprocal Trade Policy of the United States* (Philadelphia, 1938) and William S. Culbertson, *Reciprocity: A National Policy for Foreign Trade* (New York, 1937).

CHAPTER 6: THE ORDEAL OF HERBERT HOOVER

A confident belief that the Versailles settlement would prove durable permeated the air on the eve of the Great Crash. This optimism is mirrored in Frank H. Simonds, "The Fifteenth Anniversary," *Review of Reviews*, LXXX, 57–62 (August, 1929) and is later recalled by the same author in *American Foreign Policy in the Post-War Years*. Even Charles A. Beard praised the League of Nations in his 1929 article, "Prospects for Peace," cited previously.

Historians appraising President Hoover tend either to exaggerate his accomplishments or to castigate him too severely for lack of vision and understanding. Although focusing largely on domestic matters, the most erudite and judicious account is Harris G. Warren, *Herbert Hoover and the Great Depression* (New York, 1959). Foreign affairs of the period are best studied in Robert H. Ferrell, *American Diplomacy in the Great Depression* (New Haven, 1957), a brilliant book resting on an unusually broad foundation of research. Ferrell's work reduces to an historical oddity William S. Myers's panegyric *The Foreign Policies of Herbert Hoover, 1929–1933* (New York, 1940). Hoover ably defended his own record without major concessions to his detractors in his *Memoirs: The Cabinet and the Presidency, 1920–1933* [II] (New York, 1952) and *The Great Depression: 1929–1941* [III] (New York, 1952). Joseph Brandes, *Herbert Hoover and Economic Diplomacy: Department of Commerce Policy, 1921–1928* (Pittsburgh, 1962) argues that Hoover, during his Cabinet career, utterly failed to comprehend the dangerous contradiction of extending American economic involvements abroad while simultaneously restricting a healthy two-way foreign exchange. Richard Hofstadter fascinatingly scrutinizes Hoover's frame of reference in *The American Political Tradition and the Men Who Made It* (New York, 1948), pp. 279–310.

There is an impressive bibliography on the career of Hoover's Secretary of State, Henry L. Stimson. Elting E. Morison, *Turmoil and Tradition: A Study of the Life and Times of Henry L. Stimson* (Boston, 1960) is a top-notch biography enlivened by a sympathetic understanding of its subject. A dozen years before Morison's work appeared, Stimson, with the help of McGeorge Bundy, prepared a memoir cast in the third person, *On Active Service in Peace and War* (New York, 1948). In the manner of autobiographies, it is self-defensive, but the book treats fairly and frankly the differences which existed between Stimson and his chief. Richard N. Stimson, *Secretary Stimson: A Study in Statecraft* (New Brunswick, 1954) is boldly critical, lauding Hoover's devotion to peace and censoring Stimson's proclivity for risky diplomatic language and action. See also Current's sketch of Stimson's record as Secretary of State in Graebner (ed.), *An Uncertain Tradition*, pp. 168–183. For a recent and impressive assessment of Stimson's diplomacy, including a comprehensive bibliography, see Robert H. Ferrell, "Henry L. Stimson, 1929–1933," in *The American Secretaries of State and Their Diplomacy*, XI, 137–289.

Raymond G. O'Connor, *Perilous Equilibrium: The United States and the London Naval Conference of 1930* (Lawrence, Kans., 1962) constitutes the best treatment of the subject. Benjamin Sacks, *J. Ramsay MacDonald in Thought and Action: Architect for a Better World* (Albuquerque, N.M., 1952) provides rich background on the British Prime Minister who, with President Hoover, called into being the London Conference.

Few events in recent history rival the Great Depression in far-flung internal and diplomatic ramifications. Its roots are luminously explored in John K. Galbraith, *The Great Crash, 1929* (Boston, 1955). Hicks, *Republican Ascendancy* also carefully weighs the basic causes and immediate consequences of this greatest of business slumps. A number of writings describe the drastic domestic consequences of the collapse of prosperity; aftereffects which helped precipitate the introversionist American mood of the 1930's. The sordid details of hard-scrabble depression existence are vividly portrayed in Leuchtenburg, *The Perils of Prosperity;* Dixon Wecter, *The Age of the Great Depression, 1929–1941* (New York, 1948) and Frederick L. Allen, *Since Yesterday: The Nineteen-Thirties in America* (New York, 1940). For the relationship between domestic suffering and popular attitudes toward foreign affairs, see Chapter Eleven of Adler, *The Isolationist Impulse.* The depression's influence on literary themes, which reflected the introspection of the period, is estimated in Alfred Kazin's *On Native Grounds: An Interpretation of Modern American Prose Literature* (New York, 1942). "No One Has Starved," *Fortune,* VI, 19–29 (September, 1932) is a moving account of American life during the nadir of the business decline. See also the interesting collection of sources in David A. Shannon (ed.), *The Great Depression* (paperback, Englewood Cliffs, N.J., 1960). American thought in the 1930's is analyzed in Leo Gurko, *The Angry Decade* (New York, 1947). Warren, *Herbert Hoover and the Great Depression* effectively deals with the President's fumblings during the passage of the Hawley-Smoot Bill and the repercussions of that ill-fated tariff measure.

An ominous consequence of the globe-wide depression was the spread of totalitarianism. The fundamental causes for the rise of the European dictatorships are deftly analyzed in Geoffrey Brunn, *The World in the Twentieth Century* (4th ed., Boston, 1962) and Hughes, *Contemporary Europe.* Hannah Arendt, *The Origins of Totalitarianism* (New York, 1951) is a brilliant, impressionistic interpretation marred by dogmatic overstatements. For a clearer and broader analysis, consult Carl J. Friedrich and Zbigniew K. Brzezinski, *Totalitarian Dictatorship and Autocracy* (Cambridge, 1956). The origins of Nazism are explored in Rohan D'Olier Butler, *The Roots of National Socialism, 1783–1933* (New York, 1941) and Thomas L. Jarman, *The Rise and Fall of Nazi Germany* (New York, 1956). The intellectual chain which linked the older German ideologists with the shoddy Nazi theoreticians is forged in Fritz R. Stern, *The Politics of Cultural Despair: A Study in the Rise of German Ideology* (Berkeley, 1961). In "A Prelude to Hitler's Greater Germany," *American Historical Review*, LIX, 43–65 (October, 1953), Robert H. Koehl demonstrates how German expansionist ambitions, bred during the First World War, served as a blueprint for the masters of the Third Reich.

In the manner of all historical phenomena, the 1931 Japanese invasion of Manchuria stemmed from complex and interrelated causes. The episode is narrated with precision and discernment in Ferrell, *American Diplomacy* and in Leopold, *The Growth of American Foreign Policy*. Although some details of the story have been modified by subsequent findings, Griswold, *The Far Eastern Policy of the United States* is still worth reading for the Manchurian crisis. Newer and more specialized monographs subject include Reginald Bassett, *Democracy and Foreign Policy, A Case History: The Sino-Japanese Dispute, 1931–1933* (New York, 1952) and Sara R. Smith, *The Manchurian Crisis, 1931–1932: A Tragedy in International Relations* (New York, 1948). Francis C. Jones, *Manchuria Since 1931* (New York, 1949) is a brief and restrained account which neatly fits Manchuria into the general range of Japanese imperial ambitions. Takehiko Yoshihashi, *Conspiracy at Mukden* (New Haven, 1963) is a first-rate account of the incident which brings the story *au courant* with present-day knowledge. Sources which came to light after World War II were previously used by Robert H. Ferrell in his illuminating article, "The Mukden Incident: September 18–19, 1931," *Journal of Modern History*, XXVII, 66–72 (March, 1955). See also the recent general survey by William L. Neumann, *America Encounters Japan: Perry to MacArthur* (Baltimore, 1963).

The current boom in Far Eastern studies has yielded a number of penetrating works on Sino-Japanese affairs. Dorothy Borg, *American Policy and the Chinese Revolution, 1925–1928* (New York, 1947) is a pioneering work which relates kaleidoscopic changes in China to policy-making in Washington. The Chinese background to the prolonged conflict with Japan is ably sketched in Edmund O. Clubb, *20th Century China* (New York, 1964). The Japanese setting for the years of aggression is provided by William G. Beasley, *The Modern History of Japan* (New York, 1963). The part played in the exaltation of Japanese nationalism by rapid technological changes and the reaction to foreign pressures is well measured in Delmer M. Brown, *Nationalism in Japan: An Introductory Analysis* (Berkeley, 1955). In "Japanese Nationalism and Expansionism," *American Historical Review*, LX, 818–829 (July, 1955),

Hilary Conroy explains how the Japanese Liberals fell prey to the expansionist spirit, and he examines the relationship between Japanese and European hypernationalism. On all of the matters broached above, see also the standard general account by Harold M. Vinacke, *A History of the Far East in Modern Times* (6th ed., New York, 1959).

The Hoover-Stimson reaction to the Manchurian crisis, the conflicting aims of the two statesmen, and America's limited cooperation with the League in this instance have been subjected to close historical inquiry. Armin Rappaport, *Henry L. Stimson and Japan, 1931–1933* (Chicago, 1963) examines "the moods of the people" in an attempt to determine why the United States and Great Britain failed to take steps vigorous enough to halt Japan when she took to the warpath in 1931. Stimson's caution during the initial stage of the Manchurian challenge is pointed up in Paul H. Clyde, "The Diplomacy of 'Playing No Favorites': Secretary Stimson and Manchuria, 1931," *Mississippi Valley Historical Review*, XXXV, 187–202 (September, 1948). The divergent views of the President and his Secretary of State in later stages of the crisis are analyzed in Richard N. Current, "The Stimson Doctrine and the Hoover Doctrine," *American Historical Review*, LIX, 513–542 (April, 1954). While Current finds a sharp difference in the ultimate aims of the two men, other authorities, including Robert H. Ferrell, feel that Hoover and Stimson drifted far apart only after the former left the White House. The reluctance of the American public to support hard-fisted action against Japan is stressed by Ernest R. Perkins in "The Non-Application of Sanctions against Japan, 1931–1932," in Dwight E. Lee and George E. McReynolds (eds.), *Essays in History and International Relations in Honor of George Hubbard Blakeslee* (Worcester, 1949), pp. 215–232. For Stimson's first published account of the Manchurian episode, see *The Far Eastern Crisis: Recollections and Observations* (New York, 1936). Stimson's nonrecognition policy and his Democratic successor's futile efforts to use it to halt further aggression constitute the theme of Robert Langer's legalistic account, *Seizure of Territory: The Stimson Doctrine and Related Principles in Legal Theory and Diplomatic Practice* (Princeton, 1947).

There is no recent monograph covering the election of 1932. An older analysis, Roy V. Peel and Thomas C. Donnelly, *The 1932 Campaign: An Analysis* (New York, 1935) is still helpful for understanding the issues. FDR's rise to power is skillfully traced by his two major biographers: Frank Freidel, *Franklin D. Roosevelt: The Triumph* [III] (Boston, 1956); and Schlesinger, *The Crisis of the Old Order*. Although foreign affairs played a subordinate role in the campaign and election, there are interesting sidelights on Roosevelt's 1932 understanding with the ultra-isolationists in Swanberg, *Citizen Hearst.*

CHAPTER 7: THE GREAT ISOLATIONIST
ABERRATION

The diplomacy of the Franklin D. Roosevelt Era has stimulated voluminous writing. The general works here cited provide a fuller grasp of the topics covered in the present and succeeding chapters. William E. Leuchtenburg's superb *Franklin D. Roosevelt and the New Deal, 1932–1940* (New York, 1963) speedily took its place as the best one-volume work on the subject. Like its sister contributions to *The New American Nation Series*, it contains an extensive, up-to-date bibliography. Albeit Leuchtenburg surveys all aspects of FDR's first two terms, his trenchant comments on foreign affairs are shrewd and often original. James M. Burns, *Roosevelt: The Lion and the Fox* (New York, 1956) is politically oriented but most helpful in understanding the thought processes of a complex and enigmatic individual. The following two books by outstanding historians are gracefully written, cover a wide area and are generally approving of FDR: Allan Nevins, *The New Deal and World Affairs: A Chronicle of International Affairs, 1933–1945* (New Haven, 1950); and Dexter Perkins, *The New Age of Franklin D. Roosevelt, 1932–1945* (Chicago, 1957). Pratt's *Cordell Hull,* based on an exceptional probing of the primary sources, is an indispensable reference for this and the balance of these chapters. Hull's accomplishments as Secretary of State are evaluated in capsule fashion by Donald F. Drummond in Graebner (ed.), *An Uncertain Tradition,* pp. 184–209. For the course of foreign policy as viewed from Capitol Hill, see Tom Connally and Alfred Steinberg, *My Name is Tom Connally* (New York, 1954). Lloyd C. Gardner, *Economic Aspects of New Deal Diplomacy* (Madison, 1964) is a recent but inadequate book on a vital subject.

There are two useful studies of Key Pittman, a man who was miscast in his role as chairman of the Senate Foreign Relations Committee during seven long years of international turmoil. Fred L. Israel, *Nevada's Key Pittman* (Lincoln, Neb., 1963) is a critical biography which indicts its subject for devoting too much attention to silver and irrigation projects at the expense of furthering the administration's foreign policy. Wayne S. Cole, "Senator Key Pittman and American Neutrality Policies, 1933–1940," *Mississippi Valley Historical Review,* XLVI, 644–662

(March, 1960) is somewhat more understanding of the Nevadan's peculiarities and frailties.

The exciting times in which they held office led American statesmen of the Roosevelt Era to record their "inside" observations. The most important of these recollections for students of diplomacy is *The Memoirs of Cordell Hull*, 2 vols. (New York, 1948). This highly detailed chronicle reflects the intellectual image of its compiler—plodding, self-defensive, and somewhat wearisome. As might be expected from the "Old Curmudgeon," *The Secret Diary of Harold L. Ickes* (New York, 1953) is saltier, but understandably contains far less on foreign affairs. Important because Secretary of the Treasury Henry Morgenthau, Jr. made a habit of invading the province of the State Department is John M. Blum (ed.), *From the Morgenthau Diaries: Years of Crisis, 1928–1938* (Boston, 1959). Nancy H. Hooker (ed.), *The Moffat Papers: Selections from the Diplomatic Journals of Jay Pierrepont Moffat, 1919–1943* (Cambridge, 1956) is studded with interesting tidbits of gossip and information garnered by a State Department official with a propensity for news. A sampling of the aforementioned firsthand accounts will recapture for the student much of the *Zeitgeist*.

Some members of the New Deal diplomatic team cast their stories in narrative form. See William Phillips, *Venturos in Diplomacy* (Boston, 1952) and Hugh R. Wilson, *Diplomat Between Wars* (New York, 1941). The collection of lectures by Herbert Feis, *Seen from E.A.: Three International Episodes* (New York, 1947) merits special attention because the author was a respected scholar who served, among other assignments, as Adviser to the State Department on International Affairs. Also interesting and valuable are the "aside" observations of FDR's favorite, Sumner Welles, Assistant Secretary and Under Secretary of State, 1933 to 1943. Welles's *The Time for Decision* and *Seven Decisions That Shaped History* constitute the personalized interpretations of a brilliant man who left the administration after a final parting of the ways with his unforgiving chief, Secretary Hull. Roosevelt's major public statements and addresses, some of which mark important shifts in the course of American diplomacy, have been superbly edited by Samuel I. Rosenman, *The Public Papers and Addresses of Franklin D. Roosevelt*, 13 vols. (New York, 1938–1950).

Hugh R. Wilson, Jr., *Disarmament and the Cold War in the Thirties* (New York, 1963) contains helpful information on the World Disarmament Conference which met at Geneva during 1932–1933. See also John W. Wheeler-Bennett, *The Pipe Dream of Peace: The Story of the Collapse of Disarmament* (New York, 1935); the journalistic account by

John T. Whitaker, *And Fear Came* (New York, 1936) and some comments by a British conferee, Major-General Arthur C. Temperley, *The Whispering Gallery of Europe* (London, 1938).

The most comprehensive assessment of the 1933 World Economic Conference at London forms part of Arthur M. Schlesinger's monumental and colorful *The Age of Roosevelt: The Coming of the New Deal* [II] (Boston, 1959). Even though the author holds his subject in high admiration, Schlesinger suggests that FDR would have gained more by guiding the Conference to empty, face-saving resolutions than by "torpedoing" it with a lethal message. Ferrell, *American Diplomacy in the Great Depression* and Pratt, *Cordell Hull* also contain fruitful accounts of the London Economic Conference. For technical financial matters in relation to the Conference, consult Jeannette P. Nichols, "Roosevelt's Monetary Diplomacy in 1933," *American Historical Review*, LVI, 295–317 (January, 1951). Bernard Sternsher in *Rexford Tugwell and the New Deal* (New Brunswick, 1964) contends that in 1933 the nationalists who gained FDR's ear were fully aware of the importance of an international economic concert but thought the timing inopportune for a general settlement of monetary problems and an agreement on tariff reductions.

Background information on the USSR on the eve and morrow of American diplomatic recognition is most comprehensively treated in Edward H. Carr's outstanding work, *A History of Soviet Russia*, 7 vols. (New York, 1950–1954). See also Max Beloff, *The Foreign Policy of Soviet Russia, 1929–1941*, 2 vols. (Oxford, 1947–1949) and Kennan's stimulating book, *Russia and the West under Lenin and Stalin*. Sister Anne Vincent Meiburger, *Efforts of Raymond Robins toward the Recognition of Soviet Russia and the Outlawry of War, 1917–1933* (Washington, 1958) traces the campaign for recognition of Moscow waged by an ebullient reformer. McKenna's *Borah* throws light on the quixotic Senator's labors in furtherance of the same goal. Robert P. Browder, *The Origins of Soviet-American Diplomacy* (Princeton, 1953) best describes the implementation of recognition by the Roosevelt administration and its immediate consequences. See also Donald G. Bishop, *The Roosevelt-Litvinov Agreements: The American View* (Syracuse, 1965). These conventional versions should be compared with Williams, *American-Russian Relations*, where the author interprets charitably the Soviet actions which so soon disillusioned many erstwhile American champions of recognition.

The last unsuccessful effort to secure American adherence to the World Court came in 1935. There is information on the Senate's coup de grâce to the proposal in Philip C. Jessup, *Elihu Root*, 2 vols. (New York, 1938) and in Leopold, *Elihu Root and the Conservative Tradition*. The effective Coughlin-Hearst propaganda campaign against the Court is vividly described in Swanberg, *Citizen Hearst*. See also the references on the World Court listed in the bibliography for Chapter Four.

Every analysis of interwar American diplomacy must account for the ultra-isolationist mood of the 1930's. Most of the general references on isolationism cited in the listings for Chapter Two continue to be useful. However, additional writings analyze the intensification of the mood which began with the Great Depression and waned with the ripening of the Axis crisis. Chapter Eleven of Cushing Strout's *The American Image of the Old World* (New York, 1963) provides novel and penetrating reflections. Helpful insights may also be found in Bailey, *The Man in the Street*, Dahl, *Congress and Foreign Policy* and Dexter Perkins, *The Evolution of American Foreign Policy* (New York, 1948). Allan Nevins and Louis M. Hacker (eds.), *The United States and its Place in World Affairs, 1918–1943* (Boston, 1943) illustrates the tendencies toward economic autarky. Osgood, *Ideals and Self-Interest in America's Foreign Relations* contains many telling comments on the isolationist aberration of the New Deal years. See also in this regard John C. Donovan, "Congressional Isolationists and the Roosevelt Foreign Policy," *World Politics*, III, 299–316 (April, 1951). Allen W. Dulles and Hamilton F. Armstrong, *Can We Be Neutral?* (New York, 1936) is a well-reasoned primer on the subject by authors somewhat less myopic than the host of their contemporaries. Raymond L. Buell, *Isolated America* (New York, 1940) is another useful book by an informed observer. The fundamentals of the isolationist position are outlined with authority in John Bassett Moore's pontifical article, "An Appeal to Reason," *Foreign Affairs*, XI, 547–588 (July, 1933). By no means, however, should any student neglect the compact but brilliant historical analysis of interwar isolationism in William L. Langer's and S. Everett Gleason's classic work, *The Challenge to Isolation, 1937–1940* (New York, 1952), pp. 13–51.

The climate of opinion which provoked the Senate Munitions Investigating Committee can be recalled by reading the stirring article, "Arms and the Men," *Fortune*, IX, pp. 53–55 ff. (March, 1934). Agitation for curbing the munition makers was also aroused by several accusatory books of which Helmuth C. Engelbrecht and Frank C. Hanighen, *Merchants of Death: A Study of the International Armament Industry* (New York, 1934) serves as a prime example. For the recollections of a leading lobbyist who helped bring the Nye Committee into being, consult Dorothy Detzer, *Appointment on the Hill* (New York, 1948). In Cole's *Senator Gerald P. Nye and American Foreign Relations,* the North Dakotan's activities have recently come under scrutiny. Cole's findings should be compared with the revisionist views of John E. Wiltz in "The Nye Committee Revisited," *Historian,* XXIII, 211–233 (February, 1961) and *In Search of Peace: The Senate Munitions Inquiry, 1934* (Baton Rouge, 1963). Wiltz points out that the Nye Committee had no direct influence on the formulation of the Neutrality Laws, that despite some lapses on the lecture forum, Nye held more temperate views than some of his committee colleagues and that the activities of the committee ultimately may have helped undermine the isolationist citadel.

We are still awaiting a general analysis of the revisionist school of World War I historians, who reached the peak of their influence in the 1930's. The most readable and effective book of this category is Walter Millis's *Road to War: America 1914–1917* (Boston, 1935), which pronounces folly, sentimentalism, and greed as the triple causes for our intervention in a European war. More influential in the scholarly world was Charles C. Tansill's heavily documented *America Goes to War* (Boston, 1938), which concentrated on the flourishing trade in munitions and private loans as the basic reasons behind the decision for war. Harold C. Peterson, *Propaganda for War* (Norman, Okla., 1939) stressed the importance of British persuasion in whipping up the American war spirit. In *The Open Door at Home: A Trial Philosophy of National Interest* (New York, 1934), Charles A. Beard forcefully argued for American abstention from European embroilments and eloquently pleaded for increased concentration on the solution of pressing domestic problems. See also Beard's interesting piece, "Giddy Minds and Foreign Quarrels: An Estimated American Foreign Policy," *Harper's,* CLXXIX, 337–351 (September, 1939), which appeared just as the Nazi invasion of Poland ended the Long Armistice.

Recent re-evaluations of the causes of America's 1917 intervention have played havoc with many standard arguments of yesteryear's revisionists. These rejoinders are conveniently summarized in Ernest R. May, *American Intervention: 1917 and 1941* [pamphlet, publication #30, Service Center for Teachers of History: A Service of the American Historical Association] (Washington, 1960).

The lengthening of historical perspective has also produced many fecund investigations of the spate of Neutrality Acts. Walter I. Trattner, "Progressivism and World War I: A Re-Appraisal," *Mid-America,* XLIV, 131–145 (July, 1962) traces some keep-out-of-war plans for FDR's day to the Progressive rebels of a previous generation. Homer E. Socolofsky, *Arthur Capper: Publisher, Politician and Philanthropist* (Lawrence, Kans., 1962) furnishes background on one of the early advocates of an arms embargo. The catchy phrase "collective security" did not become common parlance until the New Deal Era, according to Richard N. Current, "The United States and 'Collective Security,'" in De Conde (ed.), *Isolation and Security*, pp. 33–55. The evolution of the neutrality legislation of the 1930's is meticulously traced in Robert A. Divine, *The Illusion of Neutrality* (Chicago, 1962). Divine places a good deal of the blame for these shortsighted measures on President Roosevelt, who, owing to the press of domestic concerns, delayed too long in personally directing the course of foreign policy. FDR's initial propensity to compromise with the isolationists is stressed by Divine in "Franklin D. Roosevelt and Collective Security, 1933," *Mississippi Valley Historical Review*, XLVIII, 42–59 (June, 1961).

Two contemporary articles are especially significant for the ideas which they sparked in the minds of policy makers. Cardinal principles of the "new" neutrality were laid down by the distinguished international lawyer, Charles Warren, in "Troubles of a Neutral," *Foreign Affairs*, XII, 377–395 (April, 1934). Warren prefaced his suggestion by stating that he personally desired international cooperation as the first choice of policy for the United States. Inasmuch as public opinion ruled out this approach, he favored a prior to war curtailment of traditional neutral rights by Congress. The neutrality provisions of 1937 and 1939 owed much to the views of Bernard M. Baruch as outlined in "Neutrality," *Current History*, XLIV, 33–44 (June, 1936). From Baruch's fertile mind stemmed the nucleus of the cash-carry plan, an ingenious device designed to avoid wartime incidents on the high seas without sacrificing all the profits of trade with belligerent nations.

Opposed to the champions of a revamped neutrality structure stood a coterie of international lawyers and chauvinist senators who blamed American intervention on Wilson's failure to maintain a strict and impartial neutrality. A corollary to this thesis held that the United States could avoid entanglement in future wars by an unflinching adherence to traditional neutral rights as specified by international law. This is the point of departure of Edwin M. Borchard's and William P. Lage's tendentious book, *Neutrality for the United States* (2nd ed., New Haven, 1940).

The anticipated outbreak of the Italo-Ethiopian war prodded Congress into passage of the First Neutrality Act. This conflict, of course, was rooted in the ambitions of Mussolini. Background material on Italian Fascism and its leader may be found in two recent works: S. William Halperin, *Mussolini and Italian Fascism* (Princeton, 1964); and the evaluation by a British scholar-diplomat, Sir Ivone Kirkpatrick, *Mussolini, A Study in Power* (New York, 1964). See also an older but perceptive analysis by Guiseppe A. Borgese, *Goliath: The March of Fascism* (New York, 1937).

The European machinations and fumblings associated with the Ethiopian crisis are recounted in many studies and memoirs. Hubert Cole in *Laval: A Biography* (New York, 1963) strives valiantly to refurbish a badly tarnished reputation. A member of the League secretariat, Egon F. Ranshofen-Wertheimer, has described the League's inner workings during the crisis, placing much blame on the shoulders of Secretary General Joseph Avenol, who was both incompetent and notoriously pro-Italian. See *The International Secretariat: A Great Experiment in International Administration* (New York, 1945). Hugh R. Wilson, Jr., *For Want of a Nail: The Failure of the League of Nations in Ethiopia* (New York, 1959) utilizes some interesting correspondence of a key American trouble-shooter who happened to be the author's father. In *Prelude to World War II* (London, 1953), a famous anti-Fascist Italian historian, Gaetano Salvemini, castigates British duplicity during this great muddle of western European diplomacy. *Facing the Dictators: The Memoirs of Anthony Eden, Earl of Avon* (Boston, 1962) contains interesting sidelights and rationalizations for failure to retrieve the record of his predecessor in the British Foreign Office. Ludwig F. Schaefer, *The Ethiopian Crisis: Touchstone of Appeasement?* (paperback, Boston, 1961) is a collection of contrasting interpretations.

Two recent articles concentrate on the relations of the United States to the Italo-Ethiopian crisis: Henderson B. Braddick, "A New Look at American Policy During the Italo-Ethiopian Crisis, 1935–1936," *Journal of Modern History*, XXXIV, 64–73 (March, 1962); and Robert A. Friedlander, "New Light on the Anglo-American Reaction to the Ethiopian War, 1935–1936," *Mid-America*, XLV, 115–125 (April, 1963). Brice Harris, Jr., *The United States and the Italo-Ethiopian Crisis* (Stanford, 1964) is a sturdy, widely researched monograph which, however, does not alter the main outlines of the story. John Norman, "Influence of Pro-Fascist Propaganda on American Neutrality, 1935–1936," in Lee and McReynolds (eds.), *Essays in History and International Relations in Honor of George Hubbard Blakeslee*, pp. 193–214 is an interesting account which lives up to its title.

The story of Hitler's consolidation of power, 1933–1935, is included in the massive work by a prominent American newscaster who had much experience reporting events from Nazi Berlin. While guild historians have questioned some of its details and conclusions, William L. Shirer's *The Rise and Fall of the Third Reich: A History of Nazi Germany* (New York, 1960) powerfully tells a moving and absorbing story. Social, economic, and political features of the Hitlerian regime are analyzed in Richard Grunberger, *Germany, 1918–1945* (Chester Springs, Pa., 1964). Diplomatic maneuverings of the Nazis as viewed from the embassies of some major powers are explained by Franklin Ford, "Three Observers in Berlin: Rumbold, Dodd, and François-Poncet," in Craig and Gilbert (eds.), *The Diplomats*, pp. 437–476. William E. Dodd, Jr., and Martha Dodd (eds.), *Ambassador Dodd's Diary, 1933–1938* (New York, 1941) contains the interesting entries of a major American historian who represented his country in Nazi Berlin. It should, however, be used with caution since the accuracy of some of its recordings is open to question.

Perhaps more has been written about the Spanish Civil War than about any other prelude to the Second Armageddon. The causes of this internecine struggle are acutely analyzed in Gerald Brenan, *The Spanish Labyrinth: An Account of the Social and Political Background of the Civil War* (Cambridge, Eng., 1943). See also a briefer investigation by Spain's great historian, Salvador de Madariaga, in *Spain: A Modern History* (New York, 1958), pp. 377–477. Hugh Thomas, *The Spanish Civil War* (New York, 1961) is a brilliant and comprehensive study, carefully researched, fascinatingly written, and coolly objective in tenor. Additional information on the Spanish political background may be found in Stanley G. Payne, *Falange: A History of Spanish Fascism* (Stanford, 1961).

Much has also been written of the reactions of the great powers to Spain's ordeal. Russia's role is cogently evaluated in Kennan, *Russia and the West under Lenin and Stalin*, but his conclusions invite comparison with Thomas's assessment of the Kremlin's motives and objectives. The relations of the United States to the Spanish War are treated in two studies: F. Jay Taylor, *The United States and the Spanish Civil War, 1936–1939* (New York, 1956); and Allen Guttman, *The Wound in the Heart: America and the Spanish Civil War* (New York, 1962). Taylor explains Washington's circumspect behavior in terms of conflicting isolationist, religious, and ideological pressures, and he notes a gradual American shift in favor of the Loyalists as the Fascist threat mounted. Guttman describes the dilemmas created by the Spanish situation, involving isolationists who wanted to keep hands off but feared a Fascist triumph and American Catholics who detested the church-baiting Loyalists but were dubious of the long-run effects of a Franco victory. Cole, in *Senator Gerald P. Nye and American Foreign Relations*, points out how some die-hard isolationists, including Nye and Borah, favored a relaxation of the Roosevelt-inspired arms embargo against the Madrid government. The President himself came to doubt the wisdom of his own course but in the end sided with Hull against any change in policy. Chapter Seven of Dante A. Puzzo, *Spain and the Great Powers, 1936–1941* (New York, 1962) summarizes the American reaction to the war and emphasizes the pro-Loyalist position of the United States ambassador to Madrid, Claude E. Bowers. Bowers, a prolific if occasionally careless historian and biographer, recorded his own story in *My Mission to Spain: Watching the Rehearsal for World War II* (New York, 1954).

CHAPTER 8: THE PARTIAL ECLIPSE

Most of the general works cited for the preceding chapter carry the story through the twenty-six months of Axis-spawned crises which preceded the Nazi invasion of Poland. After 1937, events overseas played a sharply increasing role in the formulation of American policy. This relationship is well developed in relevant chapters of Leopold, *The Growth of American Foreign Policy* and in Davids, *America and the World of Our Time*. Robert E. Sherwood, *Roosevelt and Hopkins: An Intimate History* (New York, 1948) is an essential book. Gracefully written by an accomplished playwright, this prize-winning work, based on Hopkins's private records, provides a view from a ringside seat.

Langer and Gleason, *The Challenge to Isolation* is the basic account of American diplomacy from 1937 to 1940. It is paralleled, in less detail, by Donald F. Drummond, *The Passing of American Neutrality, 1937–1941* (Ann Arbor, 1955). Both monographs reach similar conclusions, which generally uphold Roosevelt's major diplomatic decisions.

Dorothy Borg, *The United States and the Far Eastern Crisis of 1933–1938* (Cambridge, 1964) lends fresh perspective to a hitherto neglected phase of Japanese-American relations. Her principal thesis is that the New Deal diplomats initially exercised patient restraint toward Tokyo lest a stronger stand lead to war. For a good contemporary analysis of Japan's unwarranted assumption of hegemony in the Far East by an informed observer, consult George H. Blakeslee, "The Japanese Monroe Doctrine," *Foreign Affairs*, XI, 670–681 (July, 1933). Following the outbreak of open warfare between Japan and China in

1937, the vast majority of Americans favored the cause of Chiang Kai-shek. The roots of this emotional attachment to China and its ultimate consequences are explored in William L. Neumann, "Determinism, Destiny and Myth in the American Image of China," in Anderson (ed.), *Issues and Conflicts*, pp. 1–22. There is a brief but intelligible road map through the internal muddle of China in Allan B. Cole, *Forty Years of Chinese Communism* [pamphlet, publication #47, Service Center for Teachers of History: A Service of the American Historical Association] (Washington, 1962). Citoshi Yanaga, in *Japan Since Perry* (New York, 1949), traces the rise of the Japanese "activists" during the pre-Pearl Harbor decade.

Francis C. Jones, *Japan's New Order in East Asia: Its Rise and Fall, 1937–1945* (London, 1954) is a fundamental work by a British scholar. Jones denies the existence of a Japanese master-plan for conquest, maintaining that each territorial lunge derived from a peculiar set of circumstances. Earlier interpretations of Japanese expansionism include: Harold S. Quigley, *Far Eastern War, 1937–1941* (Boston, 1942); Claude A. Buss, *War and Diplomacy in Eastern Asia* (New York, 1941) and William C. Johnstone, *The United States and Japan's New Order* (London, 1941). U.S. Department of State, *Peace and War: United States Foreign Policy, 1931–1941* (Washington, 1942) is a convenient collection of selected documents which was designed for wartime propaganda. Herbert Feis, *The Road to Pearl Harbor: The Coming of the War Between the United States and Japan* (Princeton, 1950) is a penetrating work which skillfully traces the growing rift between Washington and Tokyo. Business groups with trans-Pacific commercial ties sought to retard strong retaliatory measures against Tokyo, according to John W. Masland, "Commercial Influences Upon American Far Eastern Policy, 1937–1941," *Pacific Historical Review*, XI, 281–299 (September, 1942).

The conventional assumption that Roosevelt's speech of October 5, 1937 marked a sharp turning point in his foreign policy is questioned by Dorothy Borg in her corrective article, "Notes on Roosevelt's 'Quarantine Speech'," *Political Science Quarterly*, LXXII, 405–443 (September, 1957), and in her book cited above. Miss Borg is convinced the President had no definite plan in mind when he delivered the Chicago address. On the other hand, John McV. Haight, Jr., in "Roosevelt and the Aftermath of the Quarantine Speech," *Review of Politics*, XXIV, 233–259 (April, 1962) maintains that FDR originally gave serious thought to implementing the "quarantine" scheme and only later abandoned the plan. The favorite argument of World War II revisionist historians, that the Chicago speech was a "big herring" drawn across the trail of unsolved New Deal domestic problems, is elaborated by Charles C. Tansill, in *The Back Door to War: The Roosevelt Foreign Policy, 1933–1941* (Chicago, 1952).

For the Welles Peace Plan of 1937, see the books by Langer and Gleason, Borg and Pratt's *Cordell Hull.* Sumner Welles's own explanation of his scheme merits consideration. He told his story for the first time in *The Time for Decision* and elaborated it in the opening chapter of *Seven Decisions That Shaped History.*

The British policy of conciliating the Axis powers is impugned in Alfred L. Rowse, *Appeasement: A Study in Political Decline, 1933–1939* (New York, 1961). This slim volume by a prominent British historian is based in part on the author's personal diary. The best work on the chief architect of appeasement is Kenneth Feiling, *The Life of Neville Chamberlain* (New York, 1946), a friendly but reasonably objective biography. The views of one of Chamberlain's most influential American sympathizers may be found in the current best seller, Richard J. Whalen, *The Founding Father: The Story of Joseph P. Kennedy* (Cleveland, 1964). Students should also see the penetrating sketch by William K. Kaufmann, "Two American Ambassadors: Bullitt and Kennedy," in Craig and Gilbert (eds.), *The Diplomats,* pp. 649–681. Richard N. Stromberg, in "American Business and the Approach of War, 1935–1941," *Journal of Economic History,* XIII, 58–78 (Winter, 1953) demonstrates that the elder Kennedy's attitude was not typical of American financial tycoons, for most of them joined in the general drift "toward unneutrality and then war."

There is no specialized study of the right-wing isolationist coalition, which reached the peak of its power during Roosevelt's second administration. Charles J. Tull, *Father Coughlin and the New Deal* (Syracuse, 1965) contains essential background information. Edward C. Blackorby has traced the evolution of various dissident groups into the Union Party of 1936, but he touches only lightly on matters relating to foreign affairs. See his "William Lemke: Agrarian Rebel and Union Party Presidential Candidate," *Mississippi Valley Historical Review,* XLIX, 67–84 (June, 1962); and his biography, *Prairie Rebel: The Public Career of William Lemke* (Lincoln, Nebr., 1963). There is a rewarding chapter on the ultra-isolationists of the Depression Decade in Strout, *The American Image of the Old World.*

Concurrent with the cresting of the isolationist wave, countervailing voices demanded American rearmament to meet the mounting threat overseas. Fred Greene, in "The Military View of American National

Policy, 1904–1940," *American Historical Review,* LXVI, 354–377 (January, 1961), places the entire subject in proper historical perspective. Gerald E. Wheeler, *Prelude to Pearl Harbor: The United States Navy and the Far East, 1921–1931* (Columbia, Mo., 1963) agrees with Greene that throughout the interwar years the strategic thinking of the admirals was more global-minded than that of the generals. This point and other related matters are treated in a fresh study by Thaddeus V. Tuleja, *Statesmen and Admirals: Quest for a Far Eastern Naval Policy* (New York, 1963). John Chalmers Vinson, "Military Force and American Policy, 1919–1939," in DeConde (ed.), *Isolation and Security,* pp. 56–81, is an illuminating sketch. Samuel E. Morison, *History of United States Naval Operations in World War II: The Rising Sun in the Pacific, 1931–April, 1942* [III] (Boston, 1948) is the work of a great historian who deals expertly with American-Japanese rivalries in the later 1930's. The best account of Congress's refusal to build up the Guam naval base is in Earl S. Pomeroy, *Pacific Outpost: American Strategy in Guam and Micronesia* (Stanford, 1951).

The climactic events which precipitated World War II have produced so abundant a literature that citations of books and articles must necessarily be highly selective. There are good standard accounts in relevant chapters of the following texts: Hughes, *Contemporary Europe;* Bruun, *The World in the Twentieth Century;* and Cyril E. Black and E. C. Helmreich, *Twentieth Century Europe: A History* (2nd rev. ed., New York, 1959). The classic epic of the coming of the war remains, of course, Winston S. Churchill, *The Second World War: The Gathering Storm* [I] (Boston, 1948). Hajo Holborn, *The Political Collapse of Europe* (New York, 1951) is a brilliant account, rich in interpretations. The failure of England's prewar diplomacy is convincingly explained in Philip A. Reynolds, *British Foreign Policy in the Inter-War Years* (London, 1954). See also Arnold Wolfers, *Britain and France Between Two Wars: Conflicting Strategies of Peace Since Versailles* (New York, 1940) and an excellent portrayal by a prominent English historian, Charles L. Mowat, *Britain Between the Wars, 1918–1940* (Chicago, 1955).

Allen L. C. Bullock, *Hitler: A Study in Tyranny* (London, 1952) is an impressive biography by an Oxford historian who made superb use of the source material uncovered at the Nuremberg trials. Opposition to the Nazi terror within the Third Reich is described in Terence C. F. Pritte, *Germans Against Hitler* (Boston, 1964). For a recent provocative assessment of Central European diplomatic trends, consult Lionel Kochan, *The Struggle for Germany, 1914–1945* (Edinburgh, 1963).

It was inevitable that sooner or later some renowned historian would turn Devil's advocate and try to absolve Hitler from the overwhelming war guilt fastened upon him by the verdict of the generation whose hopes he blighted. This Herculean task was assumed by an Oxford don, Alan J. P. Taylor, in *The Origins of the Second World War* (London, 1961). Taylor calls it "an unwanted war" growing out of egregious blunders on both sides. Although he makes some interesting points, Taylor failed, as *The Christian Science Monitor* put it, in his "grotesque attempt to stand history on its head."

There are some noteworthy treatments of the succession of crises which culminated in the Second World War. For the Austrian coup, consult Gordon Shepherd, *The Anschluss* (Philadelphia, 1963). John W. Wheeler-Bennett, *Munich: Prologue to Tragedy* (London, 1948) is a readable book by a British writer who tends to be "soft" on the appeasers. John McV. Haight, Jr., in "France, the United States and the Munich Crisis," *Journal of Modern History*, XXXII, 340–358 (December, 1960), charges that Roosevelt's failure to take a strong stand during the Czechoslovakian crisis helped persuade the French to pay Hitler's price for peace. The 1939 Nazi-Soviet Pact appears less astonishing in the light of postwar investigations. A good example of this trend is Edward H. Carr's *German-Soviet Relations Between the Two World Wars, 1919–1939* (Baltimore, 1951). Carr, a British expert on Soviet Russia, reminds his readers that the tradition of cooperation between the two powers was not forgotten even while Hitler's anti-Bolshevist tirades were being broadcast throughout the world. The tragic results of Poland's vain endeavor to play off Germany against Russia and vice versa are measured in Bohdan B. Budurowycz, *Polish-Soviet Relations, 1932–1939* (New York, 1963).

Pertinent chapters in Divine, *The Illusion of Neutrality* and in Pratt, *Cordell Hull* explain the administration's futile attempt to secure modification of the Neutrality Law before the shooting began in Europe. The President's political handicaps during this period are well explained in Milton Plesur, "The Republican Comeback of 1938," *Review of Politics*, XXIV, 525–562 (October, 1962).

CHAPTER 9: THE CONVULSION OF EUROPE

Many competent studies retrace the step-by-step movement of the United States toward full participation in the Second World War. A first-rate bibliographical article by Wayne S. Cole, "American Entry into World War II: A Historiographical Appraisal," *Mississippi Valley Historical Review*, XLIII, 595–617 (March, 1957), reveals the post-1945 polemics on the subject to be largely a carry-over of the isolationist-interventionist debate of FDR's day. May's pamphlet, *American Intervention: 1917 and 1941*, reviews this road-to-war literature in briefer compass.

Langer and Gleason, *The Challenge to Isolation* and its sequel, *The Undeclared War, 1940–1941* (New York, 1953), cast pre-Pearl Harbor American diplomacy in globe-wide perspective. These essential books, generally accepted as the classic interpretation, have been altered in some minor details by subsequent specialized research. Drummond, *The Passing of American Neutrality* is a useful survey of the same period. In general, these works imply that circumstances rather than desire for a strenuous diplomacy dictated Roosevelt's actions. Readers interested in dissent from this premise should begin with the writings of Charles A. Beard. The final literary efforts of this eminent historian accuse FDR of beguiling the American people into war with deceiving promises of peace. In *American Foreign Policy in the Making, 1932–1940* (New Haven, 1946), Beard belabored the contrast between Roosevelt's anti-war pronouncements and his actions, which veered the country toward foreign embroilments. The tone of its companion volume, *President Roosevelt and the Coming of the War, 1941* (New Haven, 1948), is even less restrained. Without making allowance for the fact that the President had to gear his diplomacy to kaleidoscopic shifts in the global power structure, Beard indicted FDR for inconsistencies and contradictions in statements and policies. Basil Rauch refuted Beard with considerable success in *Roosevelt: From Munich to Pearl Harbor* (New York, 1950)—albeit at times his refutation leans too far in the White House's direction. Robert A Divine's paperback, *The Reluctant Belligerent: American Entry into World War II* (New York, 1965), is a concise and well-balanced evaluation based on the latest published findings.

The best account of two crucial years of American relations with Hitler is Hans L. Trefousse, *Germany and American Neutrality, 1939–1941* (New York, 1951). The initial chapter of this monograph contains a thoughtful analysis of the Nazi threat to the United States. Trefousse is also the author of an interesting article, "Failure of German Intelligence in the United States, 1935–1945," *Mississippi Valley Historical Review*, XLII, 84–100 (June, 1955). He contends that the Nazi secret service in America was "singularly ineffective," and whatever pertinent information it relayed to Berlin was not put to effective use. In his *History of United States Naval Operations in World War II: The Battle of the Atlantic, September, 1939–May, 1943* [I] (Boston, 1947), Samuel E. Morison expertly explores the wartime relationship between foreign policy and naval strategy.

Two contemporary books deserve special mention: Forrest Davis and Ernest K. Lindley, *How War Came* (New York, 1942) is a journalistic account which set the pattern for vindicating Roosevelt's prewar diplomatic maneuvers. Joseph Alsop and Robert Kintner, *American White Paper: The Story of American Diplomacy and the Second World War* (New York, 1940) preserves the sense of urgency and crisis which prevailed in the United States following the fall of France. The efforts of Secretary Stimson and other "activists" to prod FDR into taking longer steps toward war are recounted in Chapter Fifteen of Stimson and Bundy, *On Active Service in Peace and War.*

Relevant chapters in Divine, *The Illusion of Neutrality*, in Pratt, *Cordell Hull*, and in Dulles, *America's Rise to World Power* explain the administration's success in securing revision of the Neutrality Law after the shooting began in Europe. Current, "The United States and 'Collective Security'," in DeConde (ed.), *Isolation and Security*, pp. 33–55, contains some shrewd insights into FDR's strategy in this and related matters. The President's talent for mobilizing public opinion is deftly analyzed in Daniel J. Boorstin, "Selling the President to the People," *Commentary*, XX, 421–427 (November, 1955). Harold F. Gosnell, *Champion Campaigner: Franklin D. Roosevelt* (New York, 1952) is a splendid assessment of FDR's political expertise by a highly competent observer. In 1939 Roosevelt was faced with the fact that some of the greatest admirers of his domestic accomplishments were strongly opposed to his unprecedented conception of neutrality. The dilemma of those men who dreaded both the spread of Fascism and American involvement in war is brilliantly described in Chapter Sixteen of Goldman, *Rendezvous With Destiny.*

The Russo-Finnish fray interrupted the tedium of the winter of 1939–1940. How this "war within a war" caused a temporary juxtaposition of isolationists and interventionists is explained in Robert Sobel, *The Origins of Interventionism: The United States and the Russo-Finnish War* (New York, 1960). Valuable information on this subject may also be found in Andrew J. Schwartz's useful little book, *America and the Russio-Finnish War* (Washington, 1960).

The Nazi blitz of 1940, culminating in the surrender of France, is covered in the Modern European History texts listed for the preceding chapter. A number of specialized accounts add interesting details on the events of those cataclysmic weeks. Jacques Bonoist-Méchin, *Sixty Days that Shook the West: The Fall of France, 1940* (New York, 1963) is a summary of events compiled by a former Nazi collaborator. For an arresting interpretation, consult Marc L. B. Bloch, *Strange Defeat* (London, 1949), a contemporary condemnation by a French medievalist executed by a Nazi firing squad. An essential weakness of the Third Republic is explored in Charles A. Micaud, *The French Right and Nazi Germany, 1933–1939: A Study of Public Opinion* (Durham, 1943). For an eye-witness account of France's ordeal by an influential British observer, see Major-General Sir Edward L. Spears, *Assignment to Catastrophe*, 2 vols. (New York, 1954–1955).

The wisdom of the American decision to recognize Vichy France has been ardently debated. Cordell Hull, smarting from widespread criticism of his Vichy policy, wanted the whole matter reviewed in the light of historical perspective. This was done with results favorable to the Roosevelt administration by William L. Langer in *Our Vichy Gamble* (New York, 1947). Langer's conclusions were sharply challenged by another outstanding authority, Louis Gottschalk, in "Our Vichy Fumble," *Journal of Modern History*, XX, 47–56 (March, 1948). Admiral William D. Leahy, American ambassador to Pétain's captive regime, justified his mission and told of his experiences in *I Was There* (New York, 1950). Chapter Four of Sumner Welles's *The Time For Decision* includes a vigorous defense of the State Department's Vichy policy.

The most spirited account of the 1940 Battle of Britain forms part of Winston S. Churchill's, *The Second World War: Their Finest Hour* [II] (Boston, 1949). Churchill's contemporary speeches are conveniently collected in his *Blood, Sweat, and Tears* (New York, 1941). Hitler's prospects for a successful landing on British soil are appraised by Walter Ansel in *Hitler Confronts England* (Durham, 1960). This German authority argues that the Nazis might well have executed "Operation Sea Lion," the code name for the invasion of England, had the German high command not been misled by some "major misconceptions." Churchill's ascent to power and the RAF's victories in the 1940 air duels over Britain are neatly summarized in Hughes, *Contemporary Europe*, pp. 313–316. There is a cogent evaluation of the threat of a total Nazi victory to American interests in Douglas Miller, *You Can't Do Business With Hitler* (Boston, 1941). This book compelled contemporary attention, for it was written on the basis of the author's six years of diplomatic experience in Nazi Berlin.

In addition to the comprehensive works cited above, competent shorter accounts of the American shift from neutrality to nonbelligerency may be found in Leopold, *The Growth of American Foreign Policy;* in Pratt, *A History of United States Foreign Policy* and in Davids, *America and the World of Our Time.* The background information on the destroyer-bases swap and the Lend-Lease Act is detailed in Churchill, *Their Finest Hour.* The student will also find valuable two books by Richard W. Van Alstyne: *American Diplomacy in Action: A Series of Case Studies* (Stanford, 1944) and *American Crisis Diplomacy: The Quest for Collective Security, 1918–1952* (Stanford, 1952). Edward R. Stettinius's *Lend Lease: Weapon for Victory* (New York, 1944) was written while the war was still in progress and is uncritical in approach, but the book does incorporate useful information on the origin and progress of this program of massive assistance. Sir Llewellyn Woodward's *British Foreign Policy in the Second World War* (London, 1962) is based on archival material and includes items pertaining to Anglo-American relations. For military planning and coordination between Washington and London prior to official American entry in the war the standard account is Chapter Twelve of Mark S. Watson, *United States Army in World War II: Chief of Staff, Prewar Plans and Preparations* [IV, Pt. I] (Washington, 1950).

The story of the two opposing pressure groups which faced each other in the protracted debate over American neutrality is well told in separate studies. Walter Johnson, *Battle Against Isolation* (Chicago, 1944) traces the formation and activities of the Committee to Defend America by Aiding the Allies. The key work on the isolationist counterpart of this group is Wayne S. Cole, *America First: The Battle Against Intervention, 1940–1941* (Madison, 1953). The role of individual opponents of intervention can be followed in Cole, *Senator Gerald P. Nye and American Foreign Relations;* in Burton K. Wheeler [with Paul F. Healy], *Yankee From the West* (New York, 1962); and in Kenneth S. Davis, *The Hero: Charles A. Lindbergh and the American Dream* (Garden City, 1959). The domestic reaction against Mussolini on the part of some erstwhile admirers is measured in John Norman, "Repudiation of Fascism by the Italian-American Press," *Journalism Quarterly,* XXXI, pp. 1–6 ff. (March, 1944). The weakness of isolationism in the South is explained in Wayne S. Cole, "America First and the South, 1940–1941," *Journal of Southern History,* XXII, 36–47 (February, 1956) and in DeConde, "The South and Isolationism," listed previously.

As yet we have no monographic treatment of the crucial election of 1940. However, there is a good deal of information on the subject in Donald B. Johnson, *The Republican Party and Wendell Willkie*

(Urbana, 1960). Concentrating on Willkie's public career, Johnson brings to life many exciting details of the campaign and election. Mary E. Dillon, *Wendell Willkie, 1892–1944* (Philadelphia, 1952) is, like Johnson, sympathetic to the GOP standard-bearer. Until FDR's major biographers reach the story of his third electoral triumph, the best view from inside the Democratic camp remains Sherwood, *Roosevelt and Hopkins.*

CHAPTER 10: EDGING TOWARD WAR

Virtually all of the larger works listed for the two preceding chapters continue to be useful because they carry the story through Pearl Harbor.

Hitler's motives for moving against Stalin were mixed. Some notion of his underlying reasons may be gained by reading pertinent parts of Cyril B. Falls, *The Second World War: A Short History* (2nd ed. rev., London, 1948) and II. Liddoll Hart, *The German Generals Talk* (New York, 1948). The Nazi dictator's long-run aims, including the subjugation of the Soviet Union, are analyzed in Gerhard L. Weinberg, "Hitler's Image of the United States," *American Historical Review*, LXIX, 1006–1021 (July, 1964). The impact of the Russian invasion on the general course of the war is assessed in Winston S. Churchill, *The Second World War: The Grand Alliance* [III] (Boston, 1950). The American reaction to the German-Soviet war is dealt with in scholarly fashion in Raymond H. Dawson, *The Decision to Aid Russia; 1941: Foreign and Domestic Politics* (Chapel Hill, 1959). Dawson holds that Roosevelt's determination to aid Stalin stemmed primarily from military considerations, and that the President's actions were justified by existing circumstances. Dawson tends to minimize the amount of determined opposition that Roosevelt faced. Inasmuch as Americans greatly underestimated the Soviet military potential, they gave relatively little thought to long-run consequences of a Soviet victory. The problem at hand was to halt the Nazi Juggernaut and it was naturally given first consideration.

The occupation of Greenland and Iceland and the halting American steps toward full convoying are well treated in Chapter Thirteen of Pratt's *Cordell Hull.* Detailed accounts of crucial naval decisions may be found in Morison, *Battle of the Atlantic* and in Ernest J. King and Walter M. Whitehill, *Fleet Admiral King: A Naval Record* (New York, 1952). The pre-Pearl Harbor argument for the creation of a "world-girdling" American defense area is forcefully presented in Eugene

Staley, "The Myth of the Continents," *Foreign Affairs*, XIX, 481–494 (April, 1941).

No single monograph concentrates on the Roosevelt-Churchill rendezvous at Argentia in August, 1941. There are, however, rewarding descriptions of this colloquy in Langer and Gleason, *The Undeclared War;* Churchill, *The Grand Alliance;* Sherwood, *Roosevelt and Hopkins* and Davis and Lindley, *How War Came.* The opening chapter of Sumner Welles, *Where Are We Heading?* (New York, 1946) provides additional interesting sidelights.

Shortly after FDR returned from Newfoundland, the *Greer* incident touched off an undeclared naval war with Germany. Suppose some compromise had been reached with Japan. Would, then, the cumulative results of repeated maritime clashes have led eventually to a declaration of war by Washington or Berlin? Trefousse, in *Germany and American Neutrality*, speculates boldly but shrewdly upon this ticklish question. The final stand of the prewar isolationists came in an unsuccessful attempt to prevent drastic revision of the 1939 Neutrality Act. Details may be found in Cole, *Senator Gerald P. Nye and American Foreign Relations.*

The coming of the war with Japan constitutes a "hot spot" in the chronicle of American diplomacy. Many scholars have dealt with the wearisome negotiations aimed at resolving the differences between Washington and Tokyo. This protracted diplomatic haggling is skillfully traced in relevant chapters of Langer and Gleason, *The Undeclared War;* and in Pratt, *Cordell Hull.* Feis, *The Road to Pearl Harbor* is a superb study based on wide research and marked by judicious restraint. But see also Morison's gifted analysis, *The Rising Sun in the Pacific, 1931–April, 1942.*

There is a growing historiography on Japanese foreign relations of the prewar era. Tokyo's quixotic understanding with Berlin is explored in Frank W. Iklé, *German-Japanese Relations, 1936–1940* (New York, 1956) and in Ernst L. Presseisen, *Germany and Japan: A Study in Totalitarian Diplomacy, 1939–1941* (The Hague, 1958). Both of these works deal with the Axis Tripartite Pact, which so vexed Japanese relations with the United States. Jones, *Japan's New Order in East Asia* is also essential for an understanding of this trouble-breeding Pact. Nicholas J. Spykman, *America's Strategy in World Politics: The United States and the Balance of Power* (New Haven, 1942) is a good contemporary assessment of the Axis alliance from the geopolitical point of view. David L. Lu, *From the Marco Polo Bridge to Pearl Harbor: Japan's Entry Into World War II* (Washington, 1961) is essential to a deeper understanding of the inner workings of Japanese diplomacy. In accord with other recent investigators, Lu insists that Tokyo did not conceive of the 1940 Pact as an "offensive weapon" against the United States. The book also seeks to explain why Japan was determined to fight through to victory in China even at the cost of an American war. Further information on prewar Japanese diplomacy may be found in John Huizenga, "Yosuke Matsuoka and the Japanese-German Alliance," in Craig and Gilbert (eds.), *The Diplomats*, pp. 615–648.

In "Mukden to Pearl Harbor," *Foreign Affairs*, XXVII, 651–664 (July, 1949), Joseph W. Ballantine makes splendid use of the sources unearthed by the International Military Tribunal for the Far East. His inquiries led him to the conclusion that at no time after the Manchurian invasion of 1931 "would it have been possible to have brought Japan to abandon her policy of territorial expansion through measures short of the application of superior force." After pruning this same material in preparation for a more specialized study, Robert J. C. Butow reached a similar verdict in *Tojo and the Coming of the War* (Princeton, 1961). See also Butow's inviting article, "The Hull-Nomura Conversations: A Fundamental Misconception," *American Historical Review*, LXV, 822–836 (July, 1960). Here he explains how the bunglings of Ambassador Nomura, an inexperienced diplomat, obfuscated American-Japanese understandings at a critical juncture in the negotiations.

Shigenori Togo, Japan's Foreign Minister from 1941–1945 completed his memoirs, *The Cause of Japan* (New York, 1956), shortly before he died in Sugamo Prison while serving a sentence for war crimes. He insisted that cardinal decisions in prewar Japan were made not by high-ranking officials but rather by a junta of supreme commanding officers little known to the outside world. On the basis of his story, some historians argue that no American concessions within the realm of political possibility could have satisfied Japanese ambitions. The influence of the ultraists in the Tokyo power structure is well explained in Yale C. Maxon, *Control of Japanese Foreign Policy: A Study of Civil-Military Rivalry, 1930–1945* (Berkeley, 1957). But the Japanese militarists who opted for war against the United States were never foolhardy enough to expect a knock-out victory. They hoped rather to force Washington to choose a negotiated peace instead of continuing a two-front war against both major Axis partners. This essential point has been made by Louis Morton in "Japan's Decision for War," in Kent R. Greenfield (ed.), *Command Decisions* (New York, 1959), pp. 63–87. However, Morton observes that the Japanese "completely overlooked the American reaction to Pearl Harbor." Toshikazu Kase [with

David N. Rowe], *Journey to the Missouri* (New Haven, 1950) is a revealing story by a former member of the Japanese Foreign Office.

Joseph C. Grew, veteran diplomat who was the last American ambassador to prewar Japan, describes the coming of the war as seen from the embassy in Tokyo. *Ten Years in Japan* (New York, 1944) is a compilation of diary entries and official correspondence. There is additional material in Grew's complete memoirs, edited by Walter Johnson and published as *Turbulent Era: A Diplomatic Record of Forty Years, 1904–1945*, 2 vols. (Boston, 1952).

A number of fertile articles concentrate on the tense weeks just before the bombs dropped from the Hawaiian skies. Immanuel C. Y. Hsu, in "Kurusu's Mission to the United States and the abortive *Modus Vivendi*," *Journal of Modern History*, XXIV, 301–307 (September, 1952) argues that Kurusu was not sent as a decoy, for Tokyo still hoped that he might work out an eleventh-hour compromise with Hull. The gist of Raymond A. Esthus's "President Roosevelt's Commitment to Britain to Intervene in a Pacific War," *Mississippi Valley Historical Review*, L, 28–38 (June, 1963) is that while FDR promised London American help in event of a Japanese attack on Allied Far Eastern territory, the President planned to secure the prior consent of Congress before honoring this pledge. The revisionist argument (based on an out-of-context quotation from Secretary Stimson's diary) that the administration plotted to have Japan fire the first shot is cleverly demolished by Richard N. Current in "How Stimson Meant to 'Maneuver' the Japanese," *ibid.*, XL, 67–74 (June, 1953). Adolph A. Hoehling, *The Week Before Pearl Harbor* (New York, 1963) is an enthralling portrait of Japanese strategy and American apathy. The author added to the known body of knowledge by skillfully interviewing surviving leading figures who were willing to tell more once official investigations had closed. But Hoehling went beyond his research findings to join the club of Roosevelt-baiters and hence some of his conclusions are questionable. The Japanese planning for the surprise attack is expertly analyzed in Robert E. Ward, "The Inside Story of the Pearl Harbor Plan," *U.S. Naval Institute Proceedings*, LXXVII, 1270–1283 (December, 1951). No one has more convincingly explained the American intelligence gap which made the astounding success of the raid possible than Roberta Wohlstetter, *Pearl Harbor: Warning and Decision* (Stanford, 1962). This distinguished book places the blame on the "uncertainty, confusion, and cross-purposes" inherent in the American chain of command and it carefully refrains from personal recrimination. Walter Millis, who achieved fame as a leading World War I revisionist, argues ably on the other side in *This Is Pearl! The United States and Japan—1941* (New York, 1947); a brilliant book which makes it clear that President Roosevelt did not desire war with Japan, let alone call it into existence. The arresting details of the attack and the might-have-beens of history that conceivably could have parried the Japanese blow are graphically described by a master investigator in Walter Lord, *Day of Infamy* (New York, 1957). Convenient documentary collections in paperback have been assembled by Paul S. Burtness and Warren U. Ober (eds.), *The Puzzle of Pearl Harbor* (Evanston, Ill., 1962) and Hans L. Trefousse, *What Happened at Pearl Harbor?* (New York, 1958).

Following the conclusion of the war that began at Pearl Harbor, a whole genre of literature indicted FDR for luring Tokyo to the attack in order to put the entire resources of the United States behind the Allied cause. These strongly prejudiced writings which, more often than not, rest on carefully winnowed evidence, must be used with caution. For a capital inventory of the earlier writings on the subject, consult Louis Morton, "Pearl Harbor in Perspective: A Bibliographical Survey," *U.S. Naval Institute Proceedings*, LXXXI, 461–468 (April, 1955). The essential revisionist arguments are marshaled together in a collection of essays edited by Harry Elmer Barnes, *Perpetual War for Perpetual Peace* (Caldwell, Ida., 1953). For the pioneering revisionist works, see John T. Flynn, *The Truth About Pearl Harbor* (New York, 1944) and the two books by Charles A. Beard mentioned in the bibliography for the preceding chapter. Another early salvo against FDR was fired by a member of the editorial staff of the Chicago *Tribune*. Consult George E. Morgenstern, *Pearl Harbor: The Story of the Secret War* (New York, 1947). In *America's Second Crusade* (Chicago, 1950), William H. Chamberlin pushed the story backward to pre-1939 diplomacy, arguing that Roosevelt ignored the legitimate grievances of the Axis powers because he wanted a general war to suit his own purposes. The President is similarly accused of courting war to achieve his own ends in Frederic R. Sanborn, *Design for War: A Study of Secret Power Politics, 1937–1941* (New York, 1951). The most elaborately documented work of this nature is Tansill, *Back Door to War—* but this book is so recriminatory in tone and so filled with non-sequiturs that the weighty research which it entailed failed to achieve its purpose. More recent books of this nature include Rear Admiral Robert A. Theobald, *The Final Secret of Pearl Harbor: The Washington Contribution to the Japanese Attack* (New York, 1954) and Husband E.

Kimmel's pathetic defense of his actions as commanding officer in Hawaii, published as *Admiral Kimmel's Story* (Chicago, 1955).

The exaggerated statements of the anti-Roosevelt writers evoked prompt and vigorous rebuttal. Captain Tracy B. Kittredge, a veteran naval historian, published a lengthy reply to Admiral Theobald. See "United States Defense Policy and Strategy, 1941," in *United States News and World Report*, XXXVII, pp. 53 ff. (December 8, 1954). Kittredge proved beyond all reasonable doubt that there had been no Pearl Harbor conspiracy hatched in Washington. Robert H. Ferrell, "Pearl Harbor and the Revisionists," *Historian*, XVII, 215–233 (Spring, 1955) and Herbert Feis, "War Came at Pearl Harbor: Suspicions Considered," *Yale Review*, XLV, 378–390 (Spring, 1956) concur strongly in this conclusion. There is a brief but clarifying analysis of Washington's misjudgments of Japan's military moves in Watson, *Chief of Staff: Prewar Plans and Preparations*, pp. 518–519.

Paul W. Schroeder's provocative book, *The Axis Alliance and Japanese-American Relations, 1941* (Ithaca, 1958) stands in a separate category. Schroeder summarily dismisses the fantastic charge that the United States purposely invited the immolation of the fleet anchored at Pearl Harbor. He is, however, severely critical of Secretary Hull for maintaining a moral rigidity which prevented the negotiation of an acceptable settlement with Japan. While this thesis appeals strongly to present-day champions of diplomatic realism, it is conjectural whether a more flexible American Far Eastern policy could have aborted a two-front war.

Index